T0214413

Lecture Notes in Computer Science 11022

Commenced Publication in 1973
Founding and Former Series Editors:
Gerhard Goos, Juris Hartmanis, and Jan van Leeuwen

Editorial Board

More information about this series at http://www.springer.com/series/7407

David N. Jansen · Pavithra Prabhakar (Eds.)

Formal Modeling and Analysis of Timed Systems

16th International Conference, FORMATS 2018
Beijing, China, September 4–6, 2018
Proceedings

 Springer

Editors
David N. Jansen (ID)
Institute of Software,
  Chinese Academy of Sciences
Beijing
China

Pavithra Prabhakar (ID)
Kansas State University
Manhattan, KS
USA

ISSN 0302-9743   ISSN 1611-3349 (electronic)
Lecture Notes in Computer Science
ISBN 978-3-030-00150-6   ISBN 978-3-030-00151-3   (eBook)
https://doi.org/10.1007/978-3-030-00151-3

Library of Congress Control Number: 2018953027

LNCS Sublibrary: SL1 – Theoretical Computer Science and General Issues

This Springer imprint is published by the registered company Springer Nature Switzerland AG
The registered company address is: Gewerbestrasse 11, 6330 Cham, Switzerland

Preface

The 16th International Conference on Formal Modeling and Analysis of Timed Systems (FORMATS 2018) was held during September 4–6, 2018, in Beijing, China. FORMATS 2018 is part of CONFESTA and was colocated with CONCUR 2018, QEST 2018, and SETTA 2018.

Control and analysis of the timing of computations is crucial to many domains of system engineering, be it, e.g., for ensuring timely response to stimuli originating in an uncooperative environment, or for synchronising components in VLSI. Reflecting this broad scope, timing aspects of systems from a variety of domains have been treated independently by different communities in computer science and control. Researchers interested in semantics, verification and performance analysis study models such as timed automata and timed Petri nets, the digital design community focuses on propagation and switching delays, while designers of embedded controllers have to take account of the time taken by controllers to compute their responses after sampling the environment, as well as of the dynamics of the controlled process during this span.

Timing-related questions in these separate disciplines do have their particularities. However, there is a growing awareness that there are basic problems (of both scientific and engineering level) that are common to all of them. In particular, all these sub-disciplines treat systems whose behaviour depends upon combinations of logical and temporal constraints; namely, constraints on the temporal distances between occurrences of successive events. Often, these constraints cannot be separated, as the intrinsic dynamics of processes couples them, necessitating models, methods, and tools facilitating their combined analysis. Reflecting this, FORMATS 2018 also accepted submissions on hybrid discrete-continuous systems and held a session on continuous dynamical systems.

FORMATS 2018 is a three-day event, featuring two invited talks, and single-track regular podium sessions.

23 Program Committee (PC) members helped to provide at least 3 reviews for most of the 29 submitted contributions, 14 of which were accepted and presented during the single-track sessions and appear as full papers in these proceedings.

A highlight of FORMATS 2018 has been the presence of two invited speakers, namely, Prof. Edward A. Lee (University of California, Berkeley) and Prof. Jyotirmoy V. Deshmukh (University of Southern California, Los Angeles). We also included their articles, which form the basis of the invited talks.

Further details on FORMATS 2018 are featured on the website:
http://lcs.ios.ac.cn/formats2018/.

Finally, a few words of acknowledgment are due. We enjoyed great institutional and financial support from the Institute of Software, Chinese Academy of Sciences, without which an international conference like FORMATS and the co-located events could not have been successfully organized. We also thank the Chinese Academy of Sciences for its financial support. Thanks to Springer for hosting the FORMATS proceedings in its

Lecture Notes in Computer Science, and to EasyChair for providing a convenient platform for coordinating the paper submission and evaluation. Thanks to the Steering Committee for support and direction, to all the PC members and additional reviewers for their work (76 reviews in total) in ensuring the quality of the contributions to FORMATS 2018, and to all the participants for contributing to this event.

June 2018   David N. Jansen
                                                                                     Pavithra Prabhakar

Organization

Program Committee

Sergiy Bogomolov	Australian National University, Australia
Borzoo Bonakdarpour	Iowa State University, USA
Patricia Bouyer	LSV, CNRS & ENS Cachan, Université Paris Saclay, France
Thao Dang	CNRS/VERIMAG, France
Martin Fränzle	Carl von Ossietzky Universität Oldenburg, Germany
Ichiro Hasuo	National Institute of Informatics, Japan
Boudewijn Haverkort	University of Twente, The Netherlands
Holger Hermanns	Saarland University, Germany
David N. Jansen	Institute of Software, Chinese Academy of Sciences, Beijing, China
Jan Křetínský	Technical University of Munich, Germany
Shankara Narayanan Krishna	IIT Bombay, India
Martin Leucker	University of Lübeck, Germany
Miroslav Pajic	Duke University, USA
David Parker	University of Birmingham, UK
Pavithra Prabhakar	Kansas State University, USA
César Sánchez	IMDEA Software Institute, Spain
Ocan Sankur	University of Rennes, Inria, CNRS, IRISA, France
Zhikun She	Beihang University, Beijing, China
Jiří Srba	Aalborg University, Denmark
B. Srivathsan	Chennai Mathematical Institute, India
Meng Sun	Peking University, China
Cong Tian	Xidian University, China
Ashutosh Trivedi	University of Colorado, Boulder, USA
Frits Vaandrager	Radboud University, The Netherlands
Mahesh Viswanathan	University of Illinois at Urbana-Champaign, USA

Additional Reviewers

Aldini, Alessandro
Busatto-Gaston, Damien
Bønneland, Frederik M.
Colange, Maximilien
Dave, Vrunda

Gupta, Ashutosh
Herbreteau, Frédéric
Kong, Hui
Krämer, Julia
Kumar, Rajesh

Li, Yi
Madnani, Khushraj
Nickovic, Dejan
Soudjani, Sadegh

Swaminathan, Mani
Taankvist, Jakob Haahr
Trtik, Marek
Zhang, Xiyue

Contents

Invited Papers

Stochastic Temporal Logic Abstractions: Challenges and Opportunities

Jyotirmoy V. Deshmukh$^{(\boxtimes)}$, Panagiotis Kyriakis, and Paul Bogdan

University of Southern California, Los Angeles, USA
{jyotirmoy.deshmukh,kyriakip,pbogdan}@usc.edu

Abstract. Reasoning about uncertainty is one of the fundamental challenges in the real-world deployment of many cyber-physical system applications. Several models for capturing environment uncertainty have been suggested in the past, and these typically are parametric models with either Markovian assumptions on the time-evolution of the system, or Gaussian assumptions on uncertainty. In this paper, we propose a framework for creating data-driven abstractions of the environment based on *Stochastic Temporal Logics*. Such logics allow combining the power of temporal logic-based absractions with powerful stochastic modeling techniques. Our framework allows constructing stochastic models using *generalized master equations*, which can be viewed as a nonparametric model capturing the dynamic evolution of the probabilities of system variables with time. Furthermore, we show how we can automatically infer temporal logic based abstractions from such a model. We give examples of applications for such a framework, and highlight some of the open problems and challenges in this approach.

1   Introduction

Reasoning about uncertainty is one of the fundamental challenges in real-world deployment of cyber-physical systems (CPS). Model-based development (MBD) has become the *de facto* paradigm for designing embedded software for CPS applications, and typical models focus on accurate representations of the time-varying dynamics of the physical processes to be controlled and models of the control software. Typically, MBD paradigms focus on worst-case behavior under environmental assumptions, but rarely analyze the system performance as it relates to stochastic uncertainty in the underlying system. There is a case to be made for probabilistic characterizations of system behavior. For example, consider a self-driving car that uses a RADAR-based sensor to estimate the positions and velocities of objects in its environment. If the software design process uses worst-case assumptions on the sensor behavior, it may lead to an overly conservative controller, or may incorrectly conclude infeasibility of a control strategy. If a tool for testing the control software uses such assumptions, it may report potential safety violations that are unrealistic. A possible solution is to express probabilistic assumptions on the environment inputs, when creating environment models for abstraction and testing of control software.

© Springer Nature Switzerland AG 2018
D. N. Jansen and P. Prabhakar (Eds.): FORMATS 2018, LNCS 11022, pp. 3–16, 2018.
https://doi.org/10.1007/978-3-030-00151-3_1

In this paper, we make a case for expressing such probabilistic assumptions as formulas in *Stochastic Temporal Logics*. A (nondeterministic) temporal logic is a formalism to express temporal relations between logical properties of time-series data (such as signals); and a traditional temporal logic formula, such as Signal Temporal Logic (STL) is interpreted over signals. Stochastic Temporal Logics, in contrast, are interpreted over stochastic processes, i.e. a (finite or infinite) collection of time-indexed random variables. Recently, there have been a few proposals for temporal logics equipped with probabilistic reasoning capabilities [14,23,28]. These logics can basically be viewed as extensions of STL that allow probabilistic predicates or chance constraints. In Sect. 2, we propose a unifying logic that uses the best features of these logics, but is equipped with quantitative semantics, similar to those for STL [9,10].

We also propose some initial techniques for *creating* such logical abstractions from data. Previous approaches on stochastic modeling of systems typically assume a *white-box* approach, i.e. the model for the system dynamics is assumed to be (at least partially) known, and the uncertainty in the environment is typically assumed to be of a parametric form, with typically well-known statistical characterizations. The key assumption in our approach is that we are provided with a *black-box* system description, i.e., we either do not have access to the symbolic equations that characterize the dynamic system behaviors, or that due to dearth of precise analytic methods to analyze the available symbolic equations, we choose to ignore them. In other words, we have the ability to stimulate a system with input signals and observe the output signals. Furthermore, we assume that the system is *stochastic*, i.e., one or more parts of the system have randomness associated with it. In the simplest case, this stochasticity can be in the way input signals are provided to the system, and in more complex cases, the stochasticity could be a result of random noise in sensing or actuation.

There are numerous challenges to create such stochastic logical abstractions from data: (1) Cyber-physical processes exhibit complex multi-scale, non-linear, non-Gaussian, and non-stationary behavior [31]; (2) intricate inter-dependence between physical phenomena can lead to complex non-Markovian and long-range memory dynamics that cannot be captured by state-of-the-art system identification and machine learning techniques [31]; (3) operating in unstructured, uncertain, dynamic and complex environments raises the issue of dealing with missing information (e.g., empirical data undersamples in space and time, some measurements for specific cyber and physical processes are missing or corrupted) [14,23,28]; (4) state-of-the-art techniques in artificial intelligence and machine learning do not provide quantitative measures of assurance when dealing with high-dimensional non-Markovian spatio-temporal fractal processes. To overcome these challenges, in Sect. 3, we propose a unique approach that draws inspiration from techniques in statistical physics, and constructs novel *generalized master equations* from data.

Finally, in Sect. 4 we show a technique that learns certain kinds of stochastic, temporal and logical abstractions from a stochastic data-driven model, such as the one identified in Sect. 3. In Sect. 6, we outline some of the key technical challenges to be overcome and in Sect. 5 some applications of using such a framework.

1.1 Related Work

There has been a recent upsurge in using real-time temporal logics such as Signal Temporal Logic [24] for expressing properties and abstractions of closed-loop cyber-physical system models [13,16,19,27]. There is also growing interesting in using temporal logic specifications for *controller synthesis* of systems with uncertainty. Under the assumption of a known stochastic dynamical model, there have been proposed approaches to find optimal control policies that maximize the probability of satisfying a given temporal logic specification by planning over stochastic abstractions [1,11,17,18]. When the underlying model is unknown, reinforcement learning based methods have been used for specifications given as LTL [26] and STL [2] formulas.

Recently, STL was extended to three probabilistic variants, Probabilistic STL (PrSTL) [28], Chance Constrained Temporal Logic (C2TL) [15], and Stochastic STL (StSTL) [23]. The atomic predicates in the logic C2TL are affine constraints on variables (or arbitrary Boolean combinations of such constraints), where the coefficients in the constraints are assumed to random variables with a Gaussian distribution. The signal variables themselves are assumed to evolve deterministically. For this logic, the authors show how the synthesis problem with a C2TL objective can be conservatively encoded as a mixed integer linear program. In [28], the authors define PrSTL that uses probabilistic atomic predicates parameterized with a time-varying random variable drawn from a given distribution. The authors then synthesize a receding horizon controller that satisfies PrSTL specifications using as a mixed integer semi-definite encoding of the synthesis problem. The work on StSTL focuses on using StSTL specification as contracts for verification using a similar MIP formulation The work on StSTL focuses on using StSTL specification as contracts for verification using a similar MIP formulation.

Also of note are approaches that use Probabilistic Computation Tree Logic (PCTL), that was introduced to expresses properties over the realizations of Markov chains and Markov Decision Processes [12] A significant amount of research has focussed on using PCTL for verification and optimal control of Markov Decision Processes [4,7,22,32].

2 Stochastic Temporal Logic

We begin by reviewing some preliminary definitions and notations.

Definition 1 (Stochastic Process). *A probability space is a triple $(\Omega, \mathcal{F}, \mathcal{P})$, where Ω is the set of all possible outcomes, $\mathcal{F}$ is the σ-algebra of all events and $\mathcal{P}$ is a probability measure. Given a measurable state-space E, a random variable $\mathbf{x}$ is measurable function $\mathbf{x} : \Omega \to E$. A stochastic process $\mathbf{x}(t)$ is a continuous collection of random variables indexed by time t that all take values in E.*

Definition 2 (Components and Dimension). *The state-space of a random variable in a stochastic process as defined in Definition 1 may be the product of single-dimension state-spaces, i.e. $E = E_1 \times \ldots \times E_k$. We then define k as the dimension of the stochastic process, and use $\mathbf{x}_j$ to define a natural projection of the process onto its jth dimension.*

In this paper, we are mostly concerned with real-valued stochastic processes which are either discrete-time or continuous-time, i.e., the index sets of the stochastic process can be finite or infinite sets.

Definition 3 (Timed Trace). *Given a stochastic process $\mathbf{x}$, a realization over the time interval $\mathcal{T} = [t_0, t_n]$ is a signal $\overline{\mathbf{x}}(t)$ obtained by sampling each time-indexed random variable in the stochastic process. A timed trace is the sequence of pairs $(t_0, \overline{\mathbf{x}}_0), \ldots, (t_n, \overline{\mathbf{x}}_n)$ obtained by sampling the realization at discrete time instances $t_0 < t_1 < \ldots < t_n$.*

We briefly review the syntax and semantics of a stochastic temporal logic. The basic building block of such a logic is a *chance constraint* or *probabilistic constraint* of the form $P(\varphi_B \geq \epsilon)$, where φ_B is an arbitrary Boolean combination of stochastic predicates. For convenience, we call φ_B a *signal predicate*.

$$\varphi_B := f(\mathbf{x}) \sim 0 \mid \neg \varphi_B \mid \varphi_B \wedge \varphi_B \mid \varphi_B \vee \varphi_B \tag{1}$$

Here, f is a *measurable* function from the state-space of the stochastic process to $\mathbb{R}$. The operator $\sim$ is an element of $\{\leq, <, >, \geq\}$, and ϵ is a real number in $[0, 1]$. In general, f may not depend on all components of $\mathbf{x}$. We use support(f) to denote the components of $\mathbf{x}$ that are used to define f. The rest of the syntax for a stochastic temporal logic is similar to that of STL:

$$\varphi := \varphi_B \mid \neg \varphi \mid \varphi \wedge \varphi \mid \varphi \vee \varphi \mid \mathbf{F}_I \mid \mathbf{G}_I \mid \varphi \mathbf{U}_I \varphi \tag{2}$$

Note that the formulas $\mathbf{F}_I \varphi$ and $\mathbf{G}_I \varphi$ are introduced as convenience, and are respectively equivalent to the formulas $true \mathbf{U}_I \varphi$, and $\neg \mathbf{F}_I \neg \varphi$. Similarly, $\varphi_1 \vee \varphi_2$ can be expressed using $\neg$ and $\wedge$ using DeMorgan's laws.

The *Boolean satisfaction semantics* of a formula of the above logic is defined recursively over the formula structure. We first define the satisfaction semantics of a chance constraint. The following equation defines the satisfaction of an atomic signal predicate by a given stochastic process $\mathbf{x}$ at time t:

$$(\mathbf{x}, t) \models P[f(\mathbf{x}) \sim 0] \geq \epsilon \equiv P[f(\mathbf{x}(t)) \sim 0] \geq \epsilon \tag{3}$$

For Boolean combinations of atomic signal predicates, we can define satisfaction using the usual laws of probability. Let $\varphi_B(t)$ denote the predicate φ_B evaluated over its subformulas at time t. Then, $P[\neg \varphi_B(t)]$ can be computed as $1 - P[\varphi_B(t)]$, while $P[\varphi_B^1(t) \wedge \varphi_B^2(t)]$ requires knowledge of either the joint probabilities of $\varphi_B^1(t)$ and $\varphi_B^2(t)$ or requires the knowledge of the conditional probability of one given the other. We now define the recursive satisfaction semantics:

$$(\mathbf{x}, t) \models P[\varphi_B] \geq \epsilon \equiv P[\varphi_B(t)] \geq \epsilon$$
$$(\mathbf{x}, t) \models \neg\varphi \equiv \neg((\mathbf{x}, t) \models \varphi)$$
$$(\mathbf{x}, t) \models \varphi_1 \wedge \varphi_2 \equiv (\mathbf{x}, t) \models \varphi_1 \wedge (\mathbf{x}, t) \models \varphi_2$$
$$(\mathbf{x}, t) \models \varphi \mathbf{U}_I \psi \equiv \exists t' \in t \oplus I : ((\mathbf{x}, t') \models \psi \wedge$$
$$\forall t'' \in [t, t') : (\mathbf{x}, t'') \models \varphi).$$

Example 1. Consider the stochastic process given by the following stochastic differential equation: $dx_t = \mu dt + \sigma dW_t$, for some positive values of the parameters μ, σ. This is essentially a Brownian motion and the PDF of the random variable x at time t is $p(x, t) = \frac{1}{\sqrt{2\pi\sigma^2 t}} e^{-\frac{(x-\mu t)^2}{2\sigma^2 t}}$. Consider the following StSTL formula

$$\phi = \mathbf{G}_{[0,1]}((P[x \leq \mu] \geq 0.5) \wedge (P[x \geq -\mu] \geq 0.5)). \tag{4}$$

We can easily verify that the formula is true: In the time interval $[0, 1]$ the mean of the process reaches its maximum value at $t = 1$. At that time the mean is equal to μ and the probability $P[x \leq \mu]$ becomes 0.5. For $t < 1$ the mean is less than μ therefore by the symmetry of the normal distribution the above probability is greater than 0.5. Similar arguments can be made for the second term of the formula.

3   Constructing Stochastic Models from Data

We now consider the stochastic modeling of data through an approach based on *generalized master equations* (GMEs)[1] [31]. Let us assume that the stochastic system is at state $\mathbf{w} \in \mathbb{R}^n$ at time t. Subsequently, it waits dt time units and then makes a transition to state $\mathbf{w} + d\mathbf{w}$. The *inter-event times* dt and *the magnitude increment* $d\mathbf{w}$ are random variables drawn from the joint probability density function $\lambda(\mathbf{w}, t)$. Using these definitions, we enumerate all possible transitions that could have led to the system being at state $\mathbf{w}$ at time t and using simple probabilistic arguments we obtain the following *Generalized Master Equation* (GME)

$$p(\mathbf{w}, t) = \Psi(t)\delta(\mathbf{w}) + \int_0^t d\tau \int_{\mathcal{R}^n} p(\mathbf{y}, \tau)\lambda(\mathbf{w} - \mathbf{y}, t - \tau)d\mathbf{y} \tag{5}$$

where $\delta(\mathbf{w})$ is the multivariate Dirac delta function and $\Psi(t)$ is the probability of making no transitions up until time t. The first term of this equation represents the trivial transition, that is, when no transition occurred up to time t and at time t the system made a transition to state $\mathbf{w}$. The second term is essentially an "enumeration" of all other possible intermediate transitions and application of the total probability theorem. This equation is a rather abstract generalization of the Brownian motion; in fact, for the simplified case of exponentially distributed inter-event times, Eq. 5 reduces to a stochastic process similar to

---

[1] Master equations are commonly used tools in statistical physics to describe time-evolution of a system [5, 6, 20].

Brownian motion with the critical difference being that $w(t)$ need not be Gaussian; it may be any distribution (potentially time-dependent). The introduction of arbitrarily distributed inter-event times aims in capturing long-term and non-Markovian behavior. In practice $\lambda(\mathbf{w}, t)$ is approximated by differentiating the given realization(s) (after removing deterministic and predictable components, as previously discussed) and estimating the probability density of the resulting time series.

We remark that the above GME formulation can also be used to represent the joint probability distribution for a number of stochastic processes. We omit the exact expression for brevity, but it can be obtained by applying the usual rules of probability to Eq. 5. Finally, constructing a model from data may can be done in a parametric or nonparametric fashion. In the former, we assume a specific form for the kernel density function λ, and attempt to estimate its parameters fro mdata. In the latter, we assume that the kernel density function is expressed as the inner product of an (infinite-dimensional) coefficient vector with an infinite set of basis functions. For example, it is possible to use wavelet functions or Fourier transforms for this purpose. In practice, we would restrict the number of basis functions used to a finite, manageable number.

4   Learning Logical Abstractions from Stochastic Models

In this section, we introduce a preliminary technique for inferring stochastic logical relations from a stochastic model. We formally define a *stochastic time-varying model* (STM) as follows:

Definition 4 (Stochastic Time-varying Model (STM)). *Let* $\mathbf{x} = (\mathbf{x}_1, \ldots, \mathbf{x}_k)$ *be a* k-*dimensional stochastic process. A stochastic time-varying model* $M(S_1, \ldots, S_m)$ *is a set* $\{p(S_1; t), p(S_2; t), \ldots, p(S_m; t)\}$, *where* $S_j \subseteq \{1, \ldots, k\}$, *and each* $p(S_j; t)$ *represents the time-varying joint PDF of the components of* $\mathbf{x}$ *indexed by elements in* S_j.

Note that M can be constructed empirically as the numeric solution of the generalized master equation (defined in Sect. 3). However, note that the definition of an STM M is quite general; for example, M could be specified in terms of analytic equations of time-varying PDFs of well-known stochastic processes (such as Brownian motion shown in Example 1). A simple technique that may be often useful is one based on *ensemble statistics*; i.e. at each time-point, representing the distribution using a number of moments of the PDF estimated from observed data. In this section, the actual method used to compute the STM is not of importance, we assume that we are given an STM that is *adequate* to create a logical abstraction w.r.t. a user-provided *template*. We formally explain these two ideas in the sequel.

Parametric Stochastic Temporal Logic (PStTL). We introduce PStTL as an extension of StSTL to define *template formulas* containing unknown parameters. A PStTL formula is then defined by modifying the previously defined grammar and allowing any constants appearing in the formula to be replaced by parameters. The set of parameters $\mathcal{P}$ is a set consisting of two disjoint sets of variables $\mathcal{P}^E$ and $\mathcal{P}^T$ of which at least one is nonempty. The parameter variables in $\mathcal{P}^E$ can take values from the state-space for the stochastic process, while the variables in $\mathcal{P}^T$ are time-parameters that take values from the time domain $\mathcal{T}$. A valuation function ν maps a parameter to a value in its domain. We denote a vector of parameter variables by $\mathbf{p}$, and extend the definition of the valuation function to map parameter vectors $\mathbf{p}$ into tuples of respective values over V or T. We define the parameter space $\mathcal{D}_P$ as a subset of $\mathcal{E}^{|\mathcal{P}^E|} \times T^{|\mathcal{P}^T|}$.

Definition 5 (Adequate Model). *Given a PStTL formula φ, we call the set of components appearing in the formula as its support variables denoted* support(φ); *this can be computed recursively computing the union of the* support *function for each subformula, and using the previously defined* support(f) *set for the signal predicates. We say that an STM $M(S_1, \ldots, S_m)$ is adequate iff there exists an $S_j \in \{S_1, \ldots, S_m\}$ such that* support(φ) $\subseteq S_j$.

In simple words, as long as it is possible to obtain the joint PDF of the stochastic process components appearing in the PStTL formula from one of the existing joint PDFs (by marginalizing unnecessary variables), then the model is adequate. We observe that a model that contains the joint PDF of all components of the stochastic process is an adequate model. However, computing the joint PDF for a large number of a high-dimensional process can be computationally intensive. Thus, given a PStTL formula, we wish to construct a *minimally adequate* STM for that formula. As the support variables of a formula are syntactically known, identifying the subset of processes to use to construct a minimally adequate STM is trivial.

4.1   Logical Abstractions Through Parameter Inference

In this subsection, we present a technique to infer parameter valuations for a given PStTL formula such that the resulting stochastic temporal logic formula is satisfied by the given STM. Given a PStTL formula $\varphi(\mathbf{p})$, a crude approach to finding a valuation ν mapping $\mathbf{p}$ to some value in $\mathcal{D}_P$ is to discretize $\mathcal{D}_P$, (say N discrete values per parameter dimension), and then test the validity of the resulting formula $\varphi(\nu(\mathbf{p}))$ over each of the $N^{|\mathcal{P}|}$ at each one of them. However, this approach does not scale as the computational complexity is $\mathcal{O}(N^{|\mathcal{P}|})$ and the accuracy of the result depends on the number of discretizations in each parameter's range (i.e. on N).

For this reason we propose an alternative method for synthesizing parameters for a large class of stochastic STL formulae that satisfy the following requirements: (a) they are monotonic with respect to each parameter, (b) for every parametrized temporal operator the sub-formula in the scope of that operator is not parametrized and (c) each parameter appears only once in the formula. The monotonicity requirement is necessitated by the fact that non-monotonic formulae can have an arbitrary high number of points at which the validity changes, therefore, we cannot expect to perform better than the grid method. The last requirement is imposed because repeated appearances of the same parameter in the formula may compromise the monotonicity. The second requirement is also necessary because nested parametric formulae may have conflicting monotonicity, meaning that the sub-formula of a parametrized temporal operator may be monotonically increasing while the operator itself monotonically decreasing (or the converse). Dealing with such nuances is left for future work.

Let us assume without loss of generality that the given formula is monotonically increasing with respect to each parameter. The method is based on the observation that, given the monotonicity assumption, it suffices to find the parameter value boundary at which the validity of the formula changes. As a preprocessing step, we verify that the boolean logic of the formula has no inconsistencies. For instance, a formula in the form $P[x > c_1] > 0.9 \wedge P[x > 5] > 1.1$ cannot be valid for any choice of c_1. Then, we decompose ϕ into a parse tree $T = T(\phi)$. Each node of T is a temporal operator, a boolean operator or (at a leaf level) an atomic stochastic temporal logic predicate. Subsequently, for a given time horizon T, we perform a time iteration and for each discretized time instance we traverse T in a breadth-wise fashion, starting from the leaves and moving upwards. Whenever we encounter a node n containing a parametrized atomic predicate or parametrized temporal operator we calculate the value of the parameter such that the formula represented by the sub-tree rooted at n is the least permissive (i.e., the value at which its validity changes). Given the assumption of increasing monotonicity, this coincides with the minimum value of the parameter for which the formula is valid.

Definition 6 (Monotonic PStTL). *A PStTL formula φ is said to be monotonically increasing in parameter $\mathbf{p}_i$ if condition (6) holds for the stochastic process $\mathbf{x}$ and is said to be monotonically decreasing in parameter c_i if condition (7) holds for $\mathbf{x}$.*

$$\nu(\mathbf{p}_i) \leq \nu'(\mathbf{p}_i) \wedge [\mathbf{x} \models \varphi(\nu(p_i))] \implies [\mathbf{x} \models \varphi(\nu(\mathbf{p}_i))] \tag{6}$$

$$\nu(\mathbf{p}_i) \geq \nu'(\mathbf{p}_i) \wedge [\mathbf{x} \models \varphi(\nu(p_i))] \implies \mathbf{x} \models \phi(\nu(\mathbf{p}_i))] \tag{7}$$

A multi-parameter formula $\varphi(\mathbf{p})$ is said to be monotonic if and only if it is monotonic in every individual parameter $\mathbf{p}_i \in \mathbf{p}$.

Let us assume without loss of generality that the given formula is monotonically increasing with respect to each parameter. The method is based on the observation that, given the monotonicity assumption, it suffices to find the parameter value boundary at which the validity of the formula changes. As a preprocessing step we verify that the boolean logic of the formula has no inconsistencies. For instance a formula in the form $P[x > c_1] > 0.9 \wedge P[x > 5] > 1.1$ cannot be valid for any choice of c_1. Then, we decompose ϕ into a parse tree $T = T(\varphi)$. Each node of T is a temporal operator, a boolean operator or (at a leaf level) an atomic predicate. Subsequently, for a given time horizon T, we perform a time iteration and for each discretized time instance we traverse T in a breadth-wise fashion, starting from the leaves and moving upwards. Whenever we encounter a node n containing a parametrized atomic predicate or parametrized temporal operator we calculate the value of the parameter such that the formula represented by the sub-tree rooted at n is the least permissive (i.e. the value at which its validity changes). Given the assumption of increasing monotonicity, this coincides with the minimum value of the parameter for which the formula is valid.

Algorithm 1. Time-Iteration Parameter Synthesis for StSTL

Inputs :
  $p(\mathbf{x}, t)$, $\phi(\mathbf{p})$, T
Procedure :
  Construct parse tree $\mathcal{T} = \mathcal{T}(\phi)$
  $(\mathbf{c}_L^*, \epsilon_L^*, \tau_L^*) \leftarrow ([], [], [])$ for all $L = 1$ to $\mathrm{depth}(\mathcal{T})$
  for $t = 1$ to T **do**
    for $L = \mathrm{depth}(\mathcal{T})$ to 1 **do**
      for all nodes n at level L **do**
        if $n := P[f(\mathbf{x}, \mathbf{c}_L) \sim 0] \geq \epsilon_L$ **then**
          $(\mathbf{c}_L^*, \epsilon_L^*) \leftarrow \mathrm{argmin}\{(\mathbf{c}_L, \epsilon_L) : (\mathbf{x}, t) \models n\}$
        else if $n := \phi_L \mathbf{U}_{[0, \tau_L]} \psi_L$ **then**
          $\tau_L^* \leftarrow \mathrm{argmin}\{\tau_L : (\mathbf{x}, t) \models n\}$
        else if $n := \phi_L(c_{L1}, \epsilon_{L1}) \mathbf{U}_{[0, T_L]} \psi_L(c_{L2}, \epsilon_{L2})$ **then**
          $(\mathbf{c}_{L1}^*, \epsilon_{L1}^*, \mathbf{c}_{L2}^*, \epsilon_{L2}^*) \leftarrow$
            $\mathrm{argmin}\{(\mathbf{c}_{L1}, \epsilon_{L1}, \mathbf{c}_{L2}, \epsilon_{L2}) : (\mathbf{x}, t) \models n\}$
        end if
      end for
    end for
  end for
Outputs : $(\mathbf{c}_L^*, \epsilon_L^*, T_L^*)$ for all $L = 1$ to $\mathrm{depth}(\mathcal{T})$

The above procedure is shown on Algorithm 1. We should note that the set of parameters $\mathcal{P}$ is decomposed for each level L of the tree to three subsets: parameters appearing as coefficients on the random variables ($\mathbf{c}_L$), parameters appearing as bounds on the probabilities (ϵ_L) and time parameters τ_L. Additionally, the notation $:=$ denotes "matches" (i.e., the condition $n := P[f(\mathbf{x}, \mathbf{c}_L) \sim 0] \geq \epsilon_L$ is true if and only if node n is a atomic predicate). Note that the first else-if matches a temporal operator parametrized by τ_L while the second one a non-parametrized temporal operator whose sub-formulae are parametrized. In the later case T_L is assumed to be constant and the parameters of the sub-formulae have been broken down to two sets. Finally, the temporal operators $\mathbf{F}$ and $\mathbf{G}$ have implicitly been included via $\mathbf{U}$.

The above algorithm essentially requires only the knowledge of the joint PDFs (or CDFs) of the process components appearing in the PStTL formula, and certain assumptions on the formula structure, but is able to automatically infer a logical abstraction from the given STM.

5   Applications

In this section, we describe some of the applications that we can tackle by constructing stochastic logical abstractions.

5.1   Controller Quality Through Environment Models

Autonomous Cyber-Physical systems (such as self-driving cars) require extensive testing and validation before they are ready for deployment in the real-world. However, currently, there is either an over-reliance on real-world physical testing (through actual driving), or testing may use overly pessimistic environment models. We wish to give the algorithms for introducing autonomy realistic environment models, and hence obtain probabilistic formal guarantees on their performance. Consider, for example, data that includes noisy RADAR measurements of the *lead gap* and *relative velocity* of a lead car, and also ground truth labels indicating the actual distance between the lead and the host and actual relative velocity. From data gathered from physical experiments, we can construct a Stochastic Temporal Logic abstraction of the error in the readings. Let e_v and e_p denote the error in the relative velocity and the position error, respectively. Then the correctness of an *adaptive cruise control* algorithm can be expressed using the following probabilistic correctness formula:

$$\mathbf{G}_{[0,T]} \left(P[e_v > 5] < 10^{-5} \wedge P[e_p > 2] < 10^{-5} \right) \implies \mathbf{G}_{[0,\tau_{lead}]} P[gap > d_{safe}] > 1 - 10^{-5} \tag{8}$$

In the above equation, τ_{lead} denotes the time window for which the car follows the lead car at a distance of greater than d_{safe} as long as the error in measurements of the relative velocity and position being greater than an acceptable threshold is small.

5.2   Causality Models for Large Inter-connected Systems

Many real-world systems consist of complex networks of interconnected cyber-physical systems. Often, when such connections are effected, these systems experience emergent behavior that was not anticipated by the designers. In such cases, designers wish to identify *why* certain physical quantities in a given component may behave in a certain way. Such an analysis requires identifying *causality relations* between signals. Similar problems arise in the domain of biological and bio-medical systems. For example, consider the problem of predicting epileptic seizures from electroencephalography (EEG) measurements [21]. In the study in [21], the researchers used 76 electrode contacts for the patient. Examination of the EEG data by a medical professional revealed two key periods relating to the seizure i.e., a pre-ictal period, just before the clinical onset, and an ictal one, corresponding to the seizure spread and to the clinical symptoms. Further statistical post-processing and analysis indicates that during the onset of an epileptic seizure, the contacts implanted in the patient's brain exhibit extremely high values of potential compared to the pre-ictal period. This suggests that this sudden decrease in potential values may indicate the onset of a seizure.

In a typical EEG setup, it is common to use several electrode contacts to measure the potential values. Let the signal measured at the ith electrode contact during the pre-ictal phase be denoted x^i_{pre} and that measured at the jth electrode during the ictal phase be x^j_{ict}. A naïve PStTL formula that indicates the onset of a seizure in the next τ seconds can be written as follows:

$$\phi_{naive} := \bigvee_{i,j} \mathbf{G} \left(P[x^i_{pre} \leq c^i_1] \geq \epsilon^i_1 \implies \mathbf{F}_{[0,\tau]} P[x^j_{ict} \geq c^j_2] \geq \epsilon^j_2 \right) \quad (9)$$

We note that even for fixed probability values, we would have to infer two parameters per pair of electrodes in the above formula. Furthermore, the generalized master equation formulation for this case would need to compute an STM with joint PDFs of signals corresponding to all the electrodes in the different phases. Thus, while creating a stochastic logical abstraction is of value, performing parameter inference efficiently requires further work. One possibility is to use information-theoretic measures such as *transfer entropy* that quantifies the amount of information flow between signals, to precisely identify the signals to use to construct the required abstraction.

6   Challenges, Open Problems, and Future Applications

In this section, we briefly enumerate some challenges to scalability, open problems, and some application domains in which we can use stochastic logical abstractions.

Anomaly Detection and Prediction. An advantage of creating a stochastic logical abstraction is that it gives us a *probabilistic prior* to represent the expected behaviors of a system. In the domain of cyber-physical security, simple priors are used to identify statistically outlying behaviors as anomalies at run-time [8,25,29,30]. There has not been any work on techniques to identify a run-time behavior as a statistical outlier w.r.t. a given stochastic temporal logic formula, and constitutes an open problem. Similarly, predictive monitoring with a stochastic model of the system is also feasible within our framework, but the algorithms to perform such monitoring have not yet been developed.

Causal Abstractions for High-Dimensional Data. Identifying precise temporal relations in high-dimensional data is challenging due to scalability concerns. Approaches such as using vector auto-regression (VAR) have been successfully shown to scale for systems where there is known linear dependence between signals [3]. However, extending such techniques to general systems with nonlinear dependence between signals is open. One approach is to compute the pairwise transfer-entropy, but this can be computationally challenging if the number of dimensions is very high.

Incremental Learning and Robustness. In this paper, we have largely focussed on building stochastic logical abstractions when we have a large existing data-set. However, in real-world settings, we often gather data incrementally, and re-computing the abstraction every time new data is available is computationally wasteful. Techniques to incrementally update the abstraction w.r.t. new data would need to be developed. Such techniques would also raise the question of *robustness* of the abstraction: Does new data cause a significant perturbation in the model? This issue can be of importance if the abstractions are deployed in a CPS which is expected to perform life-long learning. By flagging and rejecting data that can cause significant perturbations in the model, the abstraction could protect against adversarial attacks on the learning component.

Synthesis from Logical Abstractions. Finally, much of the existing work on stochastic temporal logics has focussed on synthesizing safe controllers from the given uncertainty specification on the environment. Here, many problems remain open once we do not assume any specific probability distribution on the environment uncertainty.

Acknowledgement. This work was in part supported by The Defense Advanced Research Projects Agency and DARPA Young Faculty Award under grant numbers W911NF-17-1-0076 and N66001-17-1-4044, and the US National Science Foundation (NSF) under CAREER Award CPS-1453860. The views, opinions, and/or findings contained in this article are those of the authors and should not be interpreted as representing the official views or policies, either expressed or implied, of the Defense Advanced Research Projects Agency or the Department of Defense.

References

1. Abate, A., D'Innocenzo, A., Benedetto, M.D.D.: Approximate abstractions of stochastic hybrid systems. IEEE Trans. Autom. Control **56**(11), 2688–2694 (2011)
2. Aksaray, D., Jones, A., Kong, Z., Schwager, M., Belta, C.: Q-learning for robust satisfaction of signal temporal logic specifications. In: 2016 IEEE 55th Conference on Decision and Control (CDC), pp. 6565–6570, December 2016
3. Arnold, A., Liu, Y., Abe., N.: Temporal causal modeling with graphical Granger methods. In: Proceedings of International Conference on Knowledge Discovery and Data Mining (SIGKDD-07) (2007)
4. Baier, C., Größer, M., Leucker, M., Bollig, B., Ciesinski, F.: Controller synthesis for probabilistic systems (extended abstract). In: Levy, J.-J., Mayr, E.W., Mitchell, J.C. (eds.) TCS 2004. IIFIP, vol. 155, pp. 493–506. Springer, Boston, MA (2004). https://doi.org/10.1007/1-4020-8141-3_38
5. Balescu, R.: Statistical Dynamics: Matter Out of Equilibrium. World Scientific, Singapore (1997)
6. Balescu, R.: Aspects of Anomalous Transport in Plasmas. CRC Press, Boca Raton (2005)
7. Brázdil, T., et al.: Verification of Markov decision processes using learning algorithms. In: Cassez, F., Raskin, J.-F. (eds.) ATVA 2014. LNCS, vol. 8837, pp. 98–114. Springer, Cham (2014). https://doi.org/10.1007/978-3-319-11936-6_8

8. Cardenas, A., et al.: Challenges for securing cyber physical systems. In: Workshop on Future Directions in Cyber-Physical Systems Security, vol. 5 (2009)
9. Donzé, A., Ferrère, T., Maler, O.: Efficient robust monitoring for STL. In: Sharygina, N., Veith, H. (eds.) CAV 2013. LNCS, vol. 8044, pp. 264–279. Springer, Heidelberg (2013). https://doi.org/10.1007/978-3-642-39799-8_19
10. Fainekos, G.E., Pappas, G.J.: Robustness of temporal logic specifications for continuous-time signals. Theor. Comp. Sci. **410**(42), 4262–4291 (2009)
11. Fu, J., Topcu, U.: Computational methods for stochastic control with metric interval temporal logic specifications. In: 2015 IEEE 54th Annual Conference on Decision and Control (CDC), pp. 7440–7447. IEEE (2015)
12. Hansson, H., Jonsson, B.: A logic for reasoning about time and reliability. Formal Aspects Comput. **6**(5), 512–535 (1994)
13. Hoxha, B., Abbas, H., Fainekos, G.: Benchmarks for temporal logic requirements for automotive systems. In: Frehse, G., Althoff, M. (eds.) ARCH14-15. 1st and 2nd International Workshop on Applied Verification for Continuous and Hybrid Systems. EPiC Series in Computing, vol. 34, pp. 25–30. EasyChair (2015)
14. Jha, S., Raman, V.: Automated synthesis of safe autonomous vehicle control under perception uncertainty. In: Rayadurgam, S., Tkachuk, O. (eds.) NFM 2016. LNCS, vol. 9690, pp. 117–132. Springer, Cham (2016). https://doi.org/10.1007/978-3-319-40648-0_10
15. Jha, S., Raman, V., Sadigh, D., Seshia, S.A.: Safe autonomy under perception uncertainty using chance-constrained temporal logic. J. Autom. Reason. **60**(1), 43–62 (2018)
16. Jin, X., Deshmukh, J.V., Kapinski, J., Ueda, K., Butts, K.: Powertrain control verification benchmark. In: Proceedings of the 17th International Conference on Hybrid Systems: Computation and Control, pp. 253–262. ACM (2014)
17. Julius, A.A., Pappas, G.J.: Approximations of stochastic hybrid systems. IEEE Trans. Autom. Control **54**(6), 1193–1203 (2009)
18. Kamgarpour, M., Ding, J., Summers, S., Abate, A., Lygeros, J., Tomlin, C.: Discrete time stochastic hybrid dynamical games: verification amp; controller synthesis. In: 2011 50th IEEE Conference on Decision and Control and European Control Conference, pp. 6122–6127, December 2011
19. Kapinski, J., et al.: ST-Lib: a library for specifying and classifying model behaviors. In: SAE Technical Paper. SAE (2016)
20. Klages, R., Radons, G., Radons, G., Sokolov, I.: Anomalous Transport: Foundations and Applications. Wiley, Hoboken (2008)
21. Kramer, M.A., Kolaczyk, E.D., Kirsch, H.E.: Emergent network topology at seizure onset in humans. Epilepsy Res. **79**(2), 173–186 (2008)
22. Lahijanian, M., Andersson, S.B., Belta, C.: Control of Markov decision processes from PCTL specifications. In: Proceedings of the 2011 American Control Conference, pp. 311–316, June 2011
23. Li, J., Nuzzo, P., Sangiovanni-Vincentelli, A., Xi, Y., Li, D.: Stochastic contracts for cyber-physical system design under probabilistic requirements. In: ACM/IEEE International Conference on Formal Methods and Models for System Design (2017)
24. Maler, O., Nickovic, D.: Monitoring temporal properties of continuous signals. In: Lakhnech, Y., Yovine, S. (eds.) FORMATS/FTRTFT -2004. LNCS, vol. 3253, pp. 152–166. Springer, Heidelberg (2004). https://doi.org/10.1007/978-3-540-30206-3_12
25. Pajic, M., Mangharam, R., Pappas, G.J., Sundaram, S.: Topological conditions for in-network stabilization of dynamical systems. IEEE J. Sel. Areas Commun. **31**(4), 794–807 (2013). https://doi.org/10.1109/JSAC.2013.130415

26. Rizk, A., Batt, G., Fages, F., Soliman, S.: On a continuous degree of satisfaction of temporal logic formulae with applications to systems biology. In: Heiner, M., Uhrmacher, A.M. (eds.) CMSB 2008. LNCS (LNAI), vol. 5307, pp. 251–268. Springer, Heidelberg (2008). https://doi.org/10.1007/978-3-540-88562-7_19

27. Roehm, H., Gmehlich, R., Heinz, T., Oehlerking, J., Woehrle, M.: Industrial examples of formal specifications for test case generation. In: Workshop on Applied Verification for Continuous and Hybrid Systems, ARCH@CPSWeek 2015, pp. 80–88 (2015)

28. Sadigh, D., Kapoor, A.: Safe control under uncertainty with probabilistic signal temporal logic. In: Robotics Science and Systems (2016)

29. Sundaram, S., Pajic, M., Hadjicostis, C., Mangharam, R., Pappas, G.: The wireless control network: monitoring for malicious behavior. In: 49th IEEE Conference on Decision and Control (CDC), pp. 5979–5984, December 2010. https://doi.org/10.1109/CDC.2010.5717166

30. Sundaram, S., Revzen, S., Pappas, G.: A control-theoretic approach to disseminating values and overcoming malicious links in wireless networks. Automatica **48**(11), 2894–2901 (2012)

31. Xue, Y., Bogdan, P.: Constructing compact causal mathematical models for complex dynamics. In: Proceedings of the 8th International Conference on Cyber-Physical Systems, pp. 97–107. ICCPS 2017 (2017)

32. Zhang, X., Wu, B., Lin, H.: Learning based supervisor synthesis of POMDP for PCTL specifications. In: 2015 IEEE 54th Annual Conference on Decision and Control (CDC), pp. 7470–7475. IEEE (2015)

Models of Timed Systems

Edward A. Lee$^{(\boxtimes)}$ (ID)

UC Berkeley, Berkeley, CA, USA
eal@eecs.berkeley.edu
http://eecs.berkeley.edu/~eal

Abstract. This paper analyzes the use of models for timed systems, particularly cyber-physical systems, which mix timed behavior of physical subsystems with largely untimed behavior of software. It examines how models are used in engineering and science, showing that two complementary styles for using models lead to differing conclusions about how to approach the problem of modeling timed systems. The paper argues for an increased use of an engineering style of modeling, where models are more like specifications of desired behavior and less like descriptions of some preexisting system. Finally, it argues that in the engineering style of modeling, determinism is an extremely valuable property.

Keywords: Modeling · Real-time systems · Determinism

1 Models in Science and Engineering

The most interesting cyber-physical system (CPS) applications today, such as medical devices, factory automation, and autonomous vehicles, necessarily include timing-sensitive safety-critical physical sensing and actuation[1]. The software in such systems is called real-time software because the designer has to pay attention to the timing of actions taken by the software. But what do we mean by "paying attention" to timing? Fundamentally, time only matters in computing when software interacts with the world outside the software. Without such interaction, time is irrelevant. Of course, all useful software interacts with the world outside itself, or we wouldn't bother to have the software. Hence, time matters to some degree for all software. But for many CPS applications, timing is critically important. A slow program may be annoyance, but a missed deadline in a control system could be deadly.

I have forty years of experience with cyber-physical systems. In the late 1970s, I was writing assembly code for Intel 8080s to control industrial robots. In the

This work was supported in part by the iCyPhy Research Center (Industrial Cyber-Physical Systems, supported by Denso, Ford, National Instruments, Siemens, and Toyota), and by the National Science Foundation, NSF award #1446619 (Mathematical Theory of CPS).

[1] This paper is an expanded version of [16] and borrows themes from [18].

© Springer Nature Switzerland AG 2018
D. N. Jansen and P. Prabhakar (Eds.): FORMATS 2018, LNCS 11022, pp. 17–33, 2018.
https://doi.org/10.1007/978-3-030-00151-3_2

early 1980s, I was writing assembly code for DSP chips to encode bit sequences in voice-like waveforms that could traverse the public telephone network. I designed the first fully software-defined modem at a time when modems were custom circuits.

In both cases, timing of actions was important, and the way that I would control the timing of software was to count assembly-language instructions and insert no-ops as needed. Even then, this was not easy. The computer architectures had significant complexity and I had to understand them. But I could write programs where the timing was well defined, repeatable, and precise. Today this is much more difficult.

The assembly code that I wrote can be viewed as a model. The code that I wrote provided a model of the physical actions that I wanted to occur, including when I wanted them to occur. My modeling language was assembly, which was itself built upon another model, an instruction set architecture (ISA). In the case of the programmable DSP chips I was using in the early 1980s, the timing of each instruction was an explicit part of the ISA model, one that could not be ignored. The realization of the ISA was another model, a synchronous digital logic circuit, which ultimately abstracted the physical behavior of electrons sloshing in silicon. This layering of models enabled me to work within a relatively simple paradigm, a sequence of actions with well-defined time elapsing between actions.

Today's clock frequencies are more than three orders of magnitude higher (more than 2 GHz vs. 2 MHz), but timing precision and predictably has not improved and may have actually declined. To understand the timing behavior of a program we write today, we have to model many details of the hardware and software, including the memory architecture, pipeline design, I/O subsystem, programming languages, concurrency management, and operating system design.

Today, a C program, for example, for a real-time system, is also a model, but this model does not specify timing. To control timing, we have to step outside the abstraction of the C language and make operating system calls that set priorities on threads and write to memory-mapped registers to cause hardware to trigger timer interrupts. Examining the C program alone reveals very little about timing. To understand timing, we require detailed knowledge of the operating system, the other tasks that are sharing it, the hardware associated with timer interrupts, and all other details of the microprocessor hardware, including its memory architecture and pipeline design. Knowing the ISA is insufficient.

One consequence is a subtle but important transformation in the way we use models. Forty years ago, my models specified the timing behavior, and it was incumbent on the physical system to correctly emulate my model. Today, the timing behavior emerges from the physical realization of the system. My job as an engineer has switched from designing a behavior to understanding a behavior over which I have little control.

Given behaviors that we want to understand, but did not design, a scientific approach requires building models and refining them based on observations. A whole industry has developed around models of microprocessors that can be used to estimate the worst-case execution time (WCET) of a piece of C code, for example [12, 23]. These models cannot depend only on the ISA definition. They have to include every detail of the particular implementation of the ISA, often even undocumented features [22]. And even when you get an effective model, the WCET is not the actual execution time. Most programs will execute faster, but modeling that variability is extremely difficult. As a consequence, program behavior is not repeatable. Variability in execution times can reverse the order in which actions are taken in the physical world, possibly with disastrous consequences.

The essential issue is that role that models have played in the design process has reversed. Forty years ago, my model was a specification, and it was incumbent on the physical system to behave like the model. Today, my model emulates the behavior of a physical system, and it is incumbent on my model to match that system. These two uses of models are mirror images of one another.

In a recent book, I point out that the first style of modeling is more common in engineering, and the second is more common in science. Quoting myself,

> To a scientist, the value of a model lies in how well its properties match those of a target, typically an object found in nature. ... But to an engineer ... the value of an object ... lies in how well its properties match a model. ... A scientist asks, "Can I make a model for this thing?" An engineer asks, "Can I make a thing for this model?" [18, p. 45]

If a microprocessor drops into salt water and fails to correctly execute a program, then the problem lies with the physical system, not with the model. Conversely, if a program executes faster than expected on a modern microprocessor and the order of events gets reversed, the problem lies with the model, not with the physical system. The distinction between scientific and engineering use of models is reflected in the distinction between a specification and a user manual: while they essentially contain the same information, if there is a difference between the information and the described object, then the specification is always right and the user manual is always wrong.

The engineering style of modeling has been astonishingly successful for VLSI chip design. Most chips are designed as a synchronous digital logic model. A physical piece of silicon that fails to match this logic model is not useful and will be discarded.

In science, models are used the other way around. If Newton's laws were not to describe accurately the motion of the planets, we would not hold the planets responsible and discard them. We would hold the model responsible. In science, the abstraction is required to match the physical world, the reverse of engineering.

VLSI chip design has also made very effective use of layered models. Above a synchronous digital logic model lies a Verilog or VHDL program. Above that may lie an ISA. We can keep going up in levels of abstraction, but my essential point is that at each level, the lower level is required to match the upper one. In scientific models, the responsibility is reversed. The more abstract model is required to match the less abstract one.

The consequences are profound. Consider that a scientist tries to shrink the number of relevant models, those needed to explain a physical phenomenon. In contrast, an engineer strives to grow the number of relevant models, those for which we can construct a faithful physical realization. These two styles of modeling are complementary. Most scientists and engineers use both, but rarely do they think about which they are using.

For real-time systems, I believe that the problem today is that we are doing too much science and not enough engineering. As a community, people who work in real-time systems resign themselves to the microprocessors given to us by Intel and Arm and the language given to us by Bell Labs (namely, C) as if those were artifacts found in nature. Those are magnificent engineering triumphs, but the models that they realize have little to do with timing. If we take those as given, then we are forced to use the scientific style of modeling. A price we may be paying is that real-time systems will never achieve the level of complexity and reliability of VLSI design.

There are alternatives. We could design microprocessors that give us precise and controllable timing, processors that we call PRET machines [7,25]. Then we could specify real-time behaviors, and the hardware will be required to match our specification. We have shown that such microprocessors can be designed, and that at a modest cost in hardware overhead, there is no need to sacrifice performance [17]. Given microprocessors that can deliver repeatable and controllable timing, we could design programming languages that enable us to express timing behavior. Every correct execution of those programs will deliver the same timing behavior, though we need to be careful here about what we mean by "timing behavior." Vague, intuitive notions of time will not suffice for constructing trustworthy models.

2   What Is Real Time?

In practice, when engineers talk about "real time," they may mean:

1. fast computation,
2. prioritized scheduling,
3. computation on streaming data,
4. bounded execution time,
5. temporal semantics in programs, or
6. temporal semantics in networks.

In 1988, Stankovic cataloged quite a few more possible (mis)interpretations of the term "real time" and laid out a research agenda that is dishearteningly valid today [20]. These are different views, and which view dominates has a strong effect on the choice of technical approaches to the problem.

The first, fast computation, is useful in all computation, and therefore does not deserve our attention here. Nothing about fast computation can distinguish real-time problems from non-real-time problems. In fact, many real-time systems execute on decidedly slow computers, such as microcontrollers, and timing precision, predictability, and repeatability may be far more important than speed.

The second meaning, prioritized scheduling, is the centerpiece of much work in the real-time systems community. In this approach, the requirements of the physical world are reduced to deadlines and periods, and the temporal properties of software are reduced to execution times for tasks. For cyber-physical systems, we are more interested in the closed-loop interactions of the physical and cyber parts of the system. These reductions are oversimplifications and a more holistic approach has great promise for advancing the field.

The third meaning, computation on streaming data, has become a hot area in recent years. The emerging Internet of Things (IoT) promises a flood of sensor data. Many organizations already are collecting but not effectively using vast amounts of data. Consulting and market research company Gartner calls "dark data" the "information assets that organizations collect, process and store in the course of their regular business activity, but generally fail to use for other purposes." The subtext is that those same businesses are missing an opportunity. They should be mining the data. The data has value. The research and consulting firm Forrester defines "perishable insights" as "urgent business situations (risks and opportunities) that firms can only detect and act on at a moment's notice." Fraud detection for credit cards is one example of such perishable insights. This has a real-time constraint in the sense that once a fraudulent transaction is allowed, the damage is done. In CPS, a perishable insight may be, for example, a determination of whether to apply the brakes on a car, where a wrong or late decision can be quite destructive.

Computing on streaming data means that you don't have all the data, but you have to deliver results. It differs from standard computation in that the data sets are unbounded, not just big. You can't do random access on input data, which constrains the types of algorithms you can use [1]. Because data keeps coming, programs that halt are defective, in contrast to the standard Turing-Church view of computation, where programs that fail to halt are defective.

Computing on streaming data demands different software architectures, using for example *actors* as software components rather than *objects*. Many subtle semantic questions arise. For example, when streams converge, what is the meaning of the interleaving of their elements? Are their elements simply nondeterministically interleaved, or is there more meaning to the relationship between an element of one stream and that of another? Can algorithms process potentially infinite data streams with bounded state? How is feedback handled, where processes send each other streams? What about streams that are partially ordered rather than totally ordered? And perhaps most interesting for this paper, is there any temporal semantics in the streams? That is, is there any notion of time associated with the elements of the stream, and what is the semantics of that notion of time?

The fourth meaning, bounded execution time, assumes that some deadline exists for a software execution, and that ensuring that the execution never oversteps that deadline is sufficient. This meaning is central to the sense-process-actuate programming models and is usually a basic assumption of the second meaning, prioritized scheduling. However, bounding the execution time of software is particularly problematic. The bound can only be determined for a particular implementation, where every detail of not only the software, but also the hardware on which it runs and the execution context are known. Moreover, by itself, bounding the execution time of software does not ensure predictable behavior, since it does little to ensure that the order of actions taken by the software is invariant.

The fifth meaning, temporal semantics in programs, has a long history with little practical impact. Although many experimental programming languages with some notion of time have been created, none has survived. This may be in part because temporal semantics is absent in programs from the lowest level of abstraction, in the instruction-set architecture (ISA). Reintroducing it at higher levels has proved persistently problematic. For real progress to be made, temporal semantics needs to appear throughout the abstraction stack.

The final meaning, temporal semantics in networks, is present only in specialized networks, such as those in safety critical systems including factory automation, avionics, and automotive electronics. Recent work shows, however, that temporal semantics is not entirely incompatible with commodity networks. I will say more about this below.

3   Correctness vs. Quality

All of the above interpretations of real-time computing require some measure of control over the timing of software. However, controlling timing of software is difficult. More important, achieving *repeatable* timing is difficult, and systems do not necessarily behave in the field in a manner similar to the test bench.

At the microarchitecture level, ISAs define the behavior of a microprocessor implementation in a way that makes timing irrelevant to correctness. Timing is merely a performance metric, not a correctness criterion. In contrast, arithmetic and logic *are* correctness criteria. A microprocessor that fails to take a branch when the condition evaluates to true is simply an incorrect implementation. But a microprocessor that takes a long time to take the branch is just slow. Computer architects have long exploited this property, that timing is irrelevant to correctness. They have developed clever ways to deal with deep pipelines, such as speculative execution and instruction re-ordering. They also have clever techniques to take advantage of memory heterogeneity, such as multi-level caches. These techniques, however, introduce highly variable and unpredictable timing. The goal is to speed up a typical execution, not to make executions repeatable.

The design of modern programming languages reflects the microarchitectural choice, so timing is again irrelevant to correctness. Hence, programmers have to step outside the programming abstraction to control timing, for example by writing to memory-mapped registers to set up a timer interrupt, or more indirectly, by making operating system calls to trigger context switches. The result is timing granularity that is much more coarse than what is achievable in the hardware. More important, since interrupts occur unpredictably relative to whatever is currently executing, these techniques inevitably make behavior nonrepeatable. I contend that ISAs for CPS need to be rethought to provide repeatable and precise timing.

Another reason that timing is difficult to control is operating system scheduling. Multitasking in modern operating systems is driven by timer interrupts, which disrupt the timing of programs in unpredictable ways (e.g. by affecting the cache or the pipeline state). The most widely used I/O mechanisms also rely on interrupts, again disrupting timing.

Today, most CPS applications stand to benefit enormously from being networked, an observation that underlies the current enthusiasm around IoT. But the networking technology that underlies the Internet also ignores timing. When mainstream networking pays attention to timing, the problem is put under the header "quality of service," which emphasizes that timing is viewed as a *quality* metric, not a *correctness* criterion. In contrast, reliable eventual delivery, realized by the widely used TCP protocol, is a correctness criterion.

4   Achieving Real-Time Behavior

Despite these challenges, engineers have managed to make reliable real-time systems. How? Some of the techniques used are:

1. overengineering,
2. using old technology,
3. response-time analysis,
4. real-time operating systems (RTOSs),
5. specialized networks, and
6. extensive testing and validation.

Overengineering is common because Moore's law has given us impressively fast processors. If the execution of software is essentially instantaneous with respect to the physical processes with which it is interacting, then the time it takes to execute a piece of code becomes irrelevant. However, overengineering is becoming increasingly difficult as the complexity of CPS applications increases and as technology no longer tracks Moore's law. Moreover, many CPS applications are extremely cost sensitive or energy constrained, making overengineering a poor choice.

Using old technology is also common. Safety-critical avionics software, for example, rarely uses modern programming languages, operating systems, or even interrupts. Software is written at a very low level, I/O is done through polling rather than interrupts, and multitasking is avoided. Programmable logic controllers (PLCs), widely used in industrial automation, are often programmed using ladder logic, a notation that dates back to the days when the logic of digital controllers was entirely controlled with mechanical relays. And the software executes without the help of a modern operating system, sacrificing useful capabilities such as network stacks. Many embedded systems designers avoid multicore chips, a strategy that is becoming increasingly difficult as single-core chips become more rare. And programmers often disable or lock caches, thereby getting little advantage from the memory hierarchy.

The third approach, response-time analysis, includes execution-time analysis, which puts bounds on the time it takes for sections of code to execute [23], and analysis of factors such as operating system scheduling and mutual exclusion locks. Even just the subproblem of execution-time analysis is fundamentally hard because for all modern programming languages, whether a section of code even terminates is undecidable. However, even when the execution paths through the code can be analyzed, sometimes with the help of manual annotations such as bounds on loops, the microarchitectural features mentioned above can make analysis extremely difficult. The analysis tools need a detailed model of the particular implementation of the processor that will run the code, including every minute (and often undocumented) detail. As a result, a program that has been validated using execution-time analysis is only validated for the particular piece of silicon that has been modeled. With any change in the hardware, all bets are off; even though the new hardware will correctly execute the *code*, there is no longer any assurance that the *system* behavior is correct. Manufacturers of safety-critical embedded systems, therefore, are forced to stockpile the hardware that they expect to need for the entire production run of a product. This runs counter to most basic principles in modern supply chain management for manufacturing, and it makes it impossible to take advantage of technology improvements for cost reduction, improved safety, or reduced energy consumption.

Moreover, execution-time analysis tools often need to make unrealistic assumptions, such as that interrupts are disabled, in order to get reasonable bounds. But while interrupts are disabled, the software does not react to stimuli from the outside world, so the variability in reaction time may be significantly increased, undermining the value of execution-time analysis.

In practice, designers either avoid interrupts altogether (as commonly done in avionics) or attempt to keep program segments short so that the time during which interrupts are disabled is small. Both strategies are increasingly difficult as we demand more functionality from these programs. As execution time increases, either the polling frequency decreases or the variability of the timing of other tasks that get locked out by disabled interrupts increases.

The fourth technique, RTOSs, provides real-time scheduling policies in a multitasking operating system. At the core, RTOSs use timer interrupts and priorities associated with tasks. There is a long history of strategies that can be proven optimal under (often unrealistic) assumptions, such as bounds on execution time and well-known deadlines [4]. In simple scenarios, these strategies can yield repeatable behaviors, but in more complex scenarios, they can even become chaotic [21], which makes behavior impossible to predict. Moreover, because of the reliance on interrupts, RTOSs violate the typical assumptions made for execution-time analysis, and thereby invalidate their own optimality proofs, which assume known execution times. A consequence is that when RTOSs deliver predictable timing, the precision of the resulting timing is several orders of magnitude coarser than what is in principle achievable with the underlying digital hardware.

The specialized networks that constitute the fifth approach use methods such as synchronized clocks and time-division multiple access (TDMA) to provide latency and bandwidth guarantees. Examples include CAN busses, ARINC busses, FlexRay, and TTEthernet. With the possible exception of TTEthernet, these networks are hard to integrate with the open Internet, so these systems cannot benefit from Internet connectivity nor from the economies of scale of Internet hardware and software.

The final approach, extensive testing and validation, is a laborious, brute-force engineering method. One automotive engineer described to me what he called "the mother of all test drives," where you literally drive the car a million miles in as many conditions as you can muster and hope that you have comprehensively covered all the behaviors that the cyber-physical system may exhibit in the field. But as the complexity of these systems (and their environments) increases, the likelihood that testing will be comprehensive becomes more remote.

Taken together, these techniques do make it *possible* to design safety-critical real-time embedded software, but their weaknesses suggest that it may be time to step back and reexamine the problem of real-time computing with fresh eyes. After all, microprocessors are realized in a technology, synchronous digital logic, that is capable of realizing sub-nanosecond timing precision with astonishing reliability and repeatability. It is the layers of abstraction overlaid on this technology, ISAs, programming languages, RTOSs, and networks, that discard timing. I contend that it is time for a paradigm shift where we make a commitment to deterministic models that include timing properties.

5 What Is Time?

Time, as a physical phenomenon, is poorly understood [19]. CPS engineers mostly adopt a Newtonian view, where time is a continuum that advances uniformly and identically to all observers, even though we know from relativity that the flow of time depends on the observer, and some physicists suspect from quantum field theories that time may be discrete rather than a continuum. The Newtonian view is pragmatic and has proved effective for a wide range of physical system design problems. However, it does not translate easily to the cyber world, where everything is discrete and the dynamics of programs is a sequence of steps rather than a continuous flow.

Under the Newtonian model, an instant in time can be represented as a real number. In software, real numbers are almost always approximated by floating-point numbers. This works well when modeling continuous systems because for continuous systems, by definition, small perturbations have bounded effects, so the small errors introduced in floating-point arithmetic can often be safely neglected. However, when dealing with discrete systems or with mixed discrete and continuous systems, these same errors can have bigger effects. With discrete behaviors, and hence with software, the order in which events occur, no matter how small the time difference between them, can drastically affect an outcome.

Broman et al. show that floating-point representations of time are incompatible with basic requirements for modeling hybrid systems, which mix discrete and continuous behaviors [3]. They offer an alternative, a superdense model of time with quantized resolution that exhibits a clean semantic notion of simultaneity. The key is to adopt a *model* of time, not one that attempts to solve the physics problem of what is time in the physical world, but rather one that expresses properties of real-time systems that we care about and that can be physically realized with high confidence at a reasonable cost. In other words, we need a useful temporal semantics for engineering models, rather than a model of physical time, whatever that is, given to us by nature.

What do we mean by "temporal semantics"? Consider a program that takes two distinct orchestrated actions A and B at 100 μs intervals. We can argue that it is physically impossible for these actions to be simultaneous to all observers, but that would be missing the point. Even the meaning of "100 μs intervals" is questionable in physics. Instead, we should admit that what we want is to have these actions be *logically* simultaneous and *reasonably* precise. What does this mean? It could mean that any observer of these actions within our system will at all times have counted the same number of actions A and B that have occurred. That is, if the observer has seen n A actions, then it has also seen n B actions. Note that this requirement is independent of timing precision and is most certainly physically realizable. It gives a clean semantic notion to simultaneity. This is not a scientific notion of simultaneity, but rather an engineering notion. It gives a specification that our implementation must meet.

Another example of a useful temporal semantics property is reaction time. Suppose that we have a system that reacts to sporadic discrete events, and that we wish it to react to each event with a latency no greater than 100 μs. Here, "sporadic" has a technical meaning without which we could never provide such an assurance. A sporadic stream of events is one where the time between events has a lower bound. Consider a scenario where we have two sporadic streams into a software system running on single CPU, where in each stream, the lower bound between events is 100 μs. Events arrive no more frequently than once per 100 μs, but possibly less frequently. The interleaving of events from these two streams is arbitrary, and events could even arrive simultaneously. Nevertheless, we wish to react to each event within 100 μs.

Today, we can solve this problem with interrupts, but since interrupts disrupt timing analysis, each event handler will have to disable interrupts while it handles its event. Because the timing of events in each stream is arbitrary, this interrupt-driven strategy will introduce considerable timing jitter. Suppose for example that the hander for events from stream A requires 95 μs to complete, whereas the handler for stream B requires only 5 μs. In this case, reactions to events from stream B may occur in 5 μs or in 100 μs or anything in between, depending on whether an event from stream A is being handled. This is a huge jitter compared to the reaction time.

A promising solution is the PRET machines that I already mentioned. PRET machines can give a deterministic temporal semantics to interrupt-driven reactions without any loss of performance. I will discuss next this idea of a deterministic temporal semantics and explain how it can overcome the limitations in today's real-time computing technologies.

6   A Commitment to Models

All of engineering is built on models. For the purposes of this paper, I will define a "model" of a system to be any description of the system that is not Kant's thing-in-itself (*das Ding an sich*). Mechanical engineers use Newton's laws as models for how a system will react to forces. Civil engineers use models of materials to understand how structures react to stresses. Electrical engineers model transistors as switches, logic gates as networks of switches, and digital circuits as networks of logic gates. Computer engineers model digital circuits as instruction set architectures (ISAs), programs as executions in an ISA, and applications as networks of program fragments.

Every one of these models rests on a modeling paradigm. The Java programming language, for example, is just such a modeling paradigm. What constitutes a well-formed Java program is well defined, as is the meaning of the execution of such a program. The program is a model of what a machine does when it executes the program. Synchronous digital circuits constitute another such modeling paradigm. They model what an electronic circuit does. Under the synchrony hypothesis, the latencies of logic gates are ignored, and the behavior of a network of logic gates and latches is given by Boolean algebra. Models abstract away details, and layers of models may be built one on top of another [18].

Properties of the modeling paradigm are fundamental when an engineer attempts to build confidence in a design. A synchronous digital circuit, as a model, realizes a deterministic function of its input, despite the fact that we have no useful deterministic model of the underlying physics comprising individual electrons sloshing in silicon and metal. A single-threaded Java program is also a deterministic function of its inputs. The determinism of these modeling paradigms is assumed without question by the engineer building these models. Without such determinism, we would not have billion-transistor chips and million-line programs handling our banking.

Does this mean that the execution of a Java program on a particular microprocessor chip is deterministic? This question, by itself, makes no sense. Determinism is a property of models, not of physical systems [18]. If a chip overheats or get submersed in salt water, a program will very likely not behave as expected. The physical realization has properties that the model does not have.

More to the point for this paper, the timing exhibited by the Java program is not specified in the model (the Java program itself). Whether an execution of the program is correct does not depend on the timing, so within this model, an infinite number of timing behaviors are permitted. Nevertheless, we assert that the model (the single-threaded Java program) is deterministic because the model does not include timing in its notion of the behavior of the program.

The notion of determinism is not a simple one. We can't confront uncertainty without first confronting determinism. Determinism is a deceptively simple idea that has vexed thinkers for a long time. Broadly, determinism in the physical world is the principle that everything that happens is inevitable, preordained by some earlier state of the universe or by some deity. For centuries, philosophers have debated the implications of this principle, particularly insofar as it undermines the notion of free will. If the world is deterministic, then presumably we cannot be held individually accountable for our actions because they are preordained. Determinism is quite a subtle concept, as is the notion of free will.

Earman, in his *Primer on Determinism*, admits defeat in getting a "real understanding" of the concept [6, p. 21]. Earman insists that "determinism is a doctrine about the nature of the world," but I believe that a more useful view is that determinism is a property of *models* and not a property of the physical world. This thesis does not diminish the deep questions that Earman addresses, but it certainly does make it easier to apply the concept of determinism to engineered systems. As a property of models, determinism is relatively easy to define:

> A model is deterministic if given an initial *state* of the model, and given all the *inputs* that are provided to the model, the model defines exactly one possible *behavior*.

In other words, a model is deterministic if it is not possible for it to react in two or more ways to the same conditions. Only one reaction is possible. In this definition, the italicized words must be defined within the modeling paradigm to complete the definition, specifically, "state," "input," and "behavior." Precise definitions of these words necessarily circumscribe the assumptions made by the designer. For example, if the timing of the execution of a Java program is included in the notion of "behavior," then no Java program is deterministic.

For an example of a deterministic model, if the *state* of a particle is its position $x(t)$ in a Euclidean space at a Newtonian time t, where both time and space are continuums, and if the *input* $F(t)$ is a force applied to the particle at each instant t, and the *behavior* is the motion of the particle through space, then Newton's second law provides a deterministic model.

One reason that this simple concept has been so problematic is that all too often, when speaking of determinism, the speaker is confusing the map for the territory (the model for the thing-in-itself). To even speak of determinism, we must define "input," "state," and "behavior." How can we define these things for an actual physical system? Any way we define them requires constructing a model. Hence, an assertion about determinism will actually be an assertion about the model not about the thing being modeled. Only a model can be unambiguously deterministic, which underscores Earman's struggle to pin down the concept.

Consider that any given physical system has more than one valid model. For example, a particle to which we are applying a force exhibits deterministic motion under Newton's second law but not under quantum mechanics, where the position of the particle will be given probabilistically. However, under quantum mechanics, the evolution of the particle's wave function is deterministic, following the Schrödinger equation. If the "state" and "behavior" of our model are the wave function, then the model is deterministic. If instead the state and behavior are the particle's position, then the model is nondeterministic. It makes no sense to assign determinism as a property to the particle. It is a property of the model.

If we have a deterministic model that is faithful to some physical system, then this model *may* have a particularly valuable property: the model may predict how the system will evolve in time in reaction to some input stimulus. This predictive power of a deterministic model is a key reason to seek deterministic models.

But a model can only predict aspects of behavior that lie within its modeling paradigm. My essential claim in this paper is that we should make a commitment to using models that include aspects of behavior that we care about. If we care about timing, we should use models that *do* include timing in their notion of behavior. Today, with real-time systems, we do not do that. Instead, today, timing properties emerge from a physical implementation. When we map a particular program onto a particular microprocessor, a real physical chip embedded in a real board, with real memory chips and peripherals sharing the bus, only then do we get timing properties. Timing is a property of the thing-in-itself not of the model. We have conflated the map and the territory [11].

Determinism is a key property of many of the most successful modeling paradigms in engineering. Logic gates, synchronous digital circuits, ISAs, single-threaded programs, and Newtonian mechanics are all deterministic modeling paradigms. Should we insist on deterministic modeling paradigms for CPS?

If there is anything we can be sure about, it is that we can never be sure about cyber-physical systems. We cannot know everything about them, and particularly their possible behaviors in all environments. Does this mean that we can never build confidence in a CPS realization? No, because we can build confidence in *models* of the system. While this seems to run counter to the holy grail of formal verification, it does not because formal verification proves properties of *models* of systems, not of the systems themselves. If the system itself, *das Ding an sich*, matches the model with high fidelity, then our confidence in the model translates into confidence in the system. We rely on such matching when we assume that a chip will correctly realize an ISA and correctly execute a program.

In the engineering use of models vs. the scientific one, determinism plays different roles. For an engineer, the determinism of a model is useful because it facilitates building confidence *in the model*. Logic gates, for example, are deterministic models of electrons sloshing around in silicon. The determinism of the logic gate model is valuable: it enables circuit designers to use Boolean algebra to build confidence in circuit designs that have billions of transistors. The model predicts behaviors *perfectly*, in that an engineer can determine how a logic gate model will react to any particular input, given any initial state.

Of course, the usefulness of the logic gate model also depends on our ability to build silicon structures that are extremely faithful to the model. We have learned to control the sloshing of electrons in silicon so that, with high confidence, a circuit will emulate the logic gate model billions of times per second and operate without error for years.

Some of the most valuable engineering models are deterministic. In addition to logic gates, we also have synchronous digital logic, instruction set architectures (ISAs), and programming languages, most of which are deterministic models. An ISA, for example, defines precisely what state changes should result from a sequence of instructions, and any execution that respects these, regardless of parallelism, instruction order, or timing, is a correct execution. Turing machines are also deterministic. The determinism of all these models has proved extremely valuable historically. The information technology revolution is built on the determinism of these models.

For a scientist, fundamentally, when considering the use of deterministic models, it matters quite a lot whether the physical system being modeled is also deterministic. The value of a deterministic logic gate model, however, does not depend at all on whether the sloshing of electrons in silicon is deterministic. It depends only on whether we can build silicon structures that emulate the model with high confidence. We do not need and cannot achieve perfection. As Box and Draper say, all models are wrong, but some models are useful [2], and logic gates have proved extremely useful.

I claim that for real progress to occur, we must make a commitment to deterministic models of timing and concurrency in cyber-physical systems. My essential claim is that we *can* build systems that match the behavior of such models with high confidence. This is not the same as a claim that we can construct useful deterministic models of today's cyber-physical systems. I am not making the latter claim.

What about adaptability, resilience, and fault tolerance? Any cyber-physical system will face the reality of unexpected behaviors and failures of components. Using deterministic models does not prevent us from making fault-tolerant and adaptive systems. On the contrary, it *enables* it. A deterministic model defines unambiguously what a *correct* behavior is. This enables detection of *incorrect* behaviors, an essential prerequisite to fault-tolerant adaptive systems.

The reader may protest that a deterministic model of time may be foiled by the fact that timing of programs is difficult to control. As I have pointed out, ISAs have no temporal semantics at all, and computer architects have developed a plethora of clever techniques that make timing difficult to control. But PRET machines are capable of interrupt-driven I/O that does not disrupt the timing of timing-critical tasks. I believe that PRET machines will eventually become widely available because their benefits to safety-critical systems are enormous and their performance is competitive with conventional architectures. They deliver repeatable behavior, where the behavior in the field is assured of matching their behavior on the test bench with extremely high precision and probability (at the same level of confidence as we currently get from synchronous digital logic circuits). In my expectation, it is just a matter of time before the world accepts the paradigm shift that they entail.

For distributed systems, we know from industrial practice that networks with controllable timing are realizable. Time-triggered architectures [13], TTEthernet, FlexRay, ARINC busses, and CAN bus networks all deliver some measure of controllable timing. These have been successful in specialized industrial settings, but they (mostly) don't adapt well to the open Internet. A promising development, however, is time-sensitive networking (TSN), a task group of the IEEE 802.1 working group that is developing standards that extend Internet protocols to support high-precision clock synchronization and other technologies that can enable networks with deterministic latencies and reliability delivery that are compatible with the Internet [9, 10].

To take advantage of such networks, we can leverage a deterministic programming model for distributed real-time systems called PTIDES [8, 24]. PTIDES assumes a bound on clock synchronization error and a bound on network latency, both of which can be reliably delivered with TSN. *Every* deterministic model makes assumptions about the underlying implementation, and violations of those assumptions must be treated as faults, not as performance degradations. PTIDES enables *detection* of these faults, some of which are fundamentally undetectable without a coordinated notion of time [14]. PTIDES was apparently independently reinvented at Google and deployed in a distributed database system called Spanner [5].

Despite the value of deterministic models, the real world is full of uncertainty. And even deterministic models have limitations. Chaos, complexity, and undecidability mean that deterministic models may not lead to predictable or analyzable behaviors, and incompleteness means that no set of deterministic models can cover all possible circumstances [15]. Moreover, nondeterminstic models are the only reasonable option when unknown or unknowable properties are central to the model. Hence, probabilistic and nondeterministic models will be needed. But this does not in any way undermine the value of determinism. When deterministic models work, they work spectacularly. Consider the fact that we know how to design silicon chips with billions of transistors that work as predicted the first time they are made. This simply would not be possible without the power of deterministic models.

7   Conclusion

So what is real-time computing? Today, it is an ad-hoc emergent property of physical realizations of cyber-physical systems. Tomorrow, if and when we embrace temporal semantics, real-time computing will be a model used by engineers to build high-confidence, safety-critical systems.

Acknowledgments. The author thanks David N. Jansen for very helpful suggestions.

References

1. Alur, R., Fisman, D., Raghothaman, M.: Regular programming for quantitative properties of data streams. In: Thiemann, P. (ed.) ESOP 2016. LNCS, vol. 9632, pp. 15–40. Springer, Heidelberg (2016). https://doi.org/10.1007/978-3-662-49498-1_2
2. Box, G.E.P., Draper, N.R.: Empirical Model-Building and Response Surfaces. Wiley Series in Probability and Statistics. Wiley, Hoboken (1987)
3. Broman, D., Greenberg, L., Lee, E.A., Masin, M., Tripakis, S., Wetter, M.: Requirements for hybrid cosimulation standards. In: Hybrid Systems: Computation and Control (HSCC) (2015). https://doi.org/10.1145/2728606.2728629
4. Buttazzo, G.C.: Hard Real-Time Computing Systems: Predictable Scheduling Algorithms and Applications, 2nd edn. Springer, Heidelberg (2005)
5. Corbett, J.C., et al.: Spanner: Google's globally-distributed database. In: OSDI (2012). https://doi.org/10.1145/2491245
6. Earman, J.: A Primer on Determinism, The University of Ontario Series in Philosophy of Science, vol. 32. D. Reidel Publishing Company, Dordrecht (1986)
7. Edwards, S.A., Lee, E.A.: The case for the precision timed (PRET) machine. In: Design Automation Conference (DAC) (2007)
8. Eidson, J., Lee, E.A., Matic, S., Seshia, S.A., Zou, J.: Distributed real-time software for cyber-physical systems. Proc. IEEE (Spec. Issue on CPS) 100(1), 45–59 (2012). https://doi.org/10.1109/JPROC.2011.2161237
9. Eidson, J.C.: Measurement, Control, and Communication Using IEEE 1588. Springer, London (2006). https://doi.org/10.1007/1-84628-251-9
10. Eidson, J.C., Stanton, K.B.: Timing in cyber-physical systems: the last inch problem. In: IEEE International Symposium on Precision Clock Synchronization for Measurement, Control, and Communication (ISPCS), pp. 19–24. IEEE (2015). https://doi.org/10.1109/ISPCS.2015.7324674
11. Golomb, S.W.: Mathematical models: uses and limitations. IEEE Trans. Reliab. R-20(3), 130–131 (1971). https://doi.org/10.1109/TR.1971.5216113
12. Kirner, R., Puschner, P.: Obstacles in worst-case execution time analysis. In: Symposium on Object Oriented Real-Time Distributed Computing (ISORC), pp. 333–339. IEEE (2008)
13. Kopetz, H., Bauer, G.: The time-triggered architecture. Proc. IEEE 91(1), 112–126 (2003)
14. Lamport, L.: Using time instead of timeout for fault-tolerant distributed systems. ACM Trans. Program. Lang. Syst. 6(2), 254–280 (1984)
15. Lee, E.A.: Fundamental limits of cyber-physical systems modeling. ACM Trans. Cyber-Phys. Syst. 1(1), 26 (2016). https://doi.org/10.1145/2912149
16. Lee, E.A.: What is real-time computing? A personal view. IEEE Des. Test 35(2), 64–72 (2018). https://doi.org/10.1109/MDAT.2017.2766560
17. Lee, E.A., Reineke, J., Zimmer, M.: Abstract PRET machines. In: IEEE Real-Time Systems Symposium (RTSS) (2017). Invited TCRTS award paper
18. Lee, E.A.: Plato and the Nerd – The Creative Partnership of Humans and Technology. MIT Press, Cambridge (2017)
19. Muller, R.A.: Now – The Physics of Time. W. W. Norton and Company, New York (2016)
20. Stankovic, J.A.: Misconceptions about real-time computing: a serious problem for next-generation systems. Computer 21(10), 10–19 (1988)

21. Thiele, L., Kumar, P.: Can real-time systems be chaotic? In: EMSOFT, pp. 21–30. ACM (2015)

22. Wägemann, P., Distler, T., Eichler, C., Schröder-Preikschat, W.: Benchmark generation for timing analysis. In: Real-Time Embedded Technology and Applications Symposium (RTAS). IEEE (2017)

23. Wilhelm, R., et al.: The worst-case execution-time problem - overview of methods and survey of tools. ACM Trans. Embed. Comput. Syst. (TECS) **7**(3), 1–53 (2008)

24. Zhao, Y., Lee, E.A., Liu, J.: A programming model for time-synchronized distributed real-time systems. In: Real-Time and Embedded Technology and Applications Symposium (RTAS), pp. 259–268. IEEE (2007). https://doi.org/10.1109/RTAS.2007.5

25. Zimmer, M., Broman, D., Shaver, C., Lee, E.A.: FlexPRET: a processor platform for mixed-criticality systems. In: Real-Time and Embedded Technology and Application Symposium (RTAS) (2014). http://chess.eecs.berkeley.edu/pubs/1048.html

Temporal Logics

TCTL Model Checking Lower/Upper-Bound Parametric Timed Automata Without Invariants

Étienne André[1], Didier Lime[2], and Mathias Ramparison[1(✉)]

[1] Université Paris 13, LIPN, CNRS, UMR 7030, 93430 Villetaneuse, France
`ramparison@lipn13.fr`
[2] École Centrale de Nantes, LS2N, CNRS, UMR 6597, 44000 Nantes, France

Abstract. We study timed systems in which some timing features are unknown parameters. First we consider Upper-bound Parametric Timed Automata (U-PTAs), one of the simplest extensions of timed automata with parameters, in which parameters are only used as clock upper bounds. Up to now, there have been several decidability results for the existence of parameter values in U-PTAs such that flat TCTL formulas are satisfied. We prove here that this does not extend to the full logic and that only one level of nesting leads to undecidability. This provides, to the best of our knowledge, the first problem decidable for Timed Automata with an undecidable parametric emptiness version for U-PTAs. Second we study Lower/Upper-bound Parametric Timed Automata (L/U-PTAs) in which parameters are used either as clock lower bound, or as clock upper bound, but not both. We prove that without invariants, flat TCTL is decidable for L/U-PTAs by resolving the last non investigated liveness properties.

1 Introduction

Timed automata (TAs) [AD94] are a powerful formalism for modeling concurrent real-time systems; TAs extend finite-state automata with clocks, i. e., variables evolving at the same rate, that can be compared to integers in transition guards, and possibly reset to 0.

Despite notable successes in timed model checking, TAs become less suitable to model and verify systems when some timing constants are known with some imprecision—or completely unknown. Extending TAs with *timing parameters* (unknown constants) adds one more level of abstraction, and copes with uncertainty. When allowing parameters in place of integers in guards, TAs become parametric TAs (PTAs) [AHV93]. The model checking problem becomes a parametric model checking problem: given a PTA $\mathcal{A}$ and a formula φ (expressed in e. g., TCTL [ACD93]), what are the parameter valuations v such that the

---

This work is partially supported by the ANR national research program PACS (ANR-14-CE28-0002).

D. N. Jansen and P. Prabhakar (Eds.): FORMATS 2018, LNCS 11022, pp. 37–52, 2018.
https://doi.org/10.1007/978-3-030-00151-3_3

instance of $\mathcal{A}$ in which parameters are replaced using the values given by v (denoted $v(\mathcal{A})$) satisfies φ? In the PTA literature, the main problem studied is EF-emptiness ("is the set of valuations for which given location is reachable empty?"): it is "robustly" undecidable in the sense that, even when varying the setting, undecidability is preserved. For example, EF-emptiness is undecidable even for a single bounded parameter [Mil00], even for a single rational-valued or integer-valued parameter [BBLS15], even with only one clock compared to parameters [Mil00], or with strict constraints only [Doy07] (see [And17] for a survey). In contrast, decidability is ensured in some restrictive settings such as over discrete time with a single parametric clock (i.e., compared to parameters in at least one guard) [AHV93], or over discrete or dense time with one parametric clock and arbitrarily many non-parametric clocks [BO14,BBLS15], or over discrete time with two parametric clocks and a single parameter [BO14]. But the practical power of these restrictive settings remains unclear.

In order to overcome these disappointing results, lower-bound/upper-bound parametric timed automata (L/U-PTAs) are introduced as a subclass of PTAs where each parameter either always appears as an upper bound when compared to a clock, or always as a lower bound [HRSV02]. L/U-PTAs enjoy mixed decidability results: while the EF-emptiness problem and the EF-universality problem ("Can we reach a given location, regardless of what valuations we give to the parameters?") are decidable, AF-emptiness ("is the set of valuations for which all runs eventually reach a given location empty?") is undecidable [JLR15]; as for EG-emptiness ("is the set of valuations for which one infinite or finite maximal run always remains in a given set of locations empty?"), it is decidable only when the parameter domain is bounded with closed bounds [AL17].

U-PTAs are L/U-PTAs with only upper-bound parameters [BL09], and are TAs' simplest parametric extension; since their introduction, no problem was ever shown undecidable for U-PTAs, and all their known decidability results only came from the decidability for the larger class of L/U-PTAs. In [ALR16b], we showed that, in terms of union of untimed words, U-PTAs are not more expressive than TAs. A natural question is to investigate whether their expressiveness is anyhow beyond that of TAs, or whether the parametric emptiness version of all problems decidable for TAs remains decidable for U-PTAs.

Contribution. Our first contribution is to show that the TCTL-emptiness problem ("given a TCTL formula, is the set of valuations v for which $v(\mathcal{A}) \models \varphi$ empty?") is undecidable for U-PTAs. This result comes in contrast with the fact that investigated flat TCTL formulas (namely EF, AG)—formulas that cannot be obtained by restraining another TCTL formula—are known to be decidable for U-PTAs, while others (EG and AF) are open. Our proof relies on the reduction of the halting problem of a 2-counter machine to the emptiness of the $EGAF_{=0}$ formula.

Our second contribution is that EG-emptiness is PSPACE-complete for (unbounded) integer-valued L/U-PTAs without invariants. Let us stress that EG-emptiness is undecidable for classical unbounded integer-valued L/U-PTAs with invariants [AL17], which draws a more accurate border between decidabil-

Table 1. Decidability of the emptiness problems for PTAs and subclasses

Class	U-PTAs without invariants	integer-valued L/U-PTAs without invariant	L/U-PTAs	PTAs
EF	[HRSV02]	[HRSV02]	[HRSV02]	*[AHV93, Mil00]*
AF	open	**Theorem 3**	*[JLR15]*	*[JLR15]*
EG	open	**Theorem 3**	*[AL17]*	*[AL17]*
AG	[HRSV02]	[HRSV02]	[HRSV02]	*[ALR16a]*
flat TCTL	open	**Theorem 3**	*[JLR15]*	*[AHV93]*
TCTL	**Theorem 1**	**Theorem 1**	*[JLR15]*	*[AHV93]*

ity and undecidability results regarding L/U-PTAs. Moreover, we show that EG-universality (also known as AF-emptiness) is PSPACE-complete for (unbounded) integer-valued L/U-PTAs without invariants, despite being undecidable for classical (rational- or integer-valued) L/U-PTAs with invariants [JLR15]. These results highlight the power invariants confer upon the expressiveness of L/U-PTAs. We deduce from all this that flat TCTL emptiness and universality is also decidable for integer-valued L/U-PTAs without invariants, which also makes the decidability frontier more precise with respect to nesting of TCTL formulas.

We give a summary of the known decidability results in Table 1, with our contributions in bold. We give from left to right the (un)decidability for U-PTAs, L/U-PTAs with integer-valued parameters without invariants, L/U-PTAs (the undecidability results also hold for integer-valued parameters), and PTAs. We review the emptiness of TCTL subformulas (EF, AF, EG, AG), flat TCTL and full TCTL. Decidability is given in white, whereas undecidability is given in italic grey. As U-PTAs can be seen as the simplest parametric extension of TAs, our undecidability result moves the undecidability frontier closer to TAs, and confirms that timed automata (while enjoying many decidability results) are a formalism very close to the undecidability frontier.

Outline. Section 2 recalls the necessary preliminaries. Sections 3 and 4 show that TCTL-emptiness is undecidable for U-PTAs and bounded U-PTAs, respectively. Section 5 consists of the decidability results for integer-valued L/U-PTAs without invariants. Section 6 concludes the paper and proposes some perspectives.

2 Preliminaries

We assume a set $\mathbb{X} = \{x_1, \ldots, x_H\}$ of *clocks*, i.e., real-valued variables that evolve at the same rate. A clock valuation is $w : \mathbb{X} \to \mathbb{R}_+$. We write $\mathbf{0}$ for the clock valuation assigning 0 to all clocks. Given $d \in \mathbb{R}_+$, $w + d$ is s.t. $(w + d)(x) = w(x) + d$, for all $x \in \mathbb{X}$. Given $R \subseteq \mathbb{X}$, we define the *reset* of a valuation w, denoted by $[w]_R$, as follows: $[w]_R(x) = 0$ if $x \in R$, and $[w]_R(x) = w(x)$ otherwise.

We assume a set $\mathbb{P} = \{p_1, \ldots, p_M\}$ of *parameters*. An upper-bound (resp. lower-bound) parameter p is such that, whenever it appears in a constraint

$x \bowtie p + d$ with $d \in \mathbb{N}$ then necessarily $\bowtie \in \{\leq, <\}$ (resp. $\bowtie \in \{\geq, >\}$). A parameter *valuation* v is $v : \mathbb{P} \to \mathbb{Q}_+$. An *integer* parameter *valuation* v is $v : \mathbb{P} \to \mathbb{N}$. We assume $\bowtie \in \{<, \leq, =, \geq, >\}$, $\lhd \in \{<, \leq\}$. A u-guard g (resp. an l-guard g) is a conjunction of inequalities of the form $x \bowtie d$, or $x \lhd p + d$ with p an upper-bound parameter (resp. $p + d \lhd x$ with p a lower-bound parameter) and $d \in \mathbb{N}$.

Given g, we write $w \models v(g)$ if the expression obtained by replacing each x with $w(x)$ and each p with $v(p)$ in g evaluates to true.

Let AP be a set of atomic propositions. Let us recall L/U-PTAs:

Definition 1 (L/U-PTA). *An L/U-PTA $\mathcal{A}$ is a tuple $\mathcal{A} = (\Sigma, L, \mathbf{L}, l_0, \mathbb{X}, \mathbb{P}, E)$, where:*

1. *Σ is a finite set of actions,*
2. *L is a finite set of locations,*
3. *$\mathbf{L}$ is a label function $\mathbf{L} : L \to 2^{AP}$,*
4. *$l_0 \in L$ is the initial location,*
5. *$\mathbb{X}$ is a finite set of clocks,*
6. *$\mathbb{P}$ is a finite set of parameters partitioned into lower-bound parameters and upper-bound parameters*
7. *E is a finite set of edges $e = (l, g, a, R, l')$ where $l, l' \in L$ are the source and target locations, $a \in \Sigma$, $R \subseteq \mathbb{X}$ is a set of clocks to be reset, and g is a conjunction of a u-guard and an l-guard.*

Unlike the classical definition of [HRSV02], we consider L/U-PTAs without invariants. We define a U-PTA [BL09] as an L/U-PTA where in each edge, g is a u-guard.

Given v, we denote by $v(\mathcal{A})$ the non-parametric structure where all occurrences of a parameter p_i have been replaced by $v(p_i)$. We denote as a *timed automaton* any structure $v(\mathcal{A})$, by assuming a rescaling of the constants: by multiplying all constants in $v(\mathcal{A})$ by their least common denominator, we obtain an equivalent (integer-valued) TA. A *bounded* U-PTA is a U-PTA with a bounded parameter domain that assigns to each parameter a minimum integer bound and a maximum integer bound. That is, each parameter p_i ranges in an interval $[a_i, b_i]$, with $a_i, b_i \in \mathbb{N}$. Hence, a bounded parameter domain is a hyperrectangle of dimension M.

Let us first recall the concrete semantics of TA.

Definition 2 (Semantics of a TA). *Given a L/U-PTA $\mathcal{A} = (\Sigma, L, \mathbf{L}, l_0, \mathbb{X}, \mathbb{P}, E)$, and a parameter valuation v, the semantics of $v(\mathcal{A})$ is given by the timed transition system (TTS) $(S, s_0, \to)$, with $S = \{(l, w) \in L \times \mathbb{R}_+^H\}$, $s_0 = (l_0, \mathbf{0})$ and $\to$ consists of the discrete and (continuous) delay transition relations: (i) discrete transitions: $(l, w) \overset{e}{\mapsto} (l', w')$, if $(l, w), (l', w') \in S$, and there exists $e = (l, g, a, R, l') \in E$, such that $w' = [w]_R$, and $w \models v(g)$. (ii) delay transitions: $(l, w) \overset{d}{\mapsto} (l, w + d)$, with $d \in \mathbb{R}_+$.*

Moreover we write $(l, w) \xrightarrow{e} (l', w')$ if $\exists d, w'' : (l, w) \xmapsto{d} (l, w'') \xmapsto{e} (l', w')$.

Given a TA $v(\mathcal{A})$ with concrete semantics $(S, s_0, \rightarrow)$, we refer to the states of S as the *concrete states* of $v(\mathcal{A})$. A *run* of $v(\mathcal{A})$ is a possibly infinite alternating sequence of states of $v(\mathcal{A})$ and edges starting from the initial state s_0 of the form $s_0 \xrightarrow{e_0} s_1 \xrightarrow{e_1} \cdots \xrightarrow{e_{m-1}} s_m \xrightarrow{e_m} \cdots$, such that for all $i = 0, 1, \ldots, e_i \in E$, and $(s_i, e_i, s_{i+1}) \in \rightarrow$. Given a run ρ, $\mathsf{time}(\rho)$ gives the total sum of the delays d along ρ. Given $s = (l, w)$, we say that s is reachable if s appears in a run of $v(\mathcal{A})$. By extension, we say that a label lb is reachable in $v(\mathcal{A})$ if there exists a state (l, w) that is reachable such that $lb \in \mathbf{L}(l)$. Given a set of locations $T \subseteq L$, we say that a run stays in T if all of its states (l, w) are such that $l \in T$.

A *maximal* run is a run that either contains an infinite number of discrete transitions, or that cannot be extended by a discrete transition. A maximal run is deadlocked if it is finite, i. e., contains a finite number of discrete transitions. By extension, we say that a TA is deadlocked if it contains at least one deadlocked run.

Given $ap \in AP$ and $c \in \mathbb{N}$, a TCTL formula is given by the following:

$$\varphi ::= \quad \top \quad | \quad ap \quad | \quad \neg\varphi \quad | \quad \varphi \wedge \varphi \quad | \quad \mathsf{E}\varphi\mathsf{U}_{\bowtie c}\varphi \quad | \quad \mathsf{A}\varphi\mathsf{U}_{\bowtie c}\varphi$$

A reads "always", E reads "exists", and U reads "until".

Standard abbreviations include Boolean operators as well as $\mathsf{EF}_{\bowtie c}\varphi$ for $\mathsf{E}\top\mathsf{U}_{\bowtie c}\varphi$, $\mathsf{AF}_{\bowtie c}\varphi$ for $\mathsf{A}\top\mathsf{U}_{\bowtie c}\varphi$ and $\mathsf{EG}_{\bowtie c}\varphi$ for $\neg\mathsf{AF}_{\bowtie c}\neg\varphi$. (F reads "eventually" while G reads "globally".)

Definition 3 (Semantics of TCTL). *Given a TA $v(\mathcal{A})$, the following clauses define when a state s_i of its TTS $(S, s_0, \rightarrow)$ satisfies a TCTL formula φ, denoted by $s_i \models \varphi$, by induction over the structure of φ (semantics of Boolean operators is omitted): (i) $s_i \models \mathsf{E}\varphi\mathsf{U}_{\bowtie c}\Psi$ if there is a maximal run ρ in $v(\mathcal{A})$ with $\sigma = s_i \xrightarrow{e_i} \cdots \xrightarrow{e_{j-1}} s_j$ $(i < j)$ a prefix of ρ s.t. $s_j \models \Psi$, $\mathsf{time}(\sigma) \bowtie c$, and if $i \leq k < j$, $s_k \models \varphi$, and (ii) $s_i \models \mathsf{A}\varphi\mathsf{U}_{\bowtie c}\Psi$ if for each maximal run ρ in $v(\mathcal{A})$ there exists $\sigma = s_i \xrightarrow{e_i} \cdots \xrightarrow{e_{j-1}} s_j$ $(i < j)$ a prefix of ρ s.t. $s_j \models \Psi$, $\mathsf{time}(\sigma) \bowtie c$, and if $i \leq k < j$, $s_k \models \varphi$.*

In $\mathsf{E}\varphi\mathsf{U}_{\bowtie c}\Psi$ the classical until is extended by requiring that φ be satisfied within a duration (from the current state) verifying the constraint "$\bowtie c$". Given v, an L/U-PTA $\mathcal{A}$ and a TCTL formula φ, we write $v(\mathcal{A}) \models \varphi$ when $s_0 \models \varphi$.

We define *flat TCTL* as the subset of TCTL where, in $\mathsf{E}\varphi\mathsf{U}_{\bowtie c}\varphi$ and $\mathsf{A}\varphi\mathsf{U}_{\bowtie c}\varphi$, φ must be a formula of propositional logic (a boolean combination of atomic propositions).

In this article, we address the following problems:

TCTL-emptiness problem:
INPUT: an L/U-PTA $\mathcal{A}$ and a TCTL formula φ
PROBLEM: is the set of valuations v such that $v(\mathcal{A}) \models \varphi$ empty?

More specifically, we will address in Sect. 5 the EG-emptiness (resp. EG-universality problem) i.e., whether, given an L/U-PTA $\mathcal{A}$ and a subset of its locations T, the set of parameter valuations for which there is a run in $v(\mathcal{A})$ that stays in T is empty (resp. universal).

3   Undecidability of TCTL Emptiness for U-PTAs

We exhibit here a formula that shows that TCTL emptiness is undecidable for U-PTAs.

Theorem 1. *The* EGAF$_{=0}$*-emptiness problem is undecidable for U-PTAs.*

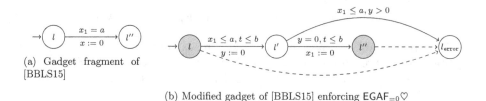

(a) Gadget fragment of [BBLS15]

(b) Modified gadget of [BBLS15] enforcing EGAF$_{=0}\heartsuit$

Fig. 1. A gadget fragment and its modification into a U-PTA

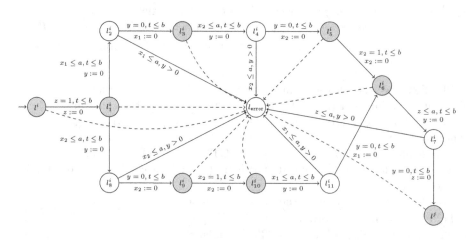

Fig. 2. Increment gadget

Proof. We reduce from the halting problem for two-counter machines, which is undecidable. Recall that a two-counter machine is a finite state machine with two integer-valued counters c_1, c_2. Two different instructions (presented for c_1 and identical for c_2) are considered: *(i)* when in state q_i, increment c_1 and go to q_j; *(ii)* when in state q_i, if $c_1 = 0$ go to q_k, otherwise decrement c_1 and go to q_j. We assume w.l.o.g. that the machine halts iff it reaches a special state q_{halt}.

We define a U-PTA that, under some conditions, will encode the machine, and for which $\mathsf{EGAF}_{=0}\heartsuit$-emptiness holds iff the machine does not halt (for some $\heartsuit \in AP$). Our U-PTA $\mathcal{A}$ uses two (possibly integer-valued) parameters a, b, and five clocks y, x_1, x_2, z, t. Each state q_i of the two-counter machine is encoded by a location l^i of $\mathcal{A}$. Each increment (resp. decrement) instruction of the two-counter machine is encoded into a U-PTA fragment depicted in Figs. 2 and 3, respectively.

Our encoding is inspired by [BBLS15] and is such that when in l^i with $w(z) = 0$ then $w(x_1)$ (resp. $w(x_2)$) represents the value of the counter c_1 (resp. c_2). However, as U-PTAs disallow constraints of the form $x = a$, we need to considerably modify the encoding. Each of our locations has exactly one label: $\heartsuit$ for the locations already present in [BBLS15] (depicted in yellow in our figures), and $\spadesuit$ for the newly introduced locations (depicted in white). In [BBLS15], the gadgets encoding the two-counter machine instructions use edges of the form of Fig. 1a. To define a proper U-PTA, we replace each of these edges by a special construction given in Fig. 1b using only inequalities of the form $x \leq a$. Our goal is to show that a run will exactly encode the two-counter machine if all guards $x \leq a$ are in fact taken when the clock valuation is exactly equal to a. Those runs are further denoted by $\rho_\heartsuit$. Consider the transformed version given in Fig. 1b: due to the $\leq$, runs exist that take the guard "too early" (i.e., before $x_1 = a$). Those are denoted by $\rho_\spadesuit$. But, in that case, observe that in l', one can either take the transition to l'' in 0-time, or spend some time in l' and then (with guard $y > 0$) go to l_{error}. Therefore on this gadget, $\mathsf{EGAF}_{=0}\heartsuit$ is true at l' iff the guard $x_1 \leq a$ from l to l' is taken at the very last moment. Note that $\mathsf{EGAF}_{=0}\heartsuit$ is trivially true in l and l'' as both locations are labeled with $\heartsuit$. (Also note that there are plenty of runs from l to l_{error} that do not encode properly the machine; they will be discarded in our reasoning later.)

We also assume a condition $t \leq b$ on all guarded transitions, where t is a clock never reset. As presented in Fig. 1b, there are transitions without guard (dashed) from l, l'' (labeled with $\heartsuit$) to l_{error}. This is done to enforce the violation of $\mathsf{EGAF}_{=0}\heartsuit$ whenever $t = b$: indeed, while $t < b$ a run can either go to l_{error} from a location labeled with $\heartsuit$, or not, but as $t = b$ every run is forced to go to l_{error}, making $\mathsf{EGAF}_{=0}\heartsuit$ false.

Increment. We give the increment gadget for c_1 in Fig. 2 (the gadget for c_2 is symmetric). Let v be a valuation, and assume we are in configuration (l^i, w), where $w(z) = 0$. First note that if $w(x_1) \geq v(a)$, there is no execution ending in l^j due to the guard $x_1 \leq a$ tested in both the upper and the lower branch in the automaton. The same reasoning is relevant for $w(x_2)$.

Assume $w(x_1), w(x_2) < v(a)$. Two cases show up: $w(x_1) \leq w(x_2)$ and $w(x_1) > w(x_2)$, which explains why we need two paths in Fig. 2. First, if $w(x_1) \leq w(x_2)$, we can perform several executions with different time delays, but those are bounded. In the following, we write w as the tuple $(w(x_1), w(x_2), w(z), w(y))$, omitting t.

From l^i, we prove that there is a unique run that reaches l^j without violating our property. It is the one that takes each transition with a u-guard $x \leq a$ at the exact moment $w(x) = v(a)$ which we describe in the following.

From (l^i, w), the unique delay to pass the transition is 1, hence we arrive in the configuration $(l_1^i, (w(x_1) + 1, w(x_2) + 1, w(y) + 1, 0))$. Here, the largest delay to pass the transition is $v(a) - w(x_1) - 1$ so a configuration we possibly obtain is $(l_2^i, (d_1, d_2, d_3, 0))$ with $(d_1, d_2, d_3) \leq (v(a), w(x_2) - w(x_1) + v(a), v(a) - w(x_1) - 1)$. If $(d_1, d_2, d_3) < (v(a), w(x_2) - w(x_1) + v(a), v(a) - w(x_1) - 1)$ then the guard $y > 0$ in the transition to l_{error} is verified, hence our property $\mathsf{EGAF}_{=0}\heartsuit$ is violated. We remove all these runs and keep the only run that ends in the exact configuration $(l_2^i, (v(a), w(x_2) - w(x_1) + v(a), v(a) - w(x_1) - 1, 0))$. As $y = 0$ holds the next configuration is $(l_3^i, (0, w(x_2) - w(x_1) + v(a), v(a) - w(x_1) - 1, 0))$. The largest delay to pass the next transition is $w(x_1) - w(x_2)$, so a configuration we possibly obtain is $(l_4^i, (d_1, d_2, d_3, 0))$ with $(d_1, d_2, d_3) \leq (w(x_1) - w(x_2), v(a), v(a) - w(x_2) - 1)$. If $(d_1, d_2, d_3) < (w(x_1) - w(x_2), v(a), v(a) - w(x_2) - 1)$ then the guard $y > 0$ in the transition to l_{error} is verified, hence our property $\mathsf{EGAF}_{=0}\heartsuit$ is violated. We remove all these runs and keep the only run that ends in the exact configuration $(l_4^i, (w(x_1) - w(x_2), v(a), v(a) - w(x_2) - 1, 0)$. As $y = 0$ holds the next configuration is $(l_5^i, (w(x_1) - w(x_2), 0, v(a) - w(x_2) - 1, 0))$. Now the unique delay to pass the transition is 1, hence as we reset x_2 we arrive in the configuration $(l_6^i, (w(x_1) - w(x_2) + 1, 0, v(a) - w(x_2), 1)$. The largest delay to pass the next transition is $w(x_2)$, so a configuration we possibly obtain is $(l_7^i, (d_1, d_2, d_3, 0))$ with $(d_1, d_2, d_3) \leq (w(x_1) + 1, w(x_2), v(a))$. If $(d_1, d_2, d_3) < (w(x_1) + 1, w(x_2), v(a))$ then the guard $y > 0$ in the transition to l_{error} is verified, hence our property $\mathsf{EGAF}_{=0}\heartsuit$ is violated. We remove all these runs and keep the only run that ends in the exact configuration $(l_7^i, (w(x_1) + 1, w(x_2), v(a), 0))$. As $y = 0$ holds the next configuration is $(l^j, (w(x_1) + 1, w(x_2), 0, 0))$, and as $w(z) = 0$, $w(x_1)$ represents the exact value of the counter c_1 increased by 1.

In its shorter form, this run is: $(l^i, w) \xrightarrow{1} (l_1^i, (w(x_1) + 1, w(x_2) + 1, w(y) + 1, 0)) \xrightarrow{v(a) - w(x_1) - 1} (l_2^i, (v(a), w(x_2) - w(x_1) + v(a), v(a) - w(x_1) - 1, 0)) \xrightarrow{0} (l_3^i, (0, w(x_2) - w(x_1) + v(a), v(a) - w(x_1) - 1, 0)) \xrightarrow{w(x_1) - w(x_2)} (l_4^i, (w(x_1) - w(x_2), v(a), v(a) - w(x_2) - 1, 0)) \xrightarrow{0} (l_5^i, (w(x_1) - w(x_2), 0, v(a) - w(x_2) - 1, 0)) \xrightarrow{1} (l_6^i, (w(x_1) - w(x_2) + 1, 0, v(a) - w(x_2), 1)) \xrightarrow{w(x_2)} (l_7^i, (w(x_1) + 1, w(x_2), v(a), 0)) \xrightarrow{0} (l^j, (w(x_1) + 1, w(x_2), 0, 0))$

Second, if $w(x_1) > w(x_2)$ we take the lower branch and apply the same reasoning.

Decrement and 0-test. The decrement and 0-test gadget is similar: we reuse the reasoning of [BBLS15], and apply the same modifications as in Fig. 1b. Note that the 0-test gadget has been completely rewritten from [BBLS15] to ensure a time elapsing of at least $a + 1$ time units when the guards are taken at the last moment.

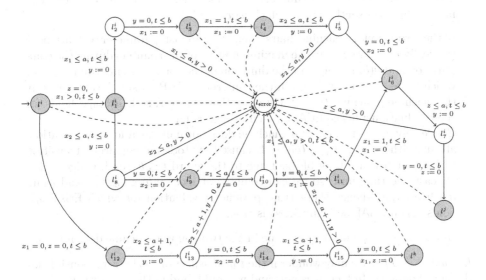

Fig. 3. Decrement gadget

We give the decrement gadget in Fig. 3. Assume we are in (l^i, w) where $w(z) = 0$ and suppose $w(x_1) > 0$. We can enter the configuration $(l_1, (w(x_1), w(x_2), 0, w(y)))$ as the guard $z = 0$ ensures no time has elapsed.

Two cases show up: $w(x_1) \leq w(x_2)$ and $w(x_1) > w(x_2)$.

First, if $w(x_1) \leq w(x_2)$, we can perform several executions with different time delays, but those are bounded. From l^i, there is a unique run that reaches l^j without violating our property. It is the one that takes each transition with a u-guard $x \leq a$ at the exact moment $w(x) = v(a)$: $(l^i, (w(x_1), w(x_2), 0, w(y)) \xrightarrow{0} (l_1^i, (w(x_1), w(x_2), 0, w(y)) \xrightarrow{v(a) - w(x_1)}$
$(l_2^i, (v(a), w(x_2) + v(a) - w(x_1), v(a) - w(x_1), 0)) \xrightarrow{0} (l_3^i, (0, w(x_2) + v(a) - w(x_1), v(a) - w(x_1), 0)) \xrightarrow{1} (l_4^i, (0, w(x_2) + v(a) - w(x_1) + 1, v(a) - w(x_1) + 1, 1)) \xrightarrow{w(x_1) - w(x_2) - 1} (l_5^i, (w(x_1) - w(x_2) - 1, v(a), v(a) - w(x_2), 0)) \xrightarrow{0} (l_6^i, (w(x_1) - w(x_2) - 1, 0, v(a) - w(x_2), 0)) \xrightarrow{w(x_2)} (l_7^i, (w(x_1) - 1, w(x_2), v(a), 0)) \xrightarrow{0} (l^j, (w(x_1) - 1, w(x_2), 0, 0)).$

Simulating the 2-counter Machine. Now, consider the runs $\rho_\spadesuit$ that take a u-guard $x \leq a$ "too early". At this moment, since after a small amount of time we have $x \leq a$ and $y > 0$ are true, there is a run that eventually reaches l_{error} and can never leave it; hence $\mathsf{EGAF}_{=0}\heartsuit$ does not hold for these runs. The same way, the runs $\rho_\spadesuit$ that take an unguarded transition to l_{error} (whether or not $t \leq b$ is true) are stuck in a location labeled by $\spadesuit$; hence $\mathsf{EGAF}_{=0}\heartsuit$ does not hold for these runs. In the following, we do not consider these runs anymore.

Now, let us consider the runs $\rho_\heartsuit$ that take each u-guard at the very last moment, which is exactly when a clock $w(x) = v(a)$.

- If the two-counter machine halts then, there exist parameter valuations v (typically $v(a)$ larger than the maximum value of the counters during the computation and $v(b)$ larger than the duration of the corresponding run in $\mathcal{A}$), for which there is a (unique) run in the constructed U-PTA simulating correctly the machine, reaching l_{halt} and staying there forever, so $\mathsf{EGAF}_{=0}\heartsuit$ holds for these valuations: hence $\mathsf{EGAF}_{=0}\heartsuit$-emptiness is false.
- Conversely, if the two-counter machine does not halt, then for any valuation, all runs either end in l_{error} (either because they took an unguarded transition to l_{error} or because they blocked due to the guard $t \leq b$—each gadget takes at least one time unit, so we can combine at most $v(b)$ gadgets—and again reached l_{error}); hence there is no parameter valuation for which $\mathsf{EGAF}_{=0}\heartsuit$ holds. Then $\mathsf{EGAF}_{=0}\heartsuit$-emptiness is true.

Therefore $\mathsf{EGAF}_{=0}\heartsuit$-emptiness is true iff the two-counter machine does not halt.

Remark 1 (CTL). We may wonder if the *timed* aspect of TCTL is responsible for the undecidability. In fact, it is not, and we could modify the proof to show that CTL itself leads to undecidability. The idea is that we remove the unguarded transitions in both the increment and the decrement and 0-test gadgets, label each location of $L \setminus \{l_{\text{error}}\}$ with $\heartsuit$, and add an unguarded self-loop on l_{halt}. We claim that EGAX-emptiness is undecidable: we show that $\mathsf{EGAX}\heartsuit$ holds for a unique run of a U-PTA that simulates a two-counter machine, with a similar reasoning.

4   Undecidability for Bounded U-PTAs

We now show that undecidability remains even when the parameter domain is bounded. Note that, if we were addressing the full class of PTAs, showing an undecidability result for bounded PTAs automatically extends to the full class of PTAs, as we can simulate any bounded PTA by an unbounded PTA (see, e. g., [ALR16b, Fig. 3]). This is not the case for U-PTAs: indeed, in [ALR16b], we showed that bounded (L/)U-PTAs are incomparable with (L/)U-PTAs; that is, it is impossible to simulate a bounded U-PTA using a U-PTA (e. g., by using a gadget that enforces parameters to be bounded), due to the nature of guards, preventing us to artificially bound a parameter both from above and from below (in fact, for U-PTAs, bounding from below is possible, but not from above). Therefore, we must study both problems. Finally note that the EG-emptiness is decidable for bounded L/U-PTAs but undecidable for L/U-PTAs [AL17], which motivates further the need to investigate both versions.

Theorem 2. *The* EGAF$_{=0}$*-emptiness is undecidable for bounded U-PTAs.*

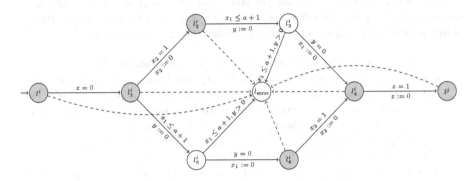

Fig. 4. Increment gadget

We reduce this time from the boundedness problem for two-counter machines (i.e., whether the value of the counters remains bounded along the execution), which is undecidable.

We define a U-PTA that, under some conditions, will encode the machine, and for which EGAF$_{=0}\heartsuit$-emptiness holds iff the counters in the machine remain bounded. The idea is as follows: we reuse a different encoding (originally from [ALR16a]), and apply the same modifications as we did in the proof of Theorem 1.

Our U-PTA $\mathcal{A}$ uses one parameter a, and four clocks y, x_1, x_2, z. Each state q_i of the two-counter machine is encoded by a location l^i of $\mathcal{A}$. Each increment instruction of the two-counter machine is encoded into a U-PTA fragment. The decrement instruction is a modification of the one in [ALR16a] using the same modifications as the increment gadget (Fig. 4).

Given v, our encoding is such that when in l^i with $w(z) = 0$ then $w(x_1)$ (resp. $w(x_2)$) represents the value of the counter c_1 (resp. c_2) encoded by $1 - v(a)c_1$ (resp. $1 - v(a)c_2$). Each of our locations has exactly one label: $\heartsuit$ for the locations already present in [ALR16a] (depicted in yellow in our figures), and $\spadesuit$ for the newly introduced locations (depicted in white).

We assume $a \in [0, 1]$. The initial encoding when $w(z) = 0$ is $w(x_1) = 1 - v(a)c_1, w(x_2) = 1 - v(a)c_2, w(y) = 0$. Suppose $w(x_2) \leq w(x_1)$. From l^i, we prove that there is a unique run, going through the upper branch of the gadget, that reaches l^j without violating our property. It is the one that takes each transition with a u-guard $x \leq a + 1$ at the exact moment $w(x) = v(a) + 1$:

$$(l^i, w) \xrightarrow{0} (l^i_1, (1 - v(a)c_1, 1 - v(a)c_2, 0, 0)) \xrightarrow{v(a)c_2} (l^i_2, (1 - v(a)c_1 +$$

$$v(a)c_2, 0, v(a)c_2, v(a)c_2)) \xrightarrow{v(a) - v(a)c_2 + v(a)c_1} (l^i_3, (v(a) + 1, v(a) - v(a)c_2 + v(a)c_1,$$

$$v(a) + v(a)c_1, 0) \xrightarrow{0} (l^i_4, (0, v(a) - v(a)c_2 + v(a)c_1, v(a) + v(a)c_1, 0) \xrightarrow{1 - v(a) - v(a)c_1}$$

$$(l^j, (1 - v(a)(c_1 + 1), 1 - v(a)c_2, 0, 1 - v(a)(c_1 + 1)))$$

The case were $w(x_2) \leq w(x_1)$ is similar, taking the lower branch of the gadget.

Now, let us consider the runs $\rho_\heartsuit$ that take each u-guard at the very last moment, which is exactly when a clock $w(x) = v(a) + 1$. (For the same reason as in the proof of Theorem 1, other runs violate the property anyway.)

– If the counters of the two-counter machine remain bounded then,
  - either the two-counter machine halts (by reaching q_{halt}) and there exist parameter valuations v (typically $v(a)$ small enough to encode the required value of the counters during the computation), for which there is a (unique) run in the constructed U-PTA simulating correctly the machine, reaching l_{halt} and staying there forever, so $EGAF_{=0}\heartsuit$ holds for these valuations: hence $EGAF_{=0}\heartsuit$-emptiness is false;
  - or the two-counter machine loops forever (and never reaches q_{halt}) with bounded values of the counters, and again there exist parameter valuations v (again small enough to encode the maximal value of the counters) for which there is an infinite (unique) run in the U-PTA simulating correctly the machine. As this run is infinite, we infinitely often visit the decrement and/or the increment gadget(s), so $EGAF_{=0}\heartsuit$ holds for these valuations: hence $EGAF_{=0}\heartsuit$-emptiness is again false.
– Conversely, if the counters of the two-counter machine are unbounded, then for any valuation, all runs either end in l_{error}, either because they took an unguarded transition to l_{error} or because they blocked due to the guard $x \leq a + 1$ —indeed when in l_6^i, we have $w(z) = v(a)(c_1 + 1)$ if c_1 is unbounded, after a sufficient number of steps we cannot pass the guard $z = 1$— and again reached l_{error}. Hence there is no parameter valuation for which $EGAF_{=0}\heartsuit$ holds. Then $EGAF_{=0}\heartsuit$-emptiness is true.

Using the same reasoning as in the proof of Theorem 1 and [ALR16a], we conclude that $EGAF_{=0}\heartsuit$-emptiness is true iff the values of the counters of the two-counter machine are unbounded.

5   Decidability of Flat-TCTL for L/U-PTAs Without Invariants

In this section, we prove that the EG-emptiness and universality problems are decidable for L/U-PTAs without invariants and with integer-valued parameters. Recall that for L/U-PTAs in their classical form with invariants (even over integer-valued parameters), these same problems are undecidable [AL17]. L/U-PTAs enjoy a well-known monotonicity property recalled in the following lemma (that corresponds to a reformulation of [HRSV02, Proposition 4.2]), stating that increasing upper-bound parameters or decreasing lower-bound parameters can only add behaviors. As our definition of L/U-PTAs does not involve invariants, our model is a subclass of L/U-PTAs as defined in [HRSV02, BL09]. Therefore, it holds for our definition of L/U-PTAs.

Lemma 1 (monotonicity). *Let $\mathcal{A}$ be an L/U-PTA without invariant and v be a parameter valuation. Let v' be a valuation such that for each upper-bound parameter p^+, $v'(p^+) \geq v(p^+)$ and for each lower-bound parameter p^-, $v'(p^-) \leq v(p^-)$. Then any run of $v(\mathcal{A})$ is a run of $v'(\mathcal{A})$.*

We will see that EG-emptiness can be reduced to the following two problems. The first one is *cycle-existence* [AL17]: given a TA $v(\mathcal{A})$, is there at least one run of $v(\mathcal{A})$ with an infinite number of discrete transitions? Before introducing the second problem, we need to have a closer look at deadlocks: recall that a state is deadlocked when no discrete transition can be taken, even after elapsing some time. As we do not have invariants, it will be either a state with no outgoing edge, or a state in which each outgoing transition contains at least one constraint on any clock x of the form $x \triangleleft k$, where k is a constant, or $x \triangleleft p^+$, where p^+ is a parameter. Indeed, for any parameter valuation, it suffices to wait enough time until all such guards are disabled—and the state becomes deadlocked. Note that with invariants, like in the L/U-PTAs of [HRSV02], this would not be sufficient: a state containing an invariant $x \triangleleft k$ and a transition containing a constraint $x \triangleleft k$ is not a deadlocked state, as the transition is forced to be taken. Formally, given an L/U-PTA[1] $\mathcal{A} = (\Sigma, L, \mathbf{L}, l_0, \mathbb{X}, \mathbb{P}, E)$, we define $L_D(\mathcal{A}) := \{l \in L \mid$ for all edges $(l, g, a, R, l') \in E$, g contains at least one constraint on a clock x of the form $x \triangleleft k$, where $k \in \mathbb{N}$, or $x \triangleleft p^+$, where $p^+ \in \mathbb{P}\}$.[2]

Now, the second problem we need to distinguish is *deadlock-existence*: given a TA $v(\mathcal{A})$, is there at least one run of $v(\mathcal{A})$ that is deadlocked, i.e., has no discrete successor (possibly after some delay)? As mentioned above, unlike the L/U-PTAs of [HRSV02], given an L/U-PTA $\mathcal{A}$, detecting deadlocks is equivalent in our L/U-PTAs without invariants to the *reachability* problem of a given location of $L_D(\mathcal{A})$. Let $v_{0/\infty}$ be the parameter valuation s.t. for each lower-bound parameter p^-, $v_{0/\infty}(p^-) = 0$ and for each upper-bound parameter p^+, $v_{0/\infty}(p^+) = \infty$.

Recall that EG T holds if either there is an infinite run staying in T, or there is a finite deadlocked run staying in T.

Lemma 2. *Let $\mathcal{A}$ be an L/U-PTA without invariant. There is a deadlock in $v(\mathcal{A})$ for some parameter valuation v iff there is $l \in L_D(\mathcal{A})$ reachable in $v_{0/\infty}(\mathcal{A})$.*

Proof. ⇒ Suppose $v(\mathcal{A})$ is deadlocked. There is a run in $v(\mathcal{A})$ ending in a state (l, w) with no possible outgoing transition. That means for all edges $(l, g, a, R, l') \in E$, guard $v(g)$ is not satisfied by $w + d$, for all $d \geq 0$. In particular, let M be the maximal constant appearing in the guards of $v_{0/\infty}(\mathcal{A})$ plus one, then g is not satisfied for $w + M$. Yet, for that clock valuation, for sure, all simple constraints of the form $k \triangleleft x$ are satisfied, so this means that g must contain at least one constraint on a clock x of the form $x \triangleleft k$, where $k \in \mathbb{N}$ and $k < w(x) + M$, or $x \triangleleft p^+$, where $p^+ \in \mathbb{P}$ and $v(p^+) < w(x) + M$. Therefore, $l \in L_D(\mathcal{A})$.

---

[1] Throughout this section, we do not use the labeling function $\mathbf{L}$.

[2] Observe that this definition also includes the locations with no outgoing edge at all.

Moreover as constraints in $v(\mathcal{A})$ are stronger than those in $v_{0/\infty}(\mathcal{A})$ (i.e., for each lower-bound parameter p^-, $v_{0/\infty}(p^-) \leq v(p^-)$ and for each upper-bound parameter p^+, $v(p^+) \leq v_{0/\infty}(p^+)$), from Lemma 1 l is reachable along a run of $v_{0/\infty}(\mathcal{A})$.

$\Leftarrow$ Conversely, let $l \in L_D(\mathcal{A})$ and suppose there is a run of $v_{0/\infty}(\mathcal{A})$ reaching (l, w), for some clock valuation w. Let v be the parameter valuation, defined as in the proof of [HRSV02, Proposition 4.4], such that (l, w) is also reachable in $v(\mathcal{A})$. That valuation assigns a finite value to upper bound parameters that we denote by μ.

Let $e = (l, g, a, R, l') \in E$. For each constraint of the form $x \lhd k$ with $k \in \mathbb{N}$ in g, define $d_1 = \max(0, \max_x(k - w(x))) + 1$. Then, for all clocks x and for all $d \geq d_1$, $w(x) + d \lhd k$ is false. Similarly, for each constraint of the form $x \lhd p^+$ with p^+ an upper-bound parameter in g, define $d_2 = \max(0, \max_x(\mu - w(x))) + 1$. Then, for all clocks x and for all $d \geq d_2$, $w(x) + d \lhd v(p^+)$ is false. Let $d_0 = \max(d_1, d_2)$ then, by construction $(l, w + d_0)$ is a deadlocked state in $v(\mathcal{A})$. $\quad\square$

Consider now a TA without invariants $\mathcal{A}$, and a subset T of its locations. We build a TA $T^+(\mathcal{A})$ as follows: first remove all locations not in T and remove all transitions to and from those removed locations. Second, add self-loops to all locations in $L_D(\mathcal{A})$, with a guard that is true, and no reset.

Lemma 3. $\mathsf{EG}(T)$ *holds if and only if there exists an infinite run in* $T^+(\mathcal{A})$.

Proof. $\Rightarrow$ Suppose $\mathsf{EG}(T)$ holds. Then there is a maximal path in $\mathcal{A}$ that stays in T. If that path is infinite then, by construction it is still possible in $T^+(\mathcal{A})$. Otherwise, it is finite and therefore it is a deadlock. From Lemma 2, this means that some location in $T \cap L_D(\mathcal{A})$ is reachable in $\mathcal{A}$, by always staying in T. Consequently that location is still reachable in $T^+(\mathcal{A})$ and since it belongs to $L_D(\mathcal{A})$, it has a self-loop in $T^+(\mathcal{A})$, which implies that there is an infinite run there.

$\Leftarrow$ In the other direction, suppose that there is an infinite run in $T^+(\mathcal{A})$. Either the corresponding infinite path never uses any of the added self-loops and therefore it is possible as is in $\mathcal{A}$, which implies $\mathsf{EG}(T)$, or it goes through $L_D(\mathcal{A})$ at least once. The latter means that some location in $L_D(\mathcal{A})$ is reachable in $\mathcal{A}$ by staying in T, and by Lemma 2, this implies that there exists a finite maximal path in $\mathcal{A}$, and finally that we have $\mathsf{EG}(T)$ in $\mathcal{A}$. $\quad\square$

Corollary 1. *The* EG-*emptiness and* EG-*universality problems are PSPACE-complete for integer-valued L/U-PTAs without invariants.*

Proof. PSPACE-hardness comes from the fact that an L/U-PTA that does not use parameters in guards is a TA and EG is PSPACE-hard for TAs [AD94].

Let $\mathcal{A}$ be an L/U-PTA and T a subset of its locations. Remark that the construction of Lemma 3 is independant of the constants in the guards, and hence can be done in the same way for a PTA, giving another PTA $T^+(\mathcal{A})$ such that, for all parameter valuations v, $T^+(v(\mathcal{A})) = v(T^+(\mathcal{A}))$. By Lemma 3, EG-emptiness (resp. EG-universality) then reduces to the emptiness (resp. universality) of the set of parameter valuations v such that $v(T^+(\mathcal{A}))$ has an infinite accepting path. We conclude by recalling that the latter problem can be solved in PSPACE for both emptiness and universality [BL09].   □

This result is important as it is the first non-trivial subclass of PTAs for which EG-universality (equivalent by negation to AF-emptiness) is decidable.

We already had the same complexity for EF-emptiness and EF-universality [HRSV02], and by negation we can get the other flat formulas of TCTL, both for universality and emptiness (e. g., AF-emptiness is "not EG-universality"). It is also easy to see that all those results would hold for flat formulas using the "until" operator. Therefore we have:

Theorem 3. *Flat-TCTL-emptiness and flat-TCTL-universality are PSPACE-complete for integer-valued L/U-PTAs without invariant.*

Remark 2. These results come without Flat-TCTL-synthesis. Indeed, suppose we can compute the set of parameters s.t. a Flat-TCTL formula is satisfied by an integer-valued L/U-PTAs without invariant, say EF, and check for the emptiness of its intersection with a set of equality constraints. Consider an integer-valued PTA $\mathcal{A}$ without invariants. For each parameter p of $\mathcal{A}$ that is used both as an upper-bound and as a lower-bound, syntactically replace its occurrences as an upper-bound (resp. lower-bound) by a new parameter p^+ (resp. p^-). We obtain an integer-valued L/U-PTAs without invariant $\mathcal{A}'$. By hypothesis, let S be the solution set of parameters valuations to the EF-synthesis problem for $\mathcal{A}'$. Let S' be the set of equality constraints $p^+ = p^-$. Therefore we can decide whether $S \cap S' = \emptyset$ and the EF-emptiness problem is decidable for integer-valued PTAs without invariants, in contradiction with the results of [BBLS15].

6   Conclusion and Perspectives

In this paper, we solved the open problem of the nested TCTL-emptiness for U-PTAs, that implies the undecidability of the whole TCTL-emptiness problem for this subclass of L/U-PTAs. Note that our proof holds even for integer-valued parameters, and even without invariants. This is a reminder that the border between undecidability and decidability problems for L/U-PTAs and its subclasses is quite thin. Unlike PTAs and bounded PTAs, U-PTAs and bounded U-PTAs are incomparable, hence we had to verify whether the same reasoning was applicable when the parameter domain is bounded. For this purpose, we used another construction to reduce to a bounded U-PTA from a two-counter machine to prove that the same TCTL-emptiness problem is also undecidable.

Moreover, we proved that EG-emptiness and universality are PSPACE-complete for (unbounded) integer-valued L/U-PTAs without invariants. This result is particularly interesting as it was undecidable with invariants [AL17]. Using existing results, we have that flat TCTL-emptiness and universality are decidable for this class, and therefore for integer-valued U-PTAs without invariants, which contrasts with our undecidability result and shows that we are there again at the frontier of decidability.

Future Work. This work opens new perspectives: where exactly the undecidability starts (in particular whether EG and AF are decidable for U-PTAs with invariants or real-valued parameters, which remains open, see Table 1), whether our proofs in Sects. 3 and 4 can be extended over bounded time, and whether the same results hold for L-PTAs (lower-bound PTAs).

Also, extending our decidability result in Theorem 3 while keeping decidability will be an interesting challenge.

References

[ACD93] Alur, R., Courcoubetis, C., Dill, D.: Model-checking in dense real-time. Inf. Comput. **104**(1), 2–34 (1993)

[AD94] Alur, R., Dill, D.L.: A theory of timed automata. Theor. Comput. Sci. **126**(2), 183–235 (1994)

[AHV93] Alur, R., Henzinger, T.A., Vardi, M.Y.: Parametric real-time reasoning. In: Kosaraju, S.R., Johnson, D.S., Aggarwal, A. (eds.) STOC, pp. 592–601. ACM, New York (1993)

[AL17] André, É., Lime, D.: Liveness in L/U-parametric timed automata. In: ACSD, pp. 9–18. IEEE (2017)

[ALR16a] André, É., Lime, D., Roux, O.H.: Decision problems for parametric timed automata. In: Ogata, K., Lawford, M., Liu, S. (eds.) ICFEM 2016. LNCS, vol. 10009, pp. 400–416. Springer, Cham (2016). https://doi.org/10.1007/978-3-319-47846-3_25

[ALR16b] André, É., Lime, D., Roux, O.H.: On the expressiveness of parametric timed automata. In: Fränzle, M., Markey, N. (eds.) FORMATS 2016. LNCS, vol. 9884, pp. 19–34. Springer, Cham (2016). https://doi.org/10.1007/978-3-319-44878-7_2

[And17] André, É.: What's decidable about parametric timed automata? Int. J. Softw. Tools Technol. Transf. (2017, to appear)

[BBLS15] Beneš, N., Bezděk, P., Larsen, K.G., Srba, J.: Language emptiness of continuous-time parametric timed automata. In: Halldórsson, M.M., Iwama, K., Kobayashi, N., Speckmann, B. (eds.) ICALP 2015. LNCS, vol. 9135, pp. 69–81. Springer, Heidelberg (2015). https://doi.org/10.1007/978-3-662-47666-6_6

[BL09] Bozzelli, L., La Torre, S.: Decision problems for lower/upper bound parametric timed automata. Formal Methods Syst. Des. **35**(2), 121–151 (2009)

[BO14] Bundala, D., Ouaknine, J.: Advances in parametric real-time reasoning. In: Csuhaj-Varjú, E., Dietzfelbinger, M., Ésik, Z. (eds.) MFCS 2014. LNCS, vol. 8634, pp. 123–134. Springer, Heidelberg (2014). https://doi.org/10.1007/978-3-662-44522-8_11

[Doy07] Doyen, L.: Robust parametric reachability for timed automata. Inf. Process. Lett. **102**(5), 208–213 (2007)

[HRSV02] Hune, T., Romijn, J., Stoelinga, M., Vaandrager, F.W.: Linear parametric model checking of timed automata. J. Logic Algebraic Program. **52–53**, 183–220 (2002)

[JLR15] Jovanović, A., Lime, D., Roux, O.H.: Integer parameter synthesis for timed automata. IEEE Trans. Softw. Eng. **41**(5), 445–461 (2015)

[Mil00] Miller, J.S.: Decidability and complexity results for timed automata and semi-linear hybrid automata. In: Lynch, N., Krogh, B.H. (eds.) HSCC 2000. LNCS, vol. 1790, pp. 296–310. Springer, Heidelberg (2000). https://doi.org/10.1007/3-540-46430-1_26

Monitoring Temporal Logic with Clock Variables

Adrián Elgyütt, Thomas Ferrère[✉], and Thomas A. Henzinger

IST Austria, Klosterneuburg, Austria
`thomas.ferrere@ist.ac.at`

Abstract. We solve the offline monitoring problem for timed propositional temporal logic (TPTL), interpreted over dense-time Boolean signals. The variant of TPTL we consider extends linear temporal logic (LTL) with *clock* variables and *reset* quantifiers, providing a mechanism to specify real-time constraints. We first describe a general monitoring algorithm based on an exhaustive computation of the set of satisfying clock assignments as a finite *union of zones*. We then propose a specialized monitoring algorithm for the one-variable case using a partition of the time domain based on the notion of *region equivalence*, whose complexity is linear in the length of the signal, thereby generalizing a known result regarding the monitoring of metric temporal logic (MTL). The region and zone representations of time constraints are known from timed automata verification and can also be used in the discrete-time case. Our prototype implementation appears to outperform previous discrete-time implementations of TPTL monitoring.

1 Introduction

Temporal logic monitoring [20] is a well-studied topic with multiple applications [17,19,23,32]. A *monitor* is a program that verifies the conformance of a single run of the system against the specification; generally speaking monitoring is one of the methods for ensuring that a system meets its specification.[1] There are two types of monitoring – online and offline. The online monitor runs simultaneously with the system, and is suitable for use on a production system to enforce a safety property of that system. The offline monitor verifies a trace of a finite length after the system execution/simulation, and is thus suitable for use in a testing scenario.

In discrete systems such as programs, behaviors can be formalized in linear temporal logic (LTL) [30]. Temporal logic abstracts time into so-called temporal modalities, such as *always*, denoted $\square$, and its dual *eventually*, denoted $\lozenge$. As an example, the typical property that every request p is followed by a grant q can be

---

[1] While temporal logic monitoring provides less guarantees than other formal methods such as model checking, the range of applicability of monitoring techniques is wider as it does not suffer from the infamous state-explosion: for monitoring purposes, all that is needed from the system model is its ability to generate execution traces.

© Springer Nature Switzerland AG 2018
D. N. Jansen and P. Prabhakar (Eds.): FORMATS 2018, LNCS 11022, pp. 53–70, 2018.
https://doi.org/10.1007/978-3-030-00151-3_4

written $\Box(p \to \Diamond q)$. In real-time systems, or in the setting of asynchronous communication, the specification not only talks of the temporal ordering of events, but also of their temporal distance. One way to specify such a distance is to integrate timing constraints into temporal modalities, as done in metric temporal logic (MTL) [25]. For instance, in MTL one can write $\Diamond_{[1,2]} q$ to specify a trace where proposition q holds eventually within 1 to 2 time units. Another way to specify the temporal distance between events is to use dedicated variables. This approach is advocated by [3] with the introduction of *timed propositional temporal logic* (TPTL). In TPTL, timing and sequential aspects are made orthogonal by the use of dedicated *clock* variables ranging over time, enabling the clean specification of temporal objectives. A clock x is a real-valued variable that measures the time elapsed from the temporal context of a formula to the temporal context of its subformulas. For this one can use *reset* quantifiers $x.\varphi$ over a formula φ, and constraints of the form $x \leq c$ (or $x \geq c$) that compare the time elapsed from the binding quantifier with some integer constant[2].

Over an integer (discrete) time domain, timing constraints can be emulated in LTL by nesting *next-time* operators, but such an encoding is cumbersome and exponential in nature as durations are represented in unary. Over a real (continuous) time domain, the *next-time* changes its meaning and one must use dedicated logics such as MTL or TPTL in order to specify timing constraints. In this setting, the one-clock fragment of TPTL is more expressive than MTL [9,21]. To translate MTL operators into TPTL, we only need one clock variable, with for instance $\Diamond_{[0,1]} p$ translating as $x.\Diamond(p \land x \leq 1)$. TPTL timing constraints may not translate to MTL when more than one temporal operator separates quantifiers and bound constraints, as in formula $x.\Diamond(p \land \Diamond(q \land x \leq 1))$.

The efficient handling of time variables in monitoring tasks is an important open problem, regardless of the underlying time domain. A practice similar to TPTL is indeed recommended in the standard specification language SVA [34], through the use of local variables of type *time*. SVA (or its *simple subset* [4]) can be used for model-checking, but is predominantly used in testing: simulation traces are systematically monitored against SVA specifications. The state-of-the-art online procedures for monitoring SVA incur an additional cost in the presence of time variables, which they often treat by spawning a new instance of the monitor at every possible variable assignment. To our knowledge, the complexity of the offline monitoring problem for SVA has not been studied.

In this paper, we solve the offline TPTL monitoring problem over continuous-time Boolean signals. The satisfaction of TPTL formulas can be characterized in terms of difference constraints on their free variables [28]. In this setting, our contribution is twofold. We first propose to compute such constraints in the form of a *union of zones*. The zone data structure underlies recent advances in continuous-time monitoring and pattern matching [6,33]. Our naïve zone-

---

[2] The original presentation of TPTL instead talks of *freeze* quantifiers that store the absolute time in variables x, y later compared using difference constraints $y - x \leq c$. We found it more convenient to work with clocks and associated *reset* quantifiers as in [31], although both presentations are equivalent.

based implementation of TPTL monitoring appears competitive relative to the existing discrete-time implementations for TPTL monitoring of [15], based on instantiating LTL monitors for every possible value of clock variables. We then propose to represent difference constraints using a partition of the time domain according to the *region equivalence*. A region is a cell in this partition, and two equivalent regions agree on the value of all subformulas. As for timed automata verification [1], this equivalence relation provides a canonical representation of the state space. The suitable inductive computation of this relation yields an algorithm with linear-time complexity relative to the trace length for monitoring the important fragment of TPTL formulas with one clock[3].

The practical performance of our zone-based and region-based algorithms is evaluated in a prototype implementation, which we compare with tool AMT [29] as baseline. Our experiments support the theoretical complexity of the region-based algorithm, which also compares to the zone-based algorithm.

Related Work. Temporal logic monitoring over continuous time is introduced by [26], who consider the logic MTL and its extension to real-valued signals called STL. Subsequently, [33] proposes an algorithm for the monitoring and matching of timed regular expressions (TRE) [5], that are regular expressions with duration constraints $\langle . \rangle_I$ requiring that the segment matching the enclosed expression also has a duration within some interval I. The work of [6] considers the monitoring of MTL with an additional time parameter standing for the horizon of the property, after which the signal is considered to end. The constructions in [6,33] use a representation of the time domain as a union of zones, which we also consider in our naïve implementation of TPTL monitoring. A recent related work [8] considers the monitoring of *metric dynamic logic* (MDL) formulas. This logic introduces modalities $\langle r \rangle_I \varphi$ requiring that φ should occur within timing interval I after a sequence of discrete events matching some regular expression r. The authors consider a weakly-monotonic, discrete model of time and obtain an algorithm with quasi-linear time complexity [8].

The decidability of TPTL offline monitoring over continuous-time domains was proved in [28] with a tight (relative to combined trace and formula size) reduction to difference constraints satisfiability. However, in the absence of fast difference constraints solvers, this does not necessarily provide a practical algorithm for large traces. In contrast our region-based algorithm comes with a linear-time guaranteed complexity relative to trace length. To the best of our knowledge, previous implementations of TPTL monitoring are as follows. The approach of [15] uses a monitor of LTL formulas as sub-routine, called on every possible valuation of time variables. This enables efficient monitoring of the sequential part of the property by reusing off-the-shelf LTL monitors, but the LTL monitor is called for every instantiation of clock variables. The number of LTL monitor instances may grow linearly with the trace length, and as a result this algorithm has a worst-case time complexity quadratic in the trace length

---

[3] This does not follow straightforwardly from [1], since TPTL does not translate to timed automata: its satisfiability over dense time is undecidable [3].

[15]. The approach of [12] proceeds by incremental rewriting of TPTL semantics, based on formalization in Maude [13]. The resulting procedure seems to suffer from similar complexity in terms of its number of rewrites.

2 Background

An essential idea in offline monitoring is that the standard (future time) operators of LTL can be realized as backward-deterministic transducers. Therefore, the whole trace can be parsed once in reverse time-order using finite memory. Let us consider a discrete time domain $\mathbb{T} = \{0, 1, \ldots, n\}$. Assuming a set of atomic propositions AP, a trace w is a function $w : \mathbb{T} \to 2^{AP}$ that we denote $w = w_0 w_1 \ldots w_n$ with $w_i \subseteq AP$ for all $i \in T$. The satisfaction relation of LTL can be characterized by a recursion on the time dimension (backwards) and on the formula structure (top-down). For the *until operator* we have:

base case: $(w, n) \models \varphi_1 \mathcal{U} \varphi_2$ iff $(w, n) \models \varphi_2$;
inductive case: $(w, i-1) \models \varphi_1 \mathcal{U} \varphi_2$ iff $(w, i-1) \models \varphi_2$, or $(w, i-1) \models \varphi_1$ and $(w, i) \models \varphi_1 \mathcal{U} \varphi_2$.

Notice that the satisfaction $\models$ of $\varphi_1 \mathcal{U} \varphi_2$ at position i only depends on the satisfaction of φ_1 and φ_2 at position i, and on the satisfaction of $\varphi_1 \mathcal{U} \varphi_2$ at $i+1$.

The LTL monitoring algorithm described in [19] first evaluates the subformulas $\varphi_1, \varphi_2, \ldots, \varphi_m$ of the main formula φ at the end of the input trace w (position n). Then for all $i = n-1, \ldots, 0$ the algorithm evaluates $\varphi_1, \varphi_2, \ldots, \varphi_m$ at time i in a bottom up fashion based on values computed at position i and $i+1$. The overall process is illustrated in Fig. 1.

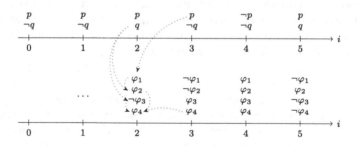

Fig. 1. Monitoring formula $(\bigcirc p \lor q) \mathcal{U} \neg q$ with subformulas $\varphi_1 \equiv \bigcirc p$, $\varphi_2 \equiv \bigcirc p \lor q$, $\varphi_3 \equiv \neg q$, and $\varphi_4 \equiv (\bigcirc p \lor q) \mathcal{U} \neg q$ by backward induction. Positions $5, 4, 3$ have been marked with satisfied subformulas, and the marking at position 2 is computed based on input values of p and q, and the values of subformulas at positions 2 and 3.

Metric temporal logic (MTL) [25] extends LTL with timed temporal modalities such as the *timed eventually*, denoted $\Diamond_I$ for timing interval I. Formula $\Diamond_{[a,b]} \varphi$ holds at time t if and only if φ holds at some time $t' \in [t+a, t+b]$. Here we consider $\mathbb{T} = [0, d] \subseteq \mathbb{R}$ to be a dense time domain. Similar to LTL, the truth value of a given formula φ is uniquely determined at time t by the truth value of its main subformulas at times $t' \geq t$.

The evolution of the truth value of a formula φ over time forms a Boolean signal, that we call *satisfaction signal*, denoted $w_\varphi[t]$ for input trace w. Monitoring MTL offline can be done by computing the entire satisfaction signal of every subformula of φ inductively, as proposed in [27]. For $\Diamond_I$, the inductive step is as follows. Assume that w_φ has value 1 over a finite set of intervals $T_0, \ldots, T_n \subseteq \mathbb{T}$, and value 0 everywhere else. Then $w_{\Diamond_I \varphi}$ will have value 1 over intervals $T_i \ominus I$ for all $i = 0, \ldots, n$, and value 0 everywhere else.[4] For all inductive cases, satisfaction signals can be computed in linear time [27]. We illustrate the resulting algorithm in Fig. 2.

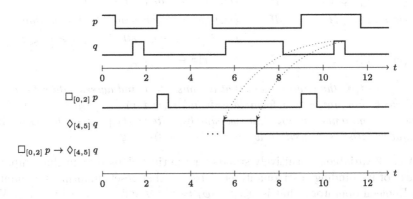

Fig. 2. Monitoring formula $\varphi = \Box_{[0,2]}p \rightarrow \Diamond_{[4,5]}q$ by inductively constructing the satisfaction signals if its subformulas. The segment of the satisfaction signal of $\Diamond_{[4,5]}q$ between times 5.5 and 7 is obtained from the segment of q between times 10.5 and 11.

3   Timed Propositional Temporal Logic

We call *time domain* a subset $\mathbb{T} \subseteq \mathbb{R}$ of the real line of the form $[0, d]$ with *duration* $d > 0$. Assume a set AP of propositional variables. A *trace* $w : \mathbb{T} \rightarrow 2^{AP}$ can be seen as a valuation of variables $p \in AP$ into Boolean signals over $\mathbb{T}$, which we write $w_p : \mathbb{T} \rightarrow \{0, 1\}$. The Boolean value of p at time t in trace w is denoted $w_p[t]$. The length of trace w is the minimal size of any partition of $\mathbb{T}$ into intervals over which the truth status of predicates w_p is constant relative to time for all $p \in AP$. We assume that every trace has a finite length denoted $|w|$.

Let $\mathbb{X}$ be a set of clock variables. An *environment* r is a valuation of clocks $x \in \mathbb{X}$ as elements of the time domain, written $r_x \in \mathbb{T}$.

Definition 1 (TPTL Syntax). *Formulas of TPTL are given by the following grammar:*

$$\varphi ::= p \mid x \leq c \mid x \geq c \mid \neg\varphi \mid \varphi \vee \varphi \mid \varphi \mathcal{U} \varphi \mid x.\varphi$$

for $p \in AP$, clock variables $x \in \mathbb{X}$, and integer constants $c \in \mathbb{N}$.

---

[4] The Minkowski difference $T_i \ominus I$ is by definition $\{t - s \in \mathbb{T} : t \in T_i \text{ and } s \in I\}$.

We also use shorthands such as $x < c$ for $\neg(x \geq c)$. The form '$x.$' in the formula $x.\varphi$ is called a *reset quantifier* and a formula is *closed* when all its variables are bound by a reset quantifier.

Definition 2 (TPTL Semantics). *The satisfaction of a TPTL formula φ relative to a trace w at time t under an environment r is according to the relation $\models$ between the tuple (w, t, r) and φ, inductively defined as follows:*

$$
\begin{aligned}
(w, t, r) &\models p & &\textit{iff} & w_p[t] &= 1 \\
(w, t, r) &\models x \leq c & &\textit{iff} & t - r_x &\leq c \\
(w, t, r) &\models \neg\varphi & &\textit{iff} & (w, t, r) &\not\models \varphi \\
(w, t, r) &\models \varphi \vee \psi & &\textit{iff} & (w, t, r) &\models \varphi \textit{ or } (w, t, r) \models \psi \\
(w, t, r) &\models \varphi \,\mathcal{U}\, \psi & &\textit{iff} & (w, t', r) &\models \psi \textit{ for some } t' > t \textit{ such that} \\
& & & & (w, t'', r) &\models \varphi \textit{ for all } t'' \textit{ with } t < t'' < t' \\
(w, t, r) &\models x.\varphi & &\textit{iff} & (w, t, r[x \leftarrow t]) &\models \varphi
\end{aligned}
$$

where $r[x \leftarrow t]$ is the environment that assigns t to x and agrees with r for every other clock. For any closed formula φ it holds $(w, t, r) \models \varphi$ iff $(w, t, r') \models \varphi$ for all environments r, r' and thus we simply write $(w, t) \models \varphi$ in that case. We say that w satisfies φ, written $w \models \varphi$, when $(w, 0) \models \varphi$.

A clock variable x intuitively stands for the time elapsed from the temporal context of its binding reset quantifier. Observe that reset quantifiers commute with Boolean operators, that is, $x.(\varphi \vee \psi) \Leftrightarrow x.\varphi \vee x.\psi$ and $x.\neg\varphi \Leftrightarrow \neg x.\varphi$. We refer the reader to [3] for a more extensive discussion of the merits of reset (or *freeze*) quantification over existential and universal quantification in the temporal logic context.

The offline monitoring problem for TPTL, which we solve in this paper, can be stated as follows: given a formula φ and a trace w, decide whether $w \models \varphi$.

4   Zone-Based Algorithm

Assume a finite set $\mathbb{X} = \{x_1, \ldots, x_k\}$ of clocks with size k, and let $\mathbb{T} = [0, d]$ be a time domain with duration d. With any TPTL formula φ and trace w we associate a *satisfaction set*, consisting of all pairs (t, r) under which w satisfies φ. For convenience we hereafter identify such time-environments pairs (t, r) with vectors in $\mathbb{T}^{k+1}$ whose first component is the value of the reference time, followed by the values of the clocks in $\mathbb{X}$.

Definition 3 (Satisfaction Set). *Let φ be a formula and w a trace. The satisfaction set of φ relative to w, denoted $[\![\varphi]\!]_w$, is defined by letting*

$$
[\![\varphi]\!]_w = \{(t, r) \in \mathbb{T}^{k+1} \; : \; (w, t, r) \models \varphi\}.
$$

Difference constraints are formulas of the form $t \bowtie a$ and $t - s \bowtie a$ for comparison operator $\bowtie \in \{<, \leq, >, \geq\}$, constant a, and real variables s, t. Satisfaction sets $[\![\varphi]\!]_w$ are definable in the first order theory of difference constraints. This theory is decidable, in particular it admits quantifier elimination [24].

Since the translation of TPTL into difference constraints can easily be made effective, a monitoring procedure for TPTL can be obtained by constructing a difference constraints formula that holds iff $w \models \varphi$, combined with a decision procedure for the first order theory of difference constraints [28]. Such an algorithm is likely to exhibit an exponential time complexity, since the problem of deciding a difference constraints formula is complete for polynomial space computations [24]. We have no hope on improving the worst-case complexity relative to the combined input size of formula and trace, given that TPTL monitoring requires polynomial space [28], already over discrete models [16]. However, we hope to reduce the complexity relative to the size of the trace alone. For this we use a polyhedral representation of the satisfaction set.

Definition 4 (Zone). *A* zone *is a subset of* $\mathbb{T}^{d+1}$ *definable as a conjunction of difference constraints.*

Zones were introduced in the context of real-time systems verification, in particular in the formal analysis of timed automata [14]. The following theorem, an immediate consequence of the discussion above, underpins our first algorithm:

Theorem 1. *For any trace w and formula φ, the set $[\![\varphi]\!]_w$ can be effectively represented as a finite union of zones.*

Given a formula φ and trace w the set $[\![\varphi]\!]_w$ can in particular be obtained by induction as follows.

- Propositional variables: The satisfaction set is a union of zones orthogonal to the time axis, of the form $[\![p]\!]_w = \bigcup_{i=1}^n J_i \times \mathbb{T}^k$.
- Timing constraints: The satisfaction set consists is the zone $[\![x \bowtie c]\!]_w = \{(t, r) \in \mathbb{T}^{k+1} : t - r_x \bowtie c\}$.
- Boolean operators: Disjunction and negation translate into the corresponding set operations $[\![\neg\varphi]\!]_w = \mathbb{T}^{k+1} \setminus [\![\varphi]\!]_w$ and $[\![\varphi \vee \psi]\!]_w = [\![\varphi]\!]_w \cup [\![\psi]\!]_w$.
- Until: Assume $[\![\varphi]\!]_w$ and $[\![\psi]\!]_w$ are given as sets of zones $\mathcal{Z}_\varphi$ and $\mathcal{Z}_\psi$, respectively. We compute zones of $[\![\varphi \, \mathcal{U} \, \psi]\!]_w$ by constructing the sequence $\mathcal{Y}_0, \dots, \mathcal{Y}_n$ up to a fixed point n as follows:

$$\mathcal{Y}_0 = \{cl_L(Z) \cap \overleftarrow{cl_R(Z)} \cap Y : Y \in \mathcal{Z}_\psi, Z \in \mathcal{Z}_\varphi\}$$

$$\mathcal{Y}_i = \{cl_L(Z) \cap \overleftarrow{Z} \cap Y : Y \in \mathcal{Y}_{i-1}, Z \in \mathcal{Z}_\varphi\} \text{ for } i > 0$$

where cl_L (respectively cl_R) take the topological closure of a zone to the left (respectively to the right) on the time component, and $\overleftarrow{Z}$ removes all lower bounds on the time component.[5] We then have $[\![\varphi \, \mathcal{U} \, \psi]\!]_w = \bigcup_{i=0}^n \mathcal{Y}_i$.

---

[5] The fixed point $\cup \mathcal{Y}_{n+1} \subseteq \bigcup_{i=0}^n \mathcal{Y}_i$ exists because only finitely many difference constraints over $\mathbb{T}$ can be built from $\mathcal{Z}_\varphi$ and $\mathcal{Z}_\psi$.

– Reset: We let $[\![x.\varphi]\!]_w = \{(t,r) \in \mathbb{T}^{k+1} \; : \; \exists s, (t, r[r_x \leftarrow s]) \in Z\}$ for $Z = [\![\varphi]\!]_w \cap \{(t,r) \in \mathbb{T}^{k+1} \; : \; t - r_x = 0\})$. All operations involved in this computation commute with $\cup$ and are standard operations over zones.

Example 1. We consider the formula $\varphi \equiv x.\Diamond(p \wedge \Diamond(q \wedge x \leq 1))$. It has subformulas p, q, $x \leq 1$, $\gamma_1 \equiv q \wedge x \leq 1$, $\gamma_2 \equiv \Diamond\gamma_1$, $\gamma_3 \equiv p \wedge \gamma_2$, $\gamma_4 \equiv \Diamond\gamma_3$, with $\varphi \equiv x.\gamma_4$. In Fig. 3 we show the satisfaction sets of each of its subformulas. Observe that the satisfaction of φ is independent of r.

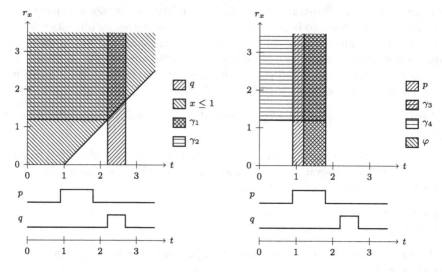

Fig. 3. Computation of the satisfaction set of formula φ on a given trace by structural induction: **(left)** satisfaction sets of subformulas q, $x \leq 1$, γ_1, and γ_2; **(right)** satisfaction sets of subformulas p, γ_3, γ_4, and φ.

For a fixed formula, the worst-case run time of this algorithm is polynomial relative to the trace length. Yet it can be more than linear. The expensive operation of complementation can be avoided by introducing a negation normal form through additional operators of conjunction and *always* (the dual of *until* can be rewritten using *always* and *until* itself). However intersecting two sets of zones can still create a quadratic number of zones. Such a phenomenon can arise when monitoring TPTL with the algorithm in this section.

Example 2. Consider the formula $\psi \equiv p \wedge \Diamond(p \wedge x = 1)$, and the family of periodic Boolean signals w_n, $n > 0$ with fixed duration $d = 2$ and period $\frac{1}{n}$, such that $w_n[t] = 1$ if and only if $\lfloor \frac{t}{2n} \rfloor$ is even. The satisfaction set $[\![\psi]\!]_w$ has $\Omega(n^2)$ zones while signal w_n has $O(n)$ time points (discontinuities).

5 Region-Based Algorithm

In this section we improve on our zone-based algorithm by moving to a representation of satisfaction sets using a notion of *region equivalence*. For simplicity we focus on the fragment of TPTL with only one clock variable x, which we denote 1-TPTL in the rest of this paper.

5.1 TPTL Formulas with One Variable

Under the present definitions, 1-TPTL is already more expressive than MTL [9]. Given a time variable x and an integer-bounded interval I, let us write $x \in I$ for the conjunction of constraints enforcing that the value of x lies in I. We can define the *timed until* operator $\mathcal{U}_I$ as the abbreviation $\varphi \mathcal{U}_I \psi \equiv x.(\varphi \mathcal{U} (x \in I \wedge \psi))$. Metric Temporal Logic (MTL) can be seen as the syntactic fragment of TPTL with the grammar $\varphi ::= p \mid \neg\varphi \mid \varphi \vee \varphi \mid \varphi \mathcal{U}_I \varphi$ for p ranging over AP and I ranging over integer-bounded intervals.

The 1-TPTL formula $\varphi_1 \equiv \Box(p \rightarrow x.\Diamond(q \wedge \Diamond(r \wedge x \leq 5)))$ was conjectured in [2] not to be expressible in MTL. The property specified by φ_1 is that every request, signified by p holding true, should be followed by two successive grants occurring within 5 time units, respectively signified by q and r holding true. It turns out that φ_1 can be expressed in MTL [9], but not when replacing the constraint $x \leq 5$ by $x \leq 1$ and assuming integer constants [21]. When allowing rational constants and past operators, MTL, 1-TPTL, and TPTL all become equivalent in expressive power [22].

Observe that formulas of 1-TPTL can contain multiple occurrences of clock variable x, as in $\varphi_2 \equiv \Diamond x.(p \mathcal{U} (x > 1 \wedge x.(q \mathcal{U} (r \mathcal{U} x \geq 2 \wedge x \leq 3))))$. Formula φ_2 expresses that eventually p holds for more than 1 time unit, after which q holds and then r holds over a period lasting between 2 and 3 time units. It could also be written as $\Diamond x.(p \mathcal{U} (x > 1 \wedge y.(q \mathcal{U} (r \mathcal{U} y \geq 2 \wedge y \leq 3))))$ for readability's sake[6].

5.2 Region Equivalence

To improve the worst-case complexity relative to the trace length, we introduce two essential changes in the algorithm of Sect. 4. We avoid overlapping polytopes, leading to combinatorial explosion, by using a grid over the 2-dimensional time domain. The number of cells (called *regions*) in the grid can still be more than linear in the trace length, as in Example 2. Instead of representing the whole set of zones explicitly, it suffices to construct this set implicitly and according to some equivalence relation. The state is maintained over a single uniform interval on the t-axis, where the input trace stays constant. Over such an interval, the

---

[6] Similar formulas with independent variables were considered in [15] in the context of monitoring. We remark that the fragment of TPTL defined there corresponds to 1-TPTL when clocks are renamed.

truth value of a formula only depends on the environment and for convenience we will represent it as a signal on the r-axis.

Let w be a trace with time sequence $0 = t_0, \ldots, t_n = d$ and φ a formula with time constants $c_1, \ldots, c_l$ and letting $c_0 = 0$ and $c_{l+1} = +\infty$. We write $r_0, \ldots, r_m$ for the ordered sequence of times in $\mathbb{T}$ each of the form $t_i - c_j$ obtained by considering all pairs of t_i and c_j for $i = 0, \ldots, n$ and $j = 0, \ldots, l$.

Definition 5 (Region). *A region relative to w and φ is a subset of $\mathbb{T}^2$ of the form $\{(t, r) \in T \times R : t - r \in I\}$ where T is of the form $\{t_i\}$ or (t_i, t_{i+1}), R is of the form $\{r_j\}$ or (r_j, r_{j+1}), and I is of the form $\{c_k\}$ or (c_k, c_{k+1}). We call T the* projection *of that region on the t-axis, and if $T \neq \{d\}$ we call* successor *the region $\{(t, r) \in T' \times R : t - r \in I\}$ where T' is adjacent to T on the right.*

Definition 6 (Equivalence). *We say that two regions A and A' are equivalent relative to w and φ, denoted $A \sim_{\varphi,w} A'$, when the following conditions apply:*

- *A and A' have the same t-axis projection;*
- *the satisfaction status of subformulas of φ relative w are the same on both A and A';*
- *if A and A' have successors B and B' then the satisfaction status of subformulas of φ relative to w are the same on both B and B'.*

Let φ be a *quantifier-free*[7] formula, and let w be a trace. The following proposition is straightforward by structural induction:

Proposition 1. *For all regions A and A' such that $A \sim_{\varphi,w} A'$ and time-environment pairs $(t, r) \in A$ and $(t', r') \in A'$ we have $(t, r) \models \varphi$ iff $(t', r') \models \varphi$.*

In order to compute the satisfaction set of a quantifier-free formula φ, time-environment pairs that lie in regions equivalent to $\sim_{\varphi,w}$ can be grouped together. Parsing the trace in reverse time-order, the number of operations per uniform time interval needed to update equivalence classes of $\sim_{\varphi,w}$ remain bounded.

For quantified subformulas we use the following notion:

Definition 7 (Satisfaction Signal). *The satisfaction signal w_φ of a closed formula φ on a trace w is a Boolean signal such that $w_\varphi[t] = 1$ if $(w, t) \models \varphi$, $w_\varphi[t] = 0$ otherwise.*

The satisfaction signal of some formula $x.\varphi$ can be obtained by intersecting the satisfaction set of φ with the diagonal $t = r$. Observe that in general, the satisfaction signal of a closed subformula is sufficient information to construct the satisfaction set of its superformulas. Applying the region equivalence to formulas with quantifiers will be made possible by incrementally replacing quantified subformulas with their satisfaction signal.

---

[7] A more general definition of *region equivalence* could be used. Our restriction of this notion to quantifier-free formulas is motivated by efficiency concerns. For instance, we aim to avoid partitioning the satisfaction set of formula $x.\Diamond(x \leq 1 \land p \land x.\Diamond(x \leq 2 \land q))$ according to timing constant $1+2$ for all subformulas. While the constant is relevant in subformula $\Diamond(x \leq 1 \land p \land x.\Diamond(x \leq 2 \land q))$, it plays no role in $\Diamond(x \leq 2 \land q)$.

5.3   Monitoring Algorithm

For a given formula φ and a trace w, the region-based algorithm computes the satisfaction signal of every subformula of the form $x.\gamma$, starting with inner-most ones (such that γ is quantifier-free). The computation of the satisfaction signal of such a subformula $x.\gamma$ is done by parsing the trace backwards and computing the satisfiability of its subformulas in each region, in a procedure similar to LTL monitoring. The satisfaction signal $w_{x.\gamma}$ is found on the diagonal and obtained by letting $w_\varphi[t] = 1$ if $(t,t) \in [\![\varphi]\!]_w$. Indeed we only need to compute the part of the satisfaction set with $r \leq t$. Once computed, the subformula $x.\gamma$ is replaced by a fresh proposition $p_{x.\gamma}$ and its satisfaction signals is added to the trace w. The satisfaction signal associated to that proposition will be used when computing superformulas, similar to MTL monitoring. Once the main formula φ has been replaced by an atomic proposition p_φ, we can conclude whether w satisfies φ by simply looking at the value of w_{p_φ} at time 0. We assume without loss of generality that the closed formula φ we monitor is of the form $x.\psi$, if this was not the case we could rewrite it as $x.\varphi$, which is equivalent since φ is closed.

Algorithm 1. Monitor

Precondition: A formula $\varphi \equiv x.\psi$, a finite trace w
 1: **function** MONITOR(φ, w)
 2:      **if** ψ contains $x.\gamma$ such that γ is quantifier-free **then**
 3:          $v \leftarrow$ SATISFY($x.\gamma, w$)
 4:          **replace** $x.\gamma$ **by** $p_{x.\gamma}$ **in** φ
 5:          $w \leftarrow w \cup (p_{x.\gamma} \mapsto v)$
 6:          **return** MONITOR(φ, w)
 7:      **else**
 8:          **return** SATISFY(φ, w)
 9:      **end if**
10: **end function**

As described, Algorithm 1 recursively searches for a subformula that does not contain any reset quantifier (lines 2, 6) until no further reset quantifiers can be found (line 8). In that case, the algorithm proceeds by computing the satisfaction signal of the found subformula by calling Algorithm 2 (line 3) and replacing it with a fresh atomic proposition $p_{x.\gamma}$ (line 4) and in addition, supplementing the trace with a Boolean satisfaction signal v for this proposition $p_{x.\gamma}$ (line 5). For a formula $x.\varphi$ where φ is quantifier-free and a trace $\mathbb{T} \to 2^{AP}$ we compute $w_{x.\varphi}$ by calling Algorithm 2.

Algorithm 2 implicitly computes the satisfaction set of all quantifier-free subformulas of φ. For simplicity, it is written and described to operate over regions rather than region equivalence classes, but operating over a single representative of each region equivalence class can easily be implemented (e.g. by keeping track of regions entering and leaving every diagonal area of the t, r plane). The algorithm starts by initializing the output trace u. Signals in the output trace

---

Algorithm 2. Satisfy

Precondition: A formula $x.\gamma$ such that γ is quantifier-free, a trace w on $[0, t_n]$

1: **function** SATISFY$(x.\gamma, w)$
2:    $u, r \leftarrow$ INITIALIZESATTRACE(w, t_n, C) ▷ r stores all time points of u
3:    **for** $t_i \in t_{n-1}, \ldots, t_0$ **do**
4:        $r' \leftarrow (r'_1, \ldots, r'_{|C|})$ where $r'_l := t_i - c_l$ for all $1 \leq l \leq |C|$
5:        $r \leftarrow$ merge(r, r') ▷ merge two lists
6:        $k \leftarrow$ largest element of r smaller than t_{i+1}
7:        **for** $r_j \in r_k, \ldots, r_0$ **do**
8:            $A, A' \leftarrow$ UPDATEREGIONS$(t_i, t_{i+1}, r_j, r_{j+1}, C)$ ▷ open interval
9:            **for** $B \in A', \ldots, A$ **do**
10:                $u \leftarrow$ UPDATESATTRACE(w, u, r_j, r_{j+1}, B)
11:            **end for**
12:            $A, A' \leftarrow$ UPDATEREGIONS(t_i, t_{i+1}, r_j, C) ▷ closed interval
13:            **for** $B \in A, \ldots, A'$ **do**
14:                $u \leftarrow$ UPDATESATTRACE(w, u, r_j, B)
15:            **end for**
16:        **end for**
17:    **end for**
18:    **return** $u_{x.\gamma}$ ▷ satisfaction signal of $x.\gamma$
19: **end function**

---

represent the satisfiability of subformulas at different environment values. The function INITIALIZESATTRACE creates m signals in the output trace u, one per subformula of γ, with time points 0, t_n, and $t_n - c$ for every $c \in C$. The values of those satisfaction signals are computed based on the signal values of w at time t_n. As we iterate over the trace (line 3), we first refine u (lines 4, 5) and we update the output trace backwards (line 7). We proceed by computing the regions relative to w contained within $T = [t_i, t_{i+1})$ and $R = (r_j, r_{j+1})$ (line 8). The function UPDATEREGIONS then only needs to compute the time constants relevant to the intervals T and R, i.e. time constants c such that $t_i \leq c + r_j \leq t_{i+1}$. Iterating backwards through the computed regions (for $B = A', \ldots, A$), we compute the satisfiability in each region inductively on the structure of the formula (function UPDATESATTRACE, line 10) and update u once we have processed the region A. The function UPDATESATTRACE updates the respective signals of u at time (r_j, r_{j+1}) based on subformulas γ_l of $x.\gamma$. For instance in the case of $\gamma_l \equiv \gamma_h \mathcal{U} \gamma_k$ over a region whose t-projection is open, we update the signal u_{γ_l} with the value of $u_{\gamma_h} \wedge (u_{\gamma_k} \vee u'_{\gamma_k} \vee u'_{\gamma_l})$, where u' is the value of u in the adjacent region to the right. Over a region whose t-projection is closed, the value of *until* is the same as in its successor region. Other operators not pose any difficulty. After we have processed the region A, we update u. We repeat the same inductive rules for the regions bounded by $T = [t_i, t_{i+1})$ and $R = \{r_j\}$. After each iteration t_i, the interval $[t_i, t_{i+1})$ of the output trace u is finalized and will remain unchanged until the end of computation, at which point we return the Boolean component of u representing the satisfaction signal of the whole formula $x.\gamma$.

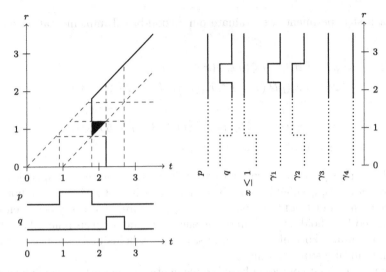

Fig. 4. Computation of the satisfaction signal of φ on a given trace. The state of the algorithm consists of the truth value of regions highlighted on the left; it is shown on the right as signals with a dotted part being updated and a plain part, final. The current time interval is $t_i = 1.8, t_{i+1} = 2.2$ and current region is $\{(r,t) \; : \; t_i < t, r < t_{i+1} - 1, t - r < 1\}$.

Example 3. We take again the formula $\varphi \equiv x.\Diamond(p \wedge \Diamond(q \wedge x \leq 1))$ with subformulas $p, q, x \leq 1, \gamma_1 \equiv q \wedge x \leq 1, \gamma_2 \equiv \Diamond\gamma_1, \gamma_3 \equiv p \wedge \gamma_2$, and $\gamma_4 \equiv \Diamond\gamma_3$ of Example 1 and illustrate the computation of its satisfaction signal in Fig. 4.

When instead computing only one representative of each equivalence class of $\sim_{\gamma,w}$, we limit the number of operations to $O(2^k)$ per uniform time interval for a subformula of size k, since there are at most 2^k equivalence classes of $\sim_{\gamma,w}$ over such an interval. The number of time points at most doubles with each time constant, so that the satisfaction signal of $w_{x.\gamma}$ has length at most $n2^k$ for a signal w of length n. Therefore we have:

Theorem 2. *The offline monitoring of a 1-TPTL formula φ of size m against a continuous-time Boolean trace w of length n can be computed in time $n2^{O(m)}$.*

6   Experimental Evaluation

We implemented both algorithms in C++. The implementation of the zone-based algorithm uses a library of the toolset IF [10] for zones computations. We then measured the execution time of monitoring several formula/trace combinations. Figures were obtained on Intel Core i5-4210u CPU with 8 GB of RAM. The input traces we considered consist of periodic Boolean signals, in which propositions $p, q, r, \ldots$ hold for 2 time units in turn. The length of a trace is determined by the number of sample points (associated to a Boolean signal changing its value). We generated traces of length 1000, 2000, 5000, 10000 and 20000 samples.

In a first experiment, we evaluate our region-based implementation on formulas

$$\varphi_1 \equiv \Box x.(p \to \Diamond(q \wedge \Diamond(x \leq 5 \wedge r)))$$
$$\varphi_2 \equiv \Diamond x.(p\,\mathcal{U}\,(x > 1 \wedge x.(q\,\mathcal{U}\,(r\,\mathcal{U}\,x \geq 2 \wedge x \leq 3))))$$
$$\varphi_3 \equiv \Box x.(p \to \Diamond(x \leq 1 \wedge q \wedge x.\Box(x \leq 1 \to \neg r)))$$
$$\varphi_4 \equiv \Box x.(p \to (\Diamond(q\,\mathcal{U}\,r) \wedge \Diamond(x \geq 3 \wedge x \leq 5 \wedge s)))$$
$$\varphi_5 \equiv (x.\Diamond(x \leq 10 \wedge p))\,\mathcal{U}\,\Box\neg q.$$

Formula φ_1 and φ_2 are two examples given in Sect. 5. Formula φ_3 specifies that whenever p holds, q should hold within 1 time unit and r should not hold for another 1 time unit from there on. Formula φ_4 requires that every occurrence of p is followed by q holding until an occurrence of r, and an occurrence of s within 3 to 5 time units. Formula φ_5 roughly says that p holds at least once every 10 time units until q stops holding.

Then, we evaluate our zone-based implementation against the same formulas and formula $\varphi_6 \equiv \Box x.(p \to \Diamond(q \wedge y.\Diamond(x \leq 5 \wedge y \geq 2 \wedge r)))$. The property expressed by φ_6 is that every request p is followed by two grants q and r within 5 time units, with q occurring at least 2 time units before r. Such a property cannot be monitored by the region-based implementation since it requires two clock variables.

We use the tool AMT [29] for MTL monitoring over continuous-time Boolean signals as our baseline. Formulas φ_3 and φ_5 are part of the MTL syntactic fragment of TPTL, and can be rewritten in MTL as $\Box(p \to \Diamond_{[0,1]}(q \wedge \Box_{[0,1]}\neg r))$ and $(\Diamond_{[0,10]}p)\,\mathcal{U}\,\Box\neg q$, respectively[8].

Table 1. Execution times (s) of monitoring formulas against periodic traces for three algorithms: our region-based (**reg**) and zone-based (**zon**) implementations, and the interval-based (**int**) implementation of MTL monitoring in the tool AMT.

$|w|$	1 000			2 000			5 000			10 000			20 000		
alg	int	reg	zon	int	reg	zon	int	reg	zon	int	reg	zon	int	reg	zon
φ_1	–	0.045	0.085	–	0.084	0.168	–	0.217	0.431	–	0.439	0.960	–	0.898	2.105
φ_2	–	0.110	0.059	–	0.160	0.132	–	0.407	0.370	–	0.814	0.739	–	1.660	1.498
φ_3	0.034	0.104	0.032	0.047	0.169	0.077	0.079	0.431	0.173	0.143	0.894	0.344	0.275	1.822	0.644
φ_4	–	0.132	0.087	–	0.259	0.268	–	0.662	0.632	–	1.348	1.416	–	2.756	3.015
φ_5	0.025	0.080	0.040	0.035	0.159	0.151	0.055	0.398	0.366	0.092	0.802	0.783	0.173	1.636	2.235
φ_6	–	–	0.242	–	–	0.390	–	–	1.001	–	–	2.111	–	–	5.009

The results are shown in Table 1. We observe that the zone-based algorithm matches closely the linear-time guaranteed performance of the region-based algorithm, and is sometimes faster. This is achieved by internally keeping zones

---

[8] Formula φ_4 could also be put in MTL form using some additional rewriting, but is not part of the MTL syntactic fragment of TPTL we defined.

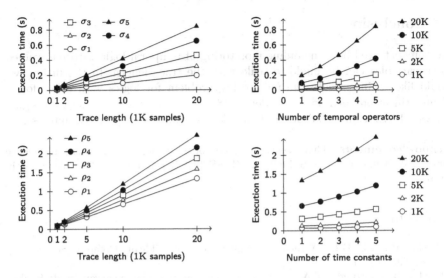

Fig. 5. Execution time for: (**left**) traces of increasing length; (**top-right**) formulas of increasing size; (**bottom-right**) formulas with increasing number of time constants.

ordered on the time axis to avoid otherwise quadratic implementation of binary operations such as intersection, see [33]. For large signal sizes the performance degrades, subject to an implementation limitation of IF (the use of a hash table for zones). The interval-based monitoring algorithm of AMT displays a speed advantage of up to 10× when monitoring formulas φ_3 and φ_5.

In a second experiment, we consider the scalability of our region-based algorithm relative to trace and formula dimensions. To demonstrate the impact of the number of operators in the formulas, we consider the family $\sigma_1 \equiv \Diamond x.(p_1 \wedge x \leq 2)$, $\sigma_2 \equiv \Diamond x.(p_1 \mathcal{U}(p_2 \wedge x \leq 4))$, up to $\sigma_5 \equiv \Diamond x.(p_1 \mathcal{U}(p_2 \mathcal{U} \ldots \mathcal{U}(p_5 \wedge x \leq 10)\ldots))$. To demonstrate the impact of the number of constants in the formula, we consider the family $\rho_i \equiv \Box x.(p_0 \rightarrow \Diamond(p_1 \wedge x \leq c_1^i \wedge \Diamond(p_2 \wedge x \leq c_2^i \wedge \ldots \wedge \Diamond(p_5 \wedge x \leq c_5^i)\ldots)))$ for $i = 1, \ldots, 5$ with constants $c_1^1 = c_2^1 = \ldots = c_5^1 = 10$; $c_1^2 = 8, c_2^2 = \ldots = c_5^2 = 10$; up to $c_1^5 = 2, c_2^5 = 4, \ldots, c_5^5 = 10$. Formulas σ_i contain an increasing number of *until* operators, while formulas ρ_i contain an increasing number of time constants.

The results are shown in Fig. 5. In the left-hand side we confirm that the execution time is linear relative to the length of the trace for a fixed formula. In the right-hand side we see that as the size of the formula, or its number of constants increases, the execution time appears to grow only slightly faster than linearly. This is expected over traces with bounded variability. More realistic benchmarks would be needed in order to fully assess the practical behavior of our algorithm relative to formula dimensions. Its asymptotic behavior in that respect is only of relative interest, given that beyond a handful of temporal operators or time constants, formulas quickly become less intelligible.

7   Conclusion

We demonstrated how the offline monitoring of temporal logic with real-valued clock variables can be made to scale with the trace length. In the future, we would like to investigate the monitoring problem for logics with other forms of quantification such as first-order [7,18], or *freeze* quantification over signal values [11]. Efficient monitoring of such logics would be of practical interest.

Acknowledgements. This research was supported in part by the Austrian Science Fund (FWF) under grants S11402-N23 (RiSE/SHiNE) and Z211-N23 (Wittgenstein Award).

References

1. Alur, R., Dill, D.L.: A theory of timed automata. Theor. Comput. Sci. **126**(2), 183–235 (1994)
2. Alur, R., Henzinger, T.A.: Logics and models of real time: a survey. In: de Bakker, J.W., Huizing, C., de Roever, W.P., Rozenberg, G. (eds.) REX 1991. LNCS, vol. 600, pp. 74–106. Springer, Heidelberg (1992). https://doi.org/10.1007/BFb0031988
3. Alur, R., Henzinger, T.A.: A really temporal logic. J. ACM (JACM) **41**(1), 181–203 (1994)
4. Armoni, R., Fisman, D., Jin, N.: SVA and PSL local variables - a practical approach. In: Sharygina, N., Veith, H. (eds.) CAV 2013. LNCS, vol. 8044, pp. 197–212. Springer, Heidelberg (2013). https://doi.org/10.1007/978-3-642-39799-8_13
5. Asarin, E., Caspi, P., Maler, O.: Timed regular expressions. J. ACM **49**(2), 172–206 (2002)
6. Asarin, E., Maler, O., Nickovic, D., Ulus, D.: Combining the temporal and epistemic dimensions for MTL monitoring. In: Abate, A., Geeraerts, G. (eds.) FORMATS 2017. LNCS, vol. 10419, pp. 207–223. Springer, Cham (2017). https://doi.org/10.1007/978-3-319-65765-3_12
7. Basin, D., Klaedtke, F., Müller, S., Zălinescu, E.: Monitoring metric first-order temporal properties. J. ACM (JACM) **62**(2), 15 (2015)
8. Basin, D., Krstić, S., Traytel, D.: Almost event-rate independent monitoring of metric dynamic logic. In: Lahiri, S., Reger, G. (eds.) RV 2017. LNCS, vol. 10548, pp. 85–102. Springer, Cham (2017). https://doi.org/10.1007/978-3-319-67531-2_6
9. Bouyer, P., Chevalier, F., Markey, N.: On the expressiveness of TPTL and MTL. In: Sarukkai, S., Sen, S. (eds.) FSTTCS 2005. LNCS, vol. 3821, pp. 432–443. Springer, Heidelberg (2005). https://doi.org/10.1007/11590156_35
10. Bozga, M., Fernandez, J.-C., Ghirvu, L., Graf, S., Krimm, J.-P., Mounier, L.: IF: a validation environment for timed asynchronous systems. In: Emerson, E.A., Sistla, A.P. (eds.) CAV 2000. LNCS, vol. 1855, pp. 543–547. Springer, Heidelberg (2000). https://doi.org/10.1007/10722167_41
11. Brim, L., Dluhoš, P., Šafránek, D., Vejpustek, T.: STL*: extending signal temporal logic with signal-value freezing operator. Inf. Comput. **236**, 52–67 (2014)
12. Chai, M., Schlingloff, H.: A rewriting based monitoring algorithm for TPTL. In: International Workshop on Concurrency, Specification and Programming (CS&P), pp. 61–72 (2013)
13. Clavel, M.: Maude: specification and programming in rewriting logic. Theor. Comput. Sci. **285**(2), 187–243 (2002)

14. Dill, D.L.: Timing assumptions and verification of finite-state concurrent systems. In: Sifakis, J. (ed.) CAV 1989. LNCS, vol. 407, pp. 197–212. Springer, Heidelberg (1990). https://doi.org/10.1007/3-540-52148-8_17

15. Dokhanchi, A., Hoxha, B., Tuncali, C.E., Fainekos, G.: An efficient algorithm for monitoring practical TPTL specifications. In: International Conference on Formal Methods and Models for System Design (MEMOCODE), pp. 184–193. IEEE (2016)

16. Feng, S., Lohrey, M., Quaas, K.: Path checking for MTL and TPTL over data words. In: Potapov, I. (ed.) DLT 2015. LNCS, vol. 9168, pp. 326–339. Springer, Cham (2015). https://doi.org/10.1007/978-3-319-21500-6_26

17. Foster, H.: Assertion-based verification: industry myths to realities (invited tutorial). In: Gupta, A., Malik, S. (eds.) CAV 2008. LNCS, vol. 5123, pp. 5–10. Springer, Heidelberg (2008). https://doi.org/10.1007/978-3-540-70545-1_3

18. Havelund, K., Peled, D., Ulus, D.: First order temporal logic monitoring with BDDs. In: Formal Methods in Computer-Aided Design FMCAD 2017, p. 116 (2017)

19. Havelund, K., Roşu, G.: Monitoring Java programs with Java pathexplorer. Electron. Notes Theor. Comput. Sci. **55**(2), 200–217 (2001)

20. Havelund, K., Roşu, G.: Synthesizing monitors for safety properties. In: Katoen, J.-P., Stevens, P. (eds.) TACAS 2002. LNCS, vol. 2280, pp. 342–356. Springer, Heidelberg (2002). https://doi.org/10.1007/3-540-46002-0_24

21. Hirshfeld, Y., Rabinovich, A.: Expressiveness of metric modalities for continuous time. In: Grigoriev, D., Harrison, J., Hirsch, E.A. (eds.) CSR 2006. LNCS, vol. 3967, pp. 211–220. Springer, Heidelberg (2006). https://doi.org/10.1007/11753728_23

22. Hunter, P., Ouaknine, J., Worrell, J.: Expressive completeness for metric temporal logic. In: Proceedings of the 2013 28th Annual ACM/IEEE Symposium on Logic in Computer Science, pp. 349–357. IEEE Computer Society (2013)

23. Kim, M., Viswanathan, M., Kannan, S., Lee, I., Sokolsky, O.: Java-MaC: a run-time assurance approach for Java programs. Form. Methods Syst. Des. **24**(2), 129–155 (2004)

24. Koubarakis, M.: Complexity results for first-order theories of temporal constraints. In: International Conference on Principles of Knowledge Representation and Reasoning (KR), pp. 379–390 (1994)

25. Koymans, R.: Specifying real-time properties with metric temporal logic. Real-Time Syst. **2**(4), 255–299 (1990)

26. Maler, O., Nickovic, D.: Monitoring temporal properties of continuous signals. In: Lakhnech, Y., Yovine, S. (eds.) FORMATS/FTRTFT -2004. LNCS, vol. 3253, pp. 152–166. Springer, Heidelberg (2004). https://doi.org/10.1007/978-3-540-30206-3_12

27. Maler, O., Nickovic, D.: Monitoring properties of analog and mixed-signal circuits. STTT **15**(3), 247–268 (2013)

28. Markey, N., Raskin, J.-F.: Model checking restricted sets of timed paths. Theor. Comput. Sci. **358**(2–3), 273–292 (2006)

29. Ničković, D., Lebeltel, O., Maler, O., Ferrère, T., Ulus, D.: AMT 2.0: qualitative and quantitative trace analysis with extended signal temporal logic. In: Beyer, D., Huisman, M. (eds.) TACAS 2018. LNCS, vol. 10806, pp. 303–319. Springer, Cham (2018). https://doi.org/10.1007/978-3-319-89963-3_18

30. Pnueli, A.: The temporal logic of programs. In: Annual Symposium on Foundations of Computer Science, SFCS 1977, pp. 46–57. IEEE Computer Society, Washington, D.C. (1977)

31. Raskin, J.-F.: Logics, automata and classical theories for deciding real time. Ph.D. thesis, Université de Namur (1999)

32. Stolz, V., Bodden, E.: Temporal assertions using AspectJ. Electron. Notes Theor. Comput. Sci. **144**(4), 109–124 (2006)
33. Ulus, D., Ferrère, T., Asarin, E., Maler, O.: Timed pattern matching. In: Legay, A., Bozga, M. (eds.) FORMATS 2014. LNCS, vol. 8711, pp. 222–236. Springer, Cham (2014). https://doi.org/10.1007/978-3-319-10512-3_16
34. Vijayaraghavan, S., Ramanathan, M.: A Practical Guide for SystemVerilog Assertions. Springer, Boston (2005). https://doi.org/10.1007/b137011

Reactive Synthesis for Robotic Swarms

Salar Moarref$^{(\boxtimes)}$ and Hadas Kress-Gazit

Cornell University, Ithaca, USA
{sm945,hadaskg}@cornell.edu

Abstract. We consider the problem of reactive synthesis for systems with *non-instantaneous* actions, i.e., it may take an arbitrary amount of time for the actions of the system to complete, and meanwhile the input from the environment may also change, possibly requiring a different response from the system. The problem can be modeled as a typical reactive synthesis problem by introducing auxiliary propositions and fairness assumptions, at the expense of additional computational complexity. We develop new realizability and synthesis algorithms that address the problem without adding auxiliary propositions or assumptions. We discuss the complexity of both approaches. We then apply our algorithms to synthesize controllers for a swarm robotic system. We implement both approaches and compare them using a specific swarm task.

1 Introduction

Given a high-level specification in a formal language such as Linear Temporal Logic (LTL), reactive synthesis is the process of computing a strategy for the system that satisfies the specification regardless of how its environment behaves. Reactive synthesis can be viewed as a game between two players: the system and its environment. The system player tries to satisfy the specification, while the environment player attempts to falsify it. The synthesized strategy is typically a finite state machine that devises an action for the system for each sequence of received inputs from the environment such that the resulting computation satisfies the specification. In this paper, we consider the problem of reactive synthesis where the actions of the system player may take an arbitrary amount of time to complete, i.e., the actions may not take effect instantaneously.

Example 1. Consider a robot that can move between three regions $\{A, B, C\}$ as shown in Fig. 1. Figure 2 shows the corresponding *region graph* where each node represents a region and edges indicate possible transitions between them. Assume that the robot decides to move from region A to B. Moving from one region to the next one is implemented by executing a (set of) underlying continuous controllers and it may take some time for the robot to exit A and enter B, i.e., the action of moving between regions does not happen instantaneously. Now assume the robot receives the value of a variable $i \in \{0, 1, 2, 3\}$ as input, and it needs to react to different values of i in order to satisfy a given specification, e.g., the robot should repeatedly visit region A if $i \in \{0, 1\}$, and visit region C if $i \in \{2, 3\}$. Due to the

© Springer Nature Switzerland AG 2018
D. N. Jansen and P. Prabhakar (Eds.): FORMATS 2018, LNCS 11022, pp. 71–87, 2018.
https://doi.org/10.1007/978-3-030-00151-3_5

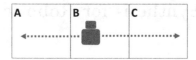

Fig. 1. Workspace for Example 1.

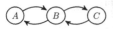

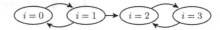

Fig. 2. A region graph.   **Fig. 3.** Possible changes in input i.

arbitrary completion times of actions, while a robot is moving toward a region, the value of the input received from the environment may change, requiring the robot to change its action, e.g., to stop moving toward region A and start moving toward C if the input changes from $i \in \{0, 1\}$ to $i \in \{2, 3\}$ as shown in Fig. 1.

Above example can be modeled as a typical reactive synthesis problem and solved using an off-the-shelf synthesis tool. Raman et al. [1] propose an approach that addresses actions with arbitrary (but finite) completion times. Roughly speaking, in [1], where the robot is perceived to be and other uncontrolled variables are considered as input propositions, and a set of *action* propositions are defined that are controlled by the system, e.g., the physical interpretation of an action proposition π_{AB} is that the robot should move from region A to region B. To reflect that the actions may take arbitrary amount of time to complete, the effects of actions are assumed to be *non-deterministic*, i.e., if the system applies action π_{AB}, then at the next step, the robot may either be in A or B. To ensure that the actions *eventually* complete, a set of *fairness assumptions* is added indicating that if the system *persists* on an action then eventually its execution is completed, e.g., if the robot persists on moving from A to B, then eventually it exits A and enters B. Thus, this approach requires the addition of auxiliary propositions and fairness assumptions, increasing the computational complexity of the synthesis. In this paper, we propose an alternative synthesis algorithm that does not require addition of auxiliary propositions and assumptions. We discuss the computational complexity of both approaches in Sect. 3.

The main motivation for this paper stems from the observation of swarm robotic systems. Swarm robotics is concerned with design and analysis of robotic systems that consist of large numbers of robots whose interaction with each other and their environment lead to collectively intelligent behaviors. The potential applications of swarm robotic systems are many, including exploration, search and rescue, and construction. Thus, it is not surprising that this research area has been very active in recent years (see [2] for a survey of the literature). However, most of the existing approaches for design and analysis of swarm robotic systems are bottom-up, where a set of local rules are designed, typically by hand, and the emergence of the collective behavior is validated through testing and simulations [3–7]. In recent work [8], we took a top-down approach and developed an abstraction and a synthesis algorithm for swarms performing non-reactive tasks. In this paper, we address the problem of synthesis for *reactive* task specifications, where the behavior of the swarm depends on environmental events.

Our approach addresses the control synthesis problem for swarms using the same philosophy of recent work regarding reactive controller synthesis from LTL specifications for single or multi-robot systems [9–17]. A common theme in these approaches is that they create a discrete abstraction of the system, compute a discrete controller that satisfies the specification over the abstraction, and then continuously implement the discrete controller, creating a hybrid controller that fulfills the high-level specification. One of the main challenges in modeling swarms is that the robots do not move instantaneously between the regions and they may execute their assigned tasks at different speeds. In this paper, we synthesize a strategy for a swarm using an abstraction that is independent of the number of robots. The synthesis algorithm takes into account that the robots may move with different speeds, and meanwhile the input values may change, requiring different responses from the robots.

Contributions. We propose realizability and synthesis algorithms for the reactive synthesis problem where the actions of the system are non-instantaneous. We compare our approach with the alternative method where a set of additional propositions and assumptions are introduced to model the problem. We then show how a robot swarm navigation problem can be modeled and solved using the two approaches. We implement our algorithms and apply them to an example to demonstrate the potential of our proposed approach.

Related work. The synthesis problem was first recognized by Church [18]. The problem of synthesizing reactive systems from a specification given in LTL was considered by Pnueli et al. [19], and shown to be doubly exponential in the size of the LTL formula [20]. Bloem et al. [21] present polynomial time algorithms for the realizability and synthesis problems for fragment of LTL known as Generalized Reactivity (1) (GR(1)). We also consider GR(1) specifications in this paper.

Extending the timing semantics of discrete-time temporal logic formulas to continuous or hybrid dynamics needs either careful definition of new semantics (see e.g. [22]) or a finite abstraction of the infinite time and state space, e.g., bisimulation relation defined for timed automata and various models of hybrid systems [23]. These bisimulations are time-abstract, i.e., they do not explicitly encode time as a continuous variable. In this paper we use a discrete abstraction that is also time-abstract where the transitions may take an arbitrary amount of time to complete. The use of verification techniques for analyzing the emergent behaviors of robotic swarms is studied in [24,25]. In this paper, we consider *synthesizing reactive* controllers for swarms of robots. Hierarchical control and planning for systems with large number of identical components from high-level temporal logic specifications is also considered in [14–16], however, there is no notion of dynamically changing environment and controllers are non-reactive.

2 Preliminaries

Let $\mathbb{Z}$ be the set of integers. For $a, b \in \mathbb{Z}$, let $[a..b] = \{x \in \mathbb{Z} \mid a \leq x \leq b\}$.

Linear Temporal Logic (LTL). LTL is a specification language with two kinds of operators: logical connectives (negation ($\neg$), disjunction ($\vee$), conjunction ($\wedge$) and implication ($\rightarrow$)) and temporal modal operators (next ($\bigcirc$), always ($\square$), eventually ($\Diamond$) and until ($\mathcal{U}$)). The formulas of LTL are defined over a set of atomic propositions (Boolean variables) $\mathcal{V}$. The syntax is given by the grammar: $\Phi := v \mid \Phi \vee \Phi \mid \neg \Phi \mid \bigcirc \Phi \mid \Phi \, \mathcal{U} \, \Phi$ for $v \in \mathcal{V}$. We define $\mathtt{True} = v \vee \neg v$, $\mathtt{False} = v \wedge \neg v$, $\Diamond \Phi = \mathtt{True} \, \mathcal{U} \, \Phi$, and $\square \Phi = \neg \Diamond \neg \Phi$. A formula with no temporal operator is a Boolean formula or a *predicate*. Given a predicate ϕ over variables $\mathcal{V}$, we say $s \in 2^{\mathcal{V}}$ satisfies ϕ, denoted by $s \models \phi$, if the formula obtained from ϕ by replacing all variables in s by $\mathtt{True}$ and all other variables by $\mathtt{False}$ is valid.

We call the set of all possible assignments to variables $\mathcal{V}$ *states* and denote them by $\Sigma_{\mathcal{V}}$, i.e., $\Sigma_{\mathcal{V}} = 2^{\mathcal{V}}$. Given a subset of variables $\mathcal{X} \subseteq \mathcal{V}$ and a state $s \in \Sigma_{\mathcal{V}}$, we denote by $s_{|\mathcal{X}}$ the projection of s to $\mathcal{X}$, i.e., $s_{|\mathcal{X}} = \{x \in \mathcal{X} \mid x \in s\}$. Given non-overlapping sets of Boolean variables $\mathcal{V}_1, \mathcal{V}_2, \cdots, \mathcal{V}_n$, we use the notation $\phi(\mathcal{V}_1, \mathcal{V}_2, \cdots, \mathcal{V}_n)$ to indicate that ϕ is a predicate over $\mathcal{V}_1 \cup \mathcal{V}_2 \cup \cdots \cup \mathcal{V}_n$. We often use predicates over $\mathcal{V} \cup \mathcal{V}'$ where $\mathcal{V}'$ is the set of primed versions of the variables in $\mathcal{V}$, i.e., $\mathcal{V}' = \{v' \mid v \in \mathcal{V}\}$. Given a predicate $\phi(\mathcal{V}_1, \mathcal{V}_2, \cdots, \mathcal{V}_n, \mathcal{V}_1', \mathcal{V}_2', \cdots, \mathcal{V}_n')$ and assignments $s_i, t_i \in \Sigma_{\mathcal{V}_i}$, we use $(s_1, s_2, \cdots, s_n, t_1', t_2', \cdots, t_n') \models \phi$ to indicate $s_1 \cup s_2 \cup \cdots \cup s_n \cup t_1' \cup t_2' \cup \cdots \cup t_n' \models \phi$ where $t_i' = \{v' \in \mathcal{V}_i' \mid v \in t_i\}$. For a set $\mathcal{Z} \subseteq \mathcal{V}$, let $Same(\mathcal{Z})$ be a predicate specifying that the values of the variables in $\mathcal{Z}$ stay unchanged during a transition. Formally, $Same(\mathcal{Z}) = \bigwedge_{z \in \mathcal{Z}} z \leftrightarrow z'$. An LTL formula over variables $\mathcal{V}$ is interpreted over infinite words $w \in (\Sigma_{\mathcal{V}})^{\omega}$. The language of an LTL formula Φ, denoted by $\mathcal{L}(\Phi)$, is the set of infinite words that satisfy Φ, i.e., $\mathcal{L}(\Phi) = \{w \in (\Sigma_{\mathcal{V}})^{\omega} \mid w \models \Phi\}$. We refer the reader to [26] for a more formal introduction.

Assume $\mathcal{V}$ is partitioned into a set of input $\mathcal{I}$ and output $\mathcal{O}$ variables, i.e., $\mathcal{V} = \mathcal{I} \uplus \mathcal{O}$. In this paper, we consider specifications of the form $\Phi = \Phi_e \rightarrow \Phi_s$ (known as GR(1) specifications [21]) where Φ_e characterizes assumptions on the environment and Φ_s specifies the correct behavior of the system. A correct implementation of the specification guarantees to satisfy Φ_s, provided that the environment satisfies Φ_e. In turn, Φ_e and Φ_s have the structure $\Phi_e = \phi_e^i \wedge \phi_e^t \wedge \phi_e^g$ and $\Phi_s = \phi_s^i \wedge \phi_s^t \wedge \phi_s^g$, where (i) ϕ_e^i and ϕ_s^i are predicates over $\mathcal{I}$ and $\mathcal{I} \cup \mathcal{O}$, respectively, characterizing the initial states, (ii) ϕ_α^t for $\alpha \in \{e, s\}$ is an LTL formula of the form $\bigwedge_i \square \psi_i$. Each subformula $\square \psi_i$ is either characterizing an invariant, in which case ψ_i is a Boolean formula over $\mathcal{I} \cup \mathcal{O}$, or it is characterizing a transition relation, in which case ψ_i is a Boolean formula over expressions v and $\bigcirc u$ where $v \in \mathcal{I} \cup \mathcal{O}$ and, $u \in \mathcal{I}$ if $\alpha = e$ and $u \in \mathcal{I} \cup \mathcal{O}$ if $\alpha = s$. (iii) ϕ_e^g and ϕ_s^g are formulas of the form $\bigwedge_i \square \Diamond \gamma_i$ characterizing fairness/liveness, where each γ_i is a predicate over $\mathcal{I} \cup \mathcal{O}$, and indicates an event that should occur infinitely often during system execution.

Game Structures. We consider two-player games played between a system and its environment. Similar to [21], a *game structure* $\mathcal{G}$ is defined as $\mathcal{G} = (\mathcal{V}, \mathcal{I}, \mathcal{O}, \theta_e, \theta_s, \tau_e, \tau_s, \Phi)$ where $\mathcal{V}$ is a finite set of Boolean variables partitioned into input variables $\mathcal{I}$ controlled by the environment and output variables $\mathcal{O}$ controlled by the system, θ_e is a predicate over $\mathcal{I}$ representing the initial states of the environment, θ_s is a predicate over $\mathcal{V}$ representing the initial states of the system, $\tau_e(\mathcal{V}, \mathcal{I}')$ is a predicate relating a state $s \in \Sigma_{\mathcal{V}}$ to a possible next input value $s_{\mathcal{I}'} \in \Sigma_{\mathcal{I}'}$, and characterizes the transition relation of the environment, $\tau_s(\mathcal{V}, \mathcal{I}', \mathcal{O}')$ is a predicate relating a state $s \in \Sigma_{\mathcal{V}}$ and an input value $s_{\mathcal{I}} \in \Sigma_{\mathcal{I}}$ to an output value $s_{\mathcal{O}} \in \Sigma_{\mathcal{O}}$, and characterizes the transition relation of the system, and Φ is the winning condition, given as an LTL formula.

A state s is *initial* if $s \models \theta_e \wedge \theta_s$. Given two states s and s' of $\mathcal{G}$, s' is a successor of s if $(s, s') \models \tau_e \wedge \tau_s$. A *play* σ of $\mathcal{G}$ is a maximal sequence of states $\sigma = s_0, s_1, \cdots$ where s_0 is initial and for each $j \geq 0$, s_{j+1} is a successor of s_j. A play $\sigma = s_0, s_1, \cdots$ is *winning* for the system if either (1) σ ends in a state s_n where there is no assignment $s_{\mathcal{I}} \in \Sigma_{\mathcal{I}}$ such that $(s_n, s'_{\mathcal{I}}) \models \tau_e$, i.e., there is no possible valid input for the environment, or (2) σ is infinite and it satisfies Φ. Otherwise, σ is winning for the environment. A *strategy* for the system is a partial function $f : M \times \Sigma_{\mathcal{V}} \times \Sigma_{\mathcal{I}} \rightarrow M \times \Sigma_{\mathcal{O}}$, where M is some *memory domain* with a designated initial value $m_0 \in M$, such that for every $s \in \Sigma_{\mathcal{V}}$, $s_{\mathcal{I}} \in \Sigma_{\mathcal{I}}$, and $m \in M$ if $(s, s'_{\mathcal{I}}) \models \tau_e$ then $(s, s'_{\mathcal{I}}, s'_{\mathcal{O}}) \models \tau_s$, where $f(m, s, s_{\mathcal{I}}) = (m', s_{\mathcal{O}})$. A play $\sigma = s_0, s_1, \cdots$ is said to be *compliant* with f if for all $i \geq 0$, $f(m_i, s_i, s_{i+1|\mathcal{I}}) = (m_{i+1}, s_{i+1|\mathcal{O}})$. Strategy f is winning for the system from a state s if all the plays starting from s that are compliant with f are winning for the system. We denote by $\mathbf{W}$ the set of states from which there is a winning strategy for the system. For the environment player, strategies and winning strategies are defined dually. $\mathcal{G}$ is said to be *winning* for the system, if for all $s_{\mathcal{I}} \in \Sigma_{\mathcal{I}}$, if $s_{\mathcal{I}} \models \theta_e$, then there exists $s_{\mathcal{O}} \in \Sigma_{\mathcal{O}}$ such that $(s_{\mathcal{I}}, s_{\mathcal{O}}) \models \theta_s$ and $(s_{\mathcal{I}}, s_{\mathcal{O}}) \models \mathbf{W}$, i.e., $(s_{\mathcal{I}}, s_{\mathcal{O}})$ is a winning state for the system. We say f is a *finite memory* strategy if M is finite. If M is a singleton, we say f is *memoryless*. Given a game structure $\mathcal{G}$, the *realizability* problem is to decide if the game is winning for the system. The *synthesis* problem is to compute a winning strategy for the system. For a GR(1) specification $\Phi = \phi_e^i \wedge \phi_e^t \wedge \phi_e^g \rightarrow \phi_s^i \wedge \phi_s^t \wedge \phi_s^g$, there is a corresponding game structure $\mathcal{G} = (\mathcal{V}, \mathcal{I}, \mathcal{O}, \theta_e, \theta_s, \tau_e, \tau_s, \phi_e^g \rightarrow \phi_s^g)$ such that any play compliant with a winning strategy for system satisfies Φ [21].

Symbolic Algorithms. Symbolic algorithms operate on sets of states, described by their characteristic functions and usually represented by binary decision diagrams (BDDs) [26]. A symbolic algorithm can manipulate sets using set-theoretic operations such as union, intersection, complementation, image and pre-image. For example, given a transition relation τ defined over $\mathcal{V}$ and a set $X \subseteq \Sigma_{\mathcal{V}}$ of states, the image operator computes the set of states that can be reached from X in a single step, and is defined as $\mathbf{img}(X) = \{v \in \Sigma_{\mathcal{V}} \mid \exists u \in X : (u, v') \models \tau\}$. The gist of symbolic algorithms for realizability and synthesis for temporal logic specifications is the controllable predecessor operator **CPre**.

Given a set of states X, $\mathbf{CPre}(X)$ is the set of states from which the system can force the game into X regardless of how the environment behaves. Formally, $\mathbf{CPre}(X) = \{s \in \Sigma_{\mathcal{V}} \mid \forall x \in \Sigma_{\mathcal{I}}. \ (s, x') \models \tau^e \rightarrow \exists y \in \Sigma_{\mathcal{O}}. \ (s, x', y') \models \tau^s \wedge (x, y) \in X\}$.

Solving GR(1) Games. Let $\mathcal{G}$ be a game where the winning condition is of the form $\Phi = \bigwedge_{i=1}^{m} \Box\Diamond a_i \rightarrow \bigwedge_{j=1}^{n} \Box\Diamond g_j$. Here a_i and g_j are predicates encoding assumptions and guarantees, respectively. We refer to such games as GR(1) games [21]. Let $j \oplus 1 = (j \bmod n) + 1$. It is shown [21] that the set of winning states $\mathbf{W}$ for GR(1) games can be computed using following μ-calculus formula:

$$
\mathbf{W} = \nu
\begin{bmatrix}
Z_1 \\
Z_2 \\
\vdots \\
Z_n
\end{bmatrix}
\begin{bmatrix}
\mu Y (\bigvee_{i=1}^{m} \nu X(g_1 \wedge \mathbf{CPre}(Z_2) \vee Y \vee \neg a_i \wedge \mathbf{CPre}(X))) \\
\mu Y (\bigvee_{i=1}^{m} \nu X(g_2 \wedge \mathbf{CPre}(Z_3) \vee Y \vee \neg a_i \wedge \mathbf{CPre}(X))) \\
\vdots \\
\mu Y (\bigvee_{i=1}^{m} \nu X(g_n \wedge \mathbf{CPre}(Z_1) \vee Y \vee \neg a_i \wedge \mathbf{CPre}(X)))
\end{bmatrix}
\tag{1}
$$

We refer the reader to [21] for thorough explanation of the above formula. Following [27], we refer to the computation of the image and pre-image of a non-empty set as a step. In [27], the complexity of a symbolic algorithm is measured by the number of steps that it takes. The choice is motivated by the larger cost normally incurred by image and pre-image computations when compared to other operations performed on sets of states like union and intersection. For GR(1) specifications, Piterman et al. [28] show that the set of winning states can be computed with $O(mn\Sigma_{\mathcal{V}}^2)$ symbolic steps in the worst case where m and n are the number of assumptions and guarantees, respectively.

Graphs and SCCs. A *directed graph* is a pair $G = (V, E)$ where V is a finite set of nodes and $E \subseteq V \times V$ is a set of edges. We say $(v_0, v_1, \cdots, v_k) \in V^*$ is a *path* of length k if for all i $(v_i, v_{i+1}) \in E$. A path is *nontrivial* if its length is nonzero, and it is *simple* if all its nodes are distinct. A *cycle* is a nontrivial path for which $v_0 = v_k$. The graph $H = (W, F)$ is a *subgraph* of G if $W \subseteq V$ and $F = E \cap (W \times W)$. For a transition relation τ defined over a set of variables $\mathcal{V}$, a corresponding directed graph $G = (V, E)$ can be defined as follows. Each state $s \in \Sigma_{\mathcal{V}}$ corresponds to a unique node $v \in V$, and each transition $(s, r') \models \tau$ corresponds to a unique edge $(v, u) \in \mathbf{E}$ where u corresponds to $r \in \Sigma_{\mathcal{V}}$.

A *strongly connected component* (SCC) of G is a maximal set $C \subseteq V$ such that for all $v, w \in C$ there is a path from v to w. For $v \in V$, we define $SCC(v)$ to be the SCC that contains v. The SCC-quotient graph of (V, E) is a graph (V^s, E^s) with $V^s = \{SCC(v) \mid v \in V\}$ and $E^s = \{(C, C') \mid C \neq C' \text{ and } \exists v \in C, v' \in C' : (v, v') \in E\}$. Since the SCC graph is acyclic, it induces a partial order, and we refer to this order when we mention *minimal* or *maximal* SCC. Specifically, a maximal SCC has no outgoing edges. In [27], Bloem et al. present a symbolic algorithm for strongly connected component decomposition of a graph that performs $\theta(|V|log|V|)$ image and pre-image computations in the worst case.

3   Reactive Synthesis with Non-instantaneous Actions

Let $\mathcal{V}$ be a set of variables partitioned into input $\mathcal{I}$ and output $\mathcal{O}$ variables. The system can change the valuations over output variables by applying actions that intuitively abstract the underlying physical controllers, e.g., the action of moving a robot between two regions is an abstraction of the physical continuous controller that implements the behavior. Let $\mathcal{A}$ be a set of actions. For each action $\mathbf{a} \in \mathcal{A}$, a partial function $\mathcal{H}^{\mathbf{a}} : \Sigma_{\mathcal{O}} \to \Sigma_{\mathcal{O}}$ is defined that maps a valuation $\mathbf{o} \in \Sigma_{\mathcal{O}}$ to the action's *effect* $\mathcal{H}^{\mathbf{a}}(\mathbf{o}) \in \Sigma_{\mathcal{O}}$, i.e., if $\mathcal{H}^{\mathbf{a}}(\mathbf{o})$ is defined, then it is the valuation over variables $\mathcal{O}$ once the execution of $\mathbf{a}$ is completed. Intuitively, $\mathcal{I}$ are those variables whose values are directly controlled by the environment, e.g., variable i in Example 1, and $\mathcal{O}$ are variables whose values are only affected by system's actions, e.g., the region where the robot is located which can change by robot's moving actions. We assume there is a special stutter action $\mathbf{a}^{\perp} \in \mathcal{A}$ with $\mathcal{H}^{\mathbf{a}^{\perp}}(\mathbf{o}) = \mathbf{o}$, i.e., $a^{\perp}$ keeps the value of propositions $\mathcal{O}$ the same.

Application of an action $\mathbf{a} \in \mathcal{A}$ at a state $s \in \Sigma_{\mathcal{V}}$ is followed by a successor state $s' \in \Sigma_{\mathcal{V}}$ and is denoted by $s \xrightarrow{\mathbf{a}} s'$. In this paper, we consider *non-instantaneous* actions that may take arbitrary number of steps to complete, and only if the system player *persists* on them by consecutive applications. Formally, for a consecutive application of an action $\mathbf{a}$ starting from a state $s_0 \in \Sigma_{\mathcal{V}}$, there exists $k \geq 1$ such that for the sequence $s_0 \xrightarrow{\mathbf{a}} s_1 \xrightarrow{\mathbf{a}} s_2 \cdots \xrightarrow{\mathbf{a}} s_k \cdots$, we have $s_{i|\mathcal{O}} = s_{0|\mathcal{O}}$ for $i < k$, and $s_{k|\mathcal{O}} = \mathcal{H}^{\mathbf{a}}(s_{0|\mathcal{O}})$, i.e., the valuations over the propositions in $\mathcal{O}$ stay unchanged up until step k, where their valuation changes due to the effect of action $\mathbf{a}$. We say an action is *instantaneous* if $k = 1$, i.e., the action takes effect in a single step. We consider the following problem:

Problem 1. Given a GR(1) specification $\varPhi$ defined over input $\mathcal{I}$ and output $\mathcal{O}$ variables, and a set of non-instantaneous actions $\mathcal{A}$, synthesize a strategy for the system that realizes $\varPhi$ considering that the actions may take arbitrary number of steps to complete, and meanwhile the values of the input variables may change.

Assumptions. We make the following assumptions in this paper. We assume that the stutter action $\mathbf{a}^{\perp}$ is instantaneous, e.g., the robot can apply the stutter action and stop immediately. Moreover, we assume that $\forall s \in \Sigma_{\mathcal{V}}, \forall \mathbf{a}_1, \mathbf{a}_2 \in \mathcal{A}$. if $\mathcal{H}^{\mathbf{a}_1}(s_{|\mathcal{O}})$ and $\mathcal{H}^{\mathbf{a}_2}(s_{|\mathcal{O}})$ are defined, then $\mathcal{H}^{\mathbf{a}_1}(s_{|\mathcal{O}}) \neq \mathcal{H}^{\mathbf{a}_2}(s_{|\mathcal{O}})$, i.e., the effects of any two actions $\mathbf{a}_1$ and $\mathbf{a}_2$ that are applicable at s are distinguishable. This assumption allows us to *infer* the actions from the computed strategies in the absence of action propositions, i.e., to know which action to apply during execution by analyzing the current and next valuations over the output variables.

3.1   Synthesis with Auxiliary Propositions [29]

One approach to solve Problem 1 is to define a set of action propositions $\varPi^{\mathcal{A}}$ where each $\pi^{\mathbf{a}} \in \varPi^{\mathcal{A}}$ corresponds to an action $\mathbf{a} \in \mathcal{A}$ [29]. Then, from the description of the actions, a set of safety assumptions over $\mathcal{O} \cup \varPi^{\mathcal{A}} \cup \mathcal{O}'$ is obtained that describes how actions can change the valuations over propositions $\mathcal{O}$. Moreover, a set of fairness assumptions $\Phi^{\mathcal{A}} = \bigwedge_{\mathbf{a} \in \mathcal{A}} \Box \Diamond \phi^{\mathbf{a}}$ are defined to indicate that if the system persists on an action, then it eventually completes. The action propositions $\pi^{\mathcal{A}}$, and additional safety and fairness assumptions are added to the original specification Φ. A synthesized strategy for the new specification, if one exists, is a solution for Problem 1. Note that the variables $\mathcal{O}$ are treated as input propositions in the new specifications to model that their values are not controlled by the system and that the system player can only change their values by applying actions. We provide an example in the next section in the context of swarm robotics, and refer the readers to [29] for further details.

The role of the action propositions and fairness assumptions in the above approach is to capture that the values of the variables $\mathcal{O}$ may not change instantaneously. Let $m_{\mathcal{A}}$ be the number of additional fairness assumptions over actions. The complexity of the above approach is bounded by $O(n(m + m_{\mathcal{A}})(2^{|\mathcal{A}|}\Sigma_{\mathcal{V}})^2)$ symbolic steps, i.e., the complexity grows linearly with the number of added assumptions, and exponentially with the number of added actions propositions in the worst case. Thus, the next natural question is how we can avoid introducing those auxiliary action propositions and fairness assumptions altogether.

3.2   Non-instantaneous-GR(1)

To model the problem without the use of the auxiliary propositions, an *action transition relation* $\tau^{\mathcal{A}}$ is obtained from descriptions of actions that intuitively describes how the system player can change the values of the output variables by applying actions. The GR(1) specification Φ and the transition relation $\tau^{\mathcal{A}}$ are then used to form a game $\mathcal{G}$. Informally, $\tau^{\mathcal{A}}$ is defined as if the actions of the system player in the resulting game $\mathcal{G}$ are instantaneous, and the realizability and synthesis algorithms are modified to capture that the actions are not, in fact, instantaneous.

Forming the Game. Action transition relation $\tau^{\mathcal{A}}$ is obtained from descriptions of actions and is defined such that it restricts the system player to take only one action at a time. Note that if there exists a winning strategy for the system player that applies multiple actions at a state, given that the actions may take arbitrary amount of time to complete and any of the applied actions may complete first, any possible successor state must be winning. Thus, the system player can deliberately apply one action and wait for it to complete before applying the next action. Moreover, $\tau^{\mathcal{A}}$ is defined such that actions are instantaneous, i.e., actions are assumed to complete in a single step. Formally, we define $\tau^{\mathcal{A}} = \bigvee_{\mathbf{a} \in \mathcal{A}} \bigvee_{\mathbf{o} \in \Sigma_{\mathcal{O}}} \mathbf{o} \wedge \mathcal{H}^{\mathbf{a}}(\mathbf{o})'$ where $\mathcal{H}^{\mathbf{a}}(\mathbf{o})'$ is $\mathcal{H}^{\mathbf{a}}(\mathbf{o})$ with propositions replaced by their primed versions [1].

Let $\mathcal{G}^{\Phi} = (\mathcal{V}, \mathcal{I}, \mathcal{O}, \theta_e, \theta_s, \tau_e, \tau_s, \phi_e^g \rightarrow \phi_s^g)$ be the GR(1) game corresponding to Φ. To solve Problem 1, we synthesize a strategy for the game $\mathcal{G} = (\mathcal{V}, \mathcal{I}, \mathcal{O}, \theta_e, \theta_s, \tau_e, \tau_s \wedge \tau^{\mathcal{A}}, \phi_e^g \rightarrow \phi_s^g)$. Intuitively, $\tau^{\mathcal{A}}$ models how the system

---

[1] If $\mathcal{H}^{\mathbf{a}}(\mathbf{o})$ is undefined for any $\mathbf{o} \in \Sigma_{\mathcal{O}}$, let $\mathcal{H}^{\mathbf{a}}(\mathbf{o}) = \texttt{False}$ in the definition of $\tau^{\mathcal{A}}$.

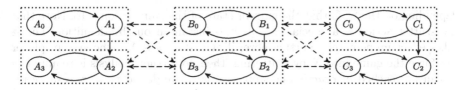

Fig. 4. Possible transitions between the states of the game.

can change the state of the game by applying actions. However, τ^A assumes more "power" for the system as it allows actions to happen instantaneously. We extend the controllable predecessor operator to take into account that an action may take an arbitrary number of steps, but if the system persists, it eventually completes. This way the auxiliary fairness assumptions are implicitly encoded into the new controllable predecessor operator.

CPre* Operator. Next, we define an extended controllable predecessor operator **CPre*** : $2^{\Sigma_\mathcal{V}} \to 2^{\Sigma_\mathcal{V}}$ that maps a set $X \subseteq \Sigma_\mathcal{V}$ of states to a set **CPre***$(X) \subseteq \Sigma_\mathcal{V}$. The operator **CPre*** is a generalization of **CPre**. Specifically, **CPre***$(X) \subseteq$ **CPre**(X). Intuitively, at any state $s \in$ **CPre***(X), upon receiving any input $x \in \Sigma_\mathcal{I}$ such that $(s, x') \models \tau_e$, there is a transition $(s, x', y') \models \tau_s$ for the system that if happens *instantaneously* (the values of the corresponding output variables change in a single step), then a state in X is reached in a *single* step. However, unlike **CPre**, the state of the game may stay within **CPre***$(X)\backslash X$ for a finite number of steps since the transitions are not instantaneous and the values of the input variables can change meanwhile.

Consider the graph shown in Fig. 4. Each node is labeled with U_i where $U \in \{A, B, C\}$ is a region occupied by the robot and i is the value of the input variable changing according to a transition relation visualized in Fig. 3. Intuitively, each node of the graph represents a state of the game. The solid edges show the transitions where the robot stays in the same region while the value of the input variable changes asynchronously. The rectangular boxes in Fig. 4 show the SCCs for subgraphs where the robot's current region does not change. To keep the figure simple, not all the possible transitions between the states of the game are shown; the dashed edges represent that there exists at least one transition between states in the corresponding SCCs.

Intuitively, there are two cases to consider when it comes to the environment player's moves: either it keeps the value of the input variable i within a SCC indefinitely, or at some point, the environment player "switches" to a different SCC. For example, starting from the node A_0 and with the robot staying put, the environment player can keep the state of the game within the SCC $\{A_0, A_1\}$, or at some point switch to $\{A_2, A_3\}$. Note that since SCC $\{A_2, A_3\}$ is maximal, the state of the game stays within $\{A_2, A_3\}$ once it is entered, unless the system takes an action to move to a different region.

Roughly speaking, **CPre***(X) are composed of those states where either the system can push the game into X by stuttering, or by persisting on some action depending on the SCC that the current state of the game belongs to. Note that the stutter action is a special case as it is instantaneous by definition, i.e., it takes effect immediately. Furthermore, if at a state $s \in \Sigma_{\mathcal{V}}$, the system player can force the game into X by stuttering, then no further analysis is required as X can be reached in *exactly* one step. Formally, we define $\tau_{\perp}^s = \tau_s \wedge same(\mathcal{O})$ as the transitions where the output variables stay unchanged. We denote by $\mathbf{CPre}^{\perp}(X)$ the set of states where the system player can force the game into X by *stuttering*, i.e., $\mathbf{CPre}^{\perp}(X) = \{s \in \Sigma_{\mathcal{V}} \mid \forall x \in \Sigma_{\mathcal{I}}. (s, x') \models \tau_e \rightarrow \exists y \in \Sigma_{\mathcal{O}}(s, x', y') \models \tau_{\perp}^s \wedge (x, y) \in X)\}$. For example, $\mathbf{CPre}^{\perp}(\{B_1\}) = \{B_0\}$, i.e., the system player can force the game into $\{B_1\}$ from B_0 simply by staying put as the only "legal" environment move is to assign $i = 1$ at the next step.

In contrast, for a state that requires changing the values of the output variables to force the game into X, we further need to consider states that can be reached due to arbitrary completion times of the actions and possible changes in the environment. First note that the environment player may keep the state of the game within an SCC forever, unless the system player persists on an action to eventually change the values of the output propositions. For example, let $X = \{C_2, C_3\}$. Observe that at state B_2 (B_3) and upon receiving $i = 3$ ($i = 2$, respectively) as the next input, the system player can move toward region C. At the next step, either the action completes by reaching C (and hence X), or the state of the game stays within $\{B_2, B_3\}$. In this example, there is a "common" action (moving toward C) for states in $\{B_2, B_3\}$ such that if the system persists on this action, it will reach X under any allowable change in the input values. On the other hand, if we add a safety constraint that moving toward C is not allowed at B_3, the system player can no longer persist on the action of moving toward C, and thus cannot force the game into X from $\{B_2, B_3\}$. Formally, for a valuation $y \in \Sigma_{\mathcal{O}}$ over output variables, we denote by $\{y\} = \{s \in \Sigma_{\mathcal{V}} \mid s_{|\mathcal{O}} = y\}$ the set of states whose valuations over $\mathcal{O}$ are the same as y. Let $\tau_e^y = \{y\} \wedge \{y\}' \wedge \tau_e$ be a transition relation where the input variables may change according to the environment transition relation τ_e while the system propositions have the valuation y and stay unchanged during the transitions. Let $G^y = (V^y, E^y)$ be the acyclic directed graph obtained from the SCC decomposition of τ_e^y [27]. For a state $s \in \Sigma_{\mathcal{V}}$ with $s_{|\mathcal{O}} = y$, we denote by $SCC(s) \in V^y$, the SCC that s belongs to. The following definition characterizes when the system player can push the game into X from the states belonging to an SCC:

Definition 1. *Given a set of states* $X \subseteq \Sigma_{\mathcal{V}}$*, we say the system player can force the game into* X *from* $SCC(s)$*, denoted by* $SCC(s) \rightsquigarrow X$*, if* (1) $SCC(s) \subseteq \mathbf{CPre}(X) \cup X$*, and* (2) $\exists y \in \Sigma_{\mathcal{O}} \forall v \in SCC(s) \cap \mathbf{CPre}(X) \forall x \in \Sigma_{\mathcal{I}}. (v, x') \models \tau_e \wedge (x, v_{|\mathcal{O}}) \in SCC(s) \backslash X \rightarrow (v, x', y') \models \tau_s \wedge (x, y) \in X$.

Intuitively, the first condition says that all the states in the $SCC(s)$ are either part of X or the system player can force the game into X from them (assuming instantaneous effects). Otherwise there is a state in the SCC for which there is no transition for the system player that even if completes instantaneously, a state in X is reached in a single step. The second condition ensures that there exists a common action with effect $y \in \Sigma_{\mathcal{O}}$ that the system can persist on to *eventually* reach X as long as the environment stays within the SCC and does not switch to a different SCC. To this end, in condition 2, only those environment transitions are considered that satisfy $(v, x') \models \tau_e \wedge (x, v_{|\mathcal{O}}) \in SCC(s) \backslash X$, i.e., the next state $(x, v_{|\mathcal{O}})$ in case the action does not take effect stays within $SCC(s)$. Note that for input values x such that $(v, x') \models \tau_e \wedge (x, v_{|\mathcal{O}}) \in X$, the system has a trivial action (stuttering) to push the state of the game into X in a single step. Thus, only the states $SCC(s) \backslash X$ need to be considered to determine if the system player has a common action for the states within an SCC. Intuitively, If condition 2 does not hold, then there is no common action for states within the $SCC(s)$, and the environment can circle in the $SCC(s)$ reaching states where the system player has to change its mind, not being able to persist on any action.

If the environment keeps the state within an SCC, then eventually the action that the system player persist on takes effect and a state in X is reached. Otherwise, the environment switches the SCC, in which case the system has to persist on an action for that SCC. Since the SCC-quotient graph is acyclic, either some system action completes in one of the SCCs, or eventually a maximal SCC is reached for which an action is guaranteed to take effect eventually. Given Definition 1, we define the **CPre*** operator:

Definition 2. *The set of states $Z = \mathbf{CPre}^*(X)$ from which the system player can push the game into X is defined recursively as (1) If $s \in \mathbf{CPre}^{\perp}(X)$ then $s \in Z$, and (2) If $s \in \mathbf{CPre}(X)$ and $SCC(s) \rightsquigarrow X$ and $\mathbf{img}(SCC(s), \tau_y) \backslash SCC(s) \subseteq Z$ where $y = s_{|\mathcal{O}}$ and $\tau_y = \{y\} \wedge \{y\}' \wedge \tau_e$, then $s \in Z$.*

Intuitively, $\mathbf{img}(SCC(s), \tau_y) \backslash SCC(s)$ are those states that can be reached due to the environment player switching the SCC while the values of the output variables stay unchanged, and they all must be in Z. Note that the SCC graph corresponding to each $y \in \Sigma_{\mathcal{O}}$ is acyclic, hence Z can be computed recursively starting from maximal SCCs. Specifically, for states $s \in \mathbf{CPre}(X)$ that $SCC(s)$ is maximal, if $SCC(s) \rightsquigarrow X$, then $s \in Z$ (since $\mathbf{img}(SCC(s), \tau_y) \backslash SCC(s) = \emptyset$).

Algorithm 1 shows the steps for computing $Z = \mathbf{CPre}^*(X)$. The set Z is initialized with $\mathbf{CPre}^{\perp}(X)$. The set of states $S = \mathbf{CPre}(X)$ where the system can force the game into X in a single step assuming instantaneous effects is computed next. In line 3, the set of valuations Y over output variables that appear in S is computed. Intuitively, only the SCCs corresponding to valuations $y \in Y$ are relevant and need to be considered since $\mathbf{CPre}^*(X) \subseteq \mathbf{CPre}(X)$. Next, the SCC-quotient graph corresponding to each y is analyzed as follows. At each iteration of the inner loop in Algorithm 1, an SCC $\mathbf{scc} \in V^y$ is picked for analysis such that all the SCCs that $\mathbf{scc}$ depends on, i.e., there is a path from $\mathbf{scc}$ to them in $\mathbf{G}^y$, have been analyzed. In line 9, it is first checked that all the transitions that leave $\mathbf{scc}$ (i.e., the environment switches to a different SCC), end up in states that are in Z. Otherwise, no state from $\mathbf{scc}$ is added to Z since the environment can switch to an SCC where the system can no longer guarantee reaching X. The conditions of Definition 1 is checked in lines 10–13 symbolically. If $\varphi = \mathtt{True}$, it means there exists a common valuation over output variables satisfying the conditions of Definition 1, in which case the states in $\mathbf{scc} \cap S$ are added to Z, and finally, $\mathbf{scc}$ is marked as analyzed.

Algorithm 1. CPre*

Data: A set of states X
Result: A set of states Z s.t. the system can force the game into X
1   $Z := \mathbf{CPre}^{\perp}(X)$;
2   $S := \mathbf{CPre}(X)$;
3   $Y := S_{|\mathcal{O}}$;
4   **for** *each* $y \in Y$ **do**
5   Let $\mathbf{G}^y = (V^y, E^y)$ be SCC-quotient of $\tau_y = \{y\} \wedge \{y\}' \wedge \tau_e$;
6   **while** *there are SCCs in* $\mathbf{G}^y$ *to be analyzed* **do**
7   Pick $\mathbf{scc} \in V^y$ s.t. $\forall \mathbf{C} \in V^y : (\mathbf{scc}, \mathbf{C}) \in E^y \rightarrow \mathbf{C}$ is marked as analyzed;
8         $\varphi := \mathtt{False}$;
9   **if** $(\mathbf{img}(\mathbf{scc}, \tau_y) \wedge \neg\mathbf{scc}) \subseteq Z$ **then**
10   **if** $\mathbf{scc} \subseteq (S \cup X)$ **then**
11             $\theta = \exists \mathcal{O}'. \; \mathbf{scc} \wedge S \wedge \tau_e \wedge (\mathbf{scc} \wedge \neg X)'$;
12             $\varphi = \exists \mathcal{O}' \; \forall \mathcal{V} \; \forall \mathcal{I}'. \; \theta \rightarrow \tau_s \wedge X'$;
13   **end**
14   **end**
15   **if** $\varphi = \mathtt{True}$ **then**
16           $Z := Z \vee (\mathbf{scc} \wedge S)$;
17   **end**
18   Mark SCC $\mathbf{scc}$ as analyzed;
19   **end**
20 **end**
21 Return Z;

Computing the Set of Winning States. The set of winning states for the system can be computed using the original algorithm for GR(1) proposed in [21] where the **CPre** operator is replaced by **CPre***. We refer to the resulting algorithm as the *Non-Instantaneous-GR(1)* algorithm. The following theorem establishes its correctness and complexity.

Theorem 1. *The Non-Instantaneous-GR(1) algorithm is sound and complete. It performs* $O(mn\Sigma_\mathcal{V}^2)$ *number of* **CPre*** *computations in the worst case.*

Since in the Non-Instantaneous-GR(1) algorithm, **CPre** is replaced by **CPre***, i.e., the symbolic steps in the original algorithm correspond to **CPre*** in the new algorithm, it follows that Non-Instantaneous-GR(1) performs $O(mn\Sigma_\mathcal{V}^2)$ number of **CPre*** computations in the worst case. Although the complexity of the proposed symbolic algorithms are measured in symbolic steps, we should note that the time needed to compute an image, pre-image or controllable predecessor is not constant, and depends on both the argument and the transition relation [27]. Moreover, the cost of symbolic computation strongly depends on the number of variables used, because the symbolic steps are often implemented using BDDs and the size of BDDs can grow exponentially with the number of variables appearing in the Boolean formula they represent [26]. Adding action propositions and fairness assumptions in the first approach not only increases the number of symbolic steps that must be performed in the worst case, but it also makes the symbolic steps more complex as the BDDs may become larger. In contrast, in the second approach, the **CPre*** manipulates BDDs that can potentially depend on a smaller number of variables. Thus, the proposed algorithm can outperform the alternative one in settings where many action propositions and fairness assumptions need to be defined. We also note that **CPre*** involves SCC-analysis that for $y \in \Sigma_{\mathcal{O}}$ can be done in $O(|\Sigma_{\mathcal{I}}|log|\Sigma_{\mathcal{I}}|)$ [27]. Since various calls to **CPre*** during the Non-Instantaneous-GR(1) algorithm may require the same SCC-decompositions (states with the same valuations over output variables may appear in **CPre*** of different arguments during the fixpoint computations), the SCC-quotient graphs can be computed, stored and shared between the calls to **CPre***. Thus, in the worst case, SCC-decompositions can be computed with effort $O(|\Sigma_{\mathcal{O}}|(|\Sigma_{\mathcal{I}}|log|\Sigma_{\mathcal{I}}|))$. In our implementation, SCC-decomposition is only done for those $y \in \Sigma_{\mathcal{O}}$ that are encountered during the **CPre*** computations.

Synthesis. The GR(1) synthesis algorithm [21] can be adapted to synthesize strategies for systems with non-instantaneous actions. Intuitively, during the fixpoint computation of winning states, the intermediate values of X and Y in the μ-calculus formula 1 are collected. These sets are then used to define n memoryless strategies $f_1, \cdots, f_n$ for the system. The strategy f_j either forces the play to visit guarantee g_j and then proceed to $Z_{j \oplus 1}$ (i.e., next goal), or eventually falsifies some assumption a_i forever. The synthesis algorithm with non-instantaneous actions follows the same idea, with the main difference being that the next valuation over output variables in the strategy must be defined in a way that satisfies the constraints of Definition 2.

4   Reactive Synthesis for Swarm Robotic Systems

In this section, we show how a swarm robotic navigation problem can be modeled and solved using the approaches outlined in the previous section. Crucial for the physical realizability of the synthesized control is the ability to model non-instantaneous actions which stem from the fact that motion takes time and robots may be moving at different speeds.

For the swarm tasks, the user provides a region graph $\mathbf{G_R} = (\mathbf{R}, \mathbf{E})$ that shows the connectivity of the work space, and a GR(1) specification Φ that describes the desired swarm behavior. For each region $\mathbf{r} \in \mathbf{R}$, let $\pi_\mathbf{r}$ be a proposition representing that a part of the swarm is in region $\mathbf{r}$. Let $\mathcal{O} = \{\pi_\mathbf{r} \mid \mathbf{r} \in \mathbf{R}\}$ be the set of region propositions. Note that unlike the case of a single robot, the truth values of the region propositions are not mutually exclusive as different parts of the swarm may occupy different regions at the same time.

Example 2. Consider the workspace shown in Fig. 5 partitioned into regions $\mathbf{R} = \{A, B, .., N\}$. It may take an arbitrary amount of time for the robots to move from one region to an adjacent region. Assume a swarm of robots, initially positioned in region D, must react to input $i \in [0..3]$ received from the environment

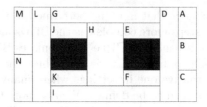

Fig. 5. Workspace

in the following manner: Always eventually, (1) if $i = 0$, then swarm must only occupy regions A, B and C, i.e., $\Box\Diamond(i = 0 \rightarrow \pi_A \wedge \pi_B \wedge \pi_C \wedge \bigwedge_{\mathbf{r}\in\mathbf{R}\backslash\{A,B,C\}} \neg\pi_\mathbf{r})$, (2) if $i = 1$, then the swarm must only occupy the corridors (regions E, F, J and K), i.e., $\Box\Diamond(i = 1 \rightarrow \pi_E \wedge \pi_F \wedge \pi_J \wedge \pi_K \wedge \bigwedge_{\mathbf{r}\in\mathbf{R}\backslash\{E,F,J,K\}} \neg\pi_\mathbf{r})$, (3) if $i = 2$, then swarm must only occupy regions G, and I, i.e., $\Box\Diamond(i = 2 \rightarrow \pi_G \wedge \pi_I \wedge \bigwedge_{\mathbf{r}\in\mathbf{R}\backslash\{G,I\}} \neg\pi_\mathbf{r})$, and (4) if $i = 3$, then swarm must only occupy regions M and N, i.e., $\Box\Diamond(i = 3 \rightarrow \pi_M \wedge \pi_N \wedge \bigwedge_{\mathbf{r}\in\mathbf{R}\backslash\{M,N\}} \neg\pi_\mathbf{r})$. We assume that the environment can assign any value from $[0..3]$ to i at each time step.

4.1   Synthesis with Auxiliary Action Propositions

We first sketch how the problem can be modeled using the auxiliary action propositions. To this end, the action propositions are automatically obtained from description of $\mathbf{G_R}$. For each edge $(\mathbf{u}, \mathbf{v}) \in \mathbf{E}$, we define a corresponding action proposition $\pi_\mathbf{uv}$ that indicates (a part of) the swarm moves from region $\mathbf{u}$ to $\mathbf{v}$. We assume that $\forall \mathbf{r} \in \mathbf{R}$. $(\mathbf{r}, \mathbf{r}) \in \mathbf{E}$, and a corresponding action $\pi_\mathbf{rr}$ is defined encoding that (a part of) the swarm remains in $\mathbf{r}$. This action is required in case a part of the swarm occupying a region must be partitioned such that a part remains in the same region, while the rest moves out of it. Let $\Pi^\mathcal{A}$ be the set of all action propositions. Note that $|\Pi^\mathcal{A}| = |\mathbf{R}| + |\mathbf{E}|$.

A set of safety assumptions for each action $\pi^\mathbf{a} \in \Pi^\mathcal{A}$ are added to the specification indicating how application of each action may change the values of region propositions. Intuitively, these safety assumptions indicate that if a part of swarm is moving from region $\mathbf{r}$ to $\mathbf{v}$, then at the next step, either regions may be occupied. Finally, a set of fairness assumptions, one for each action proposition $\pi_\mathbf{rv} \in \Pi^\mathcal{A}$ is added saying that if a part of swarm is in $\mathbf{r}$ and the system initiates moving the swarm toward $\mathbf{v}$, then eventually part of swarm moves to $\mathbf{v}$ or the system changes its mind and does not persist on the action anymore. Furthermore, an additional set of fairness assumptions are required to model that if the system persist on actions that moves the swarm out of $\mathbf{r}$ and does not take actions that move the swarm into $\mathbf{r}$, then eventually the swarm moves out of $\mathbf{r}$. Thus, we added $|\mathbf{R}| + |\mathbf{E}|$ fairness assumptions, leading to complexity $O(n(m + |\mathbf{R}| + |\mathbf{E}|)(2^{|\mathbf{R}|+|\mathbf{E}|}\Sigma_\mathcal{V})^2)$ in the worst case.

4.2 Non-instantaneous-GR(1)

Next, we explain how the swarm navigation problem can be modeled without the use of action propositions. To this end, the first step is to obtain the transition relation $\tau^{\mathcal{A}}$ for the set of actions of the swarm. $\tau^{\mathcal{A}}$ is obtained automatically from the description of the region graph $\mathbf{G_R}$ and is defined in a way that allows the system player to only move a part of the swarm from one region to the next region. Formally, let $(\mathbf{r}, \mathbf{v}) \in \mathbf{E}$ be a possible transition in the region graph. We define $\tau^{\mathcal{A}} = same(\mathcal{O}) \vee \bigvee_{(\mathbf{r},\mathbf{v})\in\mathbf{E}}(\varphi_{\mathbf{v}}^{\mathbf{r}} \vee \varphi_{\mathbf{v}}^{\neg\mathbf{r}})$ where $\varphi_{\mathbf{v}}^{\mathbf{r}} = \pi_r \wedge \neg\pi_{\mathbf{v}} \wedge \pi_r' \wedge \pi_{\mathbf{v}}' \wedge same(\mathcal{O}\backslash\{\pi_r, \pi_{\mathbf{v}}\})$, and $\varphi_{\mathbf{v}}^{\neg\mathbf{r}} = \pi_r \wedge \pi_{\mathbf{v}} \wedge \neg\pi_r' \wedge \pi_{\mathbf{v}}' \wedge same(\mathcal{O}\backslash\{\pi_r, \pi_{\mathbf{v}}\})$. Intuitively, $\varphi_{\mathbf{v}}^{\mathbf{r}}$ says that if a part of the swarm is in region $\mathbf{r}$ and region $\mathbf{v}$ is empty, then at the next step the system can move part of the swarm to region $\mathbf{v}$ such that both $\mathbf{r}$ and $\mathbf{v}$ are occupied. Similarly, $\varphi_{\mathbf{v}}^{\neg\mathbf{r}}$ indicates that if both regions $\mathbf{r}$ and $\mathbf{v}$ are occupied, then the system can evacuate region $\mathbf{r}$ by moving the subswarm to $\mathbf{v}$. All the other region propositions stay unchanged. Moreover, the system may choose to keep the region propositions the same, i.e., not to move any part of the swarm (stutter action). Note that $\tau^{\mathcal{A}}$ is written such that the system player can change the value of a region proposition in a single step, i.e., the actions are instantaneous. The non-instantaneous-GR(1) synthesis algorithm takes into account that the transitions between regions do not happen instantaneously.

4.3 Comparison

We implemented our algorithms in Java using the BDD package JDD [30]. The algorithms were run on a desktop machine with an Intel Core i7 CPU@3.40GHz and 16GB RAM. To model the problem using the approach proposed in [1], 66 action propositions and 66 fairness assumptions must be added to the specification in Example 2. We used Slugs [31] to synthesize a strategy using this approach. Although Slugs is the state-of-the-art tool for reactive synthesis, it took 54.27 min to compute a strategy. In contrast, our proposed method took 7 s to compute a strategy.

5 Conclusions and Future Work

We proposed new realizability and synthesis algorithms for reactive synthesis with non-instantaneous actions, and compared our method with the alternative approach where non-instantaneous actions are modeled through introduction of auxiliary propositions and assumptions. We applied the algorithms to synthesize controllers for swarm robotic systems, and showed that our proposed method outperforms the alternative one over an example. Nevertheless, the proposed approach has its limitations which also opens up avenues for future work. We restrict the system transition relation such that the system player can only take one action at a time (note that the alternative method allows application of multiple actions at each step). This restriction may lead to strategies that are unnecessarily large and "slow". In practice, we would like to apply more actions at each step to achieve the current goal quicker. Improving the quality of the synthesized strategies, and exploring applications of compositional synthesis [32, 33] for achieving better scalability are among the possible future directions.

Acknowledgements. This research was supported by DARPA N66001-17-2-4058.

References

1. Raman, V., Piterman, N., Finucane, C., Kress-Gazit, H.: Timing semantics for abstraction and execution of synthesized high-level robot control. IEEE Trans. Robot. **31**(3), 591–604 (2015)
2. Brambilla, M., Ferrante, E., Birattari, M., Dorigo, M.: Swarm robotics: a review from the swarm engineering perspective. Swarm Intell. **7**(1), 1–41 (2013)
3. Nouyan, S., Campo, A., Dorigo, M.: Path formation in a robot swarm. Swarm Intell. **2**(1), 1–23 (2008)
4. Soysal, O., Sahin, E.: Probabilistic aggregation strategies in swarm robotic systems. In: Proceedings 2005 IEEE Swarm Intelligence Symposium, SIS 2005, pp. 325–332. IEEE (2005)
5. Labella, T.H., Dorigo, M., Deneubourg, J.L.: Division of labor in a group of robots inspired by ants' foraging behavior. ACM Trans. Auton. Adapt. Syst. (TAAS) **1**(1), 4–25 (2006)
6. Bachrach, J., Beal, J., McLurkin, J.: Composable continuous-space programs for robotic swarms. Neural Comput. Appl. **19**(6), 825–847 (2010)
7. Balch, T., Hybinette, M.: Social potentials for scalable multi-robot formations. In: IEEE International Conference on Robotics and Automation 2000. Proceedings of ICRA 2000, vol. 1, pp. 73–80. IEEE (2000)
8. Moarref, S., Kress-Gazit, H.: Decentralized control of robotic swarms from high-level temporal logic specifications. In: International Symposium on Multi-Robot and Multi-Agent Systems. IEEE (2017, to appear)
9. Kress-Gazit, H., Fainekos, G.E., Pappas, G.J.: Temporal-logic-based reactive mission and motion planning. IEEE Trans. Robot. **25**(6), 1370–1381 (2009)
10. Wongpiromsarn, T., Topcu, U., Murray, R.M.: Receding horizon temporal logic planning. IEEE Trans. Autom. Control **57**(11), 2817–2830 (2012)
11. Kress-gazit, H., Wongpiromsarn, T., Topcu, U.: Correct, reactive robot control from abstraction and temporal logic specifications. IEEE Robot. Autom. Mag. **18**, 65–74 (2011)
12. Wongpiromsarn, T., Ulusoy, A., Belta, C., Frazzoli, E., Rus, D.: Incremental synthesis of control policies for heterogeneous multi-agent systems with linear temporal logic specifications. In: IEEE International Conference on Robotics and Automation, pp. 5011–5018. IEEE (2013)
13. Kloetzer, M., Belta, C.: Automatic deployment of distributed teams of robots from temporal logic motion specifications. IEEE Trans. Robot. **26**(1), 48–61 (2010)
14. Nilsson, P., Ozay, N.: Control synthesis for large collections of systems with mode-counting constraints. In: Proceedings of the 19th International Conference on Hybrid Systems: Computation and Control, pp. 205–214. ACM (2016)
15. Kloetzer, M., Belta, C.: Hierarchical abstractions for robotic swarms. In: Proceedings 2006 IEEE International Conference on Robotics and Automation 2006. ICRA 2006, pp. 952–957. IEEE (2006)

16. Kloetzer, M., Ding, X.C., Belta, C.: Multi-robot deployment from LTL specifications with reduced communication. In: 2011 50th IEEE Conference on Decision and Control and European Control Conference (CDC-ECC), pp. 4867–4872. IEEE (2011)

17. Kress-Gazit, H., Lahijanian, M., Raman, V.: Synthesis for robots: guarantees and feedback for robot behavior. Ann. Rev. Control Robot. Auton. Syst. **1**, 211–236 (2018)

18. Church, A.: Logic, arithmetic and automata. In: Proceedings of the International Congress of Mathematicians, pp. 23–35 (1962)

19. Pnueli, A., Rosner, R.: On the synthesis of a reactive module. In: Proceedings of the 16th ACM Symposium on Principles of Programming Languages, pp. 179–190. ACM (1989)

20. Rosner, R.: Modular synthesis of reactive systems. Ph.D. thesis, Weizmann Institute of Science (1992)

21. Bloem, R., Jobstmann, B., Piterman, N., Pnueli, A., Sa'ar, Y.: Synthesis of reactive (1) designs. J. Comput. Syst. Sci. **78**(3), 911–938 (2012)

22. Davoren, J.M., Coulthard, V., Markey, N., Moor, T.: Non-deterministic temporal logics for general flow systems. In: Alur, R., Pappas, G.J. (eds.) HSCC 2004. LNCS, vol. 2993, pp. 280–295. Springer, Heidelberg (2004). https://doi.org/10.1007/978-3-540-24743-2_19

23. Alur, R., Henzinger, T.A., Lafferriere, G., Pappas, G.J.: Discrete abstractions of hybrid systems. Proc. IEEE **88**(7), 971–984 (2000)

24. Dixon, C., Winfield, A.F., Fisher, M., Zeng, C.: Towards temporal verification of swarm robotic systems. Robot. Auton. Syst. **60**(11), 1429–1441 (2012)

25. Gjondrekaj, E., et al.: Towards a formal verification methodology for collective robotic systems. In: Aoki, T., Taguchi, K. (eds.) ICFEM 2012. LNCS, vol. 7635, pp. 54–70. Springer, Heidelberg (2012). https://doi.org/10.1007/978-3-642-34281-3_7

26. Clarke, E.M., Grumberg, O., Peled, D.: Model Checking. MIT press, Cambridge (1999)

27. Bloem, R., Gabow, H.N., Somenzi, F.: An algorithm for strongly connected component analysis in n log n symbolic steps. Form. Methods Syst. Des. **28**(1), 37–56 (2006)

28. Piterman, N., Pnueli, A., Sa'ar, Y.: Synthesis of reactive (1) designs. In: Emerson, E.A., Namjoshi, K.S. (eds.) VMCAI 2006. LNCS, vol. 3855, pp. 364–380. Springer, Heidelberg (2005). https://doi.org/10.1007/11609773_24

29. Raman, V., Kress-Gazit, H.: Synthesis for multi-robot controllers with interleaved motion. In: 2014 IEEE International Conference on Robotics and Automation (ICRA), pp. 4316–4321. IEEE (2014)

30. Vahidi, A.: JDD (2018). http://javaddlib.sourceforge.net/jdd/index.html. Accessed 16 June 2018

31. Ehlers, R., Raman, V.: Slugs: extensible GR(1) synthesis. In: Chaudhuri, S., Farzan, A. (eds.) CAV 2016. LNCS, vol. 9780, pp. 333–339. Springer, Cham (2016). https://doi.org/10.1007/978-3-319-41540-6_18

32. Alur, R., Moarref, S., Topcu, U.: Compositional synthesis of reactive controllers for multi-agent systems. In: Chaudhuri, S., Farzan, A. (eds.) CAV 2016. LNCS, vol. 9780, pp. 251–269. Springer, Cham (2016). https://doi.org/10.1007/978-3-319-41540-6_14

33. Filiot, E., Jin, N., Raskin, J.F.: Antichains and compositional algorithms for LTL synthesis. Form. Methods Syst. Des. **39**(3), 261–296 (2011)

Distributed Timed Systems

Perfect Timed Communication Is Hard

Parosh Aziz Abdulla[1], Mohamed Faouzi Atig[1(✉)],
and Shankara Narayanan Krishna[2]

[1] Uppsala University, Uppsala, Sweden
{parosh,mohamed_faouzi.atig}@it.uu.se
[2] IIT Bombay, Mumbai, India
krishnas@cse.iitb.ac.in

Abstract. We introduce the model of communicating timed automata
(CTA) that extends the classical models of finite-state processes communicating through FIFO perfect channels and timed automata, in the
sense that the finite-state processes are replaced by timed automata, and
messages inside the perfect channels are equipped with clocks representing their ages. In addition to the standard operations (resetting clocks,
checking guards of clocks) each automaton can either (1) append a message to the tail of a channel with an initial age or (2) receive the message
at the head of a channel if its age satisfies a set of given constraints. In
this paper, we show that the reachability problem is undecidable even in
the case of two timed automata connected by one unidirectional timed
channel if one allows global clocks (that the two automata can check and
manipulate). We prove that this undecidability still holds even for CTA
consisting of three timed automata and two unidirectional timed channels (and without any global clock). However, the reachability problem
becomes decidable (in **EXPTIME**) in the case of two automata linked
with one unidirectional timed channel and with no global clock. Finally,
we consider the bounded-context case, where in each context, only one
timed automaton is allowed to receive messages from one channel while
being able to send messages to all the other timed channels. In this case
we show that the reachability problem is decidable.

1 Introduction

In the last few years, several papers have been devoted to extend classical infinite-
state systems such as pushdown systems, (lossy) channel systems and Petri nets
with timed behaviors in order to obtain more accurate and precise formal models (e.g., [1,2,4,7,8,10–13,15,19–25,28]). In particular, *perfect channel systems*
have been extensively studied as a formal model for communicating protocols
[16,27]. Unfortunately, perfect channel systems are in general Turing powerful, and hence all basic decision problems (e.g., the reachability problem) are
undecidable for them [16]. To circumvent this undecidability obstacle, several
approximate techniques have been proposed in the literature including making
the channels lossy [5,18], restricting the communication topology to polyforest
architectures [26,27], or using half-duplex communication [17]. The decidability of the reachability problem can be also obtained by restricting the analysis

© Springer Nature Switzerland AG 2018
D. N. Jansen and P. Prabhakar (Eds.): FORMATS 2018, LNCS 11022, pp. 91–107, 2018.
https://doi.org/10.1007/978-3-030-00151-3_6

to only executions performing at most some fixed number of context switches (where in each context only one process is allowed to receive messages from one channel while being able to send messages to all the other channels) [26]. Another well-known technique used in the verification of perfect channel systems is that of loop acceleration where the effect of iterating a loop is computed [14].

In this paper, we introduce the model of *Communicating Timed Automata* which extends the classical models of finite-state processes communicating through FIFO perfect channels and timed automata, in the sense that the finite-state processes are replaced by timed automata, and messages inside the perfect channels are equipped with clocks representing their ages. In addition to the standard operations of timed automaton, each automaton can either (1) append a message to the tail of a channel with an initial age or (2) receive the message at the head of a channel if its age satisfies a set of given constraints. In a timed transition, the clock values and the ages of all the messages inside the perfect channels are increased uniformly. Our model subsumes both timed automata and perfect channel systems. More precisely, we obtain the latter if we do not allow the use of timed information (i.e., all the timing constraints trivially hold); and we obtain the former if we do not use the perfect channels (no message is sent or received from the channels). Observe that this model is infinite in multiple dimensions, namely we have a number of channels that may contain an unbounded number of messages each of which is equipped with a real number.

We show that the reachability problem is undecidable even in the case of two discrete timed automata connected by one unidirectional timed channel if one allows global clocks. We prove that this undecidability still holds even for the case when we have three timed automata and two unidirectional timed channels (and without any global clock). However, the reachability problem becomes decidable (in EXPTIME) in the case of two discrete timed automata linked with one unidirectional discrete timed channel and with no global clock. Finally, we consider the bounded-context case, where in each context only one timed automaton is allowed to receive messages from one channel while being able to send messages to all the other timed channels. In this case we show that the reachability is decidable even when the timed automata and the timed channels involved deal with dense time. This is quite surprising since the reachability problem for unidirectional polyforest architectures can be easily reduced to its corresponding problem in the bounded-context case in the untimed settings; however in the presence of time, polyforest architectures already give undecidability, while bounded-context stay decidable.

Related Work. Several extensions of infinite-state systems with time behaviours have been proposed in the literature (e.g., [1, 2, 4, 6–8, 10–13, 15, 19–25, 28]). The two closest to ours are those presented in [19, 25]. Both works extend perfect channel systems with time behaviours but do not associate a clock to each message (i.e., the content of each channel is still a word over a finite alphabet) as in our case. The work presented [19] shows that the reachability problem is decidable if and only if the communication topology is a polyforest while for our model the reachability problem is undecidable for polyforest architectures in general.

Furthermore, there is no simple reduction of our results to the results presented in [19]. The work presented in [25] considers dense clocks with urgent semantics. In [25], the authors show (as in our model) that the reachability problem is undecidable for three timed automata and two unidirectional timed channels; while it becomes decidable when considering two automata linked with one unidirectional timed channel. However, the used techniques for these results are quite different since we do not allow the urgent semantics.

2   Preliminaries

In this section, we introduce some notations and preliminaries which will be used throughout the paper. We use standard notation $\mathbb{N}$ for the set of naturals, along with ∞. Let $\mathcal{X}$ be a finite set of variables called *clocks*, taking on values from $\mathbb{N}$. A *valuation* on $\mathcal{X}$ is a function $\nu : \mathcal{X} \to \mathbb{N}$. We assume an arbitrary but fixed ordering on the clocks and write x_i for the clock with order i. This allows us to treat a valuation ν as a point $(\nu(x_1), \nu(x_2), \ldots, \nu(x_n)) \in \mathbb{N}^{|\mathcal{X}|}$. For a subset of clocks $X \in 2^{\mathcal{X}}$ and valuation $\nu \in \mathbb{R}_{\geq 0}^{|\mathcal{X}|}$, we write $\nu[X{:=}0]$ for the valuation where $\nu[X{:=}0](x) = 0$ if $x \in X$, and $\nu[X{:=}0](x) = \nu(x)$ otherwise. For $t \in \mathbb{N}$, write $\nu + t$ for the valuation defined by $\nu(x) + t$ for all $x \in X$. The valuation $\mathbf{0} \in \mathbb{R}_{\geq 0}^{|\mathcal{X}|}$ is a special valuation such that $\mathbf{0}(x) = 0$ for all $x \in \mathcal{X}$. A clock constraint over $\mathcal{X}$ is defined by a (finite) conjunction of constraints of the form $x \bowtie k$, where $k \in \mathbb{N}$, $x \in \mathcal{X}$, and $\bowtie \in \{<, \leq, =, >, \geq\}$. We write $\varphi(\mathcal{X})$ for the set of clock constraints. For a constraint $g \in \varphi(\mathcal{X})$, and a valuation $\nu \in \mathbb{N}^{|\mathcal{X}|}$, we write $\nu \models g$ to represent the fact that valuation ν satisfies constraint g. For example, $(1, 0, 10) \models (x_1 < 2) \wedge (x_2 = 0) \wedge (x_3 > 1)$.

Timed Automata. Let Act denote a finite set called actions. A timed automaton (TA) is a tuple $\mathcal{A} = (L, L^0, Act, \mathcal{X}, E, F)$ such that (i) L is a finite set of locations, (ii) $\mathcal{X}$ is a finite set of clocks, (iii) Act is a finite alphabet called an action set, (iv) $E \subseteq L \times \varphi(\mathcal{X}) \times Act \times 2^{\mathcal{X}} \times L$ is a finite set of transitions, and (v) $L^0, F \subseteq L$ are respectively the sets of initial and final locations and Act is a finite set of actions. A state s of a timed automaton is a pair $s = (\ell, \nu) \in L \times \mathbb{N}^{|\mathcal{X}|}$. A transition (t, e) from a state $s = (\ell, \nu)$ to a state $s' = (\ell', \nu')$ is written as $s \xrightarrow{t,e} s'$ if $e = (\ell, g, a, Y, \ell') \in E$, such that $a \in Act$, $\nu + t \models g$, and $\nu' = (\nu + t)[Y{:=}0]$. A run is a finite sequence $\rho = s_0 \xrightarrow{t_1,e_1} s_1 \xrightarrow{t_2,e_2} s_2 \cdots \xrightarrow{t_n,e_n} s_n$ of states and transitions. $\mathcal{A}$ is non-empty iff there is a run from an initial state $(l_0, \mathbf{0})$ to some state (f, ν) where $f \in F$. Note that we have defined discrete timed automata, a subclass of Alur-Dill automata [9], where clocks assume only integral values.

Region Automata. If $\mathcal{A}$ is a timed automaton, the region automaton corresponding to $\mathcal{A}$ denoted by $Reg(\mathcal{A})$ is an untimed automaton defined as follows. Let K be the maximal constant used in the constraints of A and let $[K] = \{0, 1, \ldots, K, \infty\}$. The locations of $Reg(\mathcal{A})$ are of the form $L \times [K]^{|\mathcal{X}|}$. The set of initial locations of $Reg(\mathcal{A})$ is $L_0 \times \mathbf{0}$. The transitions in $Reg(\mathcal{A})$ are of the following kinds: (i) $(l, \nu) \xrightarrow{\checkmark} (l, \nu + 1)$ denotes a time elapse of 1. If $\nu(x) + 1$

exceeds K for any clock x, then it is replaced with ∞. (ii) For each transition $e = (l, g, a, Y, l')$, we have the transition $(l, \nu) \xrightarrow{a} (l', \nu')$ if $\nu \models g$, $\nu' = \nu[Y:=0]$. It is known [9] that $Reg(\mathcal{A})$ is empty iff $\mathcal{A}$ is.

3   Communicating Timed Automata (CTA)

A communicating timed automata (CTA) $\mathcal{N} = (\mathcal{A}_1, \ldots, \mathcal{A}_n, C, \Sigma, \mathcal{T})$ consists of timed automata $\mathcal{A}_i$, a finite set C of FIFO *channels*, a finite set Σ called the *channel alphabet*, and a *network topology* $\mathcal{T}$. The network topology is a directed graph $(\{\mathcal{A}_1, \ldots, \mathcal{A}_n\}, C)$ comprising of the finite set of timed automata $\mathcal{A}_i$ as nodes, and the channels C as edges. C is given as a tuple $(c_{i,j})$; the channel from $\mathcal{A}_i$ to $\mathcal{A}_j$ is denoted by $c_{i,j}$, with the intended meaning that $\mathcal{A}_i$ writes a message from Σ to channel $c_{i,j}$ and $\mathcal{A}_j$ reads from channel $c_{i,j}$. We assume that there is atmost one channel $c_{i,j}$ from $\mathcal{A}_i$ to $\mathcal{A}_j$, for any pair $(\mathcal{A}_i, \mathcal{A}_j)$ of timed automata. Figure 1 illustrates the definition.

Each timed automaton $\mathcal{A}_i = (L_i, L_i^0, Act, \mathcal{X}_i, E_i, F_i)$ in the CTA is as explained before, with the only difference being in the transitions E_i. We assume that $\mathcal{X}_i \cap \mathcal{X}_j = \emptyset$ for $i \neq j$. A transition in E_i has the form (l_i, g, op, Y, l_i') where g, Y have the same definition as in that of a timed automaton, while $op \in Act$ is one of the following operation on the channels $c_{i,j}$:

1. nop is an empty operation that does not check or update the channel contents. Transitions having the empty operation nop are called *internal transitions*. Internal transitions of $\mathcal{A}_i$ do not change any channel contents.
2. $c_{i,j}!a$ is a write operation on channel $c_{i,j}$. The operation $c_{i,j}!a$ appends the message $a \in \Sigma$ to the tail of the channel $c_{i,j}$, and sets the age of a to be 0. The timed automaton $\mathcal{A}_i$ moves from location l_i to l_i', checking guard g, resetting clocks Y and writes message a on channel $c_{i,j}$.
3. $c_{j,i}?(a{\in}I)$ is a read operation on channel $c_{j,i}$. The operation $c_{j,i}?(a{\in}I)$ removes the message a from the head of the channel $c_{j,i}$ if its age lies in the interval I. The interval I has the form $<\ell, u>$ with $u \in \mathbb{N}$ and $\ell \in \mathbb{N}\backslash\{\infty\}$, "$<$" stands for left-open or left-closed and "$>$" for right-open or right-closed. In this case, the timed automaton $\mathcal{A}_i$ moves from location l_i to l_i', checking guard g, resetting clocks Y and reads off the oldest message a from channel $c_{j,i}$ if its age is in interval I.

Global Clocks. A clock x is said to be global in a CTA if it can be checked any of the timed automata in the CTA, and can also be reset by any of them on a transition. Note that if a clock x is not global, then it can be checked and reset only by the automata which "owns" it. The automaton A_i owns x iff $x \in \mathcal{X}_i$ (recall that $\mathcal{X}_i \cap \mathcal{X}_j = \emptyset$). The convention $\mathcal{X}_i \cap \mathcal{X}_j = \emptyset$ applies to non-global (or local) clocks. Thus, if a CTA consisting of automata $A_1, \ldots, A_n$ has global clocks, then its set of clocks can be thought of as $\biguplus \mathcal{X}_i \uplus \mathcal{G}$ where $\mathcal{G}$ is a set of global clocks, which are accessed by all of $A_1, \ldots, A_n$, while clocks of $\mathcal{X}_i$ are accessible only to A_i.

Configurations. The semantics of $\mathcal{N}$ is given by a labeled transition system $\mathcal{L}_{\mathcal{N}}$. A configuration γ of $\mathcal{N}$ is a tuple $((l_i, \nu_i)_{1 \le i \le n}, c)$ where l_i is the current control location of $\mathcal{A}_i$, and ν_i gives the valuations of clocks $\mathcal{X}_i$, $1 \le i \le n$, where $\nu_i \in \mathbb{N}^{|\mathcal{X}_i|}$. $c = (c_{i,j})$, and each channel $c_{i,j}$ is represented as a monotonic timed word $(a_1, t_1)(a_2, t_2) \ldots (a_n, t_n)$ where $a \in \Sigma$ and $t_i \le t_{i+1}$, and $t_i \in \mathbb{N}$. Given a word $c_{i,j}$ and a time $t \in \mathbb{N}$, $c_{i,j} + t$ is obtained by adding t to the ages of all messages in channel $c_{i,j}$. For $c = (c_{i,j})$, $c + t$ denotes the tuple $(c_{i,j} + t)$. The states of $\mathcal{L}_{\mathcal{N}}$ are the configurations.

Transition Relation of $\mathcal{L}_{\mathcal{N}}$ Let $\gamma_1 = ((l_1, \nu_1), \ldots, (l_n, \nu_n), c)$ and $\gamma_2 = ((l'_1, \nu'_1), \ldots, (l'_n, \nu'_n), c')$ be two configurations. The transitions $\rightarrow$ in $\mathcal{L}_{\mathcal{N}}$ are of two kinds:

1. Timed transitions $\xrightarrow{t}$: These transitions denote the passage of time $t \in \mathbb{N}$.
   $\gamma_1 \xrightarrow{t} \gamma_2$ iff $l_i = l'_i$, and $\nu'_i = \nu_i + t$, for all i and $c' = c + t$.

2. Discrete transitions $\xrightarrow{D}$. These are of the following kinds:

   (1) $\gamma_1 \xrightarrow{g,\text{nop},Y} \gamma_2$: there is a transition $l_i \xrightarrow{g,\text{nop},Y} l'_i$ in E_i, $\nu_i \models g$, $\nu'_i = \nu_i[Y := 0]$, for some i. Also, $l_k = l'_k$, $\nu_k = \nu'_k$ for all $k \ne i$, and $c_{d,h} = c'_{d,h}$ for all d, h. None of the channel contents are changed.

   (2) $\gamma_1 \xrightarrow{g,c_{i,j}!a,Y} \gamma_2$: Then, $l_k = l'_k$, $\nu_k = \nu'_k$ for all $k \ne i$, and $c_{d,h} = c'_{d,h}$ for all $(d, h) \ne (i, j)$. The transition $l_i \xrightarrow{g,c_{i,j}!a,Y} l'_i$ is in E_i, $\nu_i \models g$, $\nu'_i = \nu_i[Y := 0]$, $c_{i,j} = w \in (\Sigma \times \mathbb{N})^*$ and $c'_{i,j} = (a, 0).w$.

   (3) $\gamma_1 \xrightarrow{g,c_{j,i}?(a \in I),Y} \gamma_2$: Then, $l_k = l'_k$, $\nu_k = \nu'_k$ for all $k \ne i$, and $c_{d,h} = c'_{d,h}$ for all $(d, h) \ne (j, i)$. The transition $l_i \xrightarrow{g,c_{j,i}?(a \in I),Y} l'_i$ is in E_i, $\nu_i \models g$, $\nu'_i = \nu_i[Y := 0]$, $c_{j,i} = w.(a, t) \in (\Sigma \times \mathbb{N})^+$, $t \in I$ and $c'_{j,i} = w \in (\Sigma \times \mathbb{N})^*$.

The Reachability Problem. The initial location of $\mathcal{L}_{\mathcal{N}}$ is given by the tuple $\gamma_0 = ((l^0_1, \nu^0_1), \ldots, (l^0_n, \nu^0_n), c^0)$ where l^0_i is the initial location of A_i, $\nu^0_i = \mathbf{0}$ for all i, and c^0 is the tuple of empty channels $(\epsilon, \ldots, \epsilon)$. A control location $l_i \in L_i$ is reachable if $\gamma_0 \xrightarrow{*} ((s_i, \nu_i)_{1 \le i \le n}, c)$ such that $s_i = l_i$ (It does not matter what $(\nu_1, \ldots, \nu_n)$ and c are). An instance of the reachability problem asks whether given a CTA $\mathcal{N}$ with initial configuration γ_0, we can reach a configuration γ.

4 Acyclic CTA

In this section, we look at the reachability problem in CTA whose underlying network topology $\mathcal{T}$ is somewhat restrictive. An *acyclic CTA* is a CTA $\mathcal{N} = (A_1, \ldots, A_n, C, \Sigma, \mathcal{T})$ which has no cycles in the underlying undirected graph of $\mathcal{T}^1$. Such topologies are called polyforest topologies in [26] (left of Fig. 1). In this section, we answer the reachability question in acyclic CTA with and without global clocks by finding the thin boundary line which separates decidable and undecidable acyclic CTAs.

---

[1] Recall that the network topology $(\{A_1, \ldots, A_n\}, C)$ is a directed graph; the underlying undirected graph is obtained by considering all edges as undirected in this graph.

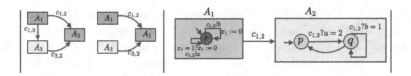

Fig. 1. The left half of the figure contains one cyclic and one acyclic topology. The right half of the figure illustrates an acyclic CTA which is not bounded context.

Theorem 1. *In the presence of global clocks, reachability is undecidable for CTA consisting of two timed automata A_1, A_2 connected by a single channel.*

A single global clock suffices; the proof can be found in [3].

Undecidable Reachability with no Global Clocks

Theorem 2. *Reachability is undecidable for acyclic CTA consisting of three one-clock timed automata without global clocks.*

Proof. We prove the undecidability by reducing the halting problem for deterministic two counter machines (see [3] for a formal definition). We consider the case of a discCTA consisting of timed automata A_1, A_2, A_3 with channels $c_{1,2}$ from A_1 to A_2 and $c_{2,3}$ from A_2 to A_3. The undecidability for the other possible topologies are discussed in [3].

The Encoding. Given a two counter machine $\mathcal{C}$, we build a discCTA $\mathcal{N}$ consisting of timed automata A_1, A_2, A_3 with channels $c_{1,2}$ from A_1 to A_2 and $c_{2,3}$ from A_2 to A_3. Corresponding to each increment, decrement and zero check instruction, we have a widget in each A_i. A widget is a "small" timed automaton, consisting of some locations and transitions between them. Corresponding to each increment/decrement instruction $\ell_i :$ inc or dec c, goto ℓ_j, or a zero check instruction $\ell_i :$ if $c = 0$, goto ℓ_j else goto ℓ_k, we have a widget $\mathcal{W}_i^{A_m}$ in each $A_m, m \in \{1, 2, 3\}$. The widgets $\mathcal{W}_i^{A_m}$ begin in a location labelled ℓ_i, and terminate in a location ℓ_j for increments/decrements, while for zero check, they begin in a location labelled ℓ_i, and terminate in a location ℓ_j or ℓ_k. Each A_m is hence obtained by superimposing (one of) the terminal location ℓ_j of a widget $\mathcal{W}_i^{A_m}$ to the initial location ℓ_j of widget $\mathcal{W}_j^{A_m}$.

We refer to initial as well as terminal locations (labelled p_{init}, p_{term}) in each $\mathcal{W}_i^{A_m}$ using the notation $(\mathcal{W}_i^{A_m}, p)$, $p \in \{p_{init}, p_{term}\}$. Note that an instruction ℓ_i can appear as initial location in a widget and a terminal location in another; thus, it is useful to remember the location along with the widget we are talking about. x_1, y_1, z_1 respectively denote the clocks used in A_1, A_2, A_3. To argue the proof of correctness, we use clocks $g_{A_1}, g_{A_2}, g_{A_3}$ respectively in A_1, A_2, A_3 which are never used in any transitions (g_{A_i} represent the total time elapse at any point in A_i).

Counter Values. The value of counter c_1 after i steps, denoted c_1^i is stored as the difference between the value of clock g_{A_2} after i steps and the value of clock

g_{A_1} after i steps. Denoting l_i to be the instruction reached after i steps, and thanks to the fact that we have locations l_i in each of A_1, A_2, A_3 corresponding to the instruction l_i, the value $c_1^i = $ (value of clock g_{A_2} at location l_i of A_2) - (value of clock g_{A_1} at location l_i of A_1). Note that A_1, A_2 are not always in sync while simulating the two counter machine: A_1 can simulate the jth instruction l_j while A_2 is simulating the ith instruction l_i for $j \geq i$, thanks to the invariant maintaining the value of c_1. When they are in sync, the value of c_1 is 0. Thus, A_1 is always ahead of A_2 or at the same step as A_2 in the simulation. The value of counter c_2 is maintained in a similar manner by A_2 and A_3. To maintain the values of c_1, c_2 correctly, the speeds of A_1, A_2, A_3 are adjusted while doing increments/decrements. For instance, to increment c_1, A_2 takes 2 units of time to go from ℓ_i to ℓ_j while A_1 takes just one unit; then the value of g_{A_2} at ℓ_j is two more than what it was at ℓ_i; likewise, the value of g_{A_1} at ℓ_j is one more than what it was at ℓ_i. The channel alphabet is $\{(\ell_i, c^+, \ell_j) \mid \ell_i : \text{inc } c \text{ goto } \ell_j\} \cup \{(\ell_i, c^-, \ell_j) \mid \ell_i : \text{dec } c \text{ goto } \ell_j\} \cup \{(\ell_i, c=0, \ell_j), (\ell_i, c>0, \ell_k) \mid \ell_i : \text{if } c = 0, \text{ then goto } \ell_j, \text{ else goto } \ell_k\} \cup \{zero_1, zero_2\}$.

1. Consider an increment instruction ℓ_i:inc c goto ℓ_j. The widgets $\mathcal{W}_i^{A_m}$ for $m = 1, 2, 3$ are described in Fig. 2. The one on the left is while incrementing c_1, while the one on the right is obtained while incrementing c_2.
2. The case of a decrement instruction is similar, and is obtained by swapping the speeds of the two automata (A_1, A_2 and A_2, A_3 respectively) in reaching ℓ_j from ℓ_i. Note that we preserve the invariant that A_1 is ahead of (or same as) A_2 which is ahead of (or same as) A_3 in the simulation of the two counter machine.
3. We finally consider a zero check instruction of the form ℓ_i:if $c_1 = 0$, then goto ℓ_j, else goto ℓ_k. The widgets $\mathcal{W}_i^{A_m}$ for $m = 1, 2, 3$ are described in Fig. 3. The one on the left is a zero check of c_1, while the one on the right is a zero check of c_2.

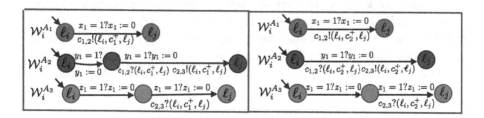

Fig. 2. Widgets corresponding to an increment c_1, c_2 instruction in A_1, A_2, A_3

Let $(\ell_0, 0, 0), (\ell_1, c_1^1, c_2^1), \ldots, (\ell_h, c_1^h, c_2^h) \ldots$ be the run of the two counter machine. ℓ_i denotes the instruction seen at the ith step and c_1^i, c_2^i respectively are the values of counters c_1, c_2 after i steps. Denote a block of transitions in A_m leading from the ith to the $(i+1)$st instruction as

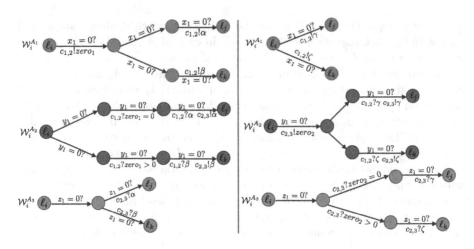

Fig. 3. Widgets corresponding to checking c_1, c_2 is 0. Let $\alpha = (\ell_i, c_1 = 0, \ell_j), \beta = (\ell_i, c_1 > 0, \ell_k), \gamma = (\ell_i, c_2 = 0, \ell_j), \zeta = (\ell_i, c_2 > 0, \ell_k)$.

$\mathcal{B}_{i,i+1} = [((\mathcal{W}_i^{A_m}, \ell_i), \nu_i^{A_m}), \ldots, ((\mathcal{W}_i^{A_m}, \ell_{i+1}), \nu_{i+1}^{A_m})]$. A run in each A_m is $\mathcal{B}_{0,1}, \mathcal{B}_{1,2}, \ldots, \mathcal{B}_{h,h+1}, \ldots$, where each block $\mathcal{B}_{h,h+1}$ of transitions in the widget $\mathcal{W}_h^{A_m}$ simulate the instruction ℓ_h, and shifts control to ℓ_{h+1}. For each m, $((\mathcal{W}_i^{A_m}, \ell_j), \nu_j^{A_m})$ represents A_m is at location ℓ_j of widget $\mathcal{W}_i^{A_m}$ with clock valuation $\nu_j^{A_m}$.

Lemma 1. *Let $\mathcal{C}$ be a two counter machine. Let c_1^h, c_2^h be the values of counters c_1, c_2 at the end of the hth instruction ℓ_h. Then there is a run of $\mathcal{N}$ which passes through widgets $\mathcal{W}_0^{A_m}, \mathcal{W}_1^{A_m}, \ldots, \mathcal{W}_h^{A_m}$ in $A_m, m \in \{1, 2, 3\}$ such that*

1. *c_1^h is the difference between the value of clock g_{A_2} on reaching location $(\mathcal{W}_h^{A_2}, \ell_h)$ and the value of clock g_{A_1} on reaching location $(\mathcal{W}_h^{A_1}, \ell_h)$. c_2^h is the difference between the value of clock g_{A_3} on reaching location $(\mathcal{W}_h^{A_3}, \ell_h)$ and the value of clock g_{A_2} on reaching location $(\mathcal{W}_h^{A_2}, \ell_h)$.*
2. *If $\mathcal{W}_h^{A_1}$ is a zero check widget for c_1 (c_2) then c_1^h (c_2^h) is 0 iff one reaches a terminal location of $\mathcal{W}_h^{A_2}$ reading α (γ) and $zero_1$ ($zero_2$) with age 0. Likewise, c_1^h (c_2^h) is > 0 iff one reaches a terminal location of $\mathcal{W}_h^{A_2}$ reading β (ζ) and $zero_1$ ($zero_2$) with age > 0.*

Machine $\mathcal{C}$ halts iff the halt widget $\mathcal{W}_{halt}^{A_m}$ is reached in $\mathcal{N}$, $m = 1, 2, 3$. [3] has the full proof.

Decidable Reachability

Theorem 3. *The reachability problem is decidable (in EXPTIME) for acyclic CTA consisting of two timed automata without global clocks.*

The proof proceeds by a reachability preserving reduction of the discCTA to a pushdown automaton. We give the proof idea here, correctness arguments and an example can be found in [3]. Given discCTA $\mathcal{N}$ consisting of $A = (L_A, L_A^0, \mathcal{X}_A, \Sigma, E_A, F_A)$ and $B = (L_B, L_B^0, \mathcal{X}_B, \Sigma, E_B, F_B)$, with a channel $c_{A,B}$ from A to B, we simulate $\mathcal{N}$ using a pushdown automaton $\mathcal{O}$ as follows.

Intermediate Notations. We start with $Reg(A)$ and $Reg(B)$, the corresponding region automata, and run them in an interleaved fashion. Let K be the maximal constant used in the guards of A, B. Let $[K] = \{0, 1, \ldots, K, \infty\}$. The locations Q_A (Q_B) of $Reg(A)$ ($Reg(B)$) are of the form $L_A \times [K]^{|\mathcal{X}_A|}$ ($L_B \times [K]^{|\mathcal{X}_B|}$). The transitions in $Reg(A), Reg(B)$ are as follows:

(i) A transition $(l, \nu) \overset{\checkmark}{\rightarrow} (l, \nu + 1)$ denotes a time elapse of 1 in both $Reg(A), Reg(B)$. If $\nu(x) + 1$ exceeds K for any clock x, then it is replaced with ∞. (ii) For each transition $e = (\ell, g, c_{A,B}!a, Y, \ell')$ in A we have the transition $(l, \nu) \overset{a}{\rightarrow} (l', \nu')$ in $Reg(A)$ if $\nu \models g$, and $\nu' = \nu[Y:=0]$. (iii) For each transition $e = (\ell, g, c_{A,B}?(a \in I), Y, \ell')$ in B we have the transition $(l, \nu) \overset{a \in I}{\rightarrow} (l', \nu')$ in $Reg(B)$ if $\nu \models g$, and $\nu' = \nu[Y:=0]$. (iv) For each internal transition $e = (\ell, g, \mathsf{nop}, Y, \ell')$ in A, B we have the transition $(l, \nu) \overset{\mathsf{nop}}{\rightarrow} (l', \nu')$ in $Reg(A), Reg(B)$ if $\nu \models g$, and $\nu' = \nu[Y:=0]$. Note that the above is an intermediate notation which will be used in the construction of the pushdown automaton $\mathcal{O}$. There is no channel between $Reg(A), Reg(B)$, and we have symbolically encoded all transitions of A, B in $Reg(A), Reg(B)$ as above.

Construction of $\mathcal{O}$: In the reduction from discCTA $\mathcal{N}$ to the pushdown automaton $\mathcal{O}$, the global time difference between A and B is stored in a counter which is part of the finite control, such that B is always ahead of A, or at the same time as A. Thus, a value $i \geq 0$ stored in the counter of finite control means that B is i units of time ahead of A. The state space of $\mathcal{O}$ is constructed using the locations of $Reg(A), Reg(B)$, and the transitions of $\mathcal{O}$ will make use of the transitions described above of $Reg(A), Reg(B)$. Internal transitions of A, B are simulated by updating the respective control locations in $Reg(A), Reg(B)$. Each unit time elapse in B results in incrementing the counter by 1, while each unit time elapse in A results in decrementing the counter. Consider a transition in A where a message m is written on the channel. The counter value when m is written tells us the time difference between B, A, and hence also the age of the message as seen from B. Assume the counter value is $i \geq 0$. If indeed m must be read in B when its age is exactly i, then B can move towards a transition where m is read, without any further time elapse. In case m must be read when its age is $j > i$, then B can execute internal transitions as well a time elapse $j - i$ so that the transition to read m is enabled. However, if m must have been read when its age is some $k < i$, then B will be unable to read m. By our interleaved execution, each time A writes a message, we make B read it before A writes further messages and proceeds. Note that this does not disallow A writing multiple messages with the same time stamp.

To ensure that the state space of $\mathcal{O}$ is finite, only counter values $\leq K$ are kept as part of the finite control of $\mathcal{O}$. When the value exceeds K, we start using the stack (with stack alphabet $\{1\}$) to keep track of the exact value $> K$. Note that we have to keep track of the exact time difference between B, A since otherwise we will not be able to check age requirements of messages correctly.

State Space of $\mathcal{O}$: Let $\hat{Q}_x = \{q_\perp, q_1, q'_\perp, q'_1 \mid q \in Q_x, x \in \{A, B\}\}^2$. Let $O_x = Q_x \cup \hat{Q}_x$ for $x \in \{A, B\}$. The state space of $\mathcal{O}$ is $O_A \times (O_B \times (\Sigma \cup \{\epsilon\})) \times ([K] \backslash \{\infty\})$, where the $\Sigma \cup \{\epsilon\}$ in $(O_B \times (\Sigma \cup \{\epsilon\}))$ is to remember the message (if any) written by A, which has to be read by B, and the last entry in the triple denotes the counter value. The stack alphabet is $\{\perp, 1\}$. The initial location of $\mathcal{O}$ is $\{((l_A^0, 0^{|\mathcal{X}_A|}), (l_B^0, 0^{|\mathcal{X}_B|}, \epsilon), 0) \mid l_A^0 \in L_A^0, l_B^0 \in L_B^0\}$ and the stack has the bottom of stack symbol $\perp$ in the initial configuration.

Transitions in $\mathcal{O}$: The transitions in $\mathcal{O}$ are as follows : For states l, l' of $\mathcal{O}$, internal transitions Δ_{int} consist of transitions of the form (l, l'); push transitions Δ_{push} consist of transitions of the form (l, a, l') for $a \in \{1, \perp\}$. Finally, we also have pop transitions Δ_{pop} of the form (l, a, l') for $a \in \{1, \perp\}$. We now describe the transitions.

1. Pop transitions Δ_{pop} : Pop transitions simulate time elapse in $Reg(A)$ as well as checking the age of a symbol being K or $> K$ while it is read from the channel.

   (a) If $(p, \nu_1) \xrightarrow{\checkmark} (p, \nu_1 + 1)$ in $Reg(A)$, and if the counter value as stored in the finite control is K, and if the stack is non-empty, then we pop the top of the stack to decrement the counter. For $l = ((p, \nu_1), (q, \nu_2, \alpha), K)$, $l' = ((p, \nu_1 + 1), (q, \nu_2, \alpha), K)$, $(l, 1, l') \in \Delta_{pop}$.

   (b) If $(p, \nu_1) \xrightarrow{\checkmark} (p, \nu_1 + 1)$ in $Reg(A)$, and if the counter value as stored in the finite control is K, and if the stack is empty, we pop $\perp$, reduce K in the finite control to $K - 1$, and push back $\perp$ to the stack. We remember that $\perp$ has been popped in the finite control, so that we push it back immediately. For $l = ((p, \nu_1), (q, \nu_2, \alpha), K), l' = ((p_\perp, \nu_1 + 1), (q, \nu_2, \alpha), K - 1)$, $(l, \perp, l') \in \Delta_{pop}$. The location $p_\perp$ tells us that $\perp$ has to be pushed back immediately.

   (c) To check that a message has age K when read, we need $i = K$, along with the fact that the stack is empty (top of stack $= \perp$). In this case, we pop $\perp$ and remember it in the finite control, and push it back. For $l = ((p, \nu_1), (q, \nu_2, \alpha), K), l' = ((p, \nu_1), (q_\perp, \nu_2, \alpha), K), (l, \perp, l') \in \Delta_{pop}$.

   (d) To check that a message has age $> K$ when read, we need $i = K$, along with the fact that the stack is non-empty (top of stack $= 1$). In this case, we pop 1 and remember it in the finite control, and push it back. For $l = ((p, \nu_1), (q, \nu_2, \alpha), K), l' = ((p, \nu_1), (q_1, \nu_2, \alpha), K), (l, 1, l') \in \Delta_{pop}$.

2. Push transitions Δ_{push} : Push transitions simulate time elapse in $Reg(B)$, and also aid in simulating checking the age of a symbol being K or $> K$ while being read from the channel.

   (a) Push $\perp$ to the stack while reducing counter value from K to $K - 1$ (1(b)). For $l = ((p_\perp, \nu_1), (q, \nu_2, \alpha), K-1)$ and $l' = ((p, \nu_1), (q, \nu_2, \alpha), K-1)$, $(l, \perp, l') \in \Delta_{push}$.

---

[2] The $q_\perp, q_1$ are used to remember the topmost symbol of the stack while in location q.

(b) Push $\perp$ to the stack before checking the age of a message is K (1(c)). For $l = ((p, \nu_1), (q_\perp, \nu_2, \alpha), K)$ and $l' = ((p, \nu_1), (q'_\perp, \nu_2, \alpha), K))$, $(l, \perp, l') \in \Delta_{push}$.

(c) Push 1 to the stack before checking the age of a message is $> K$ (1(d)). For $l = ((p, \nu_1), (q_1, \nu_2, \alpha), K)$ and $l' = ((p, \nu_1), (q'_1, \nu_2, \alpha), K)$, $(l, 1, l') \in \Delta_{push}$.

(d) If $(q, \nu_2) \overset{\checkmark}{\to} (q, \nu_2 + 1)$ in $Reg(B)$, and if the counter value as stored in the finite control is K, then we push a 1 on the stack to represent the counter value is $> K$. That is, $(l, 1, l') \in \Delta_{push}$ for $l = ((p, \nu_1), (q, \nu_2, \alpha), K)$ and $l' = ((p, \nu_1), (q, \nu_2 + 1, \alpha), K)$.

3. Internal transitions Δ_{int}: Transitions of Δ_{int} simulate internal transitions of $Reg(A), Reg(B)$ as well as $\checkmark$- transitions as follows:

(a) Let $l = ((p, \nu_1), (q, \nu_2, \alpha), i)$, $l' = ((p', \nu'_1), (q, \nu_2, \alpha), i)$ be states of $\mathcal{O}$. $(l, l') \in \Delta_{int}$ if $(p, \nu_1) \overset{nop}{\to} (p', \nu'_1)$ is an internal transition in $Reg(A)$. The same can be said of internal transitions in $Reg(B)$ updating q, ν_2, leaving α, i and (p, ν_1) unchanged.

(b) For $l = ((p, \nu_1), (q, \nu_2, \alpha), i)$ with $0 \leq i < K$, and $l' = ((p, \nu_1), (q, \nu_2 + 1, \alpha), i + 1)$, $(l, l') \in \Delta_{int}$ if $(q, \nu_2) \overset{\checkmark}{\to} (q, \nu_2 + 1)$ is a $\checkmark$-transition in $Reg(B)$. Note that $i + 1 \leq K$.

(c) For $l = ((p, \nu_1), (q, \nu_2, \alpha), i)$ with $0 < i \leq K$, and $l' = ((p, \nu_1 + 1), (q, \nu_2, \alpha), i - 1)$, $(l, l') \in \Delta_{int}$ if $(p, \nu_1) \overset{\checkmark}{\to} (p, \nu_1 + 1)$ is a $\checkmark$-transition in $Reg(A)$.

(d) For $l = ((p, \nu_1), (q, \nu_2, \epsilon), i)$, $l' = ((p', \nu'_1), (q, \nu_2, a), i)$, $(l, l') \in \Delta_{int}$ if $(p, \nu_1) \overset{a}{\to} (p', \nu'_1)$ is a transition in $Reg(A)$ corresponding to a transition from p to p' which writes a onto the channel $c_{A,B}$.

(e) For $i < K$, and $i \in I$, $l = ((p, \nu_1), (q, \nu_2, a), i)$, $l' = ((p, \nu_1), (q', \nu'_2, \epsilon), i)$, $(l, l') \in \Delta_{int}$ if $(q, \nu_2) \overset{a \in I}{\to} (q', \nu'_2)$ is a transition in $Reg(B)$ corresponding to a transition from q to q' which reads a from the channel $c_{A,B}$ and checks its age to be in interval I.

(f) To check that a message has age K when read, we need the counter value i to be K, along with the top of stack $= \perp$. See 1(c), 2(b), and then we use transition $(l, l') \in \Delta_{int}$ for $l = ((p, \nu_1), (q'_\perp, \nu_2, m), K)$, $l' = ((p, \nu_1), (r, \nu'_2, \epsilon), K)$, if $(q, \nu_2) \overset{m \in [K, K]}{\to} (r, \nu'_2)$ is a read transition in $Reg(B)$.

(g) To check that a message has age $> K$ when read, we need $i = K$, along with the fact that the stack is non-empty (top of stack $= 1$). See 1(d), 2(c), and then $(l, l') \in \Delta_{int}$ for $l = ((p, \nu_1), (q'_1, \nu_2, m), K)$, $l' = ((p, \nu_1), (r, \nu'_2, \epsilon), K)$, if $(q, \nu_2) \overset{m \in (K, \infty)}{\to} (r, \nu'_2)$ is a read transition in $Reg(B)$. (age requirements $\geq K$ are checked using this or the above).

The correctness of the construction is proved in [3] using Lemmas 2 and 3.

Lemma 2. *If $((l_A, \nu_A), (l_B, \nu_B, a), i)$ is a configuration in $\mathcal{O}$, along with a stack consisting of $1^j \perp$, then message a has age $i + j$, A is at l_A, B is at l_B, and B is $i + j$ time units ahead of A.*

Lemma 3. *Let $\mathcal{N}$ be a disc CTA with timed automata A, B connected by a channel $c_{A,B}$ from A to B. Assume that starting from an initial configuration $((l_A^0, 0^{|\mathcal{X}_A|}), (l_B^0, 0^{|\mathcal{X}_B|}), \epsilon)$ of $\mathcal{N}$, we reach configuration $((l_A, \nu_1), (l_B, \nu_2), w.(m, i))$ such that $w \in (\Sigma \times \{0, 1, \ldots, i\})^*$, and $(m, i) \in \Sigma \times [K]$ is read off by B from (l_B, ν_2). Then, from the initial configuration $((l_A^0, 0^{|\mathcal{X}_A|}), (l_B^0, 0^{|\mathcal{X}_B|}, \epsilon), 0)$ with stack contents $\perp$ of $\mathcal{O}$, we reach one of the following configurations*

(i) $((p_A, \nu_A'), (l_B, \nu_2, m), i)$ with stack contents $\perp$ if $i \leq K$,
(ii) $((p_A, \nu_A'), (l_B, \nu_2, m), h)$ with stack contents $1^j \perp, j > 0$ if $i > K$ and $h + j = i$.

Moreover, it is possible to reach (l_A, ν_1) from (p_A, ν_A') in A after elapse of i units of time. The converse is also true.

Complexity: Upper and Lower bounds The EXPTIME upper bound is easy to see, thanks to the exponential blow up incurred in the construction of $\mathcal{O}$ using the regions of A and B, and the fact that reachability in a pushdown automaton is linear. The best possible lower bound we can achieve as of now is NP-hardness, as described in [3].

4.1   Bounded Context discCTA

Before winding up with discCTA, we consider bounded context discCTA and show that the reachability problem is decidable even when having global clocks. Given a discCTA, a *context* is a sequence of transitions in the discCTA where only one automaton is *active* viz., reading from at most one fixed channel, but possibly writing to many channels that it can write to (this cannot be the one it reads from). Thus, (a) a context is simply a sequence of transitions where a single automaton A_i performs channel operations, and (b) in a context, A_i can read from at most one channel. A *context switch* happens when either a different automaton A_j, $j \neq i$ performs channel operations, or when A_i reads from a different channel.

Definition 1. *A disc CTA $\mathcal{N}$ is bounded context (disc CTA-bc) if the number of context switches in any run of $\mathcal{N}$ is bounded above by some $B \in \mathbb{N}$.*

See the right part of Fig. 1 for an example of a discCTA consisting of two processes A_1, A_2, where A_1 writes on $c_{1,2}$ to A_2. This acyclic discCTA is not bounded context. There is a run where A_1 writes an a after every one time unit, and A_2 reads an a once in two time units. There is also a run where A_1 writes b onto the channel whenever it pleases and A_2 reads it one time unit after it is written.

Theorem 4. *Reachability is decidable for disc CTA-bc, even in the presence of global clocks.*

The Idea: Let K be the maximal constant used in the discCTA with bounded context $\leq B$, and let $[K] = \{0, 1, \ldots, K, \infty\}$. For $1 \leq i \leq n$, let $A_i =$

$(L_i, L_i^0, Act, \mathcal{X}_i, E_i, F_i)$ be the n automata in the discCTA. Let $c_{i,j}$ denote the channel to which A_i writes to and A_j reads from. We translate the discCTA into a bounded phase, multistack pushdown system (BMPS) $\mathcal{M}$ preserving reachability. A multistack pushdown system (MPS) is a timed automaton with multiple untimed stacks. A *phase* in an MPS is one where a fixed stack is popped, while pushes can happen to any number of stacks. A change of phase occurs when there is a change in the stack which is popped. See [3] for a formal definition. We use Lemma 4 (proof in [3]) to obtain decidability after our reduction.

Lemma 4. *The reachability problem is decidable for BMPS.*

Encoding into BMPS. The BMPS $\mathcal{M}$ uses two stacks $W_{i,j}$ and $R_{i,j}$ to simulate channel $c_{i,j}$. The control locations of $\mathcal{M}$ keeps track of the locations and clock valuations of all the A_i, as n pairs $(p_1, \nu_1), \ldots, (p_n, \nu_n)$ with $\nu_i \in [K]$ for all i;[3] in addition, we also keep an ordered pair (A_w, b) consisting of a number $b \leq B$ to count the context switch in the discCTA and also remember the active automaton $A_w, w \in \{1, 2, \ldots, n\}$. To simulate the transitions of each A_i, we use the pairs (p_i, ν_i), keeping all pairs (p_j, ν_j) unchanged for $j \neq i$. An initial location of $\mathcal{M}$ has the form $((l_1^0, \nu_1), \ldots, (l_n^0, \nu_n), (A_i, 0))$ where $l_i^0 \in L_i^0$, $\nu_i = 0^{|\mathcal{X}_i|}$; the pair $(A_i, 0)$ denotes context 0, and A_i is some automaton which is active in context 0 (A_i writes to some channels).

Transitions of $\mathcal{M}$. The internal transitions Δ_{in} of $\mathcal{M}$ correspond to any internal transition in any of the A_is and change some (p, ν) to (q, ν') where ν' is obtained by resetting some clocks from ν. These take place irrespective of context switch.

The push and pop transitions (Δ_{push} and Δ_{pop}) of $\mathcal{M}$ are more interesting. Consider the kth context where A_j is active in the discCTA. In $\mathcal{M}$, this information is stored as (A_j, k). In the kth context, A_j can read from atmost one fixed channel $c_{l,j}$; it can also write to several channels $c_{j,i_1}, \ldots, c_{j,i_k} \neq c_{l,j}$, apart from time elapse/internal transitions. All automata other than A_j participate only in time elapse and internal transitions. When A_j writes a message m to channel c_{j,i_h} in the discCTA, it is simulated by pushing message m to stack W_{j,i_h}. All time elapses $t \in [K]$ are captured by pushing t to all stacks. Δ_{push} has transitions pushing a message m on a stack W_{i,j_k}, or pushing time elapse $t \in [K]$ on all stacks.

When A_j is ready to read from channel $c_{l,j}$ (say), the contents of stack $W_{l,j}$ are shifted to stack $R_{l,j}$ if the stack $R_{l,j}$ is empty. Assuming $R_{l,j}$ is empty, we transfer contents of $W_{l,j}$ to $R_{l,j}$. The stack to be popped is remembered in the finite control of $\mathcal{M}$: the pair (p, ν), $p \in L_j$ is replaced with $(p^{W_{l,j}}, \nu)$. As long as we keep reading symbols $t \in [K]$ from $W_{l,j}$, we remember it in the finite control of $\mathcal{M}$ by adding a tag t to locations $(p^{W_{l,j}}, \nu)$ $(p \in L_j)$ making it $((p^{W_{l,j}})_t, \nu)$. When a message m is seen on top of $W_{l,j}$, with $((p^{W_{l,j}})_t, \nu)$ in the finite control of $\mathcal{M}$, we push (m, t) to stack $R_{l,j}$, since t is indeed the time that elapsed after m was written to channel $c_{l,j}$. When we obtain $t' \in [K]$ as the top of stack $W_{l,j}$,

---

[3] The global clock valuations are maintained as a separate tuple; for simplicity, we omit this detail here. Our proof works in the presence of global clocks easily.

with $((p^{W_{l,j}})_t, \nu)$ in the finite control, we add t' to the finite control obtaining $((p^{W_{l,j}})_{t+t'}, \nu)$. The next message m' has age $t + t'$ and so on, and stack $R_{l,j}$ is populated. When $W_{l,j}$ becomes empty, the finite control is updated to $(p^{R_{l,j}}, \nu)$ and A_j starts reading from $R_{l,j}$. If $R_{l,j}$ is already non-empty when A_j starts reading, it is read off first, and when it becomes empty, we transfer $W_{l,j}$ to $R_{l,j}$. A time elapse t'' between reads and/or reads/writes of A_j is simulated by pushing t'' on all stacks, to reflect the increase in age of all messages stored in all stacks.

Phases of $\mathcal{M}$ are bounded. Each context switch in the discCTA results in $\mathcal{M}$ simulating a different automaton, or simulating the read from a different channel. Assume that every context switch of the discCTA results in some automaton reading off from some channel. Correspondingly in $\mathcal{M}$, we pop the corresponding R-stack, and if it goes empty, pop the corresponding W-stack filling up the R-stack. Once the R-stack is filled up, we continue popping it. This results in atmost two phase changes (some $R_{i,j}$ to $W_{i,j}$ and $W_{i,j}$ to $R_{i,j}$) for each context in the discCTA. An additional phase change is incurred on each context switch (a different stack $R_{k,l}$ is popped in the next context). Note that $\mathcal{M}$ does not pop a stack unless a read takes place in some automaton, and the maximum number of stacks popped is 2 per context. $\mathcal{M}$ is hence a $3B$ bounded phase MPS. A detailed proof of correctness and an example can be seen in [3].

Table 1. Summary of results for discCTA. k-discCTA represents discCTA with k discrete timed automata, $k \in \mathbb{N}$. $* -$ discCTA has finitely many discrete timed automata involved.

Acyclic discCTA	Global clocks	Channels	Reachability	Where
2-discCTA	Yes (1 global clock)	1	Undecidable	[3]
3-discCTA time	No	2	Undecidable	Theorem 2
2-discCTA	No	1	Decidable	Theorem 3
$* -$ discCTA bounded context	Yes	any	Decidable	Theorem 4

4.2   discCTA Summary

Table 1 summarizes our exhaustive characterisation for discCTA. The tightness of the lower bound (NP−hardness) of our decidability result (Theorem 3) is open. We mention the possible extensions to the model of discCTA as studied in this paper which we conjecture will preserve the decidability result in Theorem 3.

1. If we allow diagonal constraints of the form $x - y \sim c$ where x, y are clocks and $c \in \mathbb{N}$, Theorem 3 continues to hold. In the proof, given a discCTA $\mathcal{N}$ consisting of timed automata A, B connected by the channel $c_{A,B}$ from A to B, we construct a one counter automaton $\mathcal{O}$ using $Reg(A)$ and $Reg(B)$. We can easily track the difference between two clocks x, y in $Reg(A)$ or $Reg(B)$, thereby handling diagonal constraints.

2. The initial age of a newly written message in a channel is set to 0. This can be generalized in two ways : (i) allowing the initial age of a message to be some $j \in \mathbb{N}$, or (ii) assigning the value of some clock x as the initial age. The construction of $\mathcal{O}$ is such that each time A writes a message $m \in \Sigma$ to the channel, m is remembered in the finite control of $\mathcal{O}$ (transition 3(d) in the proof of Theorem 3). While simulating the read by B of the message m (transitions 3(e), (f), (g) in the proof of Theorem 3), the value i in the finite control of $\mathcal{O}$ along with the top of the stack determines whether the age of m is $< K$, $= K$ or $> K$, where K is the maximal constant used in A, B. This is used to see if the age constraint of m is met; the age of m when it is read is same as the time difference between B, A. We can adapt this for an initial age $j > 0$, by remembering (m, j) in the finite control of $\mathcal{O}$. If the counter value is $i < K$, then the age of the message is $j + i$, while if it is K and the top of stack is $\perp$, then the age of m is $j + K$, and it is $> j + K$ if the top of stack is not $\perp$. Checking the age constraint of m correctly now boils down to using $j + i$ and verifying if the constraint is satisfied.

References

1. Abdulla, P.A., Nylén, A.: Timed Petri nets and BQOs. In: Colom, J.-M., Koutny, M. (eds.) ICATPN 2001. LNCS, vol. 2075, pp. 53–70. Springer, Heidelberg (2001). https://doi.org/10.1007/3-540-45740-2_5

2. Abdulla, P.A., Atig, M.F., Cederberg, J.: Timed lossy channel systems. In: FSTTCS 2012, LIPIcs, 15–17 December 2012, Hyderabad, India, vol. 18, pp. 374–386. Schloss Dagstuhl - Leibniz-Zentrum fuer Informatik (2012)

3. Abdulla, P.A., Atig, M.F., Krishna, S.N.: What is decidable about perfect timed channels? CoRR, abs/1708.05063 (2017)

4. Abdulla, P.A., Atig, M.F., Stenman, J.: Dense-timed pushdown automata. In: Proceedings of the 27th Annual IEEE Symposium on Logic in Computer Science, LICS 2012, Dubrovnik, Croatia, 25–28 June 2012, pp. 35–44. IEEE Computer Society (2012)

5. Abdulla, P.A., Jonsson, B.: Verifying programs with unreliable channels. In: LICS. IEEE Computer Society (1993)

6. Abdulla, P., Mahata, P., Mayr, R.: Dense-timed Petri nets: checking zeneness, token liveness and boundedness. Log. Methods Comput. Sci. 3(1) (2007). https://doi.org/10.2168/LMCS-3(1:1)2007

7. Akshay, S., Gastin, P., Krishna, S.N.: Analyzing timed systems using tree automata. In: 27th International Conference on Concurrency Theory, CONCUR 2016, 23–26 August 2016, LIPIcs, Québec City, Canada, vol. 59, pp. 27:1–27:14. Schloss Dagstuhl - Leibniz-Zentrum fuer Informatik (2016)

8. Akshay, S., Genest, B., Hélouët, L.: Decidable classes of unbounded Petri nets with time and urgency. In: Kordon, F., Moldt, D. (eds.) PETRI NETS 2016. LNCS, vol. 9698, pp. 301–322. Springer, Cham (2016). https://doi.org/10.1007/978-3-319-39086-4_18

9. Alur, R., Dill, D.L.: A theory of timed automata. Theor. Comput. Sci. 126(2), 183–235 (1994)

10. Bérard, B., Cassez, F., Haddad, S., Lime, D., Roux, O.H.: Comparison of different semantics for time Petri nets. In: Peled, D.A., Tsay, Y.-K. (eds.) ATVA 2005. LNCS, vol. 3707, pp. 293–307. Springer, Heidelberg (2005). https://doi.org/10.1007/11562948_23

11. Bhave, D., Dave, V., Krishna, S.N., Phawade, R., Trivedi, A.: A perfect class of context-sensitive timed languages. In: Brlek, S., Reutenauer, C. (eds.) DLT 2016. LNCS, vol. 9840, pp. 38–50. Springer, Heidelberg (2016). https://doi.org/10.1007/978-3-662-53132-7_4

12. Bocchi, L., Lange, J., Yoshida, N.: Meeting deadlines together. In: Aceto, L., de Frutos Escrig, D. (eds.) 26th International Conference on Concurrency Theory (CONCUR 2015), Leibniz International Proceedings in Informatics (LIPIcs), Dagstuhl, Germany, vol. 42, pp. 283–296. Schloss Dagstuhl-Leibniz-Zentrum fuer Informatik (2015)

13. Bouajjani, A., Echahed, R., Robbana, R.: On the automatic verification of systems with continuous variables and unbounded discrete data structures. In: Antsaklis, P., Kohn, W., Nerode, A., Sastry, S. (eds.) HS 1994. LNCS, vol. 999, pp. 64–85. Springer, Heidelberg (1995). https://doi.org/10.1007/3-540-60472-3_4

14. Bouajjani, A., Habermehl, P.: Symbolic reachability analysis of FIFO-channel systems with nonregular sets of configurations. Theor. Comput. Sci. **221**(1–2), 211–250 (1999)

15. Bouchy, F., Finkel, A., Sangnier, A.: Reachability in timed counter systems. Electron. Notes Theor. Comput. Sci. **239**, 167–178 (2009)

16. Brand, D., Zafiropulo, P.: On communicating finite-state machines. J. ACM **30**(2), 323–342 (1983)

17. Cécé, G., Finkel, A.: Verification of programs with half-duplex communication. Inf. Comput. **202**(2), 166–190 (2005)

18. Chambart, P., Schnoebelen, P.: Mixing lossy and perfect FIFO channels. In: van Breugel, F., Chechik, M. (eds.) CONCUR 2008. LNCS, vol. 5201, pp. 340–355. Springer, Heidelberg (2008). https://doi.org/10.1007/978-3-540-85361-9_28

19. Clemente, L., Herbreteau, F., Stainer, A., Sutre, G.: Reachability of communicating timed processes. In: Pfenning, F. (ed.) FoSSaCS 2013. LNCS, vol. 7794, pp. 81–96. Springer, Heidelberg (2013). https://doi.org/10.1007/978-3-642-37075-5_6

20. Clemente, L., Lasota, S.: Timed pushdown automata revisited. In: 30th Annual ACM/IEEE Symposium on Logic in Computer Science, LICS 2015, Kyoto, Japan, 6–10 July 2015, pp. 738–749. IEEE Computer Society (2015)

21. Clemente, L., Lasota, S., Lazic, R., Mazowiecki, F.: Timed pushdown automata and branching vector addition systems. In: 32nd Annual ACM/IEEE Symposium on Logic in Computer Science, LICS 2017, Reykjavik, Iceland, 20–23 June 2017, pp. 1–12. IEEE Computer Society (2017)

22. Dang, Z.: Pushdown timed automata: a binary reachability characterization and safety verification. Theor. Comput. Sci. **302**(1–3), 93–121 (2003)

23. Emmi, M., Majumdar, R.: Decision problems for the verification of real-time software. In: Hespanha, J.P., Tiwari, A. (eds.) HSCC 2006. LNCS, vol. 3927, pp. 200–211. Springer, Heidelberg (2006). https://doi.org/10.1007/11730637_17

24. Ganty, P., Majumdar, R.: Analyzing real-time event-driven programs. In: Ouaknine, J., Vaandrager, F.W. (eds.) FORMATS 2009. LNCS, vol. 5813, pp. 164–178. Springer, Heidelberg (2009). https://doi.org/10.1007/978-3-642-04368-0_14

25. Krcal, P., Yi, W.: Communicating timed automata: the more synchronous, the more difficult to verify. In: Ball, T., Jones, R.B. (eds.) CAV 2006. LNCS, vol. 4144, pp. 249–262. Springer, Heidelberg (2006). https://doi.org/10.1007/11817963_24

26. La Torre, S., Madhusudan, P., Parlato, G.: Context-bounded analysis of concurrent queue systems. In: Ramakrishnan, C.R., Rehof, J. (eds.) TACAS 2008. LNCS, vol. 4963, pp. 299–314. Springer, Heidelberg (2008). https://doi.org/10.1007/978-3-540-78800-3_21

27. Pachl, J.K.: Reachability problems for communicating finite state machines. Ph.D. thesis, Faculty of Mathematics, University of Waterloo, Ontario (1982)

28. Trivedi, A., Wojtczak, D.: Recursive timed automata. In: Bouajjani, A., Chin, W.-N. (eds.) ATVA 2010. LNCS, vol. 6252, pp. 306–324. Springer, Heidelberg (2010). https://doi.org/10.1007/978-3-642-15643-4_23

On Persistency in Time Petri Nets

Kamel Barkaoui[1] and Hanifa Boucheneb[1,2(✉)]

[1] Laboratoire CEDRIC, Conservatoire National des Arts et Métiers,
192 rue Saint Martin, Paris Cedex 03, France
kamel.barkaoui@cnam.fr
[2] Laboratoire VeriForm, Department of Computer Engineering and Software
Engineering, École Polytechnique de Montréal, P.O. Box 6079, Station Centre-ville,
Montréal, Québec H3C 3A7, Canada
hanifa.boucheneb@polymtl.ca

Abstract. A transition of a (time) Petri net is persistent if once it is enabled, it can never become disabled through occurrences of other transitions until it is fired [5,15]. It is said to be effect-persistent if it is persistent and its effect (The effect of an enabled transition t in a marking M is defined by the set of transitions newly enabled by firing t.) is not affected by firing other transitions. This paper investigates some sufficient conditions for persistency and effect-persistency of transitions, in the context of time Petri nets (TPNs for short) that depend on the marking and the static/dynamic time information of the model. Then, it shows how to use these sufficient conditions to improve the partial order reduction technique of the TPN model.

1 Introduction

Time Petri net model (TPN for short) is among the well studied time extensions of Petri nets as it offers a good compromise between the modelling power and the verification complexity. A TPN is a Petri net where a time interval is associated with each transition. The bounds of this interval specify its minimum and maximum firing delays, relatively to its enabling date. The firing of a transition is supposed to take no time but results in a new marking. The verification of TPNs is, in general, based on the state space abstraction and the interleaving semantics. The basic idea of the state space abstraction is to regroup together all states reachable by the same firing sequence and to consider the resulting groups modulo some relation of equivalence (i.e., abstract states). Each abstract state consists of a marking and a dense convex clock/firing delay domain of its enabled transitions. Several state space abstractions are proposed in the literature for the TPNs such as the *State Class Graph (SCG)* [4], the *Contracted State Class Graph (CSCG)* [13], the *Geometric Region Graph (GRG)* [19,20], the *Strong State Class Graph (SSCG)* [4], the *Zone Based Graph (ZBG)* [10] and the *Atomic State Class Graphs (ASCGs)* [4,11,19]. All these state space abstractions preserve markings and firing sequences of the TPNs and are finite for bounded TPNs. However, they suffers from the state explosion problem.

© Springer Nature Switzerland AG 2018
D. N. Jansen and P. Prabhakar (Eds.): FORMATS 2018, LNCS 11022, pp. 108–124, 2018.
https://doi.org/10.1007/978-3-030-00151-3_7

One of the key notions that allows to attenuate the state explosion problem is the notion of persistency of transitions. A transition of a (time) Petri net is persistent if once it is enabled, it can never become disabled through occurrences of other transitions until it is fired [5, 15]. A (time) Petri net is said to be persistent if each of its transitions is persistent.

Since for a persistent Petri net, the firing of any transition will not disable the others and different interleavings of the same set of transitions lead to the same marking, a partial reduction technique should consist to select only one transition to be fired from each marking. The resulting reduced graph preserves the non-equivalent maximal firing sequences of the model (i.e., for each maximal firing sequence of the model, there is an equivalent maximal firing sequence in the reduced graph and vice-versa). Furthermore, it consists of a single finite or infinite path.

In the context of persistent time Petri nets, firing in different orders two persistent transitions from the same abstract state may lead to different abstract states whose union is not necessarily convex [7]. However, as they share the same marking, they have the same set of enabled transitions and all these transitions are persistent. Thus, for a persistent TPN, firing only one transition from each abstract state yields a reduced graph that preserves its non-equivalent maximal firing sequences. By the fact that every firing sequence of a TPN is also a firing sequence of its underlying non timed Petri net, it follows that the persistent transitions of the underlying non timed Petri net are also persistent in the TPN. The reverse is however not true. Therefore, a TPN is persistent, if its underlying non timed Petri net is persistent. The subclass of persistent TPNs includes the subclass of persistent Petri nets.

For non persistent TPNs, the notion of persistency is exploited, in the partial order reduction techniques, to select the subset of transitions to be fired from each abstract state. Nevertheless, in the context of TPNs, persistency is not sufficient to obtain reduced graphs preserving non-equivalent maximal firing sequences. Indeed, if all the enabled transitions in the current abstract state are persistent, firing only one transition is not sufficient to preserve, in the reduced graph, the non-equivalent maximal firing sequences. For instance, consider the model TPN1 and its CSCG at Fig. 1. There are two persistent and enabled transitions t_1 and t_2 in its initial marking. Firing t_1 and t_2 in both orders leads to two state classes with different behaviours. The transition t_4 is not firable from the state class reached by t_1t_2 but firable from the successor of the initial state class by t_2t_1. Thus, considering only the firing order t_1t_2 from the initial state will not cover all the non-equivalent maximal firing sequences of the model. The firing sequence $t_2t_1t_4$ will not be covered. To deal with this issue, the Partially Ordered Sets (POSETs) method is proposed in [1, 17, 18, 20].

The aim of POSETs is to compute, by exploring one sequence of transitions and fixing partially the firing order of some of its transitions, the convex hull of the abstract states reachable by some of its equivalent sequences. However, replacing abstract states by their convex hull does preserve neither boundedness nor reachability properties of the model [8]. To ensure that the computed convex hull is exactly equal to the union of abstract states reachable by firing all the sequences embedded in the partially ordered sequence, it suffices for the relaxed transitions to be persistent and their effects are independent of their firing order [7]. Such transitions are said to be effect-persistent. For example, for the model TPN1 and its initial state class, the two enabled transitions t_1 and t_2 are firable and effect-persistent. Firing t_1 (or t_2) from the initial state class without fixing any firing order constraint with the other, followed by t_2 (or t_1) will result in the union of state classes reached by firing in both orders t_1 and t_2.

In [7–9], the authors have revisited the POSETs and the stubborn sets methods in the context of time Petri nets and proposed some reduced graphs that preserve the non-equivalent firing sequences of time Petri nets. The selection procedures of the three approches stem from the fact that the persistency and the effect of an enabled transition t is preserved, if no transition can be enabled or fired before firing t and, at the same time, is in conflict with t or affects the effect of t. Their basic idea is to select a firable transition and recursively select all the enabled transitions that may alter directly/indirectly the persistency or the effect of the selected ones, until reaching a fixed point. However, in case a non firable transition t' is selected, this fixed point is not always sufficient to preserve the non-equivalent firing sequences of time Petri nets. Indeed, any sequence starting with one or more non selected transitions followed by t' may be not covered by the equivalent sequences explored by considering only the selected firable transitions. To deal with such a case it suffices to ensure that there is at least a selected transition that must be fired before t'.

The main difference between approaches in [7–9] reside in the sufficient conditions used to ensure persistency and effect-persistency of transitions. In [7], these sufficient conditions are based on the current marking and the structure of the underlying Petri nets. They do not take into account the time parameters of the model. For instance, if a transition t is selected then each enabled transition t' that may enable directly/indirectly a transition t'' in conflict with t is selected too, even if its enabledness cannot occur before firing t. In [8,9], in addition to the marking and the structure of the underlying Petri nets, both the static and the dynamic firing intervals of transitions are used to relax the sufficient conditions that ensure persistency or effect-persistency for transitions. Indeed, these time parameters allow to compute, on the one hand, a lower bound of the time needed for t'' to become enabled or firable, and, on the other hand, the maximal firing delay of t. If this lower bound is greater to the maximal firing delay of t, then t'' cannot be enabled as long as t is enabled. The approach in [8] improves the approach in [9] by better taking into account time parameters and relaxing the sufficient conditions that ensure persistency and effect persistency. For example, if a transition t is selected then [9] selects also all the enabled transitions in conflict with t in the current marking, while [8] selects only the enabled transitions in conflict with t that are firable before t. Another improvement is for the case where a non firable transition is selected. In [9], as soon as a non firable transition t is selected, all firable transitions are selected too. The approach in [8] does not select any additional transition, if there is at least a selected transition that must be fired before t'.

However in [8,9], the used lower bounds of the time needed for the transitions to become enabled or firable are based on the structure of the TPN and its static time intervals and do not take into account the current marking. This paper shows how to tighten up these lower bounds by taking into account the current marking and more accurately the structure and the static time intervals of the TPN. Then, it establishes some sufficient conditions for persistency and effect-persistency that are less restrictive than those used in [7–9]. Afterwards, it reportes some results obtained by relaxing the selection criteria used in [8].

The rest of the paper is structured as follows. Section 2 presents the TPN model, its semantics and the CSCG [13]. Section 3 is devoted to the notions of persistency and effect-persistency in time Petri nets. It provides some sufficient conditions that ensure persistency and effect-persistency for a transition. Finally, the conclusions are presented in Sect. 4.

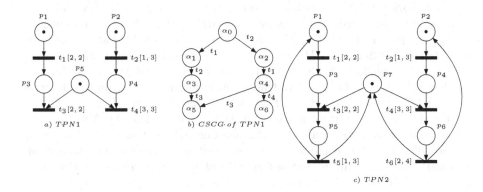

Fig. 1. TPN1, its CSCG and TPN2

2 Time Petri Nets

2.1 Definition and Semantics

Let P be a nonempty set. A multiset over P is a function $M : P \longrightarrow \mathbb{N}$, $\mathbb{N}$ being the set of natural numbers, defined also by the linear combination: $\sum_{p \in P} M(p) \times p$. We denote by P_{MS} and 0 the set of all multisets over P and the empty multiset, respectively. Let $M_1 \in P_{MS}$, $M_2 \in P_{MS}$ and $\prec \in \{\leq, =, <, >, \geq\}$. Operations on multisets are defined as usual.

Let $\mathbb{Q}^+$ and $\mathbb{R}^+$ be the sets of non-negative rational and real numbers, respectively, and $INT_{\mathbb{X}} = \{[a, b] | (a, b) \in \mathbb{X} \times (\mathbb{X} \cup \{\infty\})\}$, for $\mathbb{X} \in \{\mathbb{Q}^+, \mathbb{R}^+\}$, the set of intervals whose lower and upper bounds are in $\mathbb{X}$ and $\mathbb{X} \cup \{\infty\}$, respectively. Let $[a, b] \in INT_{\mathbb{X}}$ and $[c, d] \in INT_{\mathbb{X}}$ be two intervals, the sum of these intervals $[a, b] + [c, d]$ is the interval : $[a + c, b + d]$.

A TPN is a tuple $\mathcal{N} = (P, T, pre, post, M_0, Is)$ where: (1) P and T are finite and nonempty sets of places and transitions s.t. $P \cap T = \emptyset$, (2) pre and $post$ are the backward and forward incidence functions, respectively ($pre, post : T \longrightarrow P_{MS}$), (3) $M_0 \in P_{MS}$ is the initial marking, and (4) Is is the static firing function ($Is : T \to INT_{\mathbb{Q}+}$). $\downarrow Is(t)$ and $\uparrow Is(t)$ denote the lower and upper bounds of the static firing interval of transition t.

For $t \in T$, ${}^\bullet t = \{p \in P | pre(t)(p) > 0\}$ and $t^\bullet = \{p \in P | post(t)(p) > 0\}$ denote the sets of input and output places of t, respectively. Similarly, for $p \in P$, ${}^\bullet p = \{t \in T | post(t)(p) > 0\}$ and $p^\bullet = \{t \in T | pre(t)(p) > 0\}$ denote the sets of input and output transitions of p, respectively. We denote by $CFS(t)$ the set of transitions in structural conflict with t, i.e., $CFS(t) = \{t' \in T \mid {}^\bullet t \cap {}^\bullet t' \neq \emptyset\}$. The set of output transitions of t is denoted by $NwS(t) = \{t' \in T \mid t^\bullet \cap {}^\bullet t' \neq \emptyset\}$.

Several semantics are proposed in the literature for the TPN model [3, 12, 14]. An overview and a classification of the TPN semantics can be found in [12].

We consider here the classical and widely used semantics (i.e., the threshold, intermediate and single-server semantics).

Each marking of $\mathcal{N}$ is a multi-set over P. Let M be a marking of $\mathcal{N}$ and $t \in T$ a transition. The transition t is enabled at marking M iff all tokens required for firing t are present in M, i.e., $M \geq pre(t)$. In case t is enabled at M, its firing leads to the marking $M' = M - pre(t) + post(t)$. We denote by $En(M)$ the set of transitions enabled at M, i.e., $En(M) = \{t \in T \mid M \geq pre(t)\}$. For $t \in En(M)$, we denote by $CF(M, t)$ the set of transitions enabled at M but in conflict with t, i.e., $CF(M, t) = \{t' \in En(M) \mid t' = t \vee M \not\geq pre(t) + pre(t')\}$.

Let M' be the successor marking of M by t. We denote by $Nw(M, t)$ the set of transitions newly enabled at the marking M' reached from M by firing t. Formally, $Nw(M, t)$ contains t, if t is enabled at M', and also all transitions enabled at the marking M' but not enabled at the intermediate marking $M - pre(t)$, i.e., $Nw(M, t) = \{t' \in En(M') \mid t' = t \vee M - pre(t) \not\geq pre(t')\}$.

Starting from the initial marking M_0, the marking of $\mathcal{N}$ evolves by firing transitions at irregular intervals of time. When a transition t is newly enabled, its firing interval is set to its static firing interval. Bounds of its interval decrease synchronously with time until it is fired or disabled by a conflicting firing. Transition t is firable, if the lower bound of its firing interval reaches 0. It must fire immediately, without any additional delay, when the upper bound of its firing interval reaches 0, unless it is disabled by another firing. The firing of a transition takes no time but leads to a new marking.

Syntactically, in the context of $\mathcal{N}$, a state is defined as a pair $s = (M, I)$, where M is a marking and I is a firing interval function ($I: En(M) \to INT_{\mathbb{R}+}$). The initial state of $\mathcal{N}$ is $s_0 = (M_0, I_0)$, where $I_0(t) = Is(t)$, for all $t \in En(M_0)$.

Let $\mathcal{S} = \{(M, I) \mid M \in P_{MS} \wedge I: En(M) \to INT_{\mathbb{R}+}\}$ be the set of all syntactically correct states, $s = (M, I)$ and $s' = (M', I')$ two states of $\mathcal{S}$, $dh \in \mathbb{R}^+$ a nonnegative real number, $t \in T$ a transition and $\to$ the transition relation defined by:

- $s \xrightarrow{dh} s'$ (s' is also denoted $s + dh$) iff the state s' is reachable from state s by dh time units, i.e., $\forall t \in En(M), dh \leq \uparrow I(t), M' = M$ and

$\forall t' \in En(M'), I'(t') = [Max(0, \downarrow I(t') - dh), \uparrow I(t') - dh].$

- $s \xrightarrow{t} s'$ iff t is immediately firable from s and its firing leads to s', i.e.,
  $t \in En(M), \ \downarrow I(t) = 0, \ M' = M - pre(t) + post(t),$ and
  $$\forall t' \in En(M'), I'(t') = \begin{cases} Is(t') & \text{if } t' \in Nw(M, t) \\ I(t') & \text{otherwise.} \end{cases}$$

The semantics of $\mathcal{N}$ is defined by the transition system $(S, \rightarrow, s_0)$, where $S \subseteq \mathcal{S}$ is the set of all states reachable from s_0 by $\xrightarrow{*}$ (the reflexive and transitive closure of $\rightarrow$).

A *run* in $(S, \rightarrow, s_0)$, starting from a state s_1 of S, is a maximal sequence $\eta = s_1 \xrightarrow{dh_1} s_1 + dh_1 \xrightarrow{t_1} s_2 \xrightarrow{dh_2} s_2 + dh_2 \xrightarrow{t_2} s_3....$ By convention, for any state s_i, the relation $s_i \xrightarrow{0} s_i$ holds. Sequences $\rho = TTr(\eta) = dh_1t_1dh_2t_2...$ and $\omega = Tr(\eta) = t_1t_2...$ are called the timed trace and firing sequence (untimed trace) of η, respectively. The total elapsed time of the timed trace ρ, denoted by $time(\rho)$, is $\sum_{i=1,|\rho|} dh_i$, where $|\rho|$ is the length of the firing sequence of ρ. An infinite timed trace ρ is diverging if $time(\rho) = \infty$, otherwise it is said to be zeno. We denote by $\Pi(s)$, for $s \in S$, the set of runs of the state s. Runs of $\mathcal{N}$ are all runs of the initial state s_0.

A TPN model is said to be non-zeno if all its runs are non-zeno. Non-zeno TPNs ensure that each enabled transition will eventually become firable in the future, unless it is disabled by a conflicting transition. However, its firing can postponed indefinitely in case the upper bound of its firing interval is not bounded.

The *timed language* of $\mathcal{N}$ is the set of its timed traces. Let M be a marking. The marking M is reachable in $\mathcal{N}$ iff $\exists s \in S$ s.t. the marking of s is M. A marking M' is reachable in $\mathcal{N}$ from M iff $\exists s, s' \in S$ s.t. $s \xrightarrow{*} s'$ and the markings of s and s' are M and M', respectively. We denote by $\overrightarrow{M}^{\mathcal{N}}$ the set of markings reachable in $\mathcal{N}$ from M.

2.2 Contracted State Class Graph

The *Contracted State Class Graph (CSCG)* [13] is the quotient graph of the *State Class Graph (SCG)* [4] w.r.t. some relation of equivalence over state classes [13]. Intuitively, this relation groups together all state classes, which have the same marking and triangular constraints[1], but not necessarily the same simple atomic constraints[2].

Syntactically, a CSCG state class is defined as a pair $\alpha = (M, F)$, where M is a marking and F is a consistent conjunction of triangular atomic constraints

---

[1] Constraint of the form $x - y \leq c$, where x, y are real-valued variables and c is a rational constant.

[2] A simple atomic constraint is an atomic constraint of the form $x \leq c$ or $-x \leq c$, where x is a real-valued variable and c is a rational constant.

over the firing delays of the transitions enabled in M. The firing delay of a transition t is denoted by the non-negative real-valued variable $\underline{t}$. The formula F characterises the union of firing time domains of all states within α. By convention, $F = true$ if the number of enabled transitions in M is less than 2 (i.e., there is no triangular atomic constraint in F). A state $s' = (M', I')$ belongs to α iff $M = M'$ and its firing time domain (i.e., $\bigwedge_{t \in En(M')} \downarrow I'(t) \leq \underline{t} \leq \uparrow I'(t)$) is included in the firing time domain of α (i.e., F).

From a practical point of view, every conjunction F of triangular atomic constraints over a set of real-valued variables X is represented by means of a *Difference Bound Matrix* (DBM) [2]. The DBM of F is a square matrix D, indexed by variables of X. Each entry d_{ij} is an upper bound of $x_i - x_j$ in F (i.e., $d_{ij} = Max(c|x_i - x_j \leq c \in F))^3$. If there is no upper bound, in F, on $x_i - x_j$ with $i \neq j$, d_{ij} is ∞. Entry d_{ii} is 0. Although the same nonempty domain may be encoded by different DBM's, they have a canonical form. The canonical form of a DBM is the representation with tightest bounds on all differences between variables, computed by propagating the effect of each entry through the DBM. The DBM D of F is in canonical form iff $\forall x_i, x_j, x_k \in X, d_{ij} \leq d_{ik} + d_{kj}$. Two conjunctions of atomic constraints are equivalent (i.e., represent the same domain) iff their DBMs have the same canonical form. Canonical forms make operations over formulas much simpler [2].

The CSCG initial state class is $\alpha_0 = (M_0, F_0)$, where
$$F_0 = \bigwedge_{t_i, t_j \in En(M_0) \text{ s.t. } t_i \neq t_j} \underline{t_i} - \underline{t_j} \leq \uparrow Is(t_i) - \downarrow Is(t_j), \ \underline{t_i} \text{ and } \underline{t_j} \text{ are real-valued}$$
variables representing firing delays of transitions t_i and t_j, respectively. It keeps only the triangular atomic constraints of the SCG initial state class.

Let $\mathcal{C}_S$ be the set of all syntactically correct CSCG state classes and *succ* a successor function from $\mathcal{C}_S \times T$ to $\mathcal{C}_S \cup \{\emptyset\}$ defined by: $\forall \alpha \in \mathcal{C}_S, \forall t_f \in T$,

- $succ(\alpha, t_f) \neq \emptyset$ (i.e., t_f is firable from α) iff $t_f \in En(M)$ and the following formula is consistent (its domain is not empty): $F \wedge (\bigwedge_{t \in En(M)} \underline{t_f} - \underline{t} \leq 0)$.

  Intuitively, this formula, called the firing condition of t_f from α, means that t_f is firable from α before all other transitions enabled at M. In other words, there is at least one valuation of firing delays in F s.t. t_f has the smallest firing delay.

- If $succ(\alpha, t_f) \neq \emptyset$ then $succ(\alpha, t_f) = (M', F')$, where:
  $M' = M - pre(t_f) + post(t_f)$ and F' is computed in three steps:
  (1) Set F' to $F \wedge \bigwedge_{t \in En(M)} \underline{t_f} - \underline{t} \leq 0 \ \wedge \bigwedge_{t \in Nw(M, t_f)} \downarrow Is(t) \leq \underline{t'} - \underline{t_f} \leq \uparrow Is(t)$

  (Variables $\underline{t'}$ for $t \in Nw(M, t_f)$ are new variables introduced for representing the firing delays of the newly enabled transitions. They allow to deal with the situation where a transition t is enabled before firing t_f and newly enabled by t_f (i.e. $t \in CF(M, t_f) \cap Nw(M, t_f)$). The delay of the new instance of t is temporally represented by $\underline{t'}$, in this step);

---

3 Here, F is viewed as a set of triangular atomic constraints.

(2) Put F' in canonical form[4] and eliminate all transitions of $CF(M, t_f)$;

(3) Rename each t' into t.

We denote by $Fr(\alpha) = \{t \in T \mid succ(\alpha, t) \neq \emptyset\}$ the set of transitions firable from α. The function $succ$ is extended to sequences of transitions as follows: $\forall \omega \in T^*$, $succ(\alpha, \omega) = succ(succ(\alpha, \omega_1), \omega_2)$, where $\omega = \omega_1 \omega_2$ and, by convention, $succ(\alpha, \epsilon) = \alpha$, ϵ being the empty sequence. We denote by $\|\omega\| \subseteq T$ the set of transitions appearing in ω.

The CSCG of $\mathcal{N}$ is the structure $\mathbb{C} = (\mathcal{C}, succ, \alpha_0)$, where α_0 is the initial CSCG state class of $\mathcal{N}$ and $\mathcal{C}$ is the set of state classes accessible from α_0 by applying repeatedly the successor function $succ$, i.e., $\mathcal{C} = \{\alpha \in \mathcal{C}_S \mid \exists \omega \in T^*, \alpha = succ(\alpha_0, \omega) \neq \emptyset\}$. A sequence $\omega \in T^+$ is a firing sequence of $\mathbb{C}$ iff $succ(\alpha_0, \omega) \neq \emptyset$.

From a practical point of view, this firing rule can be implemented, using DBMs in canonical form, as follows [13]: Let $\alpha = (M, F)$ be a state class, D the DBM in canonical form of F and t_f a transition.

- $succ(\alpha, t_f) \neq \emptyset$ iff $t_f \in En(M) \wedge \forall t_i \in En(M), d_{if} \geq 0$.
- If $succ(\alpha, t_f) \neq \emptyset$, then $succ(\alpha, t_f) = (M', F')$, where M' and the canonical form of the DBM of F' are computed as follows:
  $M' = M - pre(t_f) + post(t_f)$ and $\forall(t_i, t_j) \in (En(M'))^2$,

$$d'_{ij} = \begin{cases} 0 & \text{if } i = j \\ \uparrow Is(t_i) - \downarrow Is(t_j) & \text{if } t_i, t_j \in Nw(M, t_f), \\ d_{if} - \downarrow Is(t_j) & \text{if } t_i \notin Nw(M, t_f) \wedge t_j \in Nw(M, t_f), \\ \uparrow Is(t_i) + \underset{t_u \in En(M)}{Min} d_{uj} & \text{if } t_i \in Nw(M, t_f) \wedge t_j \notin Nw(M, t_f), \\ Min(d_{ij}, d_{if} + \underset{t_u \in En(M)}{Min} d_{uj}) & \text{otherwise.} \end{cases}$$

Moreover, just after firing t_f, the minimal remaining delay of any transition $t_j \in En(M') - Nw(M, t_f)$ is $- \underset{t_u \in En(M)}{Min} d_{uj}$ [13].

This delay is the minimal value of $\underline{t_j} - \underline{t_f}$ in the domain of the firing condition of t_f from α, i.e., $F \wedge \underset{t \in En(M)}{\bigwedge} \underline{t_f} - \underline{t} \leq 0$.

Let $\alpha = (M, F)$ and $\alpha' = (M, F')$ be two state classes with the same marking M, D and D' the DBMs in canonical form of F and F', respectively. The union of state classes α and α' is not necessarily a state class [6]. The smallest enclosing state class of the union of α and α', called the convex hull of α and α' and denoted by $\alpha'' = \alpha \sqcup \alpha'$, is the state class $\alpha'' = (M, F'')$, where the DBM D'' of F'' is computed as follows: $\forall t_i, t_j \in En(M), d''_{ij} = Max(d_{ij}, d'_{ij})$. The union $\alpha \cup \alpha'$ is a state class iff $\alpha \sqcup \alpha' = \alpha \cup \alpha'$, i.e., the union of the state classes is identical to their convex hull. It is proven in [13] that the CSCG preserves markings and firing sequences of the SCG (which, in turn, preserves markings and firing sequences of $\mathcal{N}$). The CSCG of $\mathcal{N}$ is finite iff $\mathcal{N}$ is bounded. The CSCG is smaller than the SCG and has another nice feature over the SCG

---

[4] The canonical form of F' is the formula corresponding to the canonical form of its DBM.

relatively to the different interleavings of the same set of transitions. Indeed, for the TPN in Fig. 1c, from the initial state, the union of the CSCG state classes reached by sequences t_1t_2 and t_2t_1 is identical to their convex hull as the CSCG state classes reached by these sequences are $(p_3 + p_4 + p_7, -2 \leq \underline{t_3} - \underline{t_4} \leq -1)$ and $(p_3 + p_4 + p_7, -1 \leq \underline{t_3} - \underline{t_4} \leq 0)$, respectively. Their convex hull $(p_3 + p_4 + p_7, -2 \leq \underline{t_3} - \underline{t_4} \leq 0)$. Their convex hull is identical to their union. However, the union of the SCG state classes reached by sequences t_1t_2 and t_2t_1 is not identical to their convex hull. Indeed, the SCG state classes reached by these sequences are $(p_3 + p_4 + p_7, 1 \leq \underline{t_3} \leq 2 \wedge t_4 = 3 \wedge -2 \leq \underline{t_3} - \underline{t_4} \leq -1)$ and $(p_3 + p_4 + p_7, \underline{t_3} = 2 \wedge 2 \leq \underline{t_4} \leq 3 \wedge -1 \leq \underline{t_3} - \underline{t_4} \leq 0)$, respectively. Their convex hull $(p_3 + p_4 + p_7, 1 \leq \underline{t_3} \leq 2 \wedge 2 \leq \underline{t_4} \leq 3 \wedge -2 \leq \underline{t_3} - \underline{t_4} \leq 0)$ is not identical to their union, since for $\underline{t_3} = 1$ and $\underline{t_4} = 2$, the corresponding state belongs to their convex hull but does not belong to their union.

For the rest of the paper, we fix a TPN $\mathcal{N} = (P, T, pre, post, M_0, Is)$.

3   Persistent and Effect-Persistent Transitions

3.1   Definitions

For Petri nets, the notion of persistency, proposed by [16], means that no transition can disable another one. As this notion relies on the behaviour of the model, it means that there is no conflict in each reachable marking of the model. Formally, $\mathcal{N}$ is persistent iff $\forall M \in \overrightarrow{M_0}^{\mathcal{N}}, \forall t, t' \in En(M), t = t' \vee t \notin CF(M, t')$.

In the context of TPNs, this notion of persistency of transition can be defined relatively to a state or a state class. It can also be defined w.r.t. some subset of transitions. Let $s = (M, I) \in \mathcal{S}$ be a reachable state, $\alpha = (M, F)$ a reachable state class, $t \in En(M)$ a transition enabled in M and $\mu \subseteq T$ such that $t \in \mu$.

The transition t is persistent from s w.r.t. μ iff
$\forall s' = (M', I') \in \mathcal{S}, \forall t' \in T, \forall \rho \in (\mathbb{R}^+ \times T)^* \times \mathbb{R}^+,$

$$(Tr(\rho) \in (T - \mu)^* \wedge s \xrightarrow{\rho} s' \xrightarrow{t'}) \Rightarrow (t' \in \mu \vee t \notin CF(M', t')).$$

In words, from the state s, the transition t is maintained enabled as long as no transition from μ is fired. The transition t is persistent from α w.r.t. μ iff t is persistent from each state of α w.r.t μ. Note that for $\mu = \{t\}$, the definitions above correspond to the classical definition of persistency of transitions relatively to a state or a state class. Similarly, we define the notion of effect-persistent of t from s and α w.r.t μ as follows.

The transition t is effect-persistent from s w.r.t. μ iff it is persistent from s w.r.t. μ and its effect is not affected by firing transitions of $T - \mu$, i.e., $\forall s' = (M', I'), s'' = (M'', I'') \in S, \forall \rho \in (\mathbb{R}^+ \times T)^* \times \mathbb{R}^+, \forall t' \in T,$

$$(Tr(\rho) \in (T - \mu)^* \wedge s \xrightarrow{\rho} s' \xrightarrow{t'} s'') \Rightarrow$$
$$t' \in \mu \vee (t \notin CF(M', t') \wedge Nw(M', t) = Nw(M'', t)).$$

In words, from state s, the enabledness and the effects of the transition t are not affected as long as no transition of μ is fired. The transition t is effect-persistent from α w.r.t. μ iff t is effect-persistent from each state of α w.r.t μ.

We first establish, in the following, some sufficient conditions for persistency and effect-persistency of t from α w.r.t. μ. These sufficient conditions are based on the lower and upper bounds of the firing delays of transitions from α, including the non enabled ones. If a transition is enabled in α, then a lower bound and an upper bound of its firing delay, relatively to α or any other enabled transition, are provided by the time information within the state class. Otherwise, the firing delay of a non enabled transition from α is the time needed for the transition to become firable directly/indirectly from α. We show, in the following, how to compute a lower bound of this delay, even when we want to avoid some transitions. With these firing delay bounds, a sufficient condition for persistency of t from α is guaranteed, if an upper bound of its firing delay from α is strictly smaller than a lower bound of the firing delay of each transition in structural conflict with t.

3.2   Potential Firing Delays of Transitions from a State Class

Let $t, t' \in T$ be two transitions. A transition-path of $\mathcal{N}$ connecting t to t' is a sequence of transitions $t_1...t_n$, with $t = t_1, t' = t_n, n \geq 1$, such that $n = 1$ or for $i \in \{1, ..., n-1\}, \exists p_i \in post(t_i) \cap pre(t_{i+1})$ (i.e., $t_{i+1} \in NwS(t_i)$). We extend the static firing interval function to any sequence of transitions $\omega = t_1...t_n$ as follows: $Is(\omega) = Is(t_1) + ... + Is(t_n)$. Intuitively, $Is(\omega)$ gives the firing interval of the sequence ω from a marking M where t_1 is newly enabled in M and each other transition is enabled by its immediate predecessor. Let $\pi(t, t')$ be the set of transition-paths connecting t to t'. The fastest transition-paths of $\pi(t, t')$ have the smallest firing delay (i.e., $\underset{\omega \in \pi(t,t')}{Min} \downarrow Is(\omega)$). This timing information can be derived from the structure of the TPN using, for instance, the delay lower bound matrix L defined in [9] as a square matrix over the set of transitions T: $\forall t_i, t_j \in T$,

$$l_{ij} = \begin{cases} 0 & \text{if } t_i = t_j \\ \downarrow Is(t_i) & \text{if } t_i \neq t_j \wedge t_i \in NwS(t_j) \\ \infty & \text{otherwise.} \end{cases}$$

The canonical form of L, obtained by applying the Floyd-Warshall's shortest path algorithm, is denoted by $\bar{L}$. Intuitively, if t_i is not enabled when t_j is fired, then $\bar{l}_{ij}$ is a lower bound of the firing delay of t_i, relatively to the firing date of t_j. Note that $\bar{l}_{ij} = \infty$ means that there is no path connecting t_j to t_i and then t_i cannot be enabled directly or indirectly by t_j.

This lower bound is used in the partial order techniques proposed in [8,9] to establish some sufficient conditions that ensure persistency or effect-persistency for transitions. It considers neither the current marking nor the dynamic time information. Tightening up this bound might improve the approach developed in [8,9]. The idea comes from the fact that if t_i is not enabled in the current marking

M, before its enabledness, we need to fire at least one input transition for each input place p of t_i not sufficiently marked in M for t_i (i.e., $M(p) < pre(t_i)(p)$). The same process is recursively repeated for the non enabled input transitions. If t_i is enabled in M, the timing information in the state class gives the bounds of the firing delay between each enabled transition and t_i. In this way, we can retrieve a lower bound of the firing delay of t_i. Intuitively, this computing process consists in exploring in the reverse order the elementary paths connecting an enabled transition in M to the input places of t_i that are non sufficiently marked for firing t_i.

Formally, let $\alpha = (M, F)$ be a state class, D its DBM in canonical form, $t_i \in T$ and $\mu \subseteq T$ s.t. $t_i \in \mu$ a subset of transitions we want to avoid during the exploration of the firing sequences that might lead to the enabledness of t_i. Also, this set allows to explore only elementary transition-paths that lead to t_i. We define recursively a lower bound of the potential firing delay of t_i from α, in case no transition of μ is fired beforehand, by:

$$Dmin(t_i, M, F, \mu) =$$

$$\begin{cases} - \underset{t_u \in En(M)}{Min} \ d_{ui} & \text{if } t_i \in En(M), \\ \underset{p \in {}^\bullet t_i \wedge M(p) < pre(t_i)(p)}{Max} \left(\underset{t_j \in {}^\bullet p - \mu}{Min} \ Dmin(t_j, M, F, \mu \cup \{t_j\}) + \downarrow Is(t_i) \right) & \text{otherwise.} \end{cases}$$

By convention, the minimum and maximum over the empty set are ∞ and 0, respectively.

Intuitively, if t_i is enabled in M then its minimal firing delay relatively to the date of the first firing from α is $- \underset{t_u \in En(M)}{Min} \ d_{ui}$ [13]. This delay equals 0 in case t_i is firable from α [13]. Notice that this delay is independent of the transition fired first from α. Indeed, if t_f is the first transition fired from α, this delay equals the minimal value of $\underline{t_j} - \underline{t_f}$ in the domain of the firing condition of t_f from α, i.e., $F \wedge \underset{t \in En(M)}{\bigwedge} \ \underline{t_f} - \underline{t} \le 0$.

If t_i is directly enabled by some transition t_j of α, then the minimal firing delay of t_i relatively to the first firing from α is $Dmin(t_j, M, F, \mu \cup \{t_j\}) + \downarrow Is(t_i) = \downarrow Is(t_i)$, since t_j is firable from α.

Finally, if t_i is enabled indirectly from α, before its enabledness, we need to fire, for each input place p of t_i not sufficiently marked, at least one of its input transitions not in μ. Note that, thanks to μ, this recursive computation procedure of $Dmin(t_i, M, F, \mu)$ always terminates as the transition-paths explored are elementary and the number of elementary transition-paths is finite.

Example 1. Consider the model TPN2 in Fig. 1c and the reachable state class $\alpha_8 = (M_8, F_8)$, where $M_8 = p_2 + p_3 + p_7$ and $F_8 = (-1 \le \underline{t_2} - \underline{t_3} \le 1)$. Let us compute $Dmin(t_4, M_8, F_8, \{t_4\})$. By definition, $Dmin(t_4, M_8, F_8, \{t_4\}) =$

$$\left(\underset{p \in {}^\bullet t_4 \wedge M_8(p) < pre(t_4)(p)}{Max} \ \underset{t_j \in {}^\bullet p - \{t_4\}}{Min} \ Dmin(t_j, M_8, F_8, \{t_4, t_j\}) \right) + \downarrow Is(t_4)$$

$$= Dmin(t_2, M_8, F_8, \{t_2, t_4\}) + \downarrow Is(t_4) = 3.$$

The transition t_4 is not enabled in the marking M_8, as its input place p_4 is not marked. This place cannot be marked before firing its input transition t_2. Since t_2 is firable from α_8, it follows that $Dmin(t_2, M_8, F_8, \{t_2, t_4\}) = 0$ and then $Dmin(t_4, M_8, F_8, \{t_4\}) = \downarrow Is(t_4) = 3$. Note that $Dmin(t_4, M_8, F_8, \{t_1, t_4\}) = Dmin(t_4, M_8, F_8, \{t_4\})$. It means that 3 is a still a lower bound of the firing delay of t_4 from M_8, even if we avoid t_1. However, $Dmin(t_4, M_8, F_8, \{t_2, t_4\}) = \infty$. It means that from α_8, t_4 cannot be enabled before firing t_2. The transition t_4 enabled by t_2 is in conflict with t_3 but it cannot occur before t_3, as the maximal firing delay of t_3 relatively to the firing date of t_2 (i.e., $d_{32} = 1$) is smaller than the lower bound 3 of the firing delay of t_4 (i.e., $Dmin(t_4, M_8, F_8, \{t_1, t_4\}) = Dmin(t_4, M_8, F_8, \{t_4\}) = 3$). Therefore, both transitions t_2 and t_3 are persistent from α_8, as no transition in conflict with t_2 or t_3 can be fired before them.

Lemma 1 establishes some relationships between $Dmin(t, M, F, \mu)$ and the potential enabledness of t from M, without help from transitions of μ.

Lemma 1. *Let $\alpha = (M, F)$ be a state class, D the DBM of F in canonical form, $t_i \in T$, $\mu \subseteq T$ s.t. $t_i \in \mu$. Then:*

(1) $Dmin(t_i, M, F, \mu) < \infty \Rightarrow \forall s \in (M, F), \forall \rho \in (\mathbb{R}^+ \times T)^* \times \mathbb{R}^+$ s.t. $(Tr(\rho) \in (T - \mu)^* \wedge s \xrightarrow{\rho t_i})$, $time(\rho t_i) \geq Dmin(t_i, M, F, \mu)$.
   Intuitively, it means that if t_i is enabled in the current marking or in the future then $Dmin(t_i, M, F, \mu)$ is a lower bound of its firing delay, relatively to s in case no transition of μ is fired beforehand.

(2) $Dmin(t_i, M, F, \mu) = \infty \Rightarrow \forall \omega \in (T - \mu)^*, succ(\alpha, \omega t_i) = \emptyset$.
   In words, if $Dmin(t_i, M, F, \mu) = \infty$ then t_i cannot be enabled, from α, as long as no transition of μ is fired.

(3) $\forall \mu'$ s.t. $\mu' \subseteq \mu \wedge t_i \in \mu'$, $Dmin(t_i, M, F, \mu') \leq Dmin(t_i, M, F, \mu)$.
   It means that a larger set of forbidden transitions μ yields larger lower bound for the firing delay of t_i.

(4) $\forall s \in (M, F), \forall \rho \in (\mathbb{R}^+ \times T)^* \times \mathbb{R}^+, \forall s' = (M', I') \in \mathcal{S}$,

$$(s \xrightarrow{\rho} s' \wedge t_i \in En(M')) \implies time(\rho) \geq Dmin(t_i, M, F, \mu) - \downarrow Is(t_i).$$

   It means that if t_i is enabled in the current marking or in the future then it cannot be enabled before $Dmin(t_i, M, F, \mu) - \downarrow Is(t_i)$ time units.

Proof.(1) We consider 3 cases:
   (a) $t_i \in Fr(\alpha)$, (b) $t_i \in En(M) - Fr(\alpha)$ and (c) $t_i \in T - En(M)$.
   (1.a) If $t_i \in Fr(\alpha)$ then, by definition, $\forall t_u \in En(M), d_{ui} \geq 0$ and $d_{ii} = 0$. It follows that $Dmin(t_i, M, F, \mu) = - \underset{t_u \in En(M)}{Min} d_{ui} = 0$ and then

   $Dmin(t_i, M, F, \mu) \leq time(\rho t_i)$.

   (1.b) If $t_i \in En(M) - Fr(\alpha)$ then, by definition, $\exists t_u \in En(M), d_{ui} < 0$. It follows that $Dmin(t_i, M, F, \mu) = - \underset{t_u \in En(M)}{Min} d_{ui} > 0$. The trace ρ contains at least a transition and its first transition t_j is firable from α. A lower bound of the firing delay of t_i relatively to t_j is $Dmin(t_i, M, F, \mu)$. Therefore, $Dmin(t_i, M, F, \mu) \leq time(\rho t_i)$.

(1.c) If $t_i \in T - En(M)$ then the timed trace ρt_i contains at least, an input transition of t_i outside μ, for each not sufficiently marked input place of t_i. The minimal time needed to fire successively the transitions of ρ cannot be smaller than the minimal time needed for the enabledness of t_i by transitions outside μ, i.e., $Dmin(t_i, M, F, \mu) \leq time(\rho t_i)$.

(2) If $Dmin(t_i, M, F, \mu) = \infty$ then $\exists p \in {}^\bullet t_i, M(p) < pre(t_i)(p) \wedge ({}^\bullet p - \mu = \emptyset \vee (\forall t_j \in {}^\bullet p - \mu, Dmin(t_j, M, F, \mu \cup \{t_j\}) = \infty))$.

   (2.a) If $M(p) < pre(t_i)(p) \wedge {}^\bullet p - \mu = \emptyset$, then t_i is not potentially firable from α, without help from μ.

   (2.b) If $M(p) < pre(t_i)(p) \wedge \forall t_j \in {}^\bullet p - \mu, Dmin(t_j, M, F, \mu \cup \{t_j\}) = \infty$ then we repeat recursively the same development process for $Dmin(t_j, M, F, \mu \cup \{t_j\}) = \infty$, until reaching case 2.a). Consequently, t_i is not potentially firable from α.

(3) The proof is by induction on the length of the transition-paths leading to t_i and is immediate from the definitions of $Dmin(t_i, M, F, \mu)$ and $Dmin(t_i, M, F, \mu')$.

   Indeed, if $t_i \in En(M)$ then $Dmin(t_i, M, F, \mu) = Dmin(t_i, M, F, \mu')$.

   Otherwise, the proof is straightforward as, by induction, it holds that for each $t_j \in T$, s.t. $\exists p \in {}^\bullet t_i, M(p) < pre(t_i)(p) \wedge t_j \in {}^\bullet p - \mu'$, $Dmin(t_j, M, F, \mu' \cup \{t_j\}) \leq Dmin(t_j, M, F, \mu \cup \{t_j\})$. Since $\mu' \subseteq \mu$, it follows that ${}^\bullet p - \mu \subseteq {}^\bullet p - \mu'$ and then

   $$\underset{p \in {}^\bullet t_i \wedge M(p) < pre(t_i)(p)}{Max} \left(\underset{t_j \in {}^\bullet p - \mu'}{Min} Dmin(t_j, M, F, \mu' \cup \{t_j\}) + \downarrow Is(t_i) \right) \leq$$
   $$\underset{p \in {}^\bullet t_i \wedge M(p) < pre(t_i)(p)}{Max} \left(\underset{t_j \in {}^\bullet p - \mu}{Min} Dmin(t_j, M, F, \mu \cup \{t_j\}) + \downarrow Is(t_i) \right).$$

   Therefore, $Dmin(t_i, M, F, \mu') \leq Dmin(t_i, M, F, \mu)$.

(4) The proof is immediate from (1) and the fact that a transition must be maintained enabled at least $\downarrow Is(t_i)$ time units before it becomes firable. $\quad \square$

We provide in Lemmas 2 and 3 some sufficient conditions for persistency and effect-persistency for a transition from a marking or a state class w.r.t. a set of transitions.

Lemma 2. *Sufficient conditions for persistency and effect-persistency*
Let M be a marking and $t_i \in En(M)$.
1- The transition t_i is persistent from M if $\forall t_j \in En(M) - \{t_i\}$,

$$(i) \; \forall t_k \in CFS(t_i) - \{t_i\}, \; t_k \notin En(M) \wedge \bar{l}_{kj} = \infty.$$

Intuitively, (i) implies that all transitions in structural conflict with t_i are neither enabled in M nor enabled directly/indirectly by t_j.
2- The transition t_i is effect-persistent from M if $\forall t_j \in En(M) - \{t_i\}$, the both following conditions (i) and (ii) are satisfied:

$$(i) \; \forall t_k \in CFS(t_i) - \{t_i\}, \; t_k \notin En(M) \wedge \bar{l}_{kj} = \infty$$

$$(ii) \; \forall t_k \in T - \{t_i\}, (NwS(t_i) \cap (CFS(t_k) \cup NwS(t_k)) \neq \emptyset) \Rightarrow (t_k \notin En(M) \wedge \bar{l}_{kj} = \infty).$$

Intuitively, (ii) means that the effect of t_i can not be affected by firing any other transition t_k enabled in M or enabled directly/indirectly by t_j.

The proof is immediate from the fact $\bar{l}_{kj} = \infty$ means that t_j has no role in the enabledness of t_k.

Lemma 3. *Sufficient conditions for persistency and effect-persistency*
   Let $\alpha = (M, F)$ be a state class, $t_i \in En(M)$ and $\mu \subseteq T$ s.t. $t_i \in \mu$.
   1- The transition t_i is persistent from α w.r.t. μ if $\forall t_j \in Fr(\alpha) - \mu$,

(i) $\forall t_k \in CFS(t_i) - \mu$, $(\bar{l}_{kj} < \infty \vee t_k \in En(M)) \Rightarrow d_{ij} < Dmin(t_k, M, F, \mu \cup \{t_k\})$

Intuitively, (i) implies that each transition $t_k \in CFS(t_i) - \mu$ enabled in M or enabled directly/indirectly by t_j is not firable before all the transitions of μ.
2- The transition t_i is effect-persistent from α w.r.t. μ if $\forall t_j \in Fr(\alpha) - \mu$, the both following conditions (i) and (ii) are satisfied:

(i) $\forall t_k \in CFS(t_i) - \mu$, $(\bar{l}_{kj} < \infty \vee t_k \in En(M)) \Rightarrow d_{ij} < Dmin(t_k, M, F, \mu \cup \{t_k\})$.

(ii) $\forall t_k \in T - \mu, (\bar{l}_{kj} < \infty \vee t_k \in En(M)) \Rightarrow$

$$d_{ij} < Dmin(t_k, M, F, \mu \cup \{t_k\}) \vee (NwS(t_i) \cap (CFS(t_k) \cup NwS(t_k)) = \emptyset).$$

Intuitively, (ii) means that each transition $t_k \in T - \mu$, enabled in M or enabled directly/indirectly by t_j, is either not firable before all transitions of μ or its firing does not affect the effect of t_i.

Proof. It suffices to show that $d_{ij} < Dmin(t_k, M, F, \mu \cup \{t_k\})$ implies that t_k cannot be fired before t_i from α and all its direct/indirect successors by t_j, as long as no transition of μ is fired. First of all, according to the firing rule given in Sect. 2.2, it holds that for $t_j \in Fr(\alpha), d_{ij} \geq 0$. Suppose that $d_{ij} < Dmin(t_k, M, F, \mu \cup \{t_k\})$.

(1) If $Dmin(t_k, M, F, \mu \cup \{t_k\}) = \infty$ then according to Lemma 1, transition t_k is not firable directly/indirectly from α before the transitions of μ.
(2) If $Dmin(t_k, M, F, \mu \cup \{t_k\}) < \infty$ then according to Lemma 1:
$\forall s \in \alpha, \forall \rho \in (\mathbb{R}^+ \times T \times \mathbb{R}^+)^+ \cup \mathbb{R}^+$ s.t. $Tr(\rho) \in (T - \mu \cup \{t_k\})^* \wedge s \xrightarrow{\rho t_k}$
), $time(\rho t_k) \geq Dmin(t_k, M, F, \mu \cup \{t_k\})$.
   (2.a) If $Tr(\rho) = \epsilon$ then $t_k \in Fr(\alpha)$. It follows that
   $Dmin(t_k, M, F, \mu \cup \{t_k\}) = - \underset{t_u \in En(M)}{Min} d_{uk} = 0 \leq time(\rho t_k)$ and then
   $Dmin(t_k, M, F, \mu \cup \{t_k\}) \leq d_{ij}$, for $t_j \in Fr(\alpha)$, which is in contradiction with the assumption.
   (2.b) If $Tr(\rho) \neq \epsilon$ then the first transition of ρ is firable from α. Let t_j be this transition. Then, the maximal delay between the firing dates of t_i and t_j is d_{ij} as, in F, it holds that $\underline{t}_i - \underline{t}_j \leq d_{ij}$. Therefore, $d_{ij} < Dmin(t_k, M, F, \mu \cup \{t_k\})$ implies that t_k cannot be fired as long as no transition of μ is fired (see Fig. 2).

The rest of the proof is immediate. $\qquad\qquad\qquad\qquad\qquad\qquad\qquad\qquad\square$

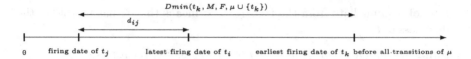

Fig. 2. Condition: $d_{ij} < Dmin(t_k, M, F, \mu \cup \{t_k\})$

Table 1. Some experimental results

TPN	RSCG'	RSCG	CSCG	SCG	TPN	RSCG'	RSCG	CSCG	SCG
KB(2) NSC	2975	7005	8542	9612	KB(3) NSC	18418	41200	45249	52597
NCSC	3853	9621	24247	27162	NCSC	26386	62471	145594	167451
CPU (s)	0	0	0	0	CPU (s)	0	0	0	0
HC(2) NSC	272	1377	3801	4325	HC(3) NSC	5222	6362	146851	168181
NCSC	345	514	10440	11819	NCSC	7824	10263	562486	643440
CPU (s)	0	0	0	0	CPU (s)	0	0	2.8	3.2
FMS(2) NSC	2819	7509	82665	91447	FMS(3) NSC	247459	392191	? > 2000000	? > 2000000
NCSC	3617	10416	233208	257080	NCSC	330988	565015		
CPU (s)	0	0	2.3	3.6	CPU (s)	4.3	7.3		
ForkJoin(2) NSC	2486	3465	11080	14360	ForkJoin(3) NSC	43816	68660	94645	119255
NCSC	3930	6607	32861	42385	NCSC	109286	185127	357449	456023
CPU (s)	0	0	1.2	1.7	CPU (s)	2.1	3.2	3.4	4.7

As discussed in Sect. 1, for a non persistent TPN, a reduced graph preserving the non-equivalent firing sequences of the TPN can be computed on-the-fly using the POSETs method and sufficient conditions of persistency and effect-persistency. These sufficient conditions of persistency and effect-persistency are used to select the subset of transitions to be fired from each state class. The ones used in [8,9] are based on the lower bounds $\bar{l}$. We report, in columns RSCG and RSCG' of Table 1, the results provided by the approach in [8] and those obtained by replacing in the sufficient conditions used in [8] the lower bounds $\bar{l}$ by $Dmin$. The models HouseConstruction (HC), FMS and Kanban (KB) are taken from the MCC (Model Checking Contest) held within Petri Nets conferences[5] and extended with firing intervals (see Table 2). The model ForkJoin is shown in Fig. 3. For each model and each graph (RSCG', RSCG, CSCG, SCG), the rows NSC, NCSC and CPU stand for the number of state classes, the number of computed state classes and the CPU time in seconds, respectively. For all the tested models, the RSCG' shows a reduction in size and time relatively to the others. However, further tests and investigation are needed to integrate more appropriately $Dmin$ and the sufficient conditions for persistency/effect-persistency established here, in a partial order reduction technique.

---

[5] http://mcc.lip6.fr.

Table 2. Static firing intervals of HC, FMS and KB

Is of HC	Is of FMS	Is of KB
$t_1[2,4]$, $t_2[2,3]$, $t_3[3,3]$	$tp_1[1,2]$, $tp_2[1,2]$, $tp_3[1,2]$	$tsynch4 - 23[1,3]$, $tsynch1 - 23[3,5]$
$t_4[1,1]$, $t_5[1,2]$, $t_6[1,2]$	$tm_1[1,1]$, $tm_2[3,4]$, $tp_3m_2[4,4]$	$tredo1[2,2]$, $tok1[3,4]$, $tback1[1,3]$
$t_7[3,3]$, $t_8[2,2]$, $t_9[1,1]$	$tp_3s[3,3]$, $tp_1m1[1,2]$, $tp_2m_2[1,1]$	$tout1[3,5]$, $tredo2[2,2]$, $tok2[3,4]$
$t_{10}[1,1]$, $t_{11}[1,2]$, $t_{12}[1,3]$	$tp_1e[5,5]$,$tp_1j[3,4]$, $tp_2j[1,1]$	$tback2[1,3]$, $tredo3[3,5]$,$tok3[2,2]$
$t_{13}[2,5]$, $t_{14}[2,2]$, $t_{15}[1,1]$	$tp_2e[1,1]$, $tp_1s[3,3]$, $tp_{12}[1,2]$	$tback3[3,4]$
$t_{16}[1,2]$, $t_{17}[1,1]$, $t_{18}[1,4]$	$tp_2s[4,4]$, $tm_3[1,1]$, $tp_{12}m_3[2,2]$	$tin4[1,3]$, $tredo4[3,5]$
	$tp_{12}s[5,5]$, $tx[2,2]$	$tback4[2,2]$, $tok4[3,4]$

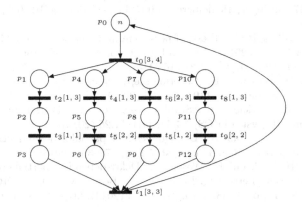

Fig. 3. Model $ForkJoin(n)$

4   Conclusion

In this paper, we have considered the TPN model and investigated the notion persistency and effect-persistency of transitions. According to its semantics, a TPN is persistent if its underlying non timed Petri net is persistent. Thus, all the sufficient conditions ensuring persistency for Petri nets are also valid for TPNs. However, the reverse is not true. A TPN can be persistent while its underlying non timed Petri net is not persistent. We have established some sufficient conditions for persistency and effect-persistency of different levels of permissiveness. The more permissive one takes into account more accurately the marking, the static and the dynamic time information of the TPN.

A nice feature of persistent TPNs is that the reachability analysis can be achieved by firing only one transition from each state class. The resulting reduced graph preserves the non-equivalent maximal firing sequences of the TPN.

For non persistent TPNs, the sufficient conditions for persistency and effect-persistency, proposed here, are less restrictive than the ones used in [7–9]. Therefore, they are useful to improve the partial order reduction techniques proposed in [7–9] for TPNs.

As future work, we will investigate more permissive sufficient conditions for persistency of TPNs.

References

1. Belluomini, W., Myers, C.J.: Timed state space exploration using POSETs. IEEE Tran. Comput.-Aided Des. Integr. Circuits **19**(5), 501–520 (2000)
2. Bengtsson, J.: Clocks, DBMs and states in timed systems. Ph.D. thesis, Department of Information Technology, Uppsala University (2002)
3. Bérard, B., Cassez, F., Haddad, S., Lime, D., Roux, O.H.: The expressive power of time Petri nets. Theor. Comput. Sci. **474**, 1–20 (2013)
4. Berthomieu, B., Vernadat, F.: State class constructions for branching analysis of time Petri nets. In: Garavel, H., Hatcliff, J. (eds.) TACAS 2003. LNCS, vol. 2619, pp. 442–457. Springer, Heidelberg (2003). https://doi.org/10.1007/3-540-36577-X_33
5. Best, E., Devillers, R.: Synthesis of persistent systems. In: Ciardo, G., Kindler, E. (eds.) PETRI NETS 2014. LNCS, vol. 8489, pp. 111–129. Springer, Cham (2014). https://doi.org/10.1007/978-3-319-07734-5_7
6. Boucheneb, H., Barkaoui, K.: Covering steps graphs of time Petri nets. Electron. Notes Theor. Comput. Sci. **239**, 155–165 (2009)
7. Boucheneb, H., Barkaoui, K.: Stubborn sets for time Petri nets. ACM Trans. Embed. Comput. Syst. (TECS) **14**(1), 11:1–11:25 (2015)
8. Boucheneb, H., Barkaoui, K.: Delay-dependent partial order reduction technique for real time systems. Real-Time Syst. **54**(2), 278–306 (2018)
9. Boucheneb, H., Barkaoui, K., Weslati, K.: Delay-dependent partial order reduction technique for time Petri nets. In: Legay, A., Bozga, M. (eds.) FORMATS 2014. LNCS, vol. 8711, pp. 53–68. Springer, Cham (2014). https://doi.org/10.1007/978-3-319-10512-3_5
10. Boucheneb, H., Gardey, G., Roux, O.H.: TCTL model checking of time Petri nets. Log. Comput. **19**(6), 1509–1540 (2009)
11. Boucheneb, H., Hadjidj, R.: CTL* model checking for time Petri nets. Theor. Comput. Sci. TCS **353**(1–3), 208–227 (2006)
12. Boucheneb, H., Lime, D., Roux, O.H.: On multi-enabledness in time Petri nets. In: Colom, J.-M., Desel, J. (eds.) PETRI NETS 2013. LNCS, vol. 7927, pp. 130–149. Springer, Heidelberg (2013). https://doi.org/10.1007/978-3-642-38697-8_8
13. Boucheneb, H., Rakkay, H.: A more efficient time Petri net state space abstraction useful to model checking timed linear properties. Fundam. Inform. **88**(4), 469–495 (2008)
14. Boyer, M., Diaz, M.: Multiple-enabledness of transitions in time Petri nets. In: 9th IEEE International Workshop on Petri Nets and Performance Models, pp. 219–228 (2001)
15. Best, E., Darondeau, P.: Decomposition theorems for bounded persistent Petri nets. In: van Hee, K.M., Valk, R. (eds.) PETRI NETS 2008. LNCS, vol. 5062, pp. 33–51. Springer, Heidelberg (2008). https://doi.org/10.1007/978-3-540-68746-7_7
16. Karp, R.M., Miller, R.E.: Parallel program schemata. J. Comput. Syst. Sci. **3**(2), 147–195 (1969)
17. Lilius, J.: Efficient state space search for time Petri nets. In: MFCS Workshop on Concurrency Algorithms and Tools, ENTCS, vol. 8, pp. 113–133 (1998)
18. Lugiez, D., Niebert, P., Zennou, S.: A partial order semantics approach to the clock explosion problem of timed automata. Theor. Comput. Sci. TCS **345**(1), 2759 (2005)
19. Yoneda, T., Ryuba, H.: CTL model checking of time Petri nets using geometric regions. EICE Trans. Inf. Syst. **E99–D**(3), 297–306 (1998)
20. Yoneda, T., Schlingloff, B.H.: Efficient verification of parallel real-time systems. Form. Methods Syst. Des. **11**(2), 187–215 (1997)

A Relational Model for Probabilistic Connectors Based on Timed Data Distribution Streams

Meng Sun[(✉)] and Xiyue Zhang

Department of Informatics and LMAM, School of Mathematical Sciences,
Peking University, Beijing, China
{sunm,zhangxiyue}@pku.edu.cn

Abstract. Connectors have shown their great potential for coordination of concurrent activities encapsulated as components and services in large-scale distributed applications. In this paper, we develop a formal model for a probabilistic extension of the channel-based coordination language Reo. The model formalizes connectors with probabilistic behavior as relations on *Timed Data Distribution Streams* (TDDSs), which specifies properties of primitive channels and complex connectors with probabilistic behavior properly. Furthermore, the implementation of this probabilistic model has been developed in Coq, which serves to demonstrate how the model can be used to prove probabilistic connectors' properties.

Keywords: Coordination · Probabilistic connector
Timed data distribution streams · Coq

1 Introduction

Coordination models that formalize the interaction among different components play a key role in the development of large-scale distributed applications, which are typically heterogeneous and geographically distributed over the internet. Such coordination models usually provide a notion of *connectors* that interconnect the components and organize the mutual interactions and communications among them in a distributed environment, where complex connectors can be compositionally constructed out of simpler ones. As an example, Reo [2,8] offers a powerful gluing mechanism for the implementation of such coordinating connectors. Primitive connectors called *channels* in Reo, such as synchronous channels, FIFO channels and timer channels, can be composed to build circuit-like connectors which serve as the glue code to exogenously coordinate the behavior of components in distributed applications.

Investigating probabilistic behavior of connectors precisely is a necessary task for developing trustworthy applications. In this paper we focus on the probabilistic aspects of Reo connectors, and provide a formal model for connectors built out of channels that might behave nondeterministically and probabilistically, such

© Springer Nature Switzerland AG 2018
D. N. Jansen and P. Prabhakar (Eds.): FORMATS 2018, LNCS 11022, pp. 125–141, 2018.
https://doi.org/10.1007/978-3-030-00151-3_8

as unreliable FIFO channels that may loose certain data items written to the buffer, or synchronous channels that may corrupt written data with some small probability. In this model, the behavior of channels (and connectors) are specified as relations of observations on the channel ends (and sink/source nodes of connectors) given by timed data distribution streams. And we also show how the model of probabilistic channels can be used in the construction of more complex connectors with probabilistic behavior. Furthermore, the model for probabilistic channels/connectors has been encoded in Coq [18] which forms an extension to our previous work on modeling and verifying connectors in Coq [13,20], and properties of such probabilistic connectors can be formally proved using Coq.

This is in fact not the first investigation on probabilistic connectors. An operational semantics for probabilistic Reo in terms of probabilistic constraint automata (PCA) has been developed by Baier in [7]. Later the Quantitative Intentional Automata (QIA) model was proposed in [5] to capture the operational semantics of connectors with stochastic behavior. The QIA model correctly captures context dependency, but it is not compositional and suffers from state explosion heavily even for simple connectors. Another model called Stochastic Timed Automata for Reo (STA_r) was developed in [15] to support both stochastic and real-time behavior of connectors in Reo. In [16], Interactive Markov Chains are adopted as a compositional semantic model for stochastic Reo connectors. The Priced Probabilistic Timed Constraint Automata model [12] enables users to reason about both probabilistic and timed behavior, as well as resource consumption. Although some of such state-based models scale up quite well, state explosion is an inherent problem in these formalisms and not avoidable by the probabilistic extension. Furthermore, modeling unbounded primitives or even bounded primitives with unbounded data domains is impossible with finite automata models, and infinite or finite but large data domains usually also cause an explosion of state space in such state-based models which becomes seriously problematic for verification.

As shown in [13,20], specifying connectors as relations on its sink and source nodes makes it possible to verify connector properties by using theorem proving techniques and we do not have to face the state space explosion problem. Properties of a complex connector can be decomposed into some subgoals which can be proved separately in theorem provers like Coq, where relations on the nodes are specified by predicates [20]. Furthermore, comparing with other works on (both deterministic and probabilistic) Reo semantics [14], our framework defines two ternary channels *replicator* and *merger*, which makes different types of connector composition operators reduced to one single flow-through composition, and thus the composition of connectors can be interpreted more explicitly than other approaches, such as TDS in the coalgebraic semantics [6]. And by separating input and output explicitly in this model, the behavior of a connector becomes easier to be described and further composed.

The paper is structured as follows. After this general introduction, we briefly summarize the coordination language Reo in Sect. 2. Section 3 presents the model of observations on the nodes of connectors with probabilistic behavior as timed data distribution streams. Section 4 specifies the model for basic (untimed and timed) Reo channels, as well as channels with probabilistic behavior, and summarizes the composing operations to build connectors from channels. In Sect. 5, we discuss the implementation of the model in Coq, and show how to prove properties of connectors. Finally, Sect. 6 concludes with some further research directions.

2 A Reo Primer

In this section, we briefly review some basic concepts in the coordination language Reo. Reo [2] is a channel-based exogenous coordination language wherein complex coordinators, called *connectors*, are compositionally constructed from simpler ones. We summarize only the main concepts in Reo here. Further details can be found in [2,8].

Sync	LossySync	FIFO1	SyncDrain	t-Timer
Channel	Channel	Channel	Channel	Channel

Fig. 1. Some basic channels in Reo

A Reo connector usually consists of a network of primitive connectors, called *channels*. A connector provides the protocol that controls and organizes the communication and cooperation among different components. Each channel has two *channel ends*. There are two types of channel ends: *source* and *sink*. A source channel end accepts data into its channel, and a sink channel end dispenses data out of its channel. It is possible for the ends of a channel to be both sinks or both sources. Figure 1 shows the graphical representation of some basic channel types in Reo whose composition allows for expressing a rich set of coordination patterns [2,3].

A *synchronous channel* has a source and a sink end. It accepts a data item through its source end iff it can simultaneously dispense the data item through its sink end. A *lossy synchronous channel* is similar to a synchronous channel except that it always accepts all data items through its source end. The data item is transferred if it is possible to be dispensed through the sink end immediately, otherwise the data item is lost. A *FIFO1 channel* represents an asynchronous channel with one buffer cell which is empty initially (this is the case in Fig. 1). If a data element d is written through the source end, it is kept in the buffer of the FIFO1 channel until being taken out through the sink end. *Synchronous drain* has two source ends and no sink end. A synchronous drain can accept a data item through one of its ends iff a data item is also available for it to simultaneously accept through the other end as well, and both data items accepted by the channel are lost. A *t-timer* channel accepts any data item at its source end and produces a *timeout* signal after a delay of t time units on its sink end.

More exotic channels permitted in Reo are omitted here and can be found in
[2,3,17]. Moreover, the set of channel types is not fixed in Reo, and new ones
can be defined freely by users according to their own interaction policies, like
the probabilistic and stochastic extensions defined in [7,9,15].

Complex connectors are constructed by composing simpler ones via the *join*
and *hiding* operations. Channels are joined together in nodes. A node consists
of a set of channel ends. The set of channel ends coincident on a node A is
disjointly partitioned into the sets of source and sink channel ends. Nodes are
categorized into *source*, *sink* and *mixed nodes* as shown in Fig. 2, depending on
whether all channel ends that coincide on a node are source ends, sink ends
or a combination of the two. The hiding operation is used to hide the internal
topology of a connector. The hidden nodes can no longer be accessed or observed
from outside. The behavior of a complex connector is formalized by means of
the data-flow at its sink and source nodes.

Fig. 2. Three types of nodes

A component can write data items to a source node that it is connected
to. The write operation succeeds only if all (source) channel ends coincident on
the node accept the data item, in which case the data item is transparently
written to every source end coincident on the node. A source node, thus, acts as
a replicator. A component can obtain data items, by an input operation, from a
sink node that it is connected to. A take operation succeeds only if at least one
of the (sink) channel ends coincident on the node offers a suitable data item.
A sink node, thus, acts as a merger. A mixed node takes a suitable data item
offered by one of its coincident sink channel ends and replicates it into all of its
coincident source channel ends.

3   Observations as Timed Data Distribution Streams

Let D be an arbitrary finite set, the elements of which are called data elements.
It will be concrete when a specific application domain is provided. We use the
symbol $\bot \in D$ to denote a corrupted data item. A *data distribution* is a total
function that maps D to the closed interval of reals $[0, 1]$. We define

$$\mathbf{PROB} =_{df} D \to [0, 1]$$

where for any member p of $\mathbf{PROB}$ the total sum of probabilities must not exceed
1: $\sum_{d \in D} p(d) \leq 1$. For any $X \subseteq D$, $p(X) = \sum_{d \in X} p(d)$. We use $\mathbf{0}$ to denote the
zero distribution $\lambda d \bullet 0$ and define

$$p_1 \leq p_2 =_{df} \forall d \in D \bullet (p_1(d) \leq p_2(d))$$

For any $p \in \mathbf{PROB}$, we have $0 \leq p$. And for any $d \in D$, we have a corresponding point distribution:
$$\eta_d =_{df} \lambda x : D \bullet (1 \triangleleft x = d \triangleright 0)$$
where the conditional expression $P \triangleleft b \triangleright Q$ equals to P if the condition b is satisfied and Q otherwise.

The set DDS of data distribution streams is defined as $DDS = \mathbf{PROB}^\omega$, i.e., the set of all sequences $\alpha = (\alpha(0), \alpha(1), \alpha(2), \cdots)$ over $\mathbf{PROB}$ where each $\alpha(i)$ is a data distribution.

Let $\mathbb{R}_+$ be the set of non-negative real numbers, which in the present context can be used to represent time moments. Let $\mathbb{R}_+^\omega$ be the set of infinite sequences $a = (a(0), a(1), a(2), \cdots)$ over $\mathbb{R}_+$, and for all a, b in $\mathbb{R}_+^\omega$,

$$a < b \qquad \text{iff} \qquad \forall n \geq 0, a(n) < b(n)$$
$$a \leq b \qquad \text{iff} \qquad \forall n \geq 0, a(n) \leq b(n)$$

For a sequence $a = (a(0), a(1), a(2), \cdots) \in \mathbb{R}_+^\omega$, and $t \in \mathbb{R}_+$, $a[+t]$ is a sequence defined as follows:

$$a[+t] = (a(0) + t, a(1) + t, a(2) + t, \cdots)$$

Furthermore, the element $a(n)$ in a sequence $a = (a(0), a(1), a(2), \cdots)$ can also be expressed in terms of derivatives $a(n) = a^{(n)}(0)$, where $a^{(n)}$ is defined by

$$a^{(0)} = a, \ a^{(1)} = (a(1), a(2), \cdots), \ a^{(k+1)} = (a^{(k)})^{(1)}$$

and sometimes we use a' instead of $a^{(1)}$ for simplicity.

The set TS of time streams is defined as

$$TS = \{a \in \mathbb{R}_+^\omega \mid (\forall n \geq 0.a(n) < a(n+1)) \wedge (\forall t \in \mathbb{R}_+.\exists k \in \mathbb{N}.a(k) > t)\}$$

Thus, a time stream $a \in TS$ consists of increasing and diverging time moments: $a(0) < a(1) < a(2) < \cdots$ and $\lim_{n \to +\infty} a(n) = +\infty$.

To specify inputs and outputs on connectors explicitly, for a connector $\mathbf{R}$, we use the mappings

$$in_\mathbf{R} : \mathcal{N}_{in} \to TDDS$$
$$out_\mathbf{R} : \mathcal{N}_{out} \to TDDS$$

to denote the observations on its source nodes and sink nodes, respectively. Here $\mathcal{N}_{in}$ and $\mathcal{N}_{out}$ are the sets of source and sink node names of $\mathbf{R}$, respectively. For every node N in a connector $\mathbf{R}$, the corresponding observation on N is specified by a *timed data distribution stream*, and $TDDS$ is the set of *timed data distribution streams* defined as $TDDS \subseteq DDS \times TS$, which is the set of pairs $\langle \alpha, a \rangle$ consisting of a data distribution stream α and a time stream a. Similar to the timed data sequence model used in [17], timed data distribution streams can be alternatively and equivalently defined as (a subset of) $(\mathbf{PROB} \times \mathbb{R}_+)^\omega$ because of the existence of the isomorphism

$$\langle \alpha, a \rangle \mapsto (\langle \alpha(0), a(0) \rangle, \langle \alpha(1), a(1) \rangle, \langle \alpha(2), a(2) \rangle, \cdots)$$

The occurrence of a data transfer at some node N of a connector is modeled by an element in the timed data distribution stream for that node, i.e., a pair of a data distribution $\alpha(i)$ and a time moment $a(i)$ when the data item is observed.

4 Relations on Timed Data Distribution Streams for Connectors

In this section we provide an overview on how channels and connectors can be formally modeled by relations of timed data distribution streams observed on the channel ends and sink/source nodes. We first see how primitive channels in Reo are specified by such relations, and then study the model of probabilistic channels. Finally we show how composite connectors can be constructed from simpler ones structurally.

We use $\mathcal{WD}$ as a predicate for well-defined TDDS types. In other words, we define the behavior only for valid streams expressed via the predicate $\mathcal{WD}$. Then, every connector $\mathbf{R}$ can be represented as follows:

$$
\begin{aligned}
\mathbf{con}: \quad & \mathbf{R}(in:in_{\mathbf{R}};out:out_{\mathbf{R}}) \\
\mathbf{in}: \quad & P(in_{\mathbf{R}}) \\
\mathbf{out}: \quad & Q(in_{\mathbf{R}},out_{\mathbf{R}})
\end{aligned}
$$

where $\mathbf{R}$ is the name of the connector, $P(in_{\mathbf{R}})$ is the condition that should be satisfied by inputs $in_{\mathbf{R}}$ on the source nodes of $\mathbf{R}$, and $Q(in_{\mathbf{R}},out_{\mathbf{R}})$ is the condition that should be satisfied by outputs $out_{\mathbf{R}}$ on the sink nodes of $\mathbf{R}$.

Furthermore, to capture the probabilistic behavior of connectors, we use $P_\tau \oplus Q$ to indicate that the probability for $P_\tau \oplus Q$ to be equal to P is τ, and the probability for $P_\tau \oplus Q$ to be equal to Q is $1-\tau$. And we use $P_1 @\tau_1 \,|\, P_2 @\tau_2 \,|\, \cdots \,|\, P_n @\tau_n$ or

$$
\begin{cases}
P_1 & @\tau_1 \\
P_2 & @\tau_2 \\
\cdots & \\
P_n & @\tau_n
\end{cases}
$$

to represent the probabilistic choice over multiple alternatives, in which the probabilities are enumerated and sum to no more than 1: $\sum_{1 \le i \le n} \tau_i \le 1$.

4.1 Primitive Reo Channels

We now start by presenting a few examples of basic channels in Reo and their corresponding models in the probabilistic setting.

The simplest form of an asynchronous channel is a FIFO channel with one buffer cell, which is denoted as **FIFO1**. A **FIFO1** channel with source end A

and sink end B is graphically represented by $A-\square\!\!\mapsto B$. The corresponding model is given as follows:

$$\mathbf{con}: \quad \mathbf{FIFO1}(in : (A \mapsto \langle \alpha, a \rangle); out : (B \mapsto \langle \beta, b \rangle))$$
$$\mathbf{in}: \quad \mathcal{WD}\langle \alpha, a \rangle$$
$$\mathbf{out}: \quad \mathcal{WD}\langle \beta, b \rangle \wedge \beta = \alpha \wedge a < b < a'$$

For a **FIFO1** channel, when the buffer is not filled, the input is accepted without immediately outputting it. The accepted data item is kept in the internal FIFO buffer of the channel. The next input can happen only after an output occurs. Note that the probabilistic distribution of every output data value over D is exactly the same as the distribution on the corresponding input, i.e., $\beta = \alpha$. Furthermore, we use $a < b < a'$ to represent the relation between the time moments for outputs and their corresponding (and next) inputs.

For the **FIFO1** channel $A-\boxed{e}\!\!\mapsto B$ where the buffer contains a data element e initially, the communication can be initiated only if the data element e can be taken through the sink end. So the first data distribution that happens on the sink end is exactly η_e, and the following ones are the same as those observed on the source end. In this case, we denote the channel by **FIFO1**$[e]$ as follows[1]:

$$\mathbf{con}: \quad \mathbf{FIFO1}[e](in : (A \mapsto \langle \alpha, a \rangle); out : (B \mapsto \langle \beta, b \rangle))$$
$$\mathbf{in}: \quad \mathcal{WD}\langle \alpha, a \rangle$$
$$\mathbf{out}: \quad \mathcal{WD}\langle \beta, b \rangle \wedge \beta = (\eta_e)^\frown \alpha \wedge b < a < b'$$

A synchronous channel transfers the data without any delay in time. So it behaves just like the identity function. The pair of I/O operations on its two ends can succeed only simultaneously. A synchronous channel with source end A and sink end B is graphically represented as $A \longrightarrow B$ and formally specified as follows:

$$\mathbf{con}: \quad \mathbf{Sync}(in : (A \mapsto \langle \alpha, a \rangle); out : (B \mapsto \langle \beta, b \rangle))$$
$$\mathbf{in}: \quad \mathcal{WD}\langle \alpha, a \rangle$$
$$\mathbf{out}: \quad \mathcal{WD}\langle \beta, b \rangle \wedge \beta = \alpha \wedge b = a$$

A lossy synchronous channel (graphically depicted as $A-\!\rightarrow B$) is similar to a normal synchronous channel, except that it always accepts all data items through its source end. If it is possible for it to simultaneously dispense the data item through its sink end, the channel transfers the data item; otherwise the data item is lost.

$$\mathbf{con}: \quad \mathbf{LossySync}(in : (A \mapsto \langle \alpha, a \rangle); out : (B \mapsto \langle \beta, b \rangle))$$
$$\mathbf{in}: \quad \mathcal{WD}\langle \alpha, a \rangle$$
$$\mathbf{out}: \quad \mathcal{WD}\langle \beta, b \rangle \wedge L(\langle \alpha, a \rangle, \langle \beta, b \rangle)$$

---

[1] Here $\frown$ is the concatenation operator on sequences. The concatenation of two sequences produces a new sequence that starts with the first sequence followed by the second sequence.

where

$$L(\langle \alpha, a\rangle, \langle \beta, b\rangle)$$
$$\equiv (\beta = (\ ) \wedge b = (\ )) \vee (a(0) \le b(0) \wedge$$
$$(L(\langle \alpha', a'\rangle, \langle \beta', b'\rangle) \wedge \alpha(0) = \beta(0)) \triangleleft a(0) = b(0) \triangleright L(\langle \alpha', a'\rangle, \langle \beta, b\rangle)))$$

The synchronous drain $A \rightarrowtail\!\!\!\leftarrow B$ is an exotic Reo channel that has two source ends A and B. Because a drain has no sink end, no data value can ever be obtained from this channel. Thus, all data accepted by this channel are lost. A synchronous drain can only accept two data items through both of its ends simultaneously.

> **con :** **SyncDrain**$(in : (A \mapsto \langle \alpha, a\rangle, B \mapsto \langle \beta, b\rangle); out : (\ ))$
>
> **in :** $\mathcal{WD}\langle \alpha, a\rangle \wedge \mathcal{WD}\langle \beta, b\rangle \wedge a = b$
>
> **out :** **true**

A filter channel $A \multimap\!\!\{p\}\!\!\to B$ specifies a filter pattern p which is a set of data values. It transfers only those data items that are matched with the pattern p and loses the rest. A write operation on the source end succeeds only if either the data item to be written does not match the pattern p or the data item matches the pattern p and it can be taken synchronously via the sink end of the channel.

> **con :** **Filter**$[p](in : (A \mapsto \langle \alpha, a\rangle); out : (B \mapsto \langle \beta, b\rangle))$
>
> **in :** $\mathcal{WD}\langle \alpha, a\rangle$
>
> **out :** $\mathcal{WD}\langle \beta, b\rangle \wedge F(\langle \alpha, a\rangle, \langle \beta, b\rangle)$

where

$$F(\langle \alpha, a\rangle, \langle \beta, b\rangle)$$
$$\equiv \begin{cases} \beta = (\ ) \wedge b = (\ ) & \text{if } \alpha = (\ ) \wedge a = (\ ) \\ \beta(0) = \alpha(0) \wedge b(0) = a(0) \wedge F(\langle \alpha', a'\rangle, \langle \beta', b'\rangle) & \text{if } \alpha(0) \in p \\ F(\langle \alpha', a'\rangle, \langle \beta, b\rangle) & \text{if } \alpha(0) \notin p \end{cases}$$

The source end of a t-timer $A \overset{t}{\multimap\!\!\to} B$ channel accepts any input value d and returns on its sink end B a *timeout* signal after a delay of t time units, where t is provided as a parameter of the channel.

> **con :** **Timer**$[t](in : (A \mapsto \langle \alpha, a\rangle); out : (B \mapsto \langle \beta, b\rangle))$
>
> **in :** $\mathcal{WD}\langle \alpha, a\rangle \wedge a[+t] \le a'$
>
> **out :** $\mathcal{WD}\langle \beta, b\rangle \wedge \beta \in \{\eta_{timeout}\}^{\omega} \wedge b = a[+t]$

4.2 Probabilistic Channels

A family of channels with probabilistic behavior are specified in the following.

A *faulty FIFO1 channel* $A \cdot \overset{\tau}{\cdot} \square \hspace{-0.3em}\rightarrow B$ might loose messages while inserting them into the buffer. Any write operation on the source end A might fail with probability τ in which case the buffer remains empty, or might be successful with probability $1 - \tau$.

> **con :** $\mathbf{FtyFIFO1}[\tau](in : (A \mapsto \langle \alpha, a \rangle); out : (B \mapsto \langle \beta, b \rangle))$
>
> **in :** $\mathcal{WD}\langle \alpha, a \rangle$
>
> **out :** $\mathcal{WD}\langle \beta, b \rangle \wedge FF(\langle \alpha, a \rangle, \langle \beta, b \rangle)$

where

$$FF(\langle \alpha, a \rangle, \langle \beta, b \rangle) \equiv \begin{cases} a(0) < b(0) < a(1) \wedge \beta(0) = \alpha(0) \wedge \\ \quad FF(\langle \alpha', a' \rangle, \langle \beta', b' \rangle) & @1 - \tau \\ a(1) < b(0) < a(2) \wedge \beta(0) = \alpha(1) \wedge \\ \quad FF(\langle \alpha^{(2)}, a^{(2)} \rangle, \langle \beta', b' \rangle) & @\tau(1 - \tau) \\ \cdots \\ a(k-1) < b(0) < a(k) \wedge \beta(0) = \alpha(k-1) \wedge \\ \quad FF(\langle \alpha^{(k)}, a^{(k)} \rangle, \langle \beta', b' \rangle) & @\tau^{k-1}(1 - \tau) \\ \cdots \\ \beta = () \wedge b = () & @\lim_{n \to \infty} \tau^n \end{cases}$$

In other words, there are infinite alternatives when we consider infinite streams on the input and the probability for $\beta = () \wedge b = ()$ is $\lim_{n \to \infty} \tau^n = 0$.

Another kind of faulty FIFO1 channel $A \hspace{-0.3em}\longrightarrow\hspace{-0.9em}\square\hspace{-0.4em} \cdot \overset{\tau}{\cdot}\hspace{-0.3em}\rightarrow B$ might loose messages from its buffer, but works perfectly for the write operation on the source end A. The difference between this channel and **FtyFIFO1** is the possibilities for the data items to be successfully stored in the buffer and to be successfully taken from the buffer to the sink end, but the models which specify the relations between observations on input and output channel ends for these two channels are exactly the same.

A *message-corrupting synchronous channel* $A - \tau \rightarrow B$ is a synchronous channel with source node A and sink node B where the delivered message is corrupted with probability τ. The value τ serves as a parameter for this channel type. If A accepts a data item, then with probability $1 - \tau$ the correct data value is obtained at B, but with probability τ, B takes a corrupted message $\perp$.

> **con :** $\mathbf{CptSync}[\tau](in : (A \mapsto \langle \alpha, a \rangle); out : (B \mapsto \langle \beta, b \rangle))$
>
> **in :** $\mathcal{WD}\langle \alpha, a \rangle$
>
> **out :** $\mathcal{WD}\langle \beta, b \rangle \wedge b = a \wedge C(\alpha, \beta)$

where

$$C(\alpha, \beta) \equiv ((\beta(0) = \eta_\perp)_\tau \oplus (\beta(0) = \alpha(0))) \wedge C(\alpha', \beta')$$

A *randomized synchronous channel* $A \overset{rand(0,1)}{\longrightarrow} B$ generates a random number $b \in \{0, 1\}$ when it is activated through an arbitrary writing action at its source end A, and the random number is synchronously taken through the sink end B.

> **con :**   **RdmSync**$[rand(0,1)](in : (A \mapsto \langle \alpha, a \rangle); out : (B \mapsto \langle \beta, b \rangle))$
>
> **in :** $\mathcal{WD}\langle \alpha, a \rangle$
>
> **out :** $\mathcal{WD}\langle \beta, b \rangle \wedge b = a \wedge R(\alpha, \beta)$

where

$$R(\alpha, \beta) \equiv ((\beta(0) = \eta_0)_{\frac{1}{2}} \oplus (\beta(0) = \eta_1)) \wedge R(\alpha', \beta')$$

A *probabilistic lossy synchronous channel* $A \overset{\tau}{-\!-\!-\!\to} B$ requires both channel ends A and B to be available to synchronize. However, the transmission of the message fails with a certain probability τ, while the correct message passing occurs with probability $1 - \tau$.

> **con :**   **ProbLossy**$[\tau](in : (A \mapsto \langle \alpha, a \rangle); out : (B \mapsto \langle \beta, b \rangle))$
>
> **in :** $\mathcal{WD}\langle \alpha, a \rangle$
>
> **out :** $\mathcal{WD}\langle \beta, b \rangle \wedge PL(\langle \alpha, a \rangle, \langle \beta, b \rangle)$

where

$$PL(\langle \alpha, a \rangle, \langle \beta, b \rangle)$$
$$\equiv PL(\langle \alpha', a' \rangle, \langle \beta, b \rangle)_\tau \oplus ((b(0) = a(0)) \wedge (\beta(0) = \alpha(0)) \wedge PL(\langle \alpha', a' \rangle, \langle \beta', b' \rangle))$$

This channel type has to be not confused with the non-probabilistic lossy synchronous channel (depicted by a dashed line without any parameter).

4.3   Composition Operators

Different channels can be composed by linking their channel ends together into nodes to build more complex connectors. The formalization of nodes sometimes becomes rather complicated, especially when an arbitrary number of incoming and outgoing edges are involved. Therefore, we introduce two ternary channels *Replicator* and *Merger*, as shown in Fig. 3, and use their combinations to capture the behavior of arbitrary source, sink or mixed nodes.

Fig. 3. Replicator and merger

Replicator is a synchronous broadcasting channel with one source end A and two sink ends B, C. The channel accepts input data values from A, and broadcasts them to B, C iff both B and C are ready to accept the data.

$$\textbf{con}: \quad \textbf{Replicator}(in : (A \mapsto \langle \alpha, a \rangle); out : (B \mapsto \langle \beta, b \rangle, C \mapsto \langle \gamma, c \rangle))$$

$$\textbf{in}: \quad \mathcal{WD}\langle \alpha, a \rangle$$

$$\textbf{out}: \quad \mathcal{WD}\langle \beta, b \rangle \wedge \mathcal{WD}\langle \gamma, c \rangle \wedge \beta = \gamma = \alpha \wedge b = c = a$$

Merger is a channel that has two source ends A, B and one sink end C, which collects inputs from either A or B and sends them to C simultaneously if C is ready to accept the data.

$$\textbf{con}: \quad \textbf{Merger}(in : (A \mapsto \langle \alpha, a \rangle, B \mapsto \langle \beta, b \rangle); out : (C \mapsto \langle \gamma, c \rangle))$$

$$\textbf{in}: \quad \mathcal{WD}\langle \alpha, a \rangle \wedge \mathcal{WD}\langle \beta, b \rangle \wedge \mathcal{DF}(a, b)$$

$$\textbf{out}: \quad \mathcal{WD}\langle \gamma, c \rangle \wedge M(\langle \alpha, a \rangle, \langle \beta, b \rangle, \langle \gamma, c \rangle)$$

where

$$\mathcal{DF}(a, b) =_{df} a(0) \neq b(0) \wedge \begin{cases} \mathcal{DF}(a', b) & \text{if } a(0) < b(0) \\ \mathcal{DF}(a, b') & \text{if } a(0) > b(0) \end{cases}$$

and the ternary relation M is defined as

$$M(\langle \alpha, a \rangle, \langle \beta, b \rangle, \langle \gamma, c \rangle)$$
$$= \begin{cases} \gamma(0) = \alpha(0) \wedge c(0) = a(0) \wedge M(\langle \alpha', a' \rangle, \langle \beta, b \rangle, \langle \gamma', c' \rangle) & \text{if } a(0) < b(0) \\ \gamma(0) = \beta(0) \wedge c(0) = b(0) \wedge M(\langle \alpha, a \rangle, \langle \beta', b' \rangle, \langle \gamma', c' \rangle) & \text{if } a(0) > b(0) \end{cases}$$

Once we have the replicator and merger defined as channels as well, the only composition operator for connectors is *flow-through*. For two connectors $\textbf{R}_1$ and $\textbf{R}_2$, suppose one sink node of $\textbf{R}_1$ and one source node of $\textbf{R}_2$ are joined together into a new node. In this case, the new node becomes a *mixed node* which behaves as a self-contained pumping station. When we compose connectors, the events on the mixed nodes happen silently and automatically whenever they can, without the participation or even the knowledge of the environment. Such mixed nodes are hidden (encapsulated) by using the existential quantifier.

For $i = 1, 2$, let

$$\textbf{con}: \quad \textbf{R}_i(in : in_{\textbf{R}_i}; out : out_{\textbf{R}_i})$$

$$\textbf{in}: \quad P_i(in_{\textbf{R}_i})$$

$$\textbf{out}: \quad Q_i(in_{\textbf{R}_i}, out_{\textbf{R}_i})$$

denote the two connectors being composed by the flow-through composition. Suppose one sink node B_1 of $\textbf{R}_1$ and one source node B_2 of $\textbf{R}_2$ are joined together into a mixed node B. Let $B_1 \mapsto \langle \beta_1, b_1 \rangle \in out_{\textbf{R}_1}$ and $B_2 \mapsto \langle \beta_2, b_2 \rangle \in in_{\textbf{R}_2}$ be the output on the node B_1 in $\textbf{R}_1$ and input on the node B_2 in $\textbf{R}_2$, respectively. Then the new connector is denoted by $\textbf{R} = \textbf{R}_{1;(B_1, B_2) \mapsto B}\textbf{R}_2$, and defined as follows:

con : $\mathbf{R}(in : (\bigcup_{i=1,2} in_{\mathbf{R}_i}) \setminus \{B_2 \mapsto \langle \beta_2, b_2 \rangle\}; out : (\bigcup_{i=1,2} out_{\mathbf{R}_i}) \setminus \{B_1 \mapsto \langle \beta_1, b_1 \rangle\})$

in : $P_1(in_{\mathbf{R}_1}) \wedge \neg(\exists \langle \beta, b \rangle . (Q_1(in_{\mathbf{R}_1}, out_{\mathbf{R}_1})[\langle \beta, b \rangle / \langle \beta_1, b_1 \rangle] \wedge$
$\neg P_2(in_{\mathbf{R}_2})[\langle \beta, b \rangle / \langle \beta_2, b_2 \rangle]))$

out : $\exists \langle \beta, b \rangle . Q_1(in_{\mathbf{R}_1}, out_{\mathbf{R}_1})[\langle \beta, b \rangle / \langle \beta_1, b_1 \rangle] \wedge Q_2(in_{\mathbf{R}_2}, out_{\mathbf{R}_2})[\langle \beta, b \rangle / \langle \beta_2, b_2 \rangle]$

where for a predicate P, if v is a variable in P, $P[u/v]$ is the predicate obtained by replacing all occurrences of v in P by u.

Example 1. We consider the randomized router given in Fig. 4 as a simple example. This connector has one source node A and two sink nodes B and C, which randomly chooses B or C (both with probability $\frac{1}{2}$) to obtain the data written at A. It is constructed by composing two synchronous channels, two filter channels, two synchronous drains, two lossy synchronous channels and one randomized synchronous channel. This connector can be easily obtained from the composition of the basic channels (with replicators at A, D, E, G) after some equivalent transformations and quantifier eliminations:

con : $\mathbf{RandRouter}(in : (A \mapsto \langle \alpha, a \rangle); out : (B \mapsto \langle \beta, b \rangle, C \mapsto \langle \gamma, c \rangle))$

in : $\mathcal{WD}\langle \alpha, a \rangle$

out : $\mathcal{WD}\langle \beta, b \rangle \wedge \mathcal{WD}\langle \gamma, c \rangle \wedge RR(\langle \alpha, a \rangle, \langle \beta, b \rangle, \langle \gamma, c \rangle)$

where

$$RR(\langle \alpha, a \rangle, \langle \beta, b \rangle, \langle \gamma, c \rangle)$$
$$\equiv (\beta(0) = \alpha(0) \wedge b(0) = a(0) \wedge RR(\langle \overrightarrow{\alpha}, \overrightarrow{a} \rangle, \langle \overrightarrow{\beta}, \overrightarrow{b} \rangle, \langle \gamma, c \rangle))_{\frac{1}{2}} \oplus$$
$$(\gamma(0) = \alpha(0) \wedge c(0) = a(0) \wedge RR(\langle \overrightarrow{\alpha}, \overrightarrow{a} \rangle, \langle \beta, b \rangle, \langle \overrightarrow{\gamma}, \overrightarrow{c} \rangle)))$$

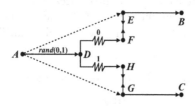

Fig. 4. Random router

5 Implementation

The implementation of this relational model for probabilistic connectors has been developed in Coq. Coq is a widely-used formal proof management system which provides a formal language called *Gallina* to write definitions, mathematical propositions and theorems, together with an environment for interactive construction of formal proofs. One of the main advantages of using Coq is that it is equipped with a set of well-developed standard libraries. For example, *Stream* provides a co-inductive definition of infinite sequences, *Reals* defines various operations and axioms on real numbers, and *Utheory* axiomatizes the properties required on the abstract type U representing the real interval $[0, 1]$. In general, quite a few axioms and theorems are predefined in such libraries. This makes it easy to support continuous time behavior and describe probabilistic channels. Moreover, any valid Coq expression can be used to depict properties, which is more powerful than just using formulas in one logic, like LTL or CTL.

The source code of the formalization in Coq is available at [19]. Compared with the initial formalization for (non-probabilistic) Reo connectors, the probabilistic behavior is captured properly in this extension. As described in Sect. 3, the observed sequences on nodes are adjusted to timed data distribution streams instead of timed data streams. But this new formalization can still be consistent with the initial one through assigning the value 1 to the companied probability of the data (i.e., the point distribution η_d instead of data item d). Based on this foundation and the specific library *Utheory*, the behavior of probabilistic channels can be characterized by the input and output timed data distribution streams properly. The probability accompanied the data will be updated accordingly when the timed data distribution pair flows through different probabilistic channels. With the definitions of channels serving as the basis, connector properties, as well as equivalence and refinement relations between different connectors can be naturally formalized as theorems in Coq and proved using tactics predefined in Coq[2].

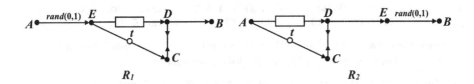

Fig. 5. Equivalence between connectors

Example 2. An interesting example of the equivalence relation between connectors is shown in Fig. 5. The two connectors are composed with the same set of basic channels but with different topologies of combination. Connector $\mathbf{R}_1$ is constructed by a randomized synchronous channel followed by a subconnector **tFIFO1** (which will be introduced in the following), while $\mathbf{R}_2$ is constructed by the subconnector **tFIFO1** and a following randomized synchronous channel. The subconnector **tFIFO1** contains a FIFO1 channel, a SyncDrain channel, a timer channel with parameter t and a Sync channel. It has been studied in [13]

---

[2] For two connectors $\mathbf{R}_1$ and $\mathbf{R}_2$, we say that $\mathbf{R}_2$ is a refinement of $\mathbf{R}_1$ (denoted by $\mathbf{R}_1 \sqsubseteq \mathbf{R}_2$) if $(P_1 \Rightarrow P_2) \wedge (P_1 \wedge Q_2 \Rightarrow Q_1)$, and they are equivalent if $\mathbf{R}_1 \sqsubseteq \mathbf{R}_2$ and $\mathbf{R}_2 \sqsubseteq \mathbf{R}_1$.

and properties related to its behavior have been proved in Coq. For the basic FIFO1 channel, the input and output timed data distribution streams will have the same data distribution but with an arbitrary time delay. Compared with the basic FIFO1 channel, the time delay is fixed by the parameter t in **tFIFO1**, apart from the same data distribution between the input and output streams.

The goal (formalized as a theorem) in this example is the equivalence relation between connectors $\mathbf{R}_1$ and $\mathbf{R}_2$ in Fig. 5. Before proving the equivalence relation, the configurations of the two connectors are first reduced to the constitution of a **RdmSync** channel and a **tFIFO1** connector with different topological orders for proof simplicity. This reduction leads to two more lemmas that need to be proved, which are the equivalence relations between the construction from basic channels and the reduced method of construction from a **RdmSync** channel and a **tFIFO1** connector. The two equivalence relations are formalized in Coq as follows:

```
1  Lemma RSync_tFIFO_eq: forall (A B: Stream TDD) (t:Time),
2       exists E: Stream TDD,
3       (RdmSync A E) /\ (t_FIFO1 E B t)
4       <->
5       (RdmSync A E) /\
6       (exists (D C:Stream TDD), (FIFO1 E D) /\ (SyncDrain D C)
7       /\ (Timert E C t) /\ (Sync D B)).
8
9  Lemma tFIFO_RSync_eq: forall (A B: Stream TDD) (t:Time),
10      exists E: Stream TDD,
11      (t_FIFO1 A E t) /\ (RdmSync E B)
12      <->
13      (exists (D C:Stream TDD), (FIFO1 A D) /\ (SyncDrain D C)
14      /\ (Timert A C t) /\ (Sync D E)) /\ (RdmSync E B).
```

Once these two equivalence relations are proved, we can establish the goal of equivalence between $\mathbf{R}_1$ and $\mathbf{R}_2$ as the following theorem:

```
1  Theorem equivalence: forall (A B:Stream TDD) (t:Time),
2    (exists E, (RdmSync A E) /\ (t_FIFO1 E B t))
3  <->
4    (exists R, (t_FIFO1 A R t) /\ (RdmSync R B)).
```

The core of the proof for this theorem is that we need to find the corresponding intermediate timed data distribution streams to complete the construction, with the construction method of the other connector provided. The equivalence proof of this example is different from the one in [20]. Unlike the proof of equivalence in [20], we cannot find one single timed data distribution stream directly serving as a match. Thus, two timed data distribution streams are constructed first and then proved as precise matches for the refinement relations in two directions, respectively. The complete proof of the theorem is available at [19].

It is straightforward to find out the reason why the commutative property is satisfied in the construction of $\mathbf{R}_1$ and $\mathbf{R}_2$ in Fig. 5. The RdmSync channel only modifies the data distribution streams while the tFIFO1 connector only transforms the time stream. As a result, the change of topological positions of these two connectors does not affect the final relation between the timed data distribution streams on the source node A and sink node B.

Actually, as this model focuses on the relations between input and output timed data distribution streams, different orders of data distribution and time stream transformations lead to the same resultant relations. Therefore, for any two connectors (or channels), as long as these two connectors transform time streams and data distribution streams exclusively, the composition order will satisfy the commutative property.

Although this example is a bit trivial, it is presented as a demonstration of the possibility to express all well-defined properties or equivalence relations between connectors and develop machine checked proof in Coq. The original formalization of classic Reo can model a certain range of scenarios, but it is not good at dealing with the uncertainty of the real world. With this probabilistic Reo extension provided, formal modeling and reasoning about uncertainty is supported. As a result, more scenarios in real world can be modeled, and the crucial issues or properties need to be considered can be further verified in Coq.

6   Conclusion and Future Work

This paper extends our previous work on the design model for (unprobabilistic) Reo connectors and introduces the relational model for probabilistic Reo connectors based on observations as timed data distribution streams. This approach provides a unified semantic model for different kinds of channels and connectors, covers different communication mechanisms encoded in Reo, and allows the combination of both deterministic and probabilistic channels in Reo. In this work, we model (both deterministic and probabilistic) channels in Reo as relations of timed data distribution streams, where the observation on each node of a connector is specified as a stream of timed data distribution. The composition of connectors is captured by flow-through composition with the help of two ternary channels *merger* and *replicator*. Our semantic model offers potential benefits in developing tool support for Reo. For example, the syntax and semantics for probabilistic Reo connectors are implemented in Coq, which makes it possible to prove connector properties, as well as equivalence and refinement relations between different connectors.

Incorporating more complex probabilistic and stochastic constraints on connectors [9,15] into our model is an interesting topic that we are now investigating. In future work, we also plan to incorporate the hybrid connectors [10], and other QoS aspects on connectors [4,5] into this model. The development of refinement and testing theories for probabilistic connectors like refinement and testing for deterministic connectors in [1,17] and integration of such theories into Coq or other existing tools for Reo [11] are of special interest and in our scope as well. On the other hand, we will investigate the inherent dynamic topology and mobility in "full" Reo based on the design model, especially context-sensitive connector behavior and reconfiguration of connectors.

Acknowledgement. The work was partially supported by the National Natural Science Foundation of China under grant no. 61772038, 61532019, 61202069 and 61272160.

References

1. Aichernig, B.K., Arbab, F., Astefanoaei, L., de Boer, F.S., Sun, M., Rutten, J.: Fault-based test case generation for component connectors. In: Proceedings of TASE 2009, pp. 147–154. IEEE Computer Society (2009)
2. Arbab, F.: Reo: a channel-based coordination model for component composition. Math. Struct. Comput. Sci. **14**(3), 329–366 (2004)
3. Arbab, F., Baier, C., de Boer, C., Rutten, J.: Models and temporal logics for timed component connectors. In: Cuellar, J.R., Liu, Z. (eds.) Proceedings of SEFM 2004, pp. 198–207. IEEE Computer Society (2004)
4. Arbab, F., Chothia, T., Meng, S., Moon, Y.-J.: Component connectors with QoS guarantees. In: Murphy, A.L., Vitek, J. (eds.) COORDINATION 2007. LNCS, vol. 4467, pp. 286–304. Springer, Heidelberg (2007). https://doi.org/10.1007/978-3-540-72794-1_16
5. Arbab, F., Chothia, T., van der Mei, R., Meng, S., Moon, Y.J., Verhoef, C.: From coordination to stochastic models of QoS. In: Field, J., Vasconcelos, V.T. (eds.) COORDINATION 2009. LNCS, vol. 5521, pp. 268–287. Springer, Heidelberg (2009). https://doi.org/10.1007/978-3-642-02053-7_14
6. Arbab, F., Rutten, J.J.M.M.: A coinductive calculus of component connectors. In: Wirsing, M., Pattinson, D., Hennicker, R. (eds.) WADT 2002. LNCS, vol. 2755, pp. 34–55. Springer, Heidelberg (2003). https://doi.org/10.1007/978-3-540-40020-2_2
7. Baier, C.: Probabilistic models for Reo connector circuits. J. Univers. Comput. Sci. **11**(10), 1718–1748 (2005)
8. Baier, C., Sirjani, M., Arbab, F., Rutten, J.: Modeling component connectors in Reo by constraint automata. Sci. Comput. Program. **61**, 75–113 (2006)
9. Baier, C., Wolf, V.: Stochastic reasoning about channel-based component connectors. In: Ciancarini, P., Wiklicky, H. (eds.) COORDINATION 2006. LNCS, vol. 4038, pp. 1–15. Springer, Heidelberg (2006). https://doi.org/10.1007/11767954_1
10. Chen, X., Sun, J., Sun, M.: A hybrid model of connectors in cyber-physical systems. In: Merz, S., Pang, J. (eds.) ICFEM 2014. LNCS, vol. 8829, pp. 59–74. Springer, Cham (2014). https://doi.org/10.1007/978-3-319-11737-9_5
11. Eclipse Coordination Tools. http://reo.project.cwi.nl/
12. He, K., Hermanns, H., Chen, Y.: Models of connected things: on priced probabilistic timed Reo. In: 2017 IEEE 41st Annual Computer Software and Applications Conference (COMPSAC), vol. 1, pp. 234–243 (2017)
13. Hong, W., Nawaz, M.S., Zhang, X., Li, Y., Sun, M.: Using Coq for formal modeling and verification of timed connectors. In: Cerone, A., Roveri, M. (eds.) SEFM 2017. LNCS, vol. 10729, pp. 558–573. Springer, Cham (2018). https://doi.org/10.1007/978-3-319-74781-1_37
14. Jongmans, S.T.Q., Arbab, F.: Overview of thirty semantic formalisms for Reo. Sci. Ann. Comput. Sci. **22**(1), 201–251 (2012)
15. Li, Y., Zhang, X., Ji, Y., Sun, M.: Capturing stochastic and real-time behavior in Reo connectors. In: Cavalheiro, S., Fiadeiro, J. (eds.) SBMF 2017. LNCS, vol. 10623, pp. 287–304. Springer, Cham (2017). https://doi.org/10.1007/978-3-319-70848-5_18

16. Oliveira, N., Silva, A., Barbosa, L.S.: IMC$_{Reo}$: interactive Markov chains for Stochastic Reo. J. Internet Serv. Inf. Secur. **5**(1), 3–28 (2015)
17. Sun, M., Arbab, F., Aichernig, B.K., Astefanoaei, L., de Boer, F.S., Rutten, J.: Connectors as designs: modeling, refinement and test case generation. Sci. Comput. Program. **77**(7–8), 799–822 (2012)
18. The Coq Proof Assistant. https://coq.inria.fr/
19. The source code of Probabilistic Reo. https://github.com/Xiyue-Selina/Prob-Reo
20. Zhang, X., Hong, W., Li, Y., Sun, M.: Reasoning about connectors in Coq. In: Kouchnarenko, O., Khosravi, R. (eds.) FACS 2016. LNCS, vol. 10231, pp. 172–190. Springer, Cham (2017). https://doi.org/10.1007/978-3-319-57666-4_11

Behavioral Equivalences

Weighted Branching Systems: Behavioural Equivalence, Behavioural Distance, and Their Logical Characterisations

Mathias Claus Jensen$^{(\boxtimes)}$, Kim Guldstrand Larsen, and Radu Mardare

Department of Computer Science, Aalborg University, Aalborg, Denmark
mathias.claus.jensen@gmail.com, {kgl,mardare}@cs.aau.dk

Abstract. In this work, we extend the notion of branching bisimulation to weighted systems. We abstract away from singular transitions and allow for bisimilar systems to match each other using finite paths of similar behaviour and weight. We show that this weighted branching bisimulation is characterised by a weighted temporal logic. Due to the restrictive nature of quantitative behavioural equivalences, we develop a notion of relative distance between weighted processes by relaxing our bisimulation by some factor. Intuitively, we allow for transitions $s \xrightarrow{w} s'$ to be matched by finite paths that accumulate a weight within the interval $[\frac{w}{\varepsilon}, w\varepsilon]$, where ε is the factor of relaxation. We extend this relaxation to our logic and show that for a class of formulae, our relaxed logic characterises our relaxed bisimulation. From this notion of relaxed bisimulation, we derive a relative pseudometric and prove robustness results. Lastly, we prove certain topological properties for classes of formulae on the open-ball topology induced by our pseudometric.

1 Introduction

For concurrent and interactive systems the notion of semantic equality has always held particular importance and in general forms the groundwork for most further reasoning about such systems. To capture this equality between systems, many behavioural preorders and equivalences have been considered, including the now classical notion of bisimulation introduced by Hennesy and Milner [HM85] and Park [Par81]. Alongside the development of behavioural equivalences, there has been an effort in describing systems with the use of various modal and temporal logics. In general, when one has a behavioural equivalence, we would like to

---

This paper is based upon unpublished ideas by Foshammer et al. [FLMX17] and the 9th semester project report [Jen18] in Computer Science by the first author at Aalborg University.

Electronic supplementary material The online version of this chapter (https://doi.org/10.1007/978-3-030-00151-3_9) contains supplementary material, which is available to authorized users.

D. N. Jansen and P. Prabhakar (Eds.): FORMATS 2018, LNCS 11022, pp. 145–161, 2018.
https://doi.org/10.1007/978-3-030-00151-3_9

produce a logic that corresponds with this equivalence, in the sense that two states are behaviourally equivalent if and only if they satisfy the same logical formulae, e.g. Hennesy Milner Logic and bisimulation [HM85].

In conjunction with this, there has also been an emphasis on discovering behavioural equivalences that allow us to abstract away from the internal behaviour of systems and only require equivalence at an external level. The original notion of observational equivalence by Milner [Mil80] serves this purpose, as does the later notion of branching bisimulation introduced by Weijland and Glabbeck in [vGW89]. Branching bisimulation has the additional property of being completely characterised by several temporal logics [DV95], including Computation Tree Logic (CTL) without the next-operator.

Today, the most common way to model concurrent systems has been by the use of process algebras such as the Calculus of Communicating Systems (CCS) introduced by Milner [Mil80] or by coalgebraic structures such as labelled transition systems (LTS). While models with only labels are sufficient for reasoning about the reactive and functional behaviour of systems, they cannot encode quantitative aspects that may be of importance to actual systems, such as time, cost, etc. This has motivated the introduction and study of weighted transition systems, for which transitions are labelled with quantities – e.g. real numbers – allowing for the modelling of consumption or production of resources, such as time and cost. Analogously to LTS, weighted transition systems also have a well-developed notion of semantic equivalence [BvBW06], namely weighted bisimulation.

In this paper, we revisit weighted transition systems with the intent of identifying behavioural equivalences similar to that of branching bisimulation; meaning we remain sensitive to quantitative behaviour, yet abstract away from internal activity. We develop a notion of weighted branching bisimulation, in which we require the transitions of behaviourally equivalent states to be matched by finite paths of equal accumulated weight.

Example 1. Consider the small weighted transition system shown below. Conceptually, we would like for t to be similar to s, as there exists a path from t that accumulates a weight of 5, thereby matching the transition $s \xrightarrow{5} s'$.

$$s \xrightarrow{5} s' \qquad t \xrightarrow{3} t' \xrightarrow{2} t''$$

As with [vGW89], we aim to characterise our weighted branching bisimulation; as such we consider a weighted extension of CTL without the next operator, for which the until operator has been equipped with closed intervals bounded by rational numbers. To this end, we develop an analogue notion image-finiteness, namely branching-finiteness, which requires that the possible ways of accumulating a weight within a particular interval from a state be finite. We show that our weighted logic characterises our notion of weighted branching bisimulation on *branching-finite* weighted Kripke structures (WKS).

Due to the restrictive nature of exact quantitative behavioural relations – i.e. the fact that small deviations in weights will cause otherwise equivalent systems to be non-equivalent – we develop a notion of expanding our weighted branching bisimulation by some real-valued factor. This approach is based upon similar work done for probabilistic systems by Giacalone et al. [GJS90] and Desharnais et al. [DGJP99]. The idea being, that if we expand our weighted branching bisimulation by $\varepsilon \in \mathbb{R}_{\geq 1}$, then any transition of weight w from bisimilar states have to be matched by finite paths of accumulated weight within the interval $[\frac{w}{\varepsilon}, w\varepsilon]$. Parallel to this, we develop a corresponding notion of expanding our logic and show that states that are expanded-weighted branching bisimilar are characterised by the expansion of our logic.

From this notion of expanding our bisimulation, we derive a distance between states: the greatest lower bound of factors, such that the states in question are expanded-weighted branching bisimilar. We show that this distance behaves much akin to a pseudometric (and that the logarithm of the distance is a pseudometric). We show that states that are within a certain distance of each other are guaranteed to satisfy similar formulae.

Lastly, we show that a particular class of formulae, the formulae using only negation on atomic propositions, are closed in the open-ball topology induced by our distance, i.e. if a sequence of states that all satisfy such a formula converge to some state, then their limit also satisfy said formula. We then define a distance between these closed formulae, namely the greatest lower bound of factors such that the satisfaction of the expanded formula implies the satisfaction of the non-expanded other and vice versa.

Related Work. Model checking of a weighted extension of CTL on weighted systems is presented by Buchholz and Kemper in [BK10].

Foshammer et al. first introduces the notion of weighted branching simulation by extending the classical notion of branching simulation with weights in [FLM16]. They also relax their systems allowing for small deviations in matching weights, thereby inducing a distance. We extend upon their work by proving similar results for a weighted branching bisimulation and for a more general class of models. Lastly, they extend their results to include parametric weights.

Efficient algorithms are given for model-checking upper-bounded WCTL formulae and completely bounded formulae are shown to be NP-hard by Jensen et al. in [JLSO16], which in turn are based upon algorithms for parametric verification presented by Christoffersen et al. in [CHM+15]. The weighted branching logic of this report is based upon the version of weighted CTL presented in these papers.

The concept of relaxing quantitative behavioural equivalences is first presented by Giacalone et al. in [GJS90]. Desharnais et al. later expands upon this work and develops the notion of a bisimulation metric, i.e. bisimilar states should be at distance 0 from each other and states relatively close together should be relatively bisimilar. A deeper analysis of metrics for weighted systems is done by Fahrenberg, Thrane and Larsen in [TFL10,LFT11,FTL11].

Larsen et al. show in [LMP12] that for discrete and continuous Markov processes, certain classes of formulae can be considered closed, open, G_δ, or F_σ under an appropriate bisimulation metric, something they call a *dynamically continuous bisimulation metric.* We show that our distance has properties very much akin to such a metric and present similar results for our weighted formulae.

2 Preliminaries

Let S be an arbitrary set. We denote the powerset of S as 2^S. Given a binary relation $\mathcal{R} \subseteq S \times S$ and two elements $s, t \in S$, we use the following short hands: $s\mathcal{R}t$ for $(s, t) \in \mathcal{R}$ and $s\mathcal{R}^c t$ for $(s, t) \notin \mathcal{R}$. Furthermore, let $\langle s_i \rangle_{i \in I} \subseteq S$ denote an indexed sequence of elements of S where $I \subseteq \mathbb{N}$. We will sometimes use the short hand $\langle s_i \rangle$ when the index set and support set are clear from context.

Given a set S, we define an *extended relative-pseudometric* on S to be a function $d : S \times S \to \mathbb{R}_{\geq 1} \cup \{\infty\}$ such that $\log d$ is an *extended pseudometric*, for an arbitrary logarithmic function $\log$. Throughout this paper, we will refer to extended relative-pseudometrics and extended pseudometrics as simply relative-pseudometrics and pseudometrics respectively.

Given a relative-pseudometric d on S and an element of $s \in S$, the open-ball of radius $\varepsilon \in \mathbb{R}_{\geq 1}$ around s is defined as $B_\varepsilon(s) = \{s' \in S \mid d(s, s') < \varepsilon\}$. We can induce a topology on S using d by taking the closure of the open-balls for arbitrary radius $\varepsilon \in \mathbb{R}_{\geq 1}$ and $s \in S$ under (possible infinite) union and finite intersection. Note that this topology would be the exact same as the one induced by the pseudometric $\log d$, as $\{s' \in S \mid d(s, s') < \varepsilon\} = \{s' \in S \mid \log d(s, s') < \log \varepsilon\}$ for all $\varepsilon \in \mathbb{R}_{\geq 1}$ and $s \in S$, where $\log \infty = \infty$.

3 Weighted Kripke Structures

In this section we introduce the weighted systems that are the subject of this research, namely *weighted Kripke structures* (WKS). A traditional Kripke structure is directed graph in which the directed edges represent possible transitions between states and where each state is assigned a set of atomic propositions, that are said to hold in that state. A WKS is the straightforward extension of requiring that the transitions between states be weighted. Kripke structures are known for being well suited for reasoning about temporal properties of systems [BCG88], which corresponds with our wish to abstract away from singular transitions and focus on branching-time.

We also clarify the notion of runs and prefixes of runs—here referring to infinite and finite paths respectively—as they will serve as the units about which we will reason regarding branching behavioural properties of weighted systems.

Lastly, we introduce a notion of non-redundant runs and define an analogue of image-finiteness for weighted branching systems, namely branching-finiteness.

Definition 1 (Weighted Kripke Structures). *Given a set of atomic propositions, AP, a weighted Kripke structure is a tuple $\mathcal{K} = (S, \to, L)$ where*

- *S is a set of states,*
- *$\to \subseteq S \times \mathbb{R}_{\geq 0} \times S$ is the weighted transition relation, and*

– $L : S \rightarrow 2^{AP}$ is the labelling function assigning sets of atomic propositions to each state.

Whenever $(s, w, s') \in \rightarrow$ we use the shorthand $s \xrightarrow{w} s'$. For a given WKS $\mathcal{K} = (S, \rightarrow, L)$ we say that it is *non-blocking* if for all $s \in S$ there exists a $w \in \mathbb{R}_{\geq 0}$ and $s' \in S$ such that $s \xrightarrow{w} s'$. In this text we only consider non-blocking WKS, and as such for all future defined WKS it will be implicitly implied that they are non-blocking. This is done for purely notational reasons and all results could easily be extended to blocking WKS. Furthermore any blocking WKS can easily be made into a non-blocking version of itself, by adding zero-loops to any blocking state.

Definition 2 (Runs). *Given a WKS $\mathcal{K} = (S, \rightarrow, L)$, a run starting in $s_0 \in S$ is a countable infinite sequence of transitions,*

$$\sigma = (s_0, w_1, s_1), (s_1, w_2, s_2), ..., (s_n, w_{n+1}, s_{n+1}), ...$$

where for all $n \in \mathbb{N}$, $s_n \in S$ and $s_n \xrightarrow{w_{n+1}} s_{n+1}$.

For $n \in \mathbb{N}$ the n-th transition of a run σ is denoted $\sigma\langle n \rangle$ and the n-th state of σ is defined as $\sigma[n] = s_n$ where $\sigma\langle n \rangle = (s_n, w_{n+1} s_{n+1})$. Furthermore, the accumulated weight of σ at position $n \in \mathbb{N}$ is defined as

$$\mathcal{W}(\sigma)(n) = \begin{cases} 0 & \text{if } n = 0 \\ \sum_{i=1}^{n} w_i, \text{ where } \sigma\langle i \rangle = (s_{i-1}, w_i, s_i) & \text{if } n > 0 \end{cases}$$

Lastly, let **Runs** be the set of all runs in $\mathcal{K}$ and for $s \in S$ let **Runs**(s) be the set of all runs starting in s.

Building upon the already well explored concepts of branching bisimulation and weighted bisimulation, we now introduce *weighted branching bisimulation* (WBB). For two states to be weighted branching bisimilar, we require that whenever one of the states can perform a weighted move, the bisimilar state can *match* this move by performing a sequence of moves that preserve behaviour a long the way, preserves the end behaviour, and accumulates the exact weight of the original move.

Definition 3 (Weighted Branching Bisimulation). *Given a WKS $\mathcal{K} = (S, \rightarrow, L)$, a weighted branching bisimulation is a relation $\mathcal{R} \subseteq S \times S$ such that whenever $s\mathcal{R}t$ then*

1. $L(s) = L(t)$,
2. *for all $s \xrightarrow{w} s'$ there exists a $\sigma \in$ **Runs**(t) and $k \in \mathbb{N}$ such that $\forall i < k : s\mathcal{R}\sigma[i]$, $s'\mathcal{R}\sigma[k]$, and $\mathcal{W}(\sigma)(k) = w$.*
3. *for all $t \xrightarrow{w} t'$ there exists a $\sigma \in$ **Runs**(s) and $k \in \mathbb{N}$ such that $\forall i < k : t\mathcal{R}\sigma[i]$, $t'\mathcal{R}\sigma[k]$, and $\mathcal{W}(\sigma)(k) = w$.*

We use $\approx$ to denote the largest weighted branching bisimulation.

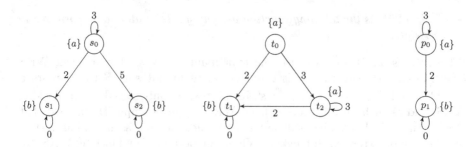

Fig. 1. A WKS where $s_0 \approx t_0$, $t_0 \approx p_0$ and $p_0 \approx s_0$.

Henceforth in this text, we will just refer to weighted branching bisimulation as our bisimulation. See Fig. 1 for an illustrated example of a WKS and bisimilar states.

While runs serve as the base for which we reason about behaviour in our WKS, a lot of the time we are only interested in computation trees of a finite height. As such, we define a concept of prefixes of runs, which are just finite sequences of transitions.

Example 2. Suppose that $\mathcal{K} = (S, \rightarrow, L)$ is a WKS where the weight of all transitions are lowerbounded by some $b \in \mathbb{R}_{\geq 0}$ where $b > 0$. If we wished to reason about all the ways a state $s \in S$ can accumulate a weight within the interval $[0, 12]$ we would only have to look at finite paths starting in s of with a length below $h = \frac{12}{b}$.

Definition 4 (Prefix). *Let* $\mathcal{K} = (S, \rightarrow, L)$ *be a WKS,* $\sigma \in$ Runs *and* $k \in \mathbb{N}$*, we denote the* prefix *of* σ *of length* k *by*

$$\sigma \uparrow k = \sigma\langle 0 \rangle, \sigma\langle 1 \rangle, ..., \sigma\langle k - 1 \rangle$$

Note the multiple otherwise different runs, may have the same prefix. In fact, for an arbitrary WKS $\mathcal{K} = (S, \rightarrow, L)$, all unique prefixes of length k can be seen as a partition of the set of runs, where we group runs together with identical prefixes.

As mentioned, prefixes will later be used to define an analogue to image-finiteness for branching systems. To this extent, we now define a function which gives us the smallest sets of prefixes that we will need to examine when wishing to reason about possible ways for a state to accumulate a weight within some interval. As with before, we are only interested in prefixes that accumulate a valid weight, but now we also prune all prefixes that has *zero-cycles* before accumulating said weight. The reason for pruning prefixes including zero-cycles is that their behaviour is dependent upon the prefixes without zero-cycles— i.e. if a run without zero-cycles cannot achieve something, then the addition of zero-cycles will not change this.

Definition 5 (Non-Redundant Prefixes). *Let* $\mathcal{K} = (S, \rightarrow, L)$ *be a WKS,* $s \in S$ *and* $[l, u] \subset \mathbb{R}_{\geq 0}$. *We denote the set of prefixes that accumulate a weight within* $[l, u]$ *without zero-cycles as*

$$P(s)([l, u]) = \left\{ \sigma \uparrow k \mid \sigma \in \mathtt{Runs}(s), k \in \mathbb{N}, \mathcal{W}(\sigma)(k) \in [l, u], \begin{array}{c} \sigma \text{ has no zero} - \text{cycles} \\ before \; k \end{array} \right\}.$$

Using this definition, we now introduce an analogue notion of finiteness for WKS to that of being image-finite, namely *branching-finite*. A WKS is *branching-finite* if and only if all the ways it can accumulate a weight within an interval, ignoring prefixes with zero-cycles of course, is finite.

Definition 6 (Finiteness in WKS). *Given a WKS* $\mathcal{K} = (S, \rightarrow, L)$, *we say that* $\mathcal{K}$ *is*

- finite *if* S *and* $\rightarrow$ *are finite,*
- image-finite *if for all* $s \in S$ *and* $w \in \mathbb{R}_{\geq 0}$, *the set* $\{s' \in S \mid s \xrightarrow{w} s'\}$ *is finite,*
- branching-finite *if for all* $s \in S$ *and* $[l, u] \subset \mathbb{R}_{\geq 0}$, *the set* $P(s)([l, u])$ *is finite.*

From this definition it is clear to see that branching-finiteness is a stronger property than image-finiteness, in the sense that if a WKS is branching-finite, then it is also image-finite. The converse is however not the case.

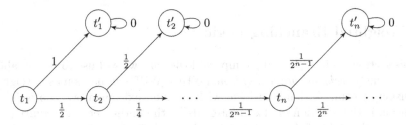

($\mathcal{K}$) Illustration of a WKS $\mathcal{K}$ that is image-finite but not branching-finite

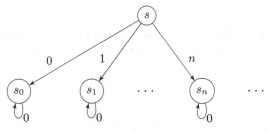

($\mathcal{G}$) Illustration of a WKS $\mathcal{G}$ that is both image-finite and branching-finite

Fig. 2. Two WKS that illustrate the difference between image-finite and branching-finite

Example 3. Consider the two WKS shown in Fig. 2. We have that the WKS $\mathcal{K}$ is image-finite, as for any state there are a total of two direct successors, $\mathcal{K}$ is however not branching-finite, as from the state t there are an infinite amount of non-redundant paths that accumulate a weight within the interval $[1, 1]$.

On the other hand, the WKS $\mathcal{G}$ is both image-finite and branching-finite. As for any given closed interval $[l, u] \subseteq \mathbb{R}_{\geq 0}$ there are a finite number of successors and a finite number of non-redundant paths that accumulate a weight within that interval.

We now produce our first lemma that states that for branching-finite WKS we can characterise our characterising prefixes using rational numbers as lower and upper bounds.

Lemma 1. *Let* $\mathcal{K} = (S, \rightarrow, L)$ *be a WKS and* $s \in S$. *For all* $[l, u] \subset \mathbb{R}_{\geq 0}$ *there exists a pair* $m, n \in \mathbb{Q}_{\geq 0}$ *such that* $[l, u] \subseteq [m, n]$ *and* $\mathcal{P}(s)([l, u]) = \mathcal{P}(s)([m, n])$.

This result is a consequence of the fact that the rationals are dense in the reals, and that the sets $\mathcal{P}(s)([l, u])$ are finite for branching-finite WKS. The lemma will prove important when we later want to characterise our behavioural relation on an otherwise real valued system with a countable logic.

Complete proofs for all lemmas and theorems can be found in either the attached appendix or in [Jen18].

4   Weighted Branching Logic

In this section we introduce the temporal logic that we will use to reason about WKS, namely *weighted branching logic* (WBL). WBL can be seen as a weighted extension of computation tree logic without the next-operator. The weighted extension is the addition of closed intervals on the until-operator, requiring the accumulated weight of the run satisfying the until also be within the given interval. Furthermore, we show that for *branching-finite* WKS, WBL characterises our bisimulation.

Definition 7 (Syntax). *Let* AP *be a set of atomic propositions. The state-formulae of weighted branching logic,* $\mathcal{L}$, *are induced by the following grammar.*

$$\mathcal{L}: \quad \phi ::= a \mid \neg\phi \mid \phi \wedge \phi \mid E\psi \mid A\psi,$$

and the path*-formulae by*

$$\psi ::= \phi \, U_{[l,u]} \, \phi,$$

where $a \in AP$ *and* $l, u \in \mathbb{Q}_{\geq 0}$.

Definition 8 (Semantics). *Let* AP *be a set of atomic propositions. The satisfiability relation,* $\models$, *is defined inductively for an arbitrary WKS* $\mathcal{K} = (S, \rightarrow, L)$, $s \in S$, *and* $\sigma \in$ Runs *as follows.*

$$
\begin{aligned}
s &\models a & &\textit{iff} & a &\in L(s) \\
s &\models \neg\phi & &\textit{iff} & \text{not } s &\models \phi \\
s &\models \phi_1 \wedge \phi_2 & &\textit{iff} & s &\models \phi_1 \text{ and } s \models \phi_2 \\
s &\models E\psi & &\textit{iff} & \exists\sigma &\in \mathrm{Runs}(s) : \sigma \models \psi \\
s &\models A\psi & &\textit{iff} & \forall\sigma &\in \mathrm{Runs}(s) : \sigma \models \psi
\end{aligned}
$$

$$
\sigma \models \phi_1 U_{[l,u]}\phi_2 \qquad \textit{iff} \qquad \exists k \in \mathbb{N} : \begin{bmatrix} \forall i < k : \sigma[i] \models \phi_1, \\ \sigma[k] \models \phi_2, \text{ and} \\ \mathcal{W}(\sigma)(k) \in [l,u] \end{bmatrix}
$$

where $a \in AP$ and $l, u \in \mathbb{Q}_{\geq 0}$.

Example 4. Let $AP = \{\mathsf{Safe}, \mathsf{Terminal}\}$ be a set of atomic propositions. Imagine a WKS $\mathcal{K} = (S, \rightarrow, L)$ that modelled some timed system where the weights on the transitions represent time. If we wished to reason about whether or not we are capable of moving from s to some terminal state through only safe states within 20 time units, we could query $E\, \mathsf{Safe}\, U_{[0,20]}\, \mathsf{Terminal}$.

The problem of model checking WBL formulae on finite WKS is NP-hard, as shown by Jonas Finnemann Jensen et al. in [JLSO16]. If we where to restrict ourselves to only considering upper bounded until formulae, then the problem of model checking would be in P, as is also shown in [JLSO16].

We conclude this section with a theorem stating, for *branching-finite* WKS, that WBL characterises our bisimulation. This result is similar to that presented by De Nicola and Vaandrager in [DV95], where they characterise the classic branching bisimulation with 3 logics, one of which is regular CTL excluding the next-operator.

Theorem 1 (Characterisation). *Let AP be a set of atomic propositions and $\mathcal{K} = (S, \rightarrow, L)$ be a branching-finite WKS. For arbitrary $s, t \in S$*

$$
s \approx t \ \textit{ iff } \ \forall\phi \in \mathcal{L} : s \models \phi \Leftrightarrow t \models \phi
$$

Proof. We show that $s \approx t$ implies $\forall\phi \in \mathcal{L} : s \models \phi \Leftrightarrow t \models \phi$. Induction on the structure of $\phi \in \mathcal{L}$. The atomic and boolean cases are trivial.

Case $\phi = E\ \phi_1\ U_{[l,u]}\ \phi_2$**:** By definition $s \models E\ \phi_1\ U_{[l,u]}\ \phi_2$ iff there exists a $\sigma \in \mathrm{Runs}(s)$ and $k \in \mathbb{N}$ such that $\forall i < k : \sigma[i] \models \phi_1, \sigma[k] \models \phi_2$, and $\mathcal{W}(\sigma)(k) \in [l,u]$. Since $s \approx t$ there must exists a matching run $\pi \in \mathrm{Runs}(t)$ and $h_k \in \mathbb{N}$ whereby induction we have that $\forall j < h_k : \pi(j) \models \phi_1$ and $\pi(h_k) \models \phi_2$. Furthermore we have that $\mathcal{W}(\pi)(h_k) = \mathcal{W}(\sigma)(k) \in [l,u]$. Hence, by definition $t \models E\ \phi_1\ U_{[l,u]}\ \phi_2$. The universal case is handled conversely as that of the existential.

We show that $s \approx t$ is implied by $\forall\phi \in \mathcal{L} : s \models \phi \Leftrightarrow t \models \phi$. We show that the relation $\mathcal{R} = \{(s,t) \in S \times S \mid \forall\phi \in \mathcal{L} : s \models \phi \Leftrightarrow t \models \phi\}$ is a weighted branching bisimulation. Suppose that $s\mathcal{R}t$ for some $s, t \in S$. Clearly $L(s) = L(t)$. For condition 2 (and 3 by symmetry), assume towards a contradiction that there exists a $s \xrightarrow{w} s'$ such that $\forall\pi \in \mathrm{Runs}(t) : \forall k \in \mathbb{N} : \exists i < k :$

$s\mathcal{R}^c\pi[i]$, $s'\mathcal{R}^c\pi[k]$, or $\mathcal{W}(\pi)(k) \neq w$. For every $\pi \uparrow k \in \mathcal{P}(t)([w,w])$ such that $s\mathcal{R}^c\sigma[i]$ there exists a $\phi_1 \in \mathcal{L}$ such that $s \models \phi$ and $\sigma[i] \not\models \phi_1$, let Φ_1 be the collection of these. Similarly let Φ_2 be the collection of distinguishing formulae for the cases where $s'\mathcal{R}^c\sigma[k]$. Clearly Φ_1 and Φ_2 are finite as $\mathcal{P}(t)([w,w])$ is finite due to $\mathcal{K}$ being *branching-finite*. By Lemma 1 we have that there exists a pair $l, u \in \mathbb{Q}_{\geq 0}$ such that $[w,w] \subseteq [l,u]$ and $\mathcal{P}(t)([w,w]) = \mathcal{P}(t)([l,u])$. We can now create a formula

$$\psi = E(\bigwedge_{\phi_1 \in \Phi_1} \phi_1)\, U_{[l,u]}(\bigwedge_{\phi_2 \in \Phi_2} \phi_2)$$

for which $\forall \sigma \uparrow k \in \mathcal{P}(t)([l,u]) : \sigma \not\models \psi$. Since no run contained in a prefix in $\mathcal{P}(t)([l,u])$ satisfies ψ, we get, without a loss of generality, that no runs satisfies ψ. This is equivalent to $t \not\models E\psi$. We now have that $s \models E\psi$ and $t \not\models E\psi$ contradicting that $s\mathcal{R}t$.   □

As a consequence of this theorem, we have that if two systems are not bisimilar, then we can produce a distinguishing formula that, in a sense, tells us how they differ.

5   Behavioural Relative Pseudometric

Requiring that paths be matched with exact weights can often be too restrictive, as small differences in weights on transitions will render otherwise similar systems non-bisimilar. Often, we will base our models on empirical data that is measured with some degree of uncertainty. As such, in this section we introduce a way of relaxing our bisimulation similar to that done for probabilistic systems by Giacalone et al. in [GJS90] and by Desharnais et al. in [DGJP99]. This is done by *expanding* the interval by which paths can match each other by some relative factor, e.g. the transition $s \xrightarrow{w} s'$ could be matched by a path of similar behaviour but with an accumulated weight within the interval $[\frac{w}{\varepsilon}, w\varepsilon]$, where ε is the relative factor of expansion. We extend this notion of expansion to our logic—by expanding the intervals on until formulae—and show that we can characterise our expanded bisimulations using this notion of expanding our formulae.

From the expansion of our bisimulation we derive a distance, namely the greatest lower bound of relative factors required for two states to be expanded bisimilar. We show this distance is a behavioural relative pseudometric and that two states within a certain distance of each other are guaranteed to have similar behaviour.

Definition 9 (Expanded WBB). *Given a WKS* $\mathcal{K} = (S, \rightarrow, L)$ *and* $\varepsilon \in \mathbb{R}_{\geq 1}$, *an* ε-*expanded weighted branching bisimulation is a relation* $\mathcal{R} \subseteq S \times S$ *such that whenever* $s\mathcal{R}t$ *then*

1. $L(s) = L(t)$
2. *for all* $s \xrightarrow{w} s'$ *there exists a* $\sigma \in \mathtt{Runs}(t)$ *and* $k \in \mathbb{N}$ *such that* $\forall i < k : s\mathcal{R}\sigma[i]$, $s'\mathcal{R}\sigma[k]$, *and* $\mathcal{W}(\sigma)(k) \in [\frac{w}{\varepsilon}, w\varepsilon]$.

3. *for all $t \xrightarrow{w} t'$ there exists a $\sigma \in \mathbf{Runs}(s)$ and $k \in \mathbb{N}$ such that $\forall i < k : t\mathcal{R}\sigma[i]$, $t'\mathcal{R}\sigma[k]$, and $\mathcal{W}(\sigma)(k) \in [\frac{w}{\varepsilon}, w\varepsilon]$.*

We use $\overset{\varepsilon}{\approx}$ to denote the largest ε-expanded weighted branching bisimulation.

Note that this expanded bisimulation relation does not form an equivalence relation, as it does not satisfy the transitive property. It is however still reflexive and symmetric. Instead of the transitive property we now have a sort of multiplicative triangular inequality, i.e. $s \overset{\varepsilon}{\approx} t$ and $t \overset{\gamma}{\approx} u$ implies $s \overset{\varepsilon\gamma}{\approx} u$, for arbitrary $s, t, u \in S$ and $\varepsilon, \gamma \in \mathbb{R}_{\geq 1}$. We also have that expanding our bisimulation by 1 does nothing, as it is the multiplicative identity. Lastly, we have that $\overset{\varepsilon}{\approx} \subseteq \overset{\varepsilon+\delta}{\approx}$, for any $\varepsilon \in \mathbb{R}_{\geq 1}$ and $\delta \geq 0$.

We now introduce a way of expanding the formulae of WBL in a way corresponding to that of expanding our bisimulation. As mentioned, this is done by expanding the intervals on all until expression that occur in any given formulae.

Definition 10 (Expansion of Formulae). *Let AP be a set of atomic propositions and $\varepsilon \in \mathbb{R}_{\geq 1}$. The ε-expansion of WBL formulae are defined for an arbitrary $\phi \in \mathcal{L}$ as*

$$\phi^\varepsilon = \begin{cases} a & \text{if } \phi = a \\ \neg(\phi_1^\varepsilon) & \text{if } \phi = \neg\phi_1 \\ \phi_1^\varepsilon \wedge \phi_2^\varepsilon & \text{if } \phi = \phi_1 \wedge \phi_2 \\ E\ \phi_1^\varepsilon\ U_{[\frac{l}{\varepsilon}, u\varepsilon]}\ \phi_2^\varepsilon & \text{if } \phi = E\ \phi_1\ U_{[l,u]}\ \phi_2 \\ A\ \phi_1^\varepsilon\ U_{[\frac{l}{\varepsilon}, u\varepsilon]}\ \phi_2^\varepsilon & \text{if } \phi = A\ \phi_1\ U_{[l,u]}\ \phi_2 \end{cases}$$

where $a \in AP$.

We canonically extend the satisfiability of until formulae to ones with real bounded intervals.

Notice here that the sets $[\![E\ \phi_1\ U_{[l,u]}\ \phi_2]\!]$ and $[\![A\ \phi_1\ U_{[l,u]}\ \phi_2]\!]$ increase as we expand the formulae in question. Similarly, we get that the sets of states $[\![\neg E\ \phi_1\ U_{[l,u]}\ \phi_2]\!]$ and $[\![\neg A\ \phi_1\ U_{[l,u]}\ \phi_2]\!]$ decrease as we expand the respective formulae. This is due to the given intervals increasing and their complement decreasing as we expand until formulae. For this reason we isolate the following positive only and negation thereof sub-logics of WBL.

$$\mathcal{L}^+ : \quad \phi ::= a \mid \neg a \mid \phi \wedge \phi \mid \phi \vee \phi \mid E\phi U_{[l,u]}\phi \mid A\phi U_{[l,u]}\phi$$
$$\mathcal{L}^- = \{\neg\phi \mid \phi \in \mathcal{L}^+\}$$

Equipped with these sub-logics we now present the following two characterisations of arbitrarily expanded weighted branching bisimulations on *branching-finite* WKS. We show that two states are expanded bisimilar if and only if one satisfy a positive only formula implies the other satisfies the same but expanded formula.

Theorem 2 (Characterisation of Expanded WBB). *Let* $\mathcal{K} = (S, \rightarrow, L)$ *be a branching-finite WKS, $s, t \in S$ and $\varepsilon \in \mathbb{R}_{\geq 1}$.*

$$s \stackrel{\varepsilon}{\approx} t \ \textit{iff} \ \forall \phi \in \mathcal{L}^+ : \begin{bmatrix} s \models \phi \implies t \models \phi^\varepsilon \\ t \models \phi \implies s \models \phi^\varepsilon \end{bmatrix}$$

The proof for Theorem 2 is almost identical to that of Theorem 1, except we now allow for the expansion of our bisimulation and positive formulae. By contrapositive, we get the following characterisation saying two states are expanded bisimilar if and only if one does not satisfy an expanded formulae implies the other does not satisfy the non-expanded formulae.

Corollary 1. *Let* $\mathcal{K} = (S, \rightarrow, L)$ *be a branching-finite WKS, $s, t \in S$ and $\varepsilon \in \mathbb{R}_{\geq 1}$.*

$$s \stackrel{\varepsilon}{\approx} t \ \textit{iff} \ \forall \phi \in \mathcal{L}^- : \begin{bmatrix} s \models \phi^\varepsilon \implies t \models \phi \\ t \models \phi^\varepsilon \implies s \models \phi \end{bmatrix}$$

The following theorem presents another interesting result regarding *branching-finite* WKS and the expansion of formulae. Namely, that if a state satisfies an expansion sequence of a positive formula, and that this expansion sequence converges to some limit, then the state also satisfies the positive formula expanded to the limit.

Theorem 3. *Let* $\mathcal{K} = (S, \rightarrow, L)$ *be a branching-finite WKS, $s \in S$, $\phi \in \mathcal{L}^+$, and $\varepsilon \in \mathbb{R}_{\geq 1}$. Furthermore, let $\langle \varepsilon_n \rangle_{n \in \mathbb{N}} \subseteq \mathbb{R}_{\geq 1}$ be a converging sequence where* $\lim_{n \to \infty} \varepsilon_n = \varepsilon$.

$$\textit{If } \forall n \in \mathbb{N} : s \models \phi^{\varepsilon_n} \textit{ then } s \models \phi^\varepsilon$$

Proof. Since $\langle \varepsilon_n \rangle_{n \in \mathbb{N}}$ is converging we can construct either an increasing or decreasing subsequence that converges to the same limit as $\langle \varepsilon_n \rangle_{n \in \mathbb{N}}$. For the case where we can construct an increasing subsequence is trivial, as $s \models \phi_n^\varepsilon$ implies $s \models \phi^\varepsilon$ for any $\varepsilon_n \leq \varepsilon$. For the case where we can construct a decreasing sequence, let $\langle \varepsilon_n \rangle_{n \in \mathbb{N}}^-$ denote this sequence. Induction on the structure of $\phi \in \mathcal{L}^+$. The atomic and boolean cases are trivial. **Case** $\phi = E \ \phi_1 \ U_{[l,u]} \ \phi_2$: We know that $\forall n \in \mathbb{N} : s \models E \ \phi_1^{\varepsilon_n} \ U_{[\frac{l}{\varepsilon_n}, u\varepsilon_n]} \ \phi_2^{\varepsilon_n}$ if and only if $\forall n \in \mathbb{N} : \exists \sigma \in \mathbf{Runs}(s)$ and $\exists k \in \mathbb{N}$ such that $\forall i < k : \sigma[i] \models \phi_1^{\varepsilon_n}$, $\sigma[k] \models \phi_2^{\varepsilon_n}$, and $\mathcal{W}(\sigma)(k) \in [\frac{l}{\varepsilon_n}, u\varepsilon_n]$. Since $\mathcal{K}$ is *branching-finite* we have that for all $n \in \mathbb{N}$, $\mathcal{P}(s)([\frac{l}{\varepsilon_n}, u\varepsilon_n])$ is finite. Additionally, as $\langle \varepsilon_n \rangle_{n \in \mathbb{N}}^-$ is a decreasing sequence we have that $\langle \mathcal{P}(s)([\frac{l}{\varepsilon_n}, u\varepsilon_n]) \rangle_{n \in \mathbb{N}}$ is a decreasing sequence of finite sets, i.e. $\mathcal{P}(t)([\frac{l}{\varepsilon_0}, u\varepsilon_0]) \supseteq \mathcal{P}(t)([\frac{l}{\varepsilon_1}, u\varepsilon_1]) \supseteq ...$ where $\exists M \in \mathbb{N} : \forall m > M : \mathcal{P}(s)([\frac{l}{\varepsilon_M}, u\varepsilon_M]) = \mathcal{P}(s)([\frac{l}{\varepsilon_m}, u\varepsilon_m]) \neq \emptyset$. This implies that there must exists a $\sigma \uparrow k \in \mathcal{P}(s)(I^{\varepsilon_M})$ whereby $\forall n \in \mathbb{N} : [\forall i < k : \sigma[i] \models \phi_1^{\varepsilon_n}, \sigma[k] \models \phi_2^{\varepsilon_n}$, and $\mathcal{W}(\sigma)(k) \in [\frac{l}{\varepsilon_n}, u\varepsilon_n]]$. By structural induction we have that $\forall i < k : \sigma[i] \models \phi_1^\varepsilon$ and $\sigma[k] \models \phi_2^\varepsilon$. Furthermore, we have that $\bigcap_{n \in \mathbb{N}} [\frac{l}{\varepsilon_n}, u\varepsilon_n] = I^\varepsilon$ and since $\forall n \in \mathbb{N} : \mathcal{W}(\sigma)(k) \in [\frac{l}{\varepsilon_n}, u\varepsilon_n]$ we have that $\mathcal{W}(\sigma)(k) \in I^\varepsilon$. Therefore, by definition $s \models E \ \phi_1^\varepsilon \ U_{[\frac{l}{\varepsilon}, u\varepsilon]} \ \phi_2^\varepsilon$. **Case** $\phi = A \ \phi_1 \ U_{[l,u]} \ \phi_2$: The universal case is handled similarly. $\qquad \square$

We now induce a relative distance from our definition of expanding our bisimulation. Precisely we define the distance between two states to be the greatest lower bounds of factors such that the two states are expanded bisimilar.

Definition 11 (Relative Distance). *Given a WKS $\mathcal{K} = (S, \rightarrow, L)$, the relative distance between two states, $s, t \in S$, is given by the function $d : S \times S \rightarrow \mathbb{R}_{\geq 1} \cup \{\infty\}$ such that*

$$d(s, t) = \inf\{\varepsilon \in \mathbb{R}_{\geq 1} \mid s \overset{\varepsilon}{\approx} t\}$$

where $\inf \emptyset = \infty$.

This distance behaves *nicely*, i.e. it behaves as a relative-pseudometric.

Proposition 1. *Let $\mathcal{K} = (S, \rightarrow, L)$ be a WKS. The distance function d is a relative-pseudometric, i.e. for $s, t, u \in S$ we have that*

1. $d(s, s) = 1$ *(Multiplicative Identity)*
2. $d(s, t) = d(t, s)$ *(Symmetry)*
3. $d(s, u) \leq d(s, t) \cdot d(t, u)$ *(Relative Triangular Inequality)*

Furthermore, we get that composing our relative-pseudometric with a logarithm result in an actual pseudometric.

Corollary 2. *Let $\mathcal{K} = (S, \rightarrow, L)$ be a WKS, $\log d$ is a pseudometric.*

More importantly, we have that this distance confers to certain behavioural properties. We have that states at distance 1 (multiplicativ identity) are bisimilar. An even stronger result is that for all states that are within a given distance of each other, say $\varepsilon \in \mathbb{R}_{\geq 1}$, we have that they are ε-expanded bisimilar with one another.

Theorem 4 (Behavioural Distance). *Let $\mathcal{K} = (S, \rightarrow, L)$ be a branching-finite WKS, $s, t \in S$, $\varepsilon \in \mathbb{R}_{\geq 1}$.*

$$d(s, t) = \varepsilon \implies s \overset{\varepsilon}{\approx} t$$

This result follows from Theorems 2 and 3 and the fact that the distance is the infimum of expansions such that two states are expanded bisimilar.

We now introduce one of the main results of this paper. Namely a robustness result regarding the distance between states and the satisfiability of positive formulae. Intuitively, the theorem states that close together states exhibit similar properties, i.e. similar formulae.

Theorem 5 (Robustness). *Let $\mathcal{K} = (S, \rightarrow, L)$ be a branching-finite WKS, $s, t \in S$, and $\varepsilon \in \mathbb{R}_{\geq 1}$.*

$$If \ d(s, t) \leq \varepsilon \ then \ \forall \phi \in \mathcal{L}^+ : s \models \phi \implies t \models \phi^\varepsilon$$

So, even if we base our models upon uncertain empirical data, we can still be certain they satisfy some given properties.

6   Topological Properties

In this section we induce a topological space from our relative distance. This is done with the purpose of reasoning about the behaviour of converging states as they approach their limit. More precisely we show that if a sequence of states all satisfying a positive formula $\phi \in \mathcal{L}^+$ converges, then the limit of this sequence also satisfies ϕ. Similar results have been shown for Markov processes and Markov logic by Larsen et al. in [LMP12].

Fig. 3. A WKS where the sequence of states $\langle s_n \rangle_{n \in \mathbb{N}}$ converges to s.

Example 5. Consider the WKS shown in Fig. 3 where a sequence of states $\langle s_n \rangle_{n \in \mathbb{N}}$—all with a single weighted self loop—converges to a state s. Clearly, we have that for all $n \in \mathbb{N}$, that $s_n \models E \top U_{[1,2]} \top$. Furthermore, we have that at the limit $s \models E \top U_{[1,2]} \top$. This property does however not hold for all formulae. Consider the negative formula $\neg E \top U_{[1,1]} \top$, again we have that for all $n \in \mathbb{N}$, that $s_n \models \neg E \top U_{[1,1]} \top$. However, at the limit we have that $s \not\models \neg E \top U_{[1,1]} \top$.

The next theorem states that positive formulae have this property, and are therefore considered *closed* in the open-ball topology induced by our behavioural relative pseudometric. I.e. if a converging sequence of states satisfy a positive formula, then so does the limit.

Theorem 6. *Let* $\mathcal{K} = (S, \rightarrow, L)$ *be a* branching-finite *WKS and* $\mathcal{T}_d$ *the open-ball topology induced by* d.

$$\text{If } \phi \in \mathcal{L}^+ \text{ then } [\![\phi]\!] \text{ is closed} \in \mathcal{T}_d$$

As direct consequence of this theorem, we get that our negative formulae are considered *open* in the open-ball topology induced by our behavioural relative pseudometric.

Corollary 3. *Let* $\mathcal{K} = (S, \rightarrow, L)$ *be a* branching-finite *WKS and* $\mathcal{T}_d$ *the open-ball topology induced by* d.

$$\text{If } \phi \in \mathcal{L}^- \text{ then } [\![\phi]\!] \text{ is open in } \mathcal{T}_d$$

Furthermore, as we consider both atomic propositions and their negation to be both positive and negative formulae, we get that they are considered *clopen*.

Corollary 4. *Let $\mathcal{K} = (S, \rightarrow, L)$ be a branching-finite WKS and $\mathcal{T}_d$ the open-ball topology induced by d.*

$$\forall a \in AP : [\![a]\!] \text{ and } [\![\neg a]\!] \text{ are clopen in } \mathcal{T}_d$$

Lastly, we conclude this section by proposing a distance for positive formulae. Inspired by the Hausdorff distance, we define the distance between two positive formulae to be the greatest lower bound of factors, such that satisfaction of the first formula implies satisfaction of the expanded second formula and vice versa.

Definition 12 (Formula Distance). *Given a WKS $\mathcal{K} = (S, \rightarrow, L)$, the distance between two formulae, $\phi, \psi \in \mathcal{L}^+$, is given by the function $d : \mathcal{L}^+ \times \mathcal{L}^+ \rightarrow \mathbb{R}_{\geq 1} \cup \{\infty\}$ such that*

$$\delta(\phi, \psi) = \inf\{\varepsilon \in \mathbb{R}_{\geq 1} \mid [\![\phi]\!] \subseteq [\![\psi^\varepsilon]\!] \text{ and } [\![\psi]\!] \subseteq [\![\phi^\varepsilon]\!]\}$$

We conclude this section by showing a robustness result similar to that of Theorem 5, but for formulae. Intuitively it states that satisfaction of a positive formula implies the satisfaction of nearby (similar) expanded formulae.

Theorem 7. *Let $\mathcal{K} = (S, \rightarrow, L)$ be a branching-finite WKS, $s \in S$, $\phi, \psi \in \mathcal{L}^+$, and $\varepsilon \in \mathbb{R}_{\geq 1}$.*

$$\text{If } s \models \phi \text{ and } \delta(\phi, \psi) \leq \varepsilon \text{ then } s \models \psi^\varepsilon$$

This result is a direct consequence of Theorem 3.

7   Conclusion and Future Work

In this paper, we extended the classical notion of branching bisimulation to that of weighted systems. We developed a notion of observable behavioural equivalence, namely our Weighted Branching Bisimulation. This allows us to class together otherwise non-bisimilar systems in the classical sense that are observably the same.

We develop a new concept of *branching-finite*, which is an analogue to image-finite but on weighted branching systems. We show that for *branching-finite* WKS, a weighted extension of CTL without the next-operator characterises our bisimulation.

We relax our bisimulation by expanding the interval by some factor wherein individual transitions can be matched by runs, thus giving us a more robust concept of bisimulation. We also introduce a way of expanding our formulae and show that for a positive subset our expansion of our bisimulation is characterised by the expansion of our formulae.

From the notion of expanding our bisimulation, we derive a distance between states: the greatest lower bound of factors such that two states are expanded bisimilar. We show that the logarithm of this distance behaves like a behavioural pseudometric on *branching-finite* WKS, and we show that states close to each other satisfy similar formulae.

Lastly, we showed that for *branching-finite* WKS, our positive formulae are closed in the open-ball topology induced by our distance.

Future Work. The computability and complexity for many of our results have been left out as our models are possibly infinite in size. For finite systems the complexity of deciding whether two systems are weighted branching bisimilar is likely to be NP-complete due to the requirement of matching transitions with runs of some exact weight and finding paths of an exact weight being NP-complete [NU02]. The computability and complexity of all our other results are still open questions however.

There is also the question of whether our bisimilation forms a congruence relation under a suitable composition of weighted processes. In fact, what a suitable composition of weighted processes is, is also an open question.

References

[BCG88] Browne, M.C., Clarke, E.M., Grumberg, O.: Characterizing finite Kripke structures in propositional temporal logic. Theor. Comput. Sci. **59**, 115–131 (1988)

[BK10] Buchholz, P., Kemper, P.: Model checking for a class of weighted automata. Discret. Event Dyn. Syst. **20**(1), 103–137 (2010)

[BvBW06] Blackburn, P., van Benthem, J.F.A.K., Wolter, F.: Handbook of Modal Logic, vol. 3. Elsevier, Amsterdam (2006)

[CHM+15] Christoffersen, P., Hansen, M., Mariegaard, A., Ringsmose, J.T., Larsen, K.G., Mardare, R.: Parametric verification of weighted systems. In: André, É., Frehse, G. (eds.) 2nd International Workshop on Synthesis of Complex Parameters, SynCoP 2015, 11 April 2015, London, United Kingdom. OASICS, vol. 44, pp. 77–90. SchlossDagstuhl - Leibniz-Zentrum fuer Informatik (2015)

[DGJP99] Desharnais, J., Gupta, V., Jagadeesan, R., Panangaden, P.: Metrics for labeled Markov systems. In: Baeten, J.C.M., Mauw, S. (eds.) CONCUR 1999. LNCS, vol. 1664, pp. 258–273. Springer, Heidelberg (1999). https://doi.org/10.1007/3-540-48320-9_19

[DV95] De Nicola, R., Vaandrager, F.W.: Three logics for branching bisimulation. J. ACM **42**(2), 458–487 (1995)

[FLM16] Foshammer, L., Larsen, K.G., Mariegaard, A.: Weighted branching simulation distance for parametric weighted Kripke structures. EPTCS **220**, 63–75 (2016)

[FLMX17] Foshammer, L., Larsen, K.G., Mardare, R., Xue, B.: Logical characterization and complexity of weighted branching preorders and distances. Unpublished Draft (2017)

[FTL11] Fahrenberg, U., Thrane, C.R., Larsen, K.G.: Distances for weighted transition systems: games and properties. EPTCS **57**, 134–147 (2011)

[GJS90] Giacalone, A., Jou, C.-C., Smolka, S.A.: Algebraic reasoning for probabilistic concurrent systems. In: Proceedings of the IFIP TC2 Working Conference on Programming Concepts and Methods. Citeseer (1990)

[HM85] Hennessy, M., Milner, R.: Algebraic laws for nondeterminism and concurrency. J. ACM **32**(1), 137–161 (1985)

[Jen18] Jensen, M.C.: Weighted branching systems: behavioural equivalence, metric structure, and their characterisations. Technical report, 9th Semester Report at Aalborg University (2018)

[JLSO16] Jensen, J.F., Larsen, K.G., Srba, J., Oestergaard, L.K.: Efficient model-checking of weighted CTL with upper-bound constraints. Int. J. Softw. Tools Technol. Transfer **18**, 409–426 (2016)

[LFT11] Larsen, K.G., Fahrenberg, U., Thrane, C.R.: Metrics for weighted transition systems: axiomatization and complexity. Theor. Comput. Sci. **412**(28), 3358–3369 (2011)

[LMP12] Larsen, K.G., Mardare, R., Panangaden, P.: Taking it to the limit: approximate reasoning for Markov processes. In: Rovan, B., Sassone, V., Widmayer, P. (eds.) MFCS 2012. LNCS, vol. 7464, pp. 681–692. Springer, Heidelberg (2012). https://doi.org/10.1007/978-3-642-32589-2_59

[Mil80] Milner, R. (ed.): A Calculus of Communicating Systems. LNCS, vol. 92. Springer, Heidelberg (1980). https://doi.org/10.1007/3-540-10235-3

[NU02] Nykänen, M., Ukkonen, E.: The exact path length problem. J. Algorithms **42**(1), 41–53 (2002)

[Par81] Park, D.: Concurrency and automata on infinite sequences. In: Deussen, P. (ed.) GI-TCS 1981. LNCS, vol. 104, pp. 167–183. Springer, Heidelberg (1981). https://doi.org/10.1007/BFb0017309

[TFL10] Thrane, C., Fahrenberg, U., Larsen, K.G.: Quantitative analysis of weighted transition systems. J. Log. Algebr. Program. **79**(7), 689–703 (2010)

[vGW89] van Glabbeek, R.J., Weijland, W.P.,: Branching time and abstraction in bisimulation semantics (extended abstract). In: IFIP Congress, pp. 613–618 (1989)

Trace Relations and Logical Preservation for Markov Automata

Arpit Sharma[✉]

Department of Electrical Engineering and Computer Science,
Indian Institute of Science Education and Research Bhopal, Bhopal, India
arpit@iiserb.ac.in

Abstract. Markov automata (MAs) have been introduced in [16] as a continuous-time version of Segala's probabilistic automata (PAs) [29]. This paper defines several variants of trace equivalence for closed MA models. These trace equivalences are obtained as a result of button pushing experiments with a black box model of MA. For every class of MA scheduler, a corresponding variant of trace equivalence has been defined. We investigate the relationship among these trace equivalences and also compare them with bisimulation for MAs. Finally, we prove that the properties specified using deterministic timed automaton (DTA) specifications and metric temporal logic (MTL) formulas are preserved under some of these trace equivalences.

Keywords: Markov · Equivalence · Trace · Bisimulation
Temporal logic

1 Introduction

Markov automata (MAs) [16] extend probabilistic automata (PAs) [29] with stochastic aspects [22]. MAs thus support non-deterministic probabilistic branching and exponentially distributed delays in continuous time. MAs are compositional, i.e., a parallel composition operator allows one to construct a complex MA from several component MAs running in parallel.

They provide a natural semantics for a variety of specifications for concurrent systems, as for example, dynamic fault trees [8,9], architectural description languages such as AADL [7,11], generalized stochastic Petri nets (GSPNs) [23], STATEMATE [6] and stochastic activity networks (SANs) [25]. They can also be used for modeling and analysis of GALS (Globally Asynchronous Locally Synchronous) hardware design [13] and shared memory mutual exclusion protocols [24]. Recently, a data rich specification language for MAs has been introduced [36]. Analyzing MAs involves applying model checking algorithms [18–20] on *closed*[1] MA models to compute the probability of linear or branching real-time objectives, e.g., long-run average, expected time, timed (interval) reachability

---

[1] A MA is said to be closed if it is not subject to any further synchronization.

© Springer Nature Switzerland AG 2018
D. N. Jansen and P. Prabhakar (Eds.): FORMATS 2018, LNCS 11022, pp. 162–178, 2018.
https://doi.org/10.1007/978-3-030-00151-3_10

[18] and Continuous Stochastic Logic (CSL) [21]. Equivalence relations are widely used for comparing and relating the behavior of stochastic models. For example, equivalences have been used to efficiently check if the implementation is an approximation of specification of the expected behavior. Additionally, equivalences are also used for reducing the size of stochastic models by combining equivalent states into a single state. For MAs, research has mainly concentrated on branching-time equivalences, e.g., strong bisimulation [16] and several variants of weak bisimulation [1,15,16,35].

This paper focuses on linear-time equivalences for closed MAs and investigates which kind of logical properties do they preserve. We use button pushing experiments on a black box model of MA (i.e., trace machine) to define several variants of trace equivalence. Our machine is equipped with an action display, a state label display, a timer and a reset button. Action and state label displays enable the external observer to observe the trace of the current run of machine $\mathcal{M}$ and timer provides the absolute time. The sequence of actions, state labels and time checks form an outcome (or timed trace), i.e., (σ, θ), of the trace machine. Since schedulers are used to resolve non-deterministic choices in MAs, we always fix a scheduler class $\mathcal{C}$ and allow the machine to execute infinitely many runs for all possible schedulers of this class. This process is repeated for every scheduler class $\mathcal{C}$ of the trace machine $\mathcal{M}$. Roughly speaking, two MAs $\mathcal{M}_1, \mathcal{M}_2$ are trace equivalent (w.r.t. scheduler class $\mathcal{C}$), denoted $\equiv_{\mathcal{C}}$, if for every scheduler $\mathcal{D} \in \mathcal{C}$ of $\mathcal{M}_1$ there exists a scheduler $\mathcal{D}' \in \mathcal{C}$ of $\mathcal{M}_2$ such that for all outcomes/timed traces (σ, θ) we have $P_{\mathcal{M}_1, \mathcal{D}}^{trace}(\sigma, \theta) = P_{\mathcal{M}_2, \mathcal{D}'}^{trace}(\sigma, \theta)$ and vice versa. Here, $P_{\mathcal{M}_1, \mathcal{D}}^{trace}(\sigma, \theta)$ denote the probability of all timed paths that are compatible with the outcome/timed trace (σ, θ) in $\mathcal{M}_1$ under scheduler $\mathcal{D}$. More specifically, we define six variants of trace equivalence on the basis of increasing power of schedulers, namely stationary deterministic (SD), stationary randomized (SR), history-dependent deterministic (HD), history-dependent randomized (HR), timed history-dependent deterministic (THD) and timed history-dependent randomized (THR) trace equivalence. We compare these trace equivalences with strong bisimulation for MAs [16]. We also study the connections among these trace equivalences.

Our main focus and motivation, however, is to investigate the preservation of linear real-time objectives under above mentioned trace equivalences. We prove that if two MAs are trace equivalent under (THD) class of schedulers then they have the same probability of satisfying a DTA specification. In addition, we study MTL [10,28], a real-time variant of LTL that is typically used for timed automata (and not for MAs). We define the semantics of MTL formulas over MA paths and prove that under (THR) trace equivalence probability of satisfying MTL formulas is preserved. Note that DTA and MTL have incomparable expressiveness [5,10,34]. Put in a nutshell, the major contributions of this paper are as follows:

- We define six variants of trace equivalence by experimenting with the trace machines, investigate the relationship between them and compare these equivalences with bisimulation for MAs.

- We prove that THD and THR trace equivalences preserve DTA and MTL specifications, respectively.

1.1   Related Work

Several linear-time equivalences for continuous-time Markov chains (CTMCs) have been investigated in [37]. Testing scenarios based on push-button experiments have been used for defining these equivalences. Trace semantics for interactive Markov chains (IMCs) have been defined in [38]. In this paper, testing scenarios using button pushing experiments have been used to define several variants of trace equivalences that arise by varying the type of schedulers. Similarly, trace semantics for continuous-time Markov decision processes have been defined in [32]. For MAs, strong and weak bisimulation relations have been defined in [16]. In [16], weak bisimulation has been defined over state probability distributions rather than over individual ones. In [14,15], it has been shown that weak bisimulation provides a sound and complete proof methodology for a touchstone equivalence called reduction barbed congruence. Notions of early and late semantics for MAs have been proposed in [35]. Using these semantics, early and late weak bisimulations have been defined and it has been proved that late weak bisimulation is weaker than all of the other variants defined in [14–16]. In [1], an expected-delay-summing weak bisimulation has been defined for MAs. Our definition of trace equivalence for MAs here builds on that investigated in [38] for IMCs. We take a similar approach and use the button pushing experiments with stochastic trace machines to define trace equivalences.

Organisation of the Paper. Section 2 briefly recalls the main concepts of MAs. Section 3 defines trace equivalence relations. Sections 4 and 5 discuss the preservation of DTA properties and MTL-formulas, respectively. Finally, Sect. 6 concludes the paper and provides pointers for future research.

2   Preliminaries

This section presents the necessary definitions and basic concepts related to Markov automata (MA) that are needed for the understanding of the rest of this paper. Let $Distr(S)$ denote the set of distribution functions over the countable set S.

Definition 1. *A* Markov automaton *(MA) is a tuple* $\mathcal{M} = (S, s_0, Act, AP, \rightarrow, \Rightarrow, L)$ *where:*

- *S is a nonempty finite set of states,*
- *s_0 is the initial state,*
- *Act is a finite set of actions,*
- *AP is a finite set of atomic propositions,*
- *$\rightarrow \subseteq S \times Act \times Distr(S)$ is the probabilistic transition relation,*
- *$\Rightarrow \subseteq S \times \mathbb{R}_{\geq 0} \times S$ is the Markovian transition relation, and*

– $L : S \to 2^{AP}$ *is a labeling function.*

We abbreviate $(s, \alpha, \mu) \in \to$ as $s \xrightarrow{\alpha} \mu$ and similarly, $(s, \lambda, s') \in \Rightarrow$ by $s \xRightarrow{\lambda} s'$. Let $PT(s)$ and $MT(s)$ denote the set of probabilistic and Markovian transitions that leave state s. A state s is *Markovian* iff $MT(s) \neq \varnothing$ and $PT(s) = \varnothing$; it is *probabilistic* iff $MT(s) = \varnothing$ and $PT(s) \neq \varnothing$. Further, s is a *hybrid* state iff $MT(s) \neq \varnothing$ and $PT(s) \neq \varnothing$; finally s is a *deadlock* state iff $MT(s) = \varnothing$ and $PT(s) = \varnothing$. In this paper we only consider those MAs that do not have any deadlock states. Let $MS \subseteq S$ and $PS \subseteq S$ denote the set of Markovian and probabilistic states in MA $\mathcal{M}$. For any Markovian state $s \in MS$ let $R(s, s') = \sum \{\lambda | s \xRightarrow{\lambda} s'\}$ be the rate to move from state s to state s'. The exit rate for state s is defined by: $E(s) = \sum_{s' \in S} R(s, s')$.

It is easy to see that a MA where $MT(s) = \varnothing$ for any state s is a probabilistic automaton (PA) [29]. A MA where $PT(s) = \varnothing$ for any state s is a continuous-time Markov chain (CTMC) [4]. The semantics of MAs can thus be given in terms of the semantics of CTMCs (for Markovian transitions) and PAs (for probabilistic transitions).

The meaning of a Markovian transition $s \xRightarrow{\lambda} s'$ is that the MA moves from state s to s' within t time units with probability $1 - e^{-\lambda \cdot t}$. If s has multiple outgoing Markovian transitions to different successors, then we speak of a race between these transitions, known as the *race condition*. In this case, the probability to move from s to s' within t time units is $\frac{R(s,s')}{E(s)} \cdot (1 - e^{-E(s) \cdot t})$.

Example 1. Consider the MA $\mathcal{M}$ shown in Fig. 1, where $S = \{s_0, s_1, s_2, s_3, s_4\}$, $AP = \{a, b, c\}$, $Act = \{\alpha, \beta\}$ and s_0 is the initial state. The set of probabilistic states is $PS = \{s_0, s_3\}$; MS contains all the other states. Note that there is no hybrid state in MA $\mathcal{M}$. Non-determinism between action transitions appears in state s_3. Similarly, race condition due to multiple Markovian transitions appears in s_1. Here we have $L(s_0) = L(s_4) = \{a\}$, $L(s_1) = \{b\}$, $L(s_2) = \{a, c\}$ and $L(s_3) = \{c\}$.

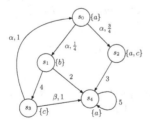

Fig. 1. An example MA $\mathcal{M}$

Note that in closed MAs all outgoing probabilistic transitions from every state $s \in S$ are labeled with $\tau \in Act$ (internal action).

Definition 2. *(Maximal progress [16]) In any closed MA, probabilistic transitions take precedence over Markovian transitions.*

Intuitively, the maximal progress assumption states that in closed MA, τ labeled transitions are not subject to interaction and thus can happen immediately[2], whereas the probability of a Markovian transition to happen immediately is zero. Accordingly, we assume that each state s has either only outgoing τ transitions or outgoing Markovian transitions. In other words, a closed MA only has probabilistic and Markovian states. We use a distinguished action $\perp \notin Act$ to indicate Markovian transitions.

Definition 3 (Timed paths). *Let $\mathcal{M} = (S, s_0, Act, AP, \rightarrow, \Rightarrow, L)$ be a MA. An infinite path π in $\mathcal{M}$ is a sequence $s_0 \xrightarrow{\sigma_0, t_0} s_1 \xrightarrow{\sigma_1, t_1} s_2 \ldots s_{n-1} \xrightarrow{\sigma_{n-1}, t_{n-1}} s_n \ldots$ where $s_i \in S$, $\sigma_i \in Act$ or $\sigma_i = \perp$, and for each i, there exists a measure μ_i such that $(s_i, \sigma_i, \mu_i) \in \rightarrow$ with $\mu_i(s_{i+1}) > 0$. For $\sigma_i \in Act$, $s_i \xrightarrow{\sigma_i, t_i} s_{i+1}$ denotes that after residing t_i time units in s_i, the MA $\mathcal{M}$ has moved via action σ_i to s_{i+1} with probability $\mu_i(s_{i+1})$. Instead, $s_i \xrightarrow{\perp, t_i} s_{i+1}$ denote that after residing t_i time units in s_i, a Markovian transition led to s_{i+1} with probability $\mu_i(s_{i+1}) = P(s_i, s_{i+1})$ where $P(s_i, s_{i+1}) = \frac{R(s_i, s_{i+1})}{E(s_i)}$. A finite path π is a finite prefix of an infinite path. The length of an infinite path π, denoted $|\pi|$ is ∞; the length of a finite path π with $n + 1$ states is n.*

Let $Paths^{\mathcal{M}} = Paths^{\mathcal{M}}_{fin} \cup Paths^{\mathcal{M}}_{\omega}$ denote the set of all paths in $\mathcal{M}$ that start in s_0, where $Paths^{\mathcal{M}}_{fin} = \bigcup_{n \in \mathbb{N}} Paths^{\mathcal{M}}_n$ is the set of all finite paths in $\mathcal{M}$ and $Paths^{\mathcal{M}}_n$ denote the set of all finite paths of length n that start in s_0. Let $Paths^{\mathcal{M}}_{\omega}$ is the set of all infinite paths in $\mathcal{M}$ that start in s_0. For infinite path $\pi = s_0 \xrightarrow{\sigma_0, t_0} s_1 \xrightarrow{\sigma_1, t_1} s_2 \ldots$ and any $i \in \mathbb{N}$, let $\pi[i] = s_i$, the $(i + 1)$th state of π. For any $t \in \mathbb{R}_{\geq 0}$, let $\pi@t$ denote the sequence of states that π occupies at time t. Note that $\pi@t$ is in general not a single state, but rather a sequence of several states, as a MA may exhibit immediate transitions and thus may occupy various states at the same time instant. Let $Act(s)$ denote the set of enabled actions from state s. Note that in case s is a Markovian state then $Act(s) = \{\perp\}$. Let $Act_{\perp} = Act \cup \{\perp\}$. Trace of an infinite path $\pi = s_0 \xrightarrow{\sigma_0, t_0} s_1 \xrightarrow{\sigma_1, t_1} s_2 \ldots s_{n-1} \xrightarrow{\sigma_{n-1}, t_{n-1}} s_n \ldots$ denoted $Trace(\pi)$ is given as $L(s_0)\sigma_0 L(s_1)\sigma_1 \ldots L(s_{n-1})\sigma_{n-1}L(s_n)\ldots$. Trace of a finite path π can be defined in an analogous manner.

Example 2. Consider an example timed path $\pi = s_0 \xrightarrow{\alpha, 0} s_1 \xrightarrow{\gamma, 0} s_3 \xrightarrow{\perp, 3} s_2 \xrightarrow{\gamma, 0} s_5$. Here we have $\pi[2] = s_3$ and $\pi@(3 - \epsilon) = \langle s_3 \rangle$, where $0 < \epsilon < 3$. Similarly, $\pi@3 = \langle s_2 s_5 \rangle$.

σ-algebra. In order to construct a measurable space over $Paths^{\mathcal{M}}_{\omega}$, we define the following sets: $\Omega = Act_{\perp} \times \mathbb{R}_{\geq 0} \times S$ and the σ-field $\mathcal{J} = (2^{Act_{\perp}} \times \mathcal{J}_R \times 2^S)$,

---

[2] We restrict to models without zenoness. In simple words, this means that τ cycles are not allowed.

where $\mathcal{J}_R$ is the Borel σ-field over $\mathbb{R}_{\geq 0}$ [3,4]. The σ-field over $Paths_n^{\mathcal{M}}$ is defined as $\mathcal{J}_{Paths_n^{\mathcal{M}}} = \sigma(\{S_0 \times M_0 \times \ldots \times M_{n-1}|S_0 \in 2^S, M_i \in \mathcal{J}, 0 \leq i \leq n-1\})$. A set $B \in \mathcal{J}_{Paths_n^{\mathcal{M}}}$ is a base of a cylinder set C if $C = Cyl(B) = \{\pi \in Paths_\omega^{\mathcal{M}}|\pi[0\ldots n] \in B\}$, where $\pi[0\ldots n]$ is the prefix of length n of the path π. The σ-field $\mathcal{J}_{Paths_\omega^{\mathcal{M}}}$ of measurable subsets of $Paths_\omega^{\mathcal{M}}$ is defined as $\mathcal{J}_{Paths_\omega^{\mathcal{M}}} = \sigma(\cup_{n=0}^{\infty}\{Cyl(B)|B \in \mathcal{J}_{Paths_n^{\mathcal{M}}}\})$.

2.1 Schedulers

Non-determinism in a MA is resolved by a scheduler. Schedulers are also known as adversaries or policies. More formally, schedulers are defined as follows:

Definition 4 (Scheduler). *A scheduler for MA $\mathcal{M} = (S, s_0, Act, AP, \rightarrow, \Rightarrow, L)$ is a measurable function $\mathcal{D} : Paths_{fin}^{\mathcal{M}} \rightarrow Distr(Act)$, such that for $n \in \mathbb{N}$,*

$$\mathcal{D}(s_0 \xrightarrow{\sigma_0,t_0} s_1 \xrightarrow{\sigma_1,t_1} \ldots \xrightarrow{\sigma_{n-1},t_{n-1}} s_n)(\alpha) > 0 \text{ implies } \alpha \in Act(s_n)$$

where $Distr(Act)$ denotes the set of all distributions on Act.

Schedulers can be classified[3] according to the way they resolve non-determinism and the information on the basis of which a decision is taken. For example, the next action can be selected with probability one (deterministic schedulers) or at random according to a specific probability distribution (randomized schedulers). Similarly, non-determinism can be resolved by only considering the current state (stationary schedulers) or complete (time-abstract/timed) history. More formally, schedulers can be classified as follows:

Definition 5 (Classes of schedulers). *A scheduler $\mathcal{D}$ for MA $\mathcal{M}$ is*

- *stationary deterministic (SD) if $\mathcal{D} : S \rightarrow Act$ such that $\mathcal{D}(s) \in Act(s)$*
- *stationary randomized (SR) if $\mathcal{D} : S \rightarrow Distr(Act)$ such that $\mathcal{D}(s)(\alpha) > 0$ implies $\alpha \in Act(s)$*
- *history-dependent deterministic (HD) if $\mathcal{D} : (S \times Act)^* \times S \rightarrow Act$ such that we have $\mathcal{D}\underbrace{(s_0 \xrightarrow{\sigma_0} s_1 \xrightarrow{\sigma_1} \ldots \xrightarrow{\sigma_{n-1}} s_n)}_{\text{time-abstract history}} \in Act(s_n)$*
- *history-dependent randomized (HR) if $\mathcal{D} : (S \times Act)^* \times S \rightarrow Distr(Act)$ such that $\mathcal{D}\underbrace{(s_0 \xrightarrow{\sigma_0} s_1 \xrightarrow{\sigma_1} \ldots \xrightarrow{\sigma_{n-1}} s_n)}_{\text{time-abstract history}}(\alpha) > 0$ implies $\alpha \in Act(s_n)$*
- *timed history-dependent deterministic (THD) if $\mathcal{D} : (S \times Act \times \mathbb{R}_{>0})^* \times S \rightarrow Act$ such that $\mathcal{D}\underbrace{(s_0 \xrightarrow{\sigma_0,t_0} s_1 \xrightarrow{\sigma_1,t_1} \ldots \xrightarrow{\sigma_{n-1},t_{n-1}} s_n)}_{\text{timed history}} \in Act(s_n)$*
- *timed history-dependent randomized (THR) scheduler has been already defined in Definition 4.*

---

[3] We only consider schedulers that make a decision as soon as a state is entered. Such schedulers are called early schedulers.

Let $Adv(\mathcal{M})$ denote the set of all schedulers of $\mathcal{M}$. Let $Adv_{\mathcal{C}}(\mathcal{M})$ denote the set of all schedulers of class $\mathcal{C}$, e.g., $Adv_{THD}(\mathcal{M})$denote the set of all THD schedulers of MA $\mathcal{M}$. Let $Paths_{\mathcal{D}}^{\mathcal{M}}$ denote the set of all infinite paths of $\mathcal{M}$ under $\mathcal{D} \in Adv(\mathcal{M})$ that start in s_0. Once the non-deterministic choices of a MA $\mathcal{M}$ have been resolved by a scheduler, say $\mathcal{D}$, the induced model obtained is purely stochastic. To that end the unique probability measure for probability space $(Paths_{\omega}^{\mathcal{M}}, \mathcal{J}_{Paths_{\omega}^{\mathcal{M}}})$ can be defined [26].

Example 3. Consider the MA $\mathcal{M}$ shown in Fig. 1. Let us assume that all the α and β labeled transitions can happen immediately. Let $\mathcal{D}$ be a SR scheduler for $\mathcal{M}$ such that $\mathcal{D}(s_3)(\alpha) = \frac{3}{4}$ and $\mathcal{D}(s_3)(\beta) = \frac{1}{4}$. Then we can compute the probability of set of paths $\mathcal{B} = Cyl(s_0, \alpha, [0, 0], s_1, \perp, [0, 4], s_3, \alpha, [0, 0], s_0)$ of $\mathcal{M}$ under $\mathcal{D}$ as follows:

$$Pr_{\mathcal{D}}(\mathcal{B}) = \frac{1}{4} \cdot \frac{4}{6} \cdot (1 - e^{-(6 \cdot 4)}) \cdot \frac{3}{4} \cdot 1 \approx .124999$$

3   Trace Equivalence Relations

This section proposes several variants of trace equivalence for closed MAs. These equivalences are obtained by performing push-button experiments with a trace machine $\mathcal{M}$. Consider the stochastic trace machine $\mathcal{M}$ shown in Fig. 2. The machine is equipped with an action display, a state label display, a timer and a reset button. Action display shows the last action that has been executed by the trace machine. For Markovian states, action display shows the distinguished action $\perp$. Note that this display is empty at the beginning of the experiment. The state label display shows the set of atomic propositions that are true in the current state of the machine $\mathcal{M}$. The timer display shows the absolute time. The reset button is used to restart the machine for another run starting from the initial state. Consider a run of the machine (under scheduler $\mathcal{D}$ of class $\mathcal{C}$) which always starts from the initial state. The state label shows the label of the current state and action display shows the last action that has been executed. Note that the action display remains unchanged until the next action is executed by the machine. The observer records the sequence of state labels, actions and time checks where each time check is recorded at an arbitrary time instant between

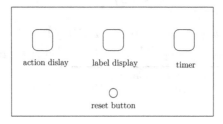

Fig. 2. Trace machine $\mathcal{M}$

the occurrence of two successive actions. The observer can press the reset button to stop the current run. Once the reset button is pressed, the action display will be empty and the state label display shows the set of atomic propositions that are true in the initial state. The machine then starts for another run and the observer again records the sequence of actions, state labels and time checks. Note that the machine needs to be executed for infinitely many runs to complete the whole experiment. It is assumed that the observer can distinguish between two successive actions that are equal. For a sequence of τ actions, state labels can be different but the recorded time checks are going to stay the same. This is because τ actions are executed immediately. An outcome of this machine is $(\sigma, \theta) = (< L(s_0)\sigma_0 L(s_1)\sigma_1 \ldots L(s_{n-1})\sigma_{n-1}L(s_n) >, < t'_0, t'_1, \ldots, t'_n >)$, where $\sigma_0, \ldots, \sigma_{n-1} \in (\{\tau\} \cup \{\bot\})$. This outcome can be interpreted as follows: for $0 \leq m < n$, action σ_m of machine is performed in the time interval $(y_m, y_{m+1}]$ where $y_m = \Sigma_{i=0}^{m} t'_i$.

Definition 6. *Let* $(\sigma, \theta) = (<L(s_0)\sigma_0 L(s_1)\sigma_1 \ldots L(s_{n-1})\sigma_{n-1}L(s_n)>, <t'_0, t'_1, \ldots, t'_n>)$ *be an outcome of* $\mathcal{M}$ *under* $\mathcal{D} \in Adv(\mathcal{M})$, *then a path* $\pi = s_0 \xrightarrow{\sigma_0, t_0} s_1 \xrightarrow{\sigma_1, t_1} s_2 \ldots s_{n-1} \xrightarrow{\sigma_{n-1}, t_{n-1}} s_n \ldots \in Paths_{\mathcal{D}}^{\mathcal{M}}$ *is said to be compatible with* (σ, θ), *denoted* $\pi \triangleright (\sigma, \theta)$, *if the following holds:*

$$Trace(\pi[0 \ldots n]) = \sigma \, and \, \Sigma_{j=0}^{i} t_j \in (y_i, y_{i+1}] \, for \, 0 \leq i < n$$

where $y_i = \Sigma_{j=0}^{i} t'_j$.

Example 4. Consider the MA $\mathcal{M}$ shown in Fig. 3 (left). An example outcome for $\mathcal{M}$ is $(\sigma, \theta) = (< \{a\}\tau\{b\}\bot\{a\}\bot\{a\} >, < 0, 0, 4, 3 >)$. An example path compatible with this outcome is $\pi = s_0 \xrightarrow{\tau, 0} s_1 \xrightarrow{\bot, 2} s_3 \xrightarrow{\bot, 4} s_3 \ldots$.

The probability of all the paths compatible with an outcome is defined as follows:

Definition 7. *Let* (σ, θ) *be an outcome of trace machine* $\mathcal{M}$ *under* $\mathcal{D} \in Adv(\mathcal{M})$. *Then the probability of all the paths compatible with* (σ, θ) *is defined as follows:*

$$P_{\mathcal{M}, \mathcal{D}}^{trace}(\sigma, \theta) = Pr_{\mathcal{D}}(\{\pi \in Paths_{\mathcal{D}}^{\mathcal{M}} | \pi \triangleright (\sigma, \theta)\})$$

Informally, $P_{\mathcal{M}, \mathcal{D}}^{trace}$ is a function that gives the probability to observe (σ, θ) in machine $\mathcal{M}$ under scheduler $\mathcal{D}$.

Definition 8 (Set of observations). *Let* $P_{\mathcal{M}, \mathcal{D}}^{trace}$ *be an observation of machine* $\mathcal{M}$ *under* $\mathcal{D} \in Adv(\mathcal{M})$. *Then the set of observations for scheduler class* $\mathcal{C}$, *denoted* $O_{\mathcal{C}}(\mathcal{M})$, *is defined as follows:*

$$O_{\mathcal{C}}(\mathcal{M}) = \{P_{\mathcal{M}, \mathcal{D}}^{trace} | \mathcal{D} \in Adv_{\mathcal{C}}(\mathcal{M})\}$$

Informally, $O_{\mathcal{C}}(\mathcal{M})$ denote a set of functions where each function assigns a probability value to every possible outcome of the trace machine, i.e., (σ, θ).

Definition 9 (Trace equivalence). *Two MAs $\mathcal{M}_1$, $\mathcal{M}_2$ are trace equivalent w.r.t. scheduler class $\mathcal{C}$ denoted $\mathcal{M}_1 \equiv_{\mathcal{C}} \mathcal{M}_2$ iff $O_{\mathcal{C}}(\mathcal{M}_1) = O_{\mathcal{C}}(\mathcal{M}_2)$.*

This definition says that for every $\mathcal{D} \in Adv_{\mathcal{C}}(\mathcal{M}_1)$ there exists a scheduler $\mathcal{D}' \in Adv_{\mathcal{C}}(\mathcal{M}_2)$ such that for all outcomes (σ, θ) we have $P^{trace}_{\mathcal{M}_1, \mathcal{D}}(\sigma, \theta) = P^{trace}_{\mathcal{M}_2, \mathcal{D}'}(\sigma, \theta)$ and vice versa.

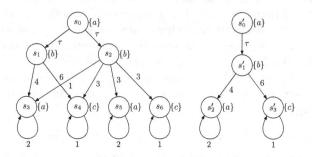

Fig. 3. MAs $\mathcal{M}$ (left) and $\mathcal{M}'$ (right)

Example 5. Consider the MAs $\mathcal{M}$ and $\mathcal{M}'$ shown in Fig. 3. These two systems are $\equiv_{SD}, \equiv_{SR}, \equiv_{HD}, \equiv_{HR}, \equiv_{THD}$ and $\equiv_{THR}$.

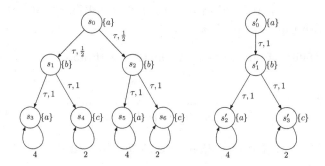

Fig. 4. MAs $\mathcal{M}$ (left) and $\mathcal{M}'$ (right)

Example 6. Consider the MAs $\mathcal{M}$ and $\mathcal{M}'$ shown in Fig. 4. These two systems are $\equiv_{SR}, \equiv_{HR}$ and $\equiv_{THR}$. Note that they are $\not\equiv_{SD}$. This is because there exists a SD-scheduler, say $\mathcal{D}$, for $\mathcal{M}$ such that the traces $\{a\}\tau\{b\}\tau\{a\}$ and $\{a\}\tau\{b\}\tau\{c\}$ have probability greater than 0, but this is not possible in $\mathcal{M}'$ for any SD-scheduler $\mathcal{D}'$. Similarly, $\mathcal{M}$, $\mathcal{M}'$ are $\not\equiv_{HD}$ and $\not\equiv_{THD}$.

3.1 Relationship Between Trace Equivalence and Bisimulation

This section investigates the relationship of bisimulation to several variants of trace equivalence defined in this paper. Informally, two states are bisimilar if they are able to mimic each other's behavior step-wise. We first recall the definition of bisimulation.

Definition 10 (Strong bisimulation [16]). *Let $\mathcal{M} = (S, s_0, Act, AP, \rightarrow, \Rightarrow, L)$ be a closed MA. An equivalence relation $\mathcal{R} \subseteq S \times S$ is a strong bisimulation on $\mathcal{M}$ if for any $(s_1, s_2) \in \mathcal{R}$ and equivalence class $C \in S/\mathcal{R}$ the following holds:*

- *$L(s_1) = L(s_2)$,*
- *$R(s_1, C) = R(s_2, C)$,*
- *$(s_1 \xrightarrow{\tau} \mu \iff s_2 \xrightarrow{\tau} \mu') \wedge \mu(C) = \mu'(C)$.*

States s_1 and s_2 are strongly bisimilar, denoted $s_1 \sim s_2$, if $(s_1, s_2) \in \mathcal{R}$ for some strong bisimulation[4] $\mathcal{R}$.

This definition of bisimulation can be easily extended to compare the behavior of two MAs $\mathcal{M}_1$ (with state space S_1) and $\mathcal{M}_2$ (with state space S_2). This can be achieved by taking the disjoint union of two state spaces ($S = S_1 \uplus S_2$) and asserting that initial states of two systems must be bisimilar with respect to S.

Example 7. Consider the MAs $\mathcal{M}$ and $\mathcal{M}'$ shown in Fig. 4. It is easy to check that these two systems are bisimilar.

Theorem 1. *The following holds:*

- $\sim \;\not\Longrightarrow\; \equiv_{SD}$ *and* $\equiv_{SD} \;\not\Longrightarrow\; \sim$
- $\sim \;\Longrightarrow\; \equiv_{SR}$ *and* $\equiv_{SR} \;\not\Longrightarrow\; \sim$
- $\sim \;\not\Longrightarrow\; \equiv_{HD}$ *and* $\equiv_{HD} \;\not\Longrightarrow\; \sim$
- $\sim \;\Longrightarrow\; \equiv_{HR}$ *and* $\equiv_{HR} \;\not\Longrightarrow\; \sim$
- $\sim \;\not\Longrightarrow\; \equiv_{THD}$ *and* $\equiv_{THD} \;\not\Longrightarrow\; \sim$
- $\sim \;\Longrightarrow\; \equiv_{THR}$ *and* $\equiv_{THR} \;\not\Longrightarrow\; \sim$

Example 8. As previously mentioned, bisimilar MAs $\mathcal{M}$ and $\mathcal{M}'$ shown in Fig. 4 are not $\equiv_{SD}$, $\equiv_{HD}$ and $\equiv_{THD}$.

3.2 Relationship Between Trace Equivalences

Next, we study the relationship between several variants of trace equivalence defined in Sect. 3. Connections among these equivalences can be understood from Fig. 5. Here a directed edge from node labeled with $\equiv_{C_1}$ to node labeled with $\equiv_{C_2}$ denote implication, i.e., $\equiv_{C_1} \Longrightarrow \equiv_{C_2}$. Similarly, an edge that connects two nodes in both the directions denote bi-implication, i.e., coincidence.

Theorem 2. *The following holds:*

- $\equiv_{SD} \;\Longrightarrow\; \equiv_{SR}$, $\equiv_{SD} \;\Longrightarrow\; \equiv_{HD}$, $\equiv_{SD} \;\Longrightarrow\; \equiv_{HR}$, $\equiv_{SD} \;\Longrightarrow\; \equiv_{THD}$, $\equiv_{SD} \;\Longrightarrow\; \equiv_{THR}$

---

[4] Note that the definition of strong bisimulation has been slightly modified to take into account the state labels.

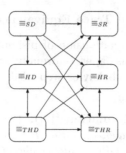

Fig. 5. Connections among six trace equivalences

- $\equiv_{SR} \not\Longrightarrow \equiv_{SD}$, $\equiv_{SR} \not\Longrightarrow \equiv_{HD}$, $\equiv_{SR} \Longrightarrow \equiv_{HR}$, $\equiv_{SR} \not\Longrightarrow \equiv_{THD}$, $\equiv_{SR} \Longrightarrow$
  $\equiv_{THR}$
- $\equiv_{HD} \Longrightarrow \equiv_{SD}$, $\equiv_{HD} \Longrightarrow \equiv_{SR}$, $\equiv_{HD} \Longrightarrow \equiv_{THD}$, $\equiv_{HD} \Longrightarrow \equiv_{HR}$, $\equiv_{HD} \Longrightarrow$
  $\equiv_{THR}$
- $\equiv_{HR} \not\Longrightarrow \equiv_{SD}$, $\equiv_{HR} \Longrightarrow \equiv_{SR}$, $\equiv_{HR} \not\Longrightarrow \equiv_{HD}$, $\equiv_{HR} \not\Longrightarrow \equiv_{THD}$, $\equiv_{HR} \Longrightarrow$
  $\equiv_{THR}$
- $\equiv_{THD} \Longrightarrow \equiv_{SD}$, $\equiv_{THD} \Longrightarrow \equiv_{SR}$, $\equiv_{THD} \Longrightarrow \equiv_{HD}$, $\equiv_{THD} \Longrightarrow \equiv_{HR}$, $\equiv_{THD}$
  $\Longrightarrow \equiv_{THR}$
- $\equiv_{THR} \not\Longrightarrow \equiv_{SD}$, $\equiv_{THR} \Longrightarrow \equiv_{SR}$, $\equiv_{THR} \not\Longrightarrow \equiv_{HD}$, $\equiv_{THR} \Longrightarrow \equiv_{HR}$, $\equiv_{THR}$
  $\not\Longrightarrow \equiv_{THD}$

4   Deterministic Timed Automaton

In order to investigate the kind of real-time properties for closed MAs that are preserved by THD trace equivalence, we study in this section linear real-time objectives that are given by Deterministic Timed Automata (DTAs) [2]. We first recall the definition of DTA.

Definition 11 (DTA). *A deterministic timed automaton (DTA) is a tuple $\mathcal{A} = (\Sigma, \mathcal{X}, Q, q_0, F, \rightarrow)$ where:*

- *Σ is a finite alphabet,*
- *$\mathcal{X}$ is a finite set of clocks,*
- *Q is a nonempty finite set of locations with the initial location $q_0 \in Q$,*
- *$F \subseteq Q$ is a set of accepting (or final) locations,*
- *$\rightarrow \subseteq Q \times \Sigma \times \mathcal{CC}(\mathcal{X}) \times 2^{\mathcal{X}} \times Q$ is the edge relation satisfying:*

$$\left(q \xrightarrow{a,g,X} q' \text{ and } q \xrightarrow{a,g',X'} q'' \text{ with } g \neq g'\right) \quad \Longrightarrow \quad g \cap g' = \emptyset.$$

Intuitively, the edge $q \xrightarrow{a,g,X} q'$ asserts that the DTA $\mathcal{A}$ can move from location q to q' when the input symbol is a and the guard g holds, while the clocks in X should be reset when entering q' (all other clocks keep their value). DTAs are deterministic as they have a single initial location, and outgoing edges of a location labeled with the same input symbol are required to have disjoint guards. In this way, the next location is uniquely determined for a given location and a given set of clock values. In case no guard is satisfied in a location for a given clock valuation, time can progress. If the advance of time will never reach a situation in which a guard holds, the DTA will stay in that location *ad infinitum*. Note that DTAs do not have location invariants. The semantics of a DTA is given by an infinite-state transition system [2]. Next, we define the notion of paths, i.e., runs or executions of a DTA. This is done using some auxiliary notions. A *clock valuation* η for a set $\mathcal{X}$ of clocks is a function $\eta : \mathcal{X} \to \mathbb{R}_{\geq 0}$, assigning to each clock $x \in \mathcal{X}$ its current value $\eta(x)$. The clock valuation η over $\mathcal{X}$ satisfies the clock constraint g, denoted $\eta \models g$, iff the values of the clocks under η fulfill g. For instance, $\eta \models x - y > c$ iff $\eta(x) - \eta(y) > c$. Other cases are defined analogously. For $d \in \mathbb{R}_{\geq 0}$, $\eta + d$ denotes the clock valuation where all clocks of η are increased by d. That is, $(\eta + d)(x) = \eta(x) + d$ for all clocks $x \in \mathcal{X}$. Clock *reset* for a subset $X \subseteq \mathcal{X}$, denoted by $\eta[X := 0]$, is the valuation η' defined by: $\forall x \in X.\eta'(x) := 0$ and $\forall x \notin X.\eta'(x) := \eta(x)$. The valuation that assigns 0 to all the clocks is denoted by $\mathbf{0}$. An (infinite) path of DTA $\mathcal{A}$ has the form $\rho = q \xrightarrow{a_0, t_0} q_1 \xrightarrow{a_1, t_1} \ldots$ such that $\eta_0 = \mathbf{0}$, and for all $j \geq 0$, it holds $t_j > 0$, $\eta_j + t_j \models g_j$, $\eta_{j+1} = (\eta_j + t_j)[X_j := 0]$, where η_j is the clock evaluation on entering q_j. Here, g_j is the guard of the j-th edge taken in the DTA and X_j the set of clock to be reset on that edge. A path ρ is accepted by $\mathcal{A}$ if $q_i \in F$ for some $i \geq 0$. Since the DTA is deterministic, the successor location is uniquely determined; for convenience we write $q' = succ(q, a, g)$.

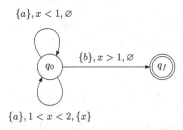

{a}, x < 1, ∅

{b}, x > 1, ∅

q_0

q_f

{a}, 1 < x < 2, {x}

Fig. 6. An example DTA $\mathcal{A}$

Example 9. Consider the DTA $\mathcal{A}$ shown in Fig. 6, where $\Sigma = \{a, b\}$, $Q = \{q_0, q_f\}$, $\mathcal{X} = \{x\}$, $F = \{q_f\}$ and q_0 is the initial location. An example timed path is $q_0 \xrightarrow{a, 1.4} q_0 \xrightarrow{b, 2.1} q_f$.

A path in a MA $\mathcal{M}$ can be "matched" by a path through DTA $\mathcal{A}$ by regarding sets of atomic propositions in $\mathcal{M}$ as input symbols of $\mathcal{A}$. Such a path is accepted, if at some point an accepting location in the DTA is reached:

Definition 12 (Path acceptance). *Let MA* $\mathcal{M} = (S, s_0, Act, AP, \rightarrow, \Rightarrow, L)$
and DTA $\mathcal{A} = (2^{AP}, \mathcal{X}, Q, q_0, F, \rightarrow)$. *The MA path* $\pi = s_0 \xrightarrow{\sigma_0, t_0} s_1 \xrightarrow{\sigma_1, t_1} s_2 \ldots$
is accepted by $\mathcal{A}$ *if there exists a corresponding DTA path*

$$q_0 \xrightarrow{L(s_0), t_0} \underbrace{succ(q_0, L(s_0), g_0)}_{=q_1} \xrightarrow{L(s_1), t_1} \underbrace{succ(q_1, L(s_1), g_1)}_{=q_2} \ldots$$

such that $q_j \in F$ *for some* $j \geq 0$. *Here,* $\eta_0 = \mathbf{0}$, g_i *is the (unique) guard in* q_i
(if it exists) such that $\eta_i + t_i \models g_i$ *and* $\eta_{i+1} = (\eta_i + t_i)[X_i := 0]$, *and* η_i *is the
clock evaluation on entering* q_i, *for* $i \geq 0$. *Let* $Paths^{\mathcal{M}}(\mathcal{A}) = \{\pi \in Paths^{\mathcal{M}} \mid \pi$ *is accepted by DTA* $\mathcal{A}\}^5$.

Definition 13 (Probability of accepted paths). *For MA* $\mathcal{M}$, $\mathcal{D} \in Adv(\mathcal{M})$
and DTA $\mathcal{A}$, *let* $Pr_{\mathcal{D}}(\mathcal{M} \models \mathcal{A}) = Pr_{\mathcal{D}}(Paths^{\mathcal{M}}(\mathcal{A}))$.

$Pr_{\mathcal{D}}(\mathcal{M} \models \mathcal{A})$ denote the probability of all paths of $\mathcal{M}$ under scheduler $\mathcal{D}$ that
are accepted by DTA $\mathcal{A}$.

Definition 14 (Max probability). *For MA* $\mathcal{M}$ *and DTA* $\mathcal{A}$, *let* $Pr^{max}(\mathcal{M} \models \mathcal{A}) = \sup\limits_{\mathcal{D} \in Adv(\mathcal{M})} Pr_{\mathcal{D}}(\mathcal{M} \models \mathcal{A})$.

In simple words, $Pr^{max}(\mathcal{M} \models \mathcal{A})$ is the maximum probability of MA $\mathcal{M}$ satisfying a DTA $\mathcal{A}$ computed over all possible schedulers of $\mathcal{M}$, i.e., $Adv(\mathcal{M})$.
$Pr^{min}(\mathcal{M} \models \mathcal{A})$ can be defined in an analogous manner. For MAs, THD schedulers suffice for computing $Pr^{max}(\mathcal{M} \models \mathcal{A})$ and $Pr^{min}(\mathcal{M} \models \mathcal{A})$ [12,27].

Theorem 3 (Preservation of DTA). *Let* $\mathcal{M}_1$, $\mathcal{M}_2$ *be two MAs such that*
$\mathcal{M}_1 \equiv_{THD} \mathcal{M}_2$. *Then for any DTA* $\mathcal{A}$ *we have:*

$$Pr^{max}(\mathcal{M}_1 \models \mathcal{A}) = Pr^{max}(\mathcal{M}_2 \models \mathcal{A})$$

$$Pr^{min}(\mathcal{M}_1 \models \mathcal{A}) = Pr^{min}(\mathcal{M}_2 \models \mathcal{A})$$

In simple words this theorem states that if two MAs are THD trace equivalent,
then their maximum (resp. minimum) probability to satisfy any DTA specification coincides.

Corollary 1. *THD trace equivalence preserves maximum and minimum transient state probabilities.*

5   Metric Temporal Logic

In this section we show that THR trace equivalence for closed MAs preserves
the probability of satisfying MTL specifications. Note that the expressive power
of MTL is different from that of DTA. For example, property specified using

---

[5] For any MA $\mathcal{M}$ and DTA $\mathcal{A}$, the set $Paths^{\mathcal{M}}(\mathcal{A})$ is measurable [17].

an MTL formula $\lozenge^{[0,100]}\square^{[0,5]}a$ cannot be expressed using DTA. On the other hand, the following DTA property cannot be expressed using MTL: what is the probability to reach a given target state within the deadline, while avoiding forbidden states and not staying too long in any of the dangerous states on the way [34]. We now recall the syntax and semantics of Metric Temporal Logic [10,28].

Definition 15 (Syntax of MTL). *Let AP be a set of atomic propositions, then the formulas of MTL are built from AP using Boolean connectives, and time-constrained versions of the* until *operator U as follows:*

$$\varphi ::= tt \mid a \mid \neg\varphi \mid \varphi \wedge \varphi \mid \varphi\, U^I\, \varphi$$

where $I \subseteq \mathbb{R}_{\geq 0}$ is a non-empty interval with rational bounds, and $a \in AP$.

Next, we define the semantics of MTL formulas over MA paths.

Definition 16 (Semantics of MTL formulas). *The meaning of MTL formulas is defined by means of a satisfaction relation, denoted by $\models$, between a MA $\mathcal{M}$, one of its paths π, MTL formula φ, and time $t \in \mathbb{R}_{\geq 0}$. Let $\pi = s_0 \xrightarrow{\sigma_0, t_0} s_1 \ldots s_{n-1} \xrightarrow{\sigma_{n-1}, t_{n-1}} s_n \ldots$ be a finite or infinite path of $\mathcal{M}$, then $(\pi, t) \models \varphi$ is defined inductively by:*

$$(\pi, t) \models tt$$
$$(\pi, t) \models a \qquad iff\ a \in L(\pi@t)$$
$$(\pi, t) \models \neg\varphi \qquad iff\ not(\pi, t) \models \varphi$$
$$(\pi, t) \models \varphi_1 \wedge \varphi_2 \quad iff\ (\pi, t) \models \varphi_1\ and\ (\pi, t) \models \varphi_2$$
$$(\pi, t) \models \varphi_1\, U^I\, \varphi_2 \quad iff\ \exists t' \in t{+}I.\ ((\pi, t') \models \varphi_2 \wedge \forall t \leq t'' < t'.(\pi, t'') \models \varphi_1).$$

Timed variant of standard temporal operator $\lozenge$ ("eventually") is derived in the following way: $\lozenge^I \varphi = tt\, U^I\, \varphi$. Similarly, timed variant of $\square$ ("globally") is derived as follows: $\square^I \varphi = \neg(\lozenge^I \neg\varphi)$. Let $Paths^{\mathcal{M}}(\varphi) = \{\pi \in Paths^{\mathcal{M}} \mid \pi \models \varphi\}$[6].

Definition 17. *For MA $\mathcal{M}$, $\mathcal{D} \in Adv(\mathcal{M})$ and MTL formula φ, let $Pr_{\mathcal{D}}(\mathcal{M} \models \varphi) = Pr_{\mathcal{D}}(Paths^{\mathcal{M}}(\varphi))$.*

$Pr_{\mathcal{D}}(\mathcal{M} \models \varphi)$ denote the probability of all paths of $\mathcal{M}$ under scheduler $\mathcal{D}$ that satisfy an MTL formula φ.

Definition 18 (Maximum probability of MTL). *For MA $\mathcal{M}$ and MTL formula φ, $Pr^{max}(\mathcal{M} \models \varphi) = \sup_{\mathcal{D} \in Adv(\mathcal{M})} Pr_{\mathcal{D}}(\mathcal{M} \models \varphi)$.*

$Pr^{min}(\mathcal{M} \models \varphi)$ can be defined in an analogous manner.

---

[6] Note that paths satisfying an MTL formula φ can be written as a set of cylinder sets [34].

Theorem 4 (Preservation of MTL). *Let* $\mathcal{M}_1$, $\mathcal{M}_2$ *be two MAs such that* $\mathcal{M}_1 \equiv_{THR} \mathcal{M}_2$. *Then for any MTL formula* φ *we have:*

$$Pr^{max}(\mathcal{M}_1 \models \varphi) = Pr^{max}(\mathcal{M}_2 \models \varphi)$$

$$Pr^{min}(\mathcal{M}_1 \models \varphi) = Pr^{min}(\mathcal{M}_2 \models \varphi)$$

This theorem asserts that THR-trace equivalent MAs have the same maximum (resp. minimum) probability of satisfying any MTL formula φ.

Corollary 2. *THR trace equivalence preserves maximum and minimum transient state probabilities.*

6   Conclusions and Future Work

This paper presented several variants of trace equivalence for closed MAs. We investigated the relationship among these trace relations and also compared them with bisimulation for MAs. Finally, we proved that trace equivalent MAs have the same probability of satisfying DTA and MTL properties. This research work can be extended in several directions which are as follows:

- Investigate the relationship between trace equivalences and several variants of weak bisimulation [15,16,35].
- Investigate the relationship between trace equivalences and weighted Markovian equivalence [30,31,33].
- Study ready trace and failure trace semantics.
- Use button pushing experiments to define (approximate) trace equivalences for open MAs.

References

1. Aldini, A., Bernardo, M.: Expected-delay-summing weak bisimilarity for Markov automata. In: QAPL. EPTCS, vol. 194, pp. 1–15 (2015)
2. Alur, R., Dill, D.L.: A theory of timed automata. Theor. Comput. Sci. **126**(2), 183–235 (1994)
3. Ash, R.B., Doleans-Dade, C.A.: Probability and Measure Theory. Academic Press, New York (2000)
4. Baier, C., Haverkort, B.R., Hermanns, H., Katoen, J.-P.: Model-checking algorithms for continuous-time Markov chains. IEEE Trans. Softw. Eng. **29**(6), 524–541 (2003)
5. Baier, C., Katoen, J.-P.: Principles of Model Checking. MIT Press, Cambridge (2008)
6. Böde, E., et al.: Compositional dependability evaluation for STATEMATE. IEEE Trans. Softw. Eng. **35**(2), 274–292 (2009)
7. Boudali, H., Crouzen, P., Haverkort, B.R., Kuntz, M., Stoelinga, M.: Architectural dependability evaluation with arcade. In: DSN, pp. 512–521. IEEE Computer Society (2008)

8. Boudali, H., Crouzen, P., Stoelinga, M.: A compositional semantics for dynamic fault trees in terms of interactive Markov chains. In: Namjoshi, K.S., Yoneda, T., Higashino, T., Okamura, Y. (eds.) ATVA 2007. LNCS, vol. 4762, pp. 441–456. Springer, Heidelberg (2007). https://doi.org/10.1007/978-3-540-75596-8_31

9. Boudali, H., Crouzen, P., Stoelinga, M.: Dynamic fault tree analysis using input/output interactive Markov chains. In: DSN, pp. 708–717. IEEE Computer Society (2007)

10. Bouyer, P.: From qualitative to quantitative analysis of timed systems. Mémoire d'habilitation, Université Paris 7, Paris, France, January 2009

11. Bozzano, M., Cimatti, A., Katoen, J., Nguyen, V.Y., Noll, T., Roveri, M.: Safety, dependability and performance analysis of extended AADL models. Comput. J. **54**(5), 754–775 (2011)

12. Chen, T., Han, T., Katoen, J.-P., Mereacre, A.: Observing continuous-time MDPs by 1-clock timed automata. In: Delzanno, G., Potapov, I. (eds.) RP 2011. LNCS, vol. 6945, pp. 2–25. Springer, Heidelberg (2011). https://doi.org/10.1007/978-3-642-24288-5_2

13. Coste, N., Hermanns, H., Lantreibecq, E., Serwe, W.: Towards performance prediction of compositional models in industrial GALS designs. In: Bouajjani, A., Maler, O. (eds.) CAV 2009. LNCS, vol. 5643, pp. 204–218. Springer, Heidelberg (2009). https://doi.org/10.1007/978-3-642-02658-4_18

14. Deng, Y., Hennessy, M.: On the semantics of Markov automata. In: Aceto, L., Henzinger, M., Sgall, J. (eds.) ICALP 2011. LNCS, vol. 6756, pp. 307–318. Springer, Heidelberg (2011). https://doi.org/10.1007/978-3-642-22012-8_24

15. Deng, Y., Hennessy, M.: On the semantics of Markov automata. Inf. Comput. **222**, 139–168 (2013)

16. Eisentraut, C., Hermanns, H., Zhang, L.: On probabilistic automata in continuous time. In: LICS, pp. 342–351 (2010)

17. Fu, H.: Approximating acceptance probabilities of CTMC-paths on multi-clock deterministic timed automata. In: HSCC, pp. 323–332. ACM (2013)

18. Guck, D., Hatefi, H., Hermanns, H., Katoen, J.-P., Timmer, M.: Modelling, reduction and analysis of Markov automata. In: Joshi, K., Siegle, M., Stoelinga, M., D'Argenio, P.R. (eds.) QEST 2013. LNCS, vol. 8054, pp. 55–71. Springer, Heidelberg (2013). https://doi.org/10.1007/978-3-642-40196-1_5

19. Guck, D., Hatefi, H., Hermanns, H., Katoen, J., Timmer, M.: Analysis of timed and long-run objectives for Markov automata. LMCS **10**(3) (2014)

20. Guck, D., Timmer, M., Hatefi, H., Ruijters, E., Stoelinga, M.: Modelling and analysis of Markov reward automata. In: Cassez, F., Raskin, J.-F. (eds.) ATVA 2014. LNCS, vol. 8837, pp. 168–184. Springer, Cham (2014). https://doi.org/10.1007/978-3-319-11936-6_13

21. Hatefi, H., Hermanns, H.: Model checking algorithms for Markov automata. ECE-ASST **53** (2012)

22. Hermanns, H.: Interactive Markov Chains: And the Quest for Quantified Quality. Springer, Heidelberg (2002). https://doi.org/10.1007/3-540-45804-2

23. Hermanns, H., Katoen, J., Neuhäußer, M.R., Zhang, L.: GSPN model checking despite confusion. Technical report, RWTH Aachen University (2010)

24. Mateescu, R., Serwe, W.: A study of shared-memory mutual exclusion protocols using CADP. In: Kowalewski, S., Roveri, M. (eds.) FMICS 2010. LNCS, vol. 6371, pp. 180–197. Springer, Heidelberg (2010). https://doi.org/10.1007/978-3-642-15898-8_12

25. Meyer, J.F., Movaghar, A., Sanders, W.H.: Stochastic activity networks: structure, behavior, and application. In: PNPM, pp. 106–115. IEEE Computer Society (1985)

26. Neuhäußer, M.R.: Model checking non-deterministic and randomly timed systems. Ph.D. thesis, RWTH Aachen University. Ph.D. dissertation, RWTH Aachen University (2015)

27. Neuhäußer, M.R., Stoelinga, M., Katoen, J.-P.: Delayed nondeterminism in continuous-time Markov decision processes. In: de Alfaro, L. (ed.) FoSSaCS 2009. LNCS, vol. 5504, pp. 364–379. Springer, Heidelberg (2009). https://doi.org/10.1007/978-3-642-00596-1_26

28. Ouaknine, J., Worrell, J.: Some recent results in metric temporal logic. In: Cassez, F., Jard, C. (eds.) FORMATS 2008. LNCS, vol. 5215, pp. 1–13. Springer, Heidelberg (2008). https://doi.org/10.1007/978-3-540-85778-5_1

29. Segala, R.: Modelling and verification of randomized distributed real time systems. Ph.D. thesis, MIT (1995)

30. Sharma, A.: Reduction techniques for non-deterministic and probabilistic systems. Ph.D. dissertation, RWTH Aachen (2015)

31. Sharma, A.: Interactive Markovian equivalence. In: Reinecke, P., Di Marco, A. (eds.) EPEW 2017. LNCS, vol. 10497, pp. 33–49. Springer, Cham (2017). https://doi.org/10.1007/978-3-319-66583-2_3

32. Sharma, A.: Trace relations and logical preservation for continuous-time Markov decision processes. In: Hung, D., Kapur, D. (eds.) ICTAC 2017. LNCS, vol. 10580, pp. 192–209. Springer, Cham (2017). https://doi.org/10.1007/978-3-319-67729-3_12

33. Sharma, A.: Non-bisimulation based behavioral relations for Markov automata. In: Jansen, D.N., Prabhakar, P. (eds.) FORMATS 2018. LNCS, vol. 11022, pp. 179–196. Springer, Cham (2018)

34. Sharma, A., Katoen, J.-P.: Weighted lumpability on Markov chains. In: Clarke, E., Virbitskaite, I., Voronkov, A. (eds.) PSI 2011. LNCS, vol. 7162, pp. 322–339. Springer, Heidelberg (2012). https://doi.org/10.1007/978-3-642-29709-0_28

35. Song, L., Zhang, L., Godskesen, J.C.: Late weak bisimulation for Markov automata. CoRR, abs/1202.4116 (2012)

36. Timmer, M., Katoen, J.-P., van de Pol, J., Stoelinga, M.I.A.: Efficient modelling and generation of Markov automata. In: Koutny, M., Ulidowski, I. (eds.) CONCUR 2012. LNCS, vol. 7454, pp. 364–379. Springer, Heidelberg (2012). https://doi.org/10.1007/978-3-642-32940-1_26

37. Wolf, V., Baier, C., Majster-Cederbaum, M.E.: Trace machines for observing continuous-time Markov chains. ENTCS **153**(2), 259–277 (2006)

38. Wolf, V., Baier, C., Majster-Cederbaum, M.E.: Trace semantics for stochastic systems with nondeterminism. Electr. Notes Theor. Comput. Sci. **164**(3), 187–204 (2006)

Non-bisimulation Based Behavioral Relations for Markov Automata

Arpit Sharma[(⊠)]

Department of Electrical Engineering and Computer Science,
Indian Institute of Science Education and Research Bhopal, Bhopal, India
arpit@iiserb.ac.in

Abstract. Markov automata (MAs) [16] extend probabilistic automata (PAs) [29] with stochastic aspects [22]. This paper defines two equivalence relations, namely, weighted Markovian equivalence (WME) and weak weighted Markovian equivalence (WWME) for the subclass of closed MAs. We define the quotient system under these relations and investigate their relationship with strong bisimulation and weak bisimulation, respectively. Next, we show that both WME and WWME can be used for repeated minimization of closed MAs. Finally, we prove that properties specified using deterministic timed automaton (DTA) specifications and metric temporal logic (MTL) formulas are preserved under WME and WWME quotienting.

Keywords: Markov · Equivalence · Bisimulation · Linear-time
Temporal logic

1 Introduction

Markov automata (MAs) have been introduced in [16] as a continuous-time version of Segala's probabilistic automata (PAs) [29]. MAs thus support non-deterministic probabilistic branching and exponentially distributed delays in continuous time. MAs are compositional, i.e., a parallel composition operator allows one to construct a complex MA from several component MAs running in parallel.

They provide a natural semantics for a variety of specifications for concurrent systems, as for example, dynamic fault trees [7,8], architectural description languages such as AADL [6,10], generalized stochastic Petri nets (GSPNs) [24], STATEMATE [5] and stochastic activity networks (SANs) [26]. They can also be used for modeling and analysis of GALS (Globally Asynchronous Locally Synchronous) hardware design [12] and shared memory mutual exclusion protocols [25]. Recently, a data rich specification language for MAs has been introduced [35]. Analyzing MAs involves applying model checking algorithms [18–20] on *closed*[1] MA models to compute the probability of linear or branching real-time

---

[1] A MA is said to be closed if it is not subject to any further synchronization.

© Springer Nature Switzerland AG 2018
D. N. Jansen and P. Prabhakar (Eds.): FORMATS 2018, LNCS 11022, pp. 179–196, 2018.
https://doi.org/10.1007/978-3-030-00151-3_11

objectives, e.g., long-run average, expected time, timed (interval) reachability [18] and Continuous Stochastic Logic (CSL) [21].

Equivalence relations are used to compare the behavior of MAs [14,16,34]. Abstraction techniques based on equivalence relations reduce the state space of MAs, by aggregating equivalent states into a single state. The reduced state space obtained under an equivalence relation, called a quotient, can then be used for analysis provided it preserves a rich class of properties of interest. Strong and weak bisimulation [13,14,16] are two well known equivalence relations for MAs. Strong bisimulation for MAs preserves time-bounded reachability probabilities [23]. Note that bisimulation is too restrictive as it requires equivalent states to simulate their mutual stepwise behavior. Due to this reason, for certain classes of stochastic systems, e.g., incremental service systems [4], bisimulation fails to provide any state space reduction. Additionally, if the properties to be verified belong to the class of linear real-time properties, e.g., timed reachability, MTL and DTA specifications, it is often desirable to use an alternate equivalence relation for reducing the size of system. This is especially true if the bisimulation has already failed to provide significant state space reduction.

This paper proposes a novel theoretical framework for the state space reduction of the subclass of closed MAs, i.e., that do not allow non-determinism between action transitions. We define weighted Markovian equivalence (WME) and weak weighted Markovian equivalence (WWME) for closed MAs. Unlike bisimulation which compares states on the basis of their direct successors, WME considers a *two-step* perspective. Before explaining the idea of WME, let us recall that every state of a closed MA can either have Markovian transitions or τ-labeled probabilistic transitions. Accordingly, every state can either be a Markovian state or a probabilistic state, respectively. Every Markovian transition is labeled with a positive real number λ. This parameter indicates the rate of the exponential distribution, i.e., the probability of a λ-labeled transition to be enabled within t time units equals $1 - e^{-\lambda \cdot t}$. Similarly, every probabilistic transition relates a state and a τ action to a probability distribution over the set of states.

Two probabilistic states s and s' are WME equivalent if for each pair of their direct predecessors *weighted probability* to directly move to any equivalence class via the equivalence class $[s] = [s']$ coincides. In the same way, two Markovian states s and s' are WME equivalent if for each pair of their direct predecessors *weighted rate* to directly move to any equivalence class via the equivalence class $[s] = [s']$ coincides. In the weak setting, two probabilistic states s and s' are weak WME equivalent if for each pair of their direct predecessors (that are not in $[s]$) *weak weighted probability* to move to any equivalence class (other than $[s]$) in two or more steps via the equivalence class $[s]$ coincides. Note that all the extra steps are taken within $[s]$.

Contributions. The main contributions of this paper are as follows:

– We provide a structural definition of WME on closed MAs, define quotient under WME and investigate its relationship with strong bisimulation [16].

- We provide a structural definition of weak WME on closed MAs, define quotient under WWME and investigate its relationship with weak bisimulation [16].
- Finally, we prove that properties specified using DTA specifications and MTL formulas are preserved under WME and WWME quotienting.

1.1 Related Work

In [3], Bernardo considered Markovian testing equivalence over sequential Markovian process calculus (SMPC), and coined the term T-lumpability [4] for the induced state-level aggregation where T stands for testing. His testing equivalence is a congruence w.r.t. parallel composition, and preserves transient as well as steady-state probabilities. Bernardo's T-lumpability has been reconsidered in [30,33] where weighted lumpability (WL) is defined as a structural notion on CTMCs. Note that DTA and MTL specifications are preserved under WL [30]. In [36], several linear-time equivalences (Markovian trace equivalence, failure and ready trace equivalence) for CTMCs have been investigated. Testing scenarios based on push-button experiments have been used for defining these equivalences.

For interactive Markov chains (IMCs), strong and weak bisimulation relations have been defined in [23]. This paper proves that strong and weak bisimulation preserve time-bounded reachability properties. In [31] strong and weak variants of interactive Markovian equivalence (IME) have been defined over states of a IMC. IME preserves the probability of timed-bounded reachability properties. For MAs, strong and weak bisimulation relations have been defined in [16]. In [16], weak bisimulation has been defined over state probability distributions rather than over individual ones. In [14], it has been shown that weak bisimulation provides a sound and complete proof methodology for a touchstone equivalence called reduction barbed congruence. Notions of early and late semantics for MAs have been proposed in [15,34]. Using these semantics, early and late weak bisimulations have been defined and it has been proved that late weak bisimulation is weaker than all of the other variants defined in [13,14,16]. Recently, an expected-delay-summing weak bisimulation has been defined for MAs [1]. Our definition of (weak) WME here builds on that investigated in [30,33] for CTMCs.

Organisation of the paper. Section 2 briefly recalls the main concepts of MA. Section 3 defines WME and investigates its relationship with strong bisimulation. Section 4 defines the weaker variant of WME and investigates its relationship with weak bisimulation. Section 5 proves the preservation of DTA properties. Section 6 proves the preservation of MTL properties. Finally, Sect. 7 concludes the paper and provides pointers for future research.

2 Preliminaries

This section presents the necessary definitions and basic concepts related to Markov automata (MA) that are needed for the understanding of the rest of this paper. Let $Distr(S)$ denote the set of distribution functions over the countable set S.

Definition 1. *A* Markov automaton *(MA) is a tuple* $\mathcal{M} = (S, s_0, Act, AP, \rightarrow, \Rightarrow, L)$ *where:*

- S *is a nonempty finite set of states,*
- s_0 *is the initial state,*
- Act *is a finite set of actions,*
- AP *is a finite set of atomic propositions,*
- $\rightarrow \subseteq S \times Act \times Distr(S)$ *is the probabilistic transition relation,*
- $\Rightarrow \subseteq S \times \mathbb{R}_{>0} \times S$ *is the Markovian transition relation, and*
- $L : S \rightarrow 2^{AP}$ *is a labeling function.*

We abbreviate $(s, \alpha, \mu) \in \rightarrow$ as $s \xrightarrow{\alpha} \mu$ and similarly, $(s, \lambda, s') \in \Rightarrow$ by $s \xRightarrow{\lambda} s'$. Let $PT(s)$ and $MT(s)$ denote the set of probabilistic and Markovian transitions that leave state s. A state s is *Markovian* iff $MT(s) \neq \varnothing$ and $PT(s) = \varnothing$; it is *probabilistic* iff $MT(s) = \varnothing$ and $PT(s) \neq \varnothing$. Further, s is a *hybrid* state iff $MT(s) \neq \varnothing$ and $PT(s) \neq \varnothing$; finally s is a *deadlock* state iff $MT(s) = \varnothing$ and $PT(s) = \varnothing$. In this paper we only consider those MAs that do not have any deadlock states. Let $MS \subseteq S$ and $PS \subseteq S$ denote the set of Markovian and probabilistic states in MA $\mathcal{M}$. For any Markovian state $s \in MS$ let $R(s, s') = \sum\{\lambda | s \xRightarrow{\lambda} s'\}$ be the rate to move from state s to state s'. The exit rate for state s is defined by: $E(s) = \sum_{s' \in S} R(s, s')$.

The meaning of a Markovian transition $s \xRightarrow{\lambda} s'$ is that the MA moves from state s to s' within t time units with probability $1 - e^{-\lambda \cdot t}$. If s has multiple outgoing Markovian transitions to different successors, then we speak of a race between these transitions, known as the *race condition*. In this case, the probability to move from s to s' within t time units is $\frac{R(s,s')}{E(s)} \cdot (1 - e^{-E(s) \cdot t})$. Note that in closed MAs all outgoing probabilistic transitions from every state $s \in S$ are labeled with $\tau \in Act$ (internal action).

Definition 2 *(Maximal progress [23]). In any closed MA, probabilistic transitions take precedence over Markovian transitions.*

Intuitively, the maximal progress assumption states that in closed MA, τ labeled transitions are not subject to interaction and thus can happen immediately[2], whereas the probability of a Markovian transition to happen immediately is zero. Accordingly, we assume that each state s has either only outgoing τ transitions or outgoing Markovian transitions. In other words, a closed MA only has probabilistic and Markovian states. We use a distinguished action $\perp \notin Act$ to indicate Markovian transitions.

---

[2] We restrict to models without zenoness. In simple words, this means that τ cycles are not allowed.

Definition 3 (Timed paths). *Let $\mathcal{M} = (S, s_0, Act, AP, \rightarrow, \Rightarrow, L)$ be a MA. An infinite* path π *in $\mathcal{M}$ is a sequence* $s_0 \xrightarrow{\sigma_0, t_0} s_1 \xrightarrow{\sigma_1, t_1} s_2 \dots s_{n-1} \xrightarrow{\sigma_{n-1}, t_{n-1}} s_n \dots$ *where $s_i \in S$, $\sigma_i \in Act$ or $\sigma_i = \bot$, and for each i, there exists a measure μ_i such that $(s_i, \sigma_i, \mu_i) \in \rightarrow$ with $\mu_i(s_{i+1}) > 0$. For $\sigma_i \in Act$, $s_i \xrightarrow{\sigma_i, t_i} s_{i+1}$ denotes that after residing t_i time units in s_i, the MA $\mathcal{M}$ has moved via action σ_i to s_{i+1} with probability $\mu_i(s_{i+1})$. Instead, $s_i \xrightarrow{\bot, t_i} s_{i+1}$ denote that after residing t_i time units in s_i, a Markovian transition led to s_{i+1} with probability $\mu_i(s_{i+1}) = P(s_i, s_{i+1})$ where $P(s_i, s_{i+1}) = \frac{R(s_i, s_{i+1})}{E(s_i)}$. A finite path π is a finite prefix of an infinite path. The length of an infinite path π, denoted $|\pi|$ is ∞; the length of a finite path π with $n + 1$ states is n.*

Let $Paths^{\mathcal{M}} = Paths_{fin}^{\mathcal{M}} \cup Paths_{\omega}^{\mathcal{M}}$ denote the set of all paths in $\mathcal{M}$ that start in s_0, where $Paths_{fin}^{\mathcal{M}} = \bigcup_{n \in \mathbb{N}} Paths_n^{\mathcal{M}}$ is the set of all finite paths in $\mathcal{M}$ and $Paths_n^{\mathcal{M}}$ denote the set of all finite paths of length n that start in s_0. Let $Paths_{\omega}^{\mathcal{M}}$ is the set of all infinite paths in $\mathcal{M}$ that start in s_0. For infinite path $\pi = s_0 \xrightarrow{\sigma_0, t_0} s_1 \xrightarrow{\sigma_1, t_1} s_2 \dots$ and any $i \in \mathbb{N}$, let $\pi[i] = s_i$, the $(i+1)$th state of π. For any $t \in \mathbb{R}_{\geq 0}$, let $\pi@t$ denote the sequence of states that π occupies at time t. Note that $\pi@t$ is in general not a single state, but rather a sequence of several states, as a MA may exhibit immediate transitions and thus may occupy various states at the same time instant. Let $Act(s)$ denote the set of enabled actions from state s. Note that in case s is a Markovian state then $Act(s) = \{\bot\}$. Let $Act_{\bot} = Act \cup \{\bot\}$. The usual cylinder set construction yields a σ-algebra of measurable subsets of paths [27,32].

Assumptions. Throughout this paper we make the following assumptions:

1. Every state of a MA $\mathcal{M}$ has at least one predecessor. This is not a restriction, as any MA $\mathcal{M} = (S, s_0, Act, AP, \rightarrow, \Rightarrow, L)$ can be transformed into an equivalent MA $(S', s_0', Act, AP', \rightarrow', \Rightarrow, L')$ which fulfills this condition. This is done by adding a new state $\hat{s}$ to S equipped with a self-loop and which has a transition to each state in S without predecessors. Let all the outgoing transitions from $\hat{s}$ be labeled with τ. To distinguish this state from the others we set $L'(\hat{s}) = \#$ with $\# \notin AP$ (All other labels, states and transitions remain unaffected). Let $s_0' = s_0$. It follows that all states in $S' = S \cup \{\hat{s}\}$ have at least one predecessor. Moreover, the reachable state space of both MA coincides.
2. We assume that the initial state s_0 of a MA is distinguished from all other states by a unique label, say \$. This assumption implies that for any equivalence that groups equally labeled states, $\{s_0\}$ constitutes a separate equivalence class.
3. We also assume that for every state s of a MA $\mathcal{M}$, non-determinism between action transitions is not allowed[3].

For convenience, we neither show the state $\hat{s}$ nor the label \$ in figures.

---

[3] Since our closed MA models do not allow multiple action transitions, schedulers are not required for resolving non-deterministic choices.

3 Weighted Markovian Equivalence

Before defining weighted Markovian equivalence, we first define some auxiliary concepts. All the definitions presented in this section are relative to a closed MA $\mathcal{M} = (S, s_0, Act, AP, \rightarrow, \Rightarrow, L)$, where $Act = \{\tau\}$. For any state $s \in S$ and $Act = \{\tau\}$, the set of τ-predecessors of s is defined by: $Pred(s, \tau) = \{s' \in S | \exists \mu : s' \xrightarrow{\tau} \mu \wedge \mu(s) > 0\}$ and $Pred(s) = \{s' \in S | R(s', s) > 0\} \cup Pred(s, \tau)$. Let for $C \subseteq S$, $Pred(C) = \bigcup_{s \in C} Pred(s)$. Similarly, the set of τ-successors of any state s is defined by: $Post(s, \tau) = \{s' \in S | \exists \mu : s \xrightarrow{\tau} \mu \wedge \mu(s') > 0\}$ and $Post(s) = \{s' \in S | R(s, s') > 0\} \cup Post(s, \tau)$. Let $Post(C) = \bigcup_{s \in C} Post(s)$.

Definition 4 (Probabilistic closed). *Let $C \subseteq S$, then C is said to be probabilistic closed iff $C \subseteq PS \wedge Pred(C) \subseteq PS$.*

Definition 5 (Markovian closed). *Let $C \subseteq S$, then C is said to be Markovian closed iff $C \subseteq MS \wedge Pred(C) \subseteq MS$.*

Let $P(S)$ denote the set of all possible subsets of S that are probabilistic closed. Let $M(S)$ denote the set of all possible subsets of S that are Markovian closed.

Example 1. Consider the MA shown in Fig. 1 (left). Let $C = \{s_1, s_2\}$ and $D = \{s_5, s_6, s_7\}$. Here C is probabilistic closed since $C \subseteq PS$ and $Pred(C) = \{s_0\} \subseteq PS$. Similarly, D is Markovian closed.

Definition 6. *For $s, s' \in S$ and $C \subseteq S$, the function $pbr : S \times S \times 2^S \rightarrow \mathbb{R}_{\geq 0}$ is defined by:*

$$pbr(s, s', C) = \begin{cases} \frac{\mu(s')}{\mu(C)} & \text{if } s' \in C \text{ and } \mu(C) > 0 \\ 0 & \text{otherwise.} \end{cases}$$

where $(s, \tau, \mu) \in \rightarrow$ and $\mu(C) = \sum_{s' \in C} \mu(s')$.

Example 2. Consider the MA shown in Fig. 1 (left). Let $C = \{s_1, s_2\}$. Then $pbr(s_0, s_1, C) = \frac{1}{3}$, $pbr(s_0, s_2, C) = \frac{2}{3}$.

Definition 7 (Weighted probability). *For $s \in S$, and $C, D \subseteq S$, the function $wp : S \times 2^S \times 2^S \rightarrow \mathbb{R}_{\geq 0}$ is defined by:*

$$wp(s, C, D) = \sum_{s' \in C} pbr(s, s', C) \cdot \mu'(D)$$

where $(s', \tau, \mu') \in \rightarrow$.

Example 3. Consider the MA shown in Fig. 1 (left). Let $C = \{s_1, s_2\}$ and $D = \{s_3\}$. Then $wp(s_0, C, D) = \frac{1}{3} \cdot 1 + \frac{2}{3} \cdot 0 = \frac{1}{3}$. Similarly, for $D = \{s_4\}$, $wp(s_0, C, D) = \frac{1}{3} \cdot 0 + \frac{2}{3} \cdot 1 = \frac{2}{3}$.

Definition 8. *For $s, s' \in S$ and $C \subseteq S$, the function $P : S \times S \times 2^S \to \mathbb{R}_{\geq 0}$ is defined by:*

$$P(s, s', C) = \begin{cases} \frac{P(s,s')}{P(s,C)} & \text{if } s' \in C \text{ and } P(s, C) > 0 \\ 0 & \text{otherwise.} \end{cases}$$

where $P(s, s') = \frac{R(s,s')}{E(s)}$ and $P(s, C) = \sum_{s' \in C} P(s, s')$.

Intuitively, $P(s, s', C)$ is the probability to move from state s to s' under the condition that s moves to some state in C.

Example 4. Consider the MA shown in Fig. 1 (left). Let $C = \{s_5, s_6, s_7\}$. Then $P(s_3, s_5, C) = \frac{1}{3}$, $P(s_3, s_6, C) = \frac{2}{3}$, $P(s_4, s_6, C) = \frac{2}{3}$ and $P(s_4, s_7, C) = \frac{1}{3}$.

Definition 9 (Weighted rate). *For $s \in S$, and $C, D \subseteq S$, the function $wr : S \times 2^S \times 2^S \to \mathbb{R}_{\geq 0}$ is defined by:*

$$wr(s, C, D) = \sum_{s' \in C} P(s, s', C) \cdot R(s', D)$$

where $R(s', D) = \sum_{s'' \in D} R(s', s'')$.

Intuitively, $wr(s, C, D)$ is the (weighted) rate to move from s to some states in D in two steps via states of C.

Example 5. Consider the example in Fig. 1 (left). Let $C = \{s_5, s_6, s_7\}$ and $D = \{s_8\}$. Then $wr(s_3, C, D) = P(s_3, s_5, C) \cdot R(s_5, D) + P(s_3, s_6, C) \cdot R(s_6, D) = \frac{1}{3} \cdot 0 + \frac{2}{3} \cdot 2 = \frac{4}{3}$. Similarly, for $D = \{s_9\}$, $wr(s_3, C, D) = P(s_3, s_5, C) \cdot R(s_5, D) + P(s_3, s_6, C) \cdot R(s_6, D) = \frac{1}{3} \cdot 2 + \frac{2}{3} \cdot 0 = \frac{2}{3}$.

Definition 10 (WME). *Equivalence $\mathcal{R}$ on S is a weighted Markovian equivalence (WME) if we have:*

1. $\forall (s_1, s_2) \in \mathcal{R}$ *it holds:* $L(s_1) = L(s_2)$ *and* $E(s_1) = E(s_2)$,
2. $\forall C \in S/\mathcal{R}$ *s.t.* $C \in P(S)$, $\forall D \in S/\mathcal{R}$ *and* $\forall s', s'' \in Pred(C)$: $wp(s', C, D) = wp(s'', C, D)$,
3. $\forall C \in S/\mathcal{R}$ *s.t.* $C \in M(S)$, $\forall D \in S/\mathcal{R}$ *and* $\forall s', s'' \in Pred(C)$: $wr(s', C, D) = wr(s'', C, D)$,
4. $\forall C \in S/\mathcal{R}$ *s.t.* $C \notin P(S) \wedge C \notin M(S)$: $|C| = 1$.

States s_1, s_2 are WM related, denoted by $s_1 \equiv s_2$, if $(s_1, s_2) \in \mathcal{R}$ for some WME $\mathcal{R}$.

Example 6. For the closed MA in Fig. 1 (left), the equivalence relation induced by the partitioning $\{\{s_0\}, \{s_1, s_2\}, \{s_3\}, \{s_4\}, \{s_5, s_6, s_7\}, \{s_8\}, \{s_9\}, \{s_{10}\}\}$ is a WME relation.

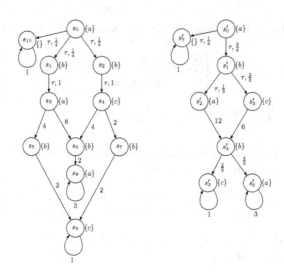

Fig. 1. MA $\mathcal{M}$ (left) and its quotient under a WME $\mathcal{R}$ (right)

3.1   Quotient MA

Definition 11. *For a WME relation $\mathcal{R}$ on $\mathcal{M}$, the quotient MA $\mathcal{M}/_\mathcal{R}$ is defined by $\mathcal{M}/_\mathcal{R} = (S/_\mathcal{R}, s_0', Act, AP, \rightarrow', \Rightarrow', L')$ where:*

- *$S/_\mathcal{R}$ is the set of all equivalence classes under $\mathcal{R}$,*
- *$s_0' = C$ where $s_0 \in C = [s_0]_\mathcal{R}$,*
- *$\rightarrow' \subseteq S/_\mathcal{R} \times Act \times Distr(S/_\mathcal{R})$ is defined by $\dfrac{C \in P(S) \wedge p = wp(s', C, D),\ s' \in Pred(C)}{C \xrightarrow{\tau} \mu' \wedge \mu'(D) = p}$
  and $\dfrac{C \notin P(S) \wedge \exists s \in C : s \xrightarrow{\tau} \mu \wedge p = \mu(D)}{C \xrightarrow{\tau} \mu' \wedge \mu'(D) = p}$,*
- *$\Rightarrow' \subseteq S/_\mathcal{R} \times \mathbb{R}_{\geq 0} \times S/_\mathcal{R}$ is defined by $\dfrac{C \in M(S) \wedge \lambda = wr(s', C, D),\ s' \in Pred(C)}{C \xrightarrow{\lambda} D}$ and
  $\dfrac{C \notin M(S) \wedge \lambda = R(s, D),\ s \in C}{C \xrightarrow{\lambda} D}$,*
- *$L'(C) = L(s)$, where $s \in C$.*

Example 7 (Quotient). The quotient MA for the Fig. 1 (left) under the WME relation with partition $\{\{s_0\}, \{s_1, s_2\}, \{s_3\}, \{s_4\}, \{s_5, s_6, s_7\}, \{s_8\}, \{s_9\}, \{s_{10}\}\}$ is shown in Fig. 1 (right).

Next, we show that any closed MA $\mathcal{M}$ and its quotient under WME relation are $\equiv$-related.

Definition 12. *Any MA $\mathcal{M}$ and its quotient $\mathcal{M}/_\mathcal{R}$ under WME $\mathcal{R}$ are $\equiv$-related, denoted by $\mathcal{M} \equiv \mathcal{M}/_\mathcal{R}$, if and only if there exists a WME relation $\mathcal{R}^*$ defined on the disjoint union of state space $S \uplus S/_\mathcal{R}$ such that*

$$\forall C \in S/_\mathcal{R}, \forall s \in C \implies (s, C) \in \mathcal{R}^*.$$

Theorem 1. *Let $\mathcal{M}$ be a closed MA and $\mathcal{R}$ be a WME on $\mathcal{M}$. Then $\mathcal{M} \equiv \mathcal{M}/_\mathcal{R}$.*

Proposition 1. *Union of WMEs is not necessarily a WME.*

In simple words, it is possible that $\mathcal{R}_1, \mathcal{R}_2$ are two WMEs on S s.t. $\mathcal{R}_1 \cup \mathcal{R}_2$ is not a WME. Intuitively, it means that the original closed MA $\mathcal{M}$ can be reduced in different ways.

3.2 Repeated Minimization

Next, we show that WME can be used for repeated minimization of a closed MA. Intuitively, this means that if a quotient system $\mathcal{M}'$ has been obtained from a closed MA $\mathcal{M}$ under WME $\mathcal{R}$, then it might still be possible to further reduce $\mathcal{M}'$ to $\mathcal{M}''$ under some WME $\mathcal{R}'$.

Example 8. Consider the example in Fig. 2 (left). MA in Fig. 2 (middle) is the quotient for the WME induced by the partition $\{\{s_0\}, \{s_1, s_2\}, \{s_3, s_4\}, \{s_5\}, \{s_6\}, \{s_7\}, \{s_8\}\}$. MA shown in Fig. 2 (right) is the quotient of MA shown in Fig. 2 (middle) for WME induced by the partition $\{\{s_0'\}, \{s_1'\}, \{s_2', s_3'\}, \{s_4'\}, \{s_5'\}, \{s_6'\}\}$. It is easy to check that s_3, s_4, s_5 in the original system cannot be merged in one shot, since s_1 can reach states labeled with atomic propositions a and b in two steps via s_3 and s_4 respectively, but s_2 cannot reach these states. This is no longer a problem once s_1 and s_2 are merged as shown in Fig. 2 (middle) as s_2', s_3' now have a single predecessor, i.e., s_1'.

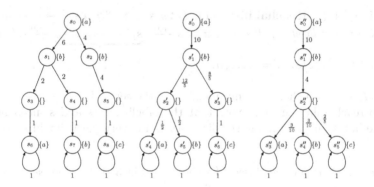

Fig. 2. Repeated minimization

3.3 Strong Bisimulation vs WME

Next, we investigate the relationship between WME and strong bisimulation for MAs [16].

Definition 13 (Strong bisimulation [16]). *Let* $\mathcal{M} = (S, s_0, Act, AP, \rightarrow, \Rightarrow, L)$ *be a closed MA. An equivalence relation* $\mathcal{R} \subseteq S \times S$ *is a strong bisimulation on* $\mathcal{M}$ *if for any* $(s_1, s_2) \in \mathcal{R}$ *and equivalence class* $C \in S/_{\mathcal{R}}$ *the following holds:*

- $L(s_1) = L(s_2)$,
- $R(s_1, C) = R(s_2, C)$,
- $(s_1 \xrightarrow{\tau} \mu \iff s_2 \xrightarrow{\tau} \mu') \wedge \mu(C) = \mu'(C)$.

States s_1 and s_2 are strongly bisimilar, denoted $s_1 \sim s_2$, if $(s_1, s_2) \in \mathcal{R}$ for some strong bisimulation[4] $\mathcal{R}$.

Strong bisimulation is rigid as it requires that each individual step should be mimicked.

Example 9. Consider the closed MA shown in Fig. 1 (left). Here s_5 and s_7 are bisimilar, i.e., $s_5 \sim s_7$.

Proposition 2. $\sim \not\Rightarrow \equiv$ *and* $\equiv \not\Rightarrow \sim$.

This proposition says that bisimulation and WME are incomparable.

4   Weak Weighted Markovian Equivalence

In this section we define weak weighted Markovian equivalence (WWME). It is a variant of WME that abstracts from stutter steps, also referred to as internal or non-observable steps. We first define some auxiliary concepts followed by the definition of WWME.

Definition 14 (+ Reachability set). *Let $s, s' \in S$. Then $s \xrightarrow{\tau^+} s'$ denote the set of all finite τ-labeled paths, i.e., $\pi = s \xrightarrow{\tau,0} \underbrace{s_1 \xrightarrow{\tau,0} s_2 \ldots s_n}_{n} \xrightarrow{\tau,0} s'$, where $n \geq 0$ and $L(s) = L(s_i), i = 1, \ldots, n$.*

Remark 1. If $n = 0$ then the only member of the set $s \xrightarrow{\tau^+} s'$ is $s \xrightarrow{\tau,0} s'$, i.e., one step reachability in MA. Note that the labeling of s and s' need not be the same but s and all the intermediate states in every path should be equally labeled.

Example 10. Consider the closed MA shown in Fig. 3 (left). Here $s_7 \xrightarrow{\tau^+} s_{11}$ is the set of two finite paths $\pi_1 = s_7 \xrightarrow{\tau,0} s_8 \xrightarrow{\tau,0} s_{11}$ and $\pi_2 = s_7 \xrightarrow{\tau,0} s_9 \xrightarrow{\tau,0} s_{11}$.

Definition 15. $Pr(s \xrightarrow{\tau^+} s') = \sum\limits_{\pi \in s \xrightarrow{\tau^+} s'} Pr(\pi)$, *where* $Pr(\pi) = \mu_0(s_1) \cdot \mu_1(s_2) \ldots \mu_{n-1}(s_n) \cdot \mu'(s')$.

Example 11. Consider the MA shown in Fig. 3 (left). Here $Pr(s_7 \xrightarrow{\tau^+} s_{11}) = Pr(\pi_1) + Pr(\pi_2) = \frac{2}{3} \cdot 1 + \frac{1}{3} \cdot \frac{1}{4} = \frac{3}{4}$.

---

[4] Note that the definition of strong bisimulation has been slightly modified to take into account the state labels.

Definition 16. *Let $s \in S$ and $D \subseteq S$. Let $s \xrightarrow{\tau^+} D$ denote the set* $\bigcup_{s' \in D} s \xrightarrow{\tau^+} s'$.

In simple words, $s \xrightarrow{\tau^+} D$ denote the set of all finite τ-labeled paths that start from s and end in some $s' \in D$.

Definition 17 (Probability of $s \xrightarrow{\tau^+} D$). *Let $s \in S$ and $D \subseteq S$. Then* $Pr(s \xrightarrow{\tau^+} D) = \Sigma_{s' \in D} Pr(s \xrightarrow{\tau^+} s')$.

Definition 18 (Weak weighted probability). *For $s \in S$, and $C, D \subseteq S$, the function $wwp : S \times 2^S \times 2^S \to \mathbb{R}_{\geq 0}$ is defined by:*

$$wwp(s, C, D) = \sum_{s' \in C} pbr(s, s', C) \cdot Pr(s' \xrightarrow{\tau^+} D)$$

Example 12. Consider the MA shown in Fig. 3 (left). Let $C = \{s_5, s_6, s_7, s_8, s_9\}$ and $D = \{s_{11}\}$. Then $wwp(s_4, C, D) = pbr(s_4, s_7, C) \cdot Pr(s_7 \xrightarrow{\tau^+} D) = 1 \cdot (\frac{2}{3} \cdot 1 + \frac{1}{3} \cdot \frac{1}{4}) = \frac{3}{4}$. Similarly, for $D = \{s_{10}\}$, $wwp(s_4, C, D) = pbr(s_4, s_7, C) \cdot Pr(s_7 \xrightarrow{\tau^+} D) = 1 \cdot \frac{1}{3} \cdot \frac{3}{4} = \frac{1}{4}$.

Definition 19 (WWME). *Equivalence $\mathcal{R}$ on S is a weak interactive Markovian equivalence (WIME) if we have:*

1. $\forall (s_1, s_2) \in \mathcal{R}$ *it holds:* $L(s_1) = L(s_2)$ *and* $E(s_1) = E(s_2)$,
2. $\forall C \in S/_{\mathcal{R}}$ *s.t.* $C \in P(S)$, $\forall D \in S/_{\mathcal{R}} \setminus \{C\}$ *and* $\forall s', s'' \in Pred(C) \setminus C$: $wwp(s', C, D) = wwp(s'', C, D)$,
3. $\forall C \in S/_{\mathcal{R}}$ *s.t.* $C \in M(S)$, $\forall D \in S/_{\mathcal{R}}$ *and* $\forall s', s'' \in Pred(C)$: $wr(s', C, D) = wr(s'', C, D)$,
4. $\forall C \in S/_{\mathcal{R}}$ *s.t.* $C \notin P(S) \wedge C \notin M(S)$, *we have* $|C| = 1$.

States s_1, s_2 are WWM related, denoted by $s_1 \cong s_2$, if $(s_1, s_2) \in \mathcal{R}$ for some WMME $\mathcal{R}$.

Example 13. For MA shown in Fig. 3 (left), the relation induced by the partitioning $\{\{s_0\}, \{s_1, s_2\}, \{s_3\}, \{s_4\}, \{s_5, s_6, s_7, s_8, s_9\}, \{s_{10}\}, \{s_{11}\}\}$ is a WWME relation.

4.1 Quotient MA

Definition 20. *For WMME relation $\mathcal{R}$ on $\mathcal{M}$, the quotient MA $\mathcal{M}/_{\mathcal{R}}$ is defined by $\mathcal{M}/_{\mathcal{R}} = (S/_{\mathcal{R}}, s_0', Act, AP, \to', \Rightarrow', L')$ where:*

- *$S/_{\mathcal{R}}$ is the set of all equivalence classes under $\mathcal{R}$,*
- *$s_0' = C$ where $s_0 \in C = [s_0]_{\mathcal{R}}$,*
- *$\to' \subseteq S/_{\mathcal{R}} \times Act \times Distr(S/_{\mathcal{R}})$:* $\dfrac{C \in P(S) \wedge p = wwp(s', C, D),\ s' \in Pred(C) \setminus C, C \neq D}{C \xrightarrow{\tau} \mu' \wedge \mu'(D) = p}$ *and*

$\dfrac{C \notin P(S) \wedge \exists s \in C : s \xrightarrow{\tau} \mu \wedge p = \mu(D), C \neq D}{C \xrightarrow{\tau} \mu' \wedge \mu'(D) = p}$,

- $\Rightarrow' \subseteq S/_{\mathcal{R}} \times \mathbb{R}_{\geq 0} \times S/_{\mathcal{R}}$ is defined by $\dfrac{C \in M(S) \wedge \lambda = wr(s', C, D),\ s' \in Pred(C)}{C \xrightarrow{\lambda} D}$ and $\dfrac{C \notin M(S) \wedge \lambda = R(s, D),\ s \in C}{C \xrightarrow{\lambda} D}$,
- $L'(C) = L(s)$, where $s \in C$.

Example 14. The quotient MA for the Fig. 3 (left) under the WWME relation with partition $\{\{s_0\}, \{s_1, s_2\}, \{s_3\}, \{s_4\}, \{s_5, s_6, s_7, s_8, s_9\}, \{s_{10}\}, \{s_{11}\}\}$ is shown in Fig. 3 (right).

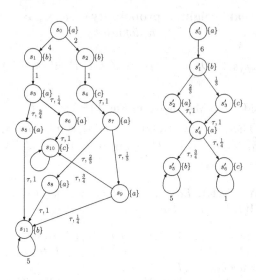

Fig. 3. MA $\mathcal{M}$ (left) and its quotient under a WWME $\mathcal{R}$ (right)

Definition 21. *Any MA $\mathcal{M}$ and its quotient $\mathcal{M}/_{\mathcal{R}}$ under WWME $\mathcal{R}$ are $\cong$-related, denoted by $\mathcal{M} \cong \mathcal{M}/_{\mathcal{R}}$, if and only if there exists a WMME relation $\mathcal{R}^*$ defined on the disjoint union of state space $S \uplus S/_{\mathcal{R}}$ such that*

$$\forall C \in S/_{\mathcal{R}}, \forall s \in C \implies (s, C) \in \mathcal{R}^*.$$

Theorem 2. *Let $\mathcal{M}$ be a closed MA and $\mathcal{R}$ be a WWME on $\mathcal{M}$. Then $\mathcal{M} \cong \mathcal{M}/_{\mathcal{R}}$.*

Proposition 3. *Union of WWME is not necessarily a WWME.*

Remark 2. WWMEs can be used for repeated minimization of a closed MA.

4.2   Weak Bisimulation Vs WWME

Next, we investigate the relationship between WWME and weak bisimulation for MAs [16]. Due to space limit we do not provide the definition of weak bisimulation (denoted $\approx$), but refer the interested reader to appendix and [16].

Proposition 4. $\approx \;\not\Longrightarrow\; \cong$ *and* $\cong \;\not\Longrightarrow\; \approx$.

This proposition says that weak bisimulation and WWME are incomparable.

Theorem 3. $\equiv$ *is strictly finer than* $\cong$.

This theorem asserts that WWME can achieve a larger state space reduction as compared to WME.

5 Deterministic Timed Automaton

In order to investigate the kind of real-time properties for MAs that are preserved by WME and WWME, we study in this section linear real-time objectives that are given by Deterministic Timed Automata (DTAs) [2].

Definition 22 (DTA). *A deterministic timed automaton (DTA) is a tuple* $\mathcal{A} = (\Sigma, \mathcal{X}, Q, q_0, F, \rightarrow)$ *where:*

- Σ *is a finite alphabet,*
- $\mathcal{X}$ *is a finite set of clocks,*
- Q *is a nonempty finite set of locations with the initial location* $q_0 \in Q$,
- $F \subseteq Q$ *is a set of accepting (or final) locations,*
- $\rightarrow \;\subseteq Q \times \Sigma \times \mathcal{CC}(\mathcal{X}) \times 2^{\mathcal{X}} \times Q$ *is the edge relation satisfying:*

$$\left(q \xrightarrow{a,g,X} q' \wedge q \xrightarrow{a,g',X'} q'', g \neq g'\right) \implies g \cap g' = \varnothing.$$

Intuitively, the edge $q \xrightarrow{a,g,X} q'$ asserts that the DTA $\mathcal{A}$ can move from location q to q' when the input symbol is a and the guard g holds, while the clocks in X should be reset when entering q' (all other clocks keep their value). DTAs are deterministic as they have a single initial location, and outgoing edges of a location labeled with the same input symbol are required to have disjoint guards. In this way, the next location is uniquely determined for a given location and a given set of clock values. In case no guard is satisfied in a location for a given clock valuation, time can progress. If the advance of time will never reach a situation in which a guard holds, the DTA will stay in that location *ad infinitum*. Note that DTAs do not have location invariants. The semantics of a DTA is given by an infinite-state transition system [2]. Next, we define the notion of paths, i.e., runs or executions of a DTA. This is done using some auxiliary notions. A *clock valuation* η for a set $\mathcal{X}$ of clocks is a function $\eta : \mathcal{X} \rightarrow \mathbb{R}_{\geq 0}$, assigning to each clock $x \in \mathcal{X}$ its current value $\eta(x)$. The clock valuation η over $\mathcal{X}$ satisfies the clock constraint g, denoted $\eta \models g$, iff the values of the clocks under η fulfill g. For instance, $\eta \models x - y > c$ iff $\eta(x) - \eta(y) > c$. Other cases are defined analogously. For $d \in \mathbb{R}_{\geq 0}$, $\eta + d$ denotes the clock valuation where all clocks of η are increased by d. That is, $(\eta + d)(x) = \eta(x) + d$ for all clocks $x \in \mathcal{X}$. Clock *reset* for a subset $X \subseteq \mathcal{X}$, denoted by $\eta[X := 0]$, is the valuation η' defined by: $\forall x \in X.\eta'(x) := 0$ and $\forall x \notin X.\eta'(x) := \eta(x)$. The valuation that assigns

0 to all the clocks is denoted by $\mathbf{0}$. An (infinite) path of DTA $\mathcal{A}$ has the form $\rho = q \xrightarrow{a_0, t_0} q_1 \xrightarrow{a_1, t_1} \dots$ such that $\eta_0 = \mathbf{0}$, and for all $j \geq 0$, it holds $t_j > 0$, $\eta_j + t_j \models g_j$, $\eta_{j+1} = (\eta_j + t_j)[X_j := 0]$, where η_j is the clock evaluation on entering q_j. Here, g_j is the guard of the j-th edge taken in the DTA and X_j the set of clock to be reset on that edge. A path ρ is accepted by $\mathcal{A}$ if $q_i \in F$ for some $i \geq 0$. Since the DTA is deterministic, the successor location is uniquely determined; for convenience we write $q' = succ(q, a, g)$. A path in a MA $\mathcal{M}$ can be "matched" by a path through DTA $\mathcal{A}$ by regarding sets of atomic propositions in $\mathcal{M}$ as input symbols of $\mathcal{A}$. Such a path is accepted, if at some point an accepting location in the DTA is reached:

Definition 23 (Path acceptance). *Let MA $\mathcal{M} = (S, s_0, Act, AP, \rightarrow, \Rightarrow, L)$ and DTA $\mathcal{A} = (2^{AP}, \mathcal{X}, Q, q_0, F, \rightarrow)$. The MA path $\pi = s_0 \xrightarrow{\sigma_0, t_0} s_1 \xrightarrow{\sigma_1, t_1} s_2 \dots$ is accepted by $\mathcal{A}$ if there exists a corresponding DTA path*

$$q_0 \xrightarrow{L(s_0), t_0} \underbrace{succ(q_0, L(s_0), g_0)}_{=q_1} \xrightarrow{L(s_1), t_1} \underbrace{succ(q_1, L(s_1), g_1)}_{=q_2} \dots$$

such that $q_j \in F$ for some $j \geq 0$. Here, $\eta_0 = \mathbf{0}$, g_i is the (unique) guard in q_i (if it exists) such that $\eta_i + t_i \models g_i$ and $\eta_{i+1} = (\eta_i + t_i)[X_i := 0]$, and η_i is the clock evaluation on entering q_i, for $i \geq 0$. Let $Paths^{\mathcal{M}}(\mathcal{A}) = \{\pi \in Paths^{\mathcal{M}} \mid \pi$ is accepted by DTA $\mathcal{A}\}$[5].

Definition 24 (Probability of accepted paths). *For MA $\mathcal{M}$ and DTA $\mathcal{A}$, let $Pr(\mathcal{M} \models \mathcal{A}) = Pr(Paths^{\mathcal{M}}(\mathcal{A}))$*

Theorem 4 (Preservation of DTA under WME). *For any MA $\mathcal{M}$, a WME $\mathcal{R}$ on $\mathcal{M}$ and DTA $\mathcal{A}$:*

$$Pr(\mathcal{M} \models \mathcal{A}) = Pr(\mathcal{M}/_{\mathcal{R}} \models \mathcal{A})$$

Theorem 5 (Preservation of DTA under WWME). *For any MA $\mathcal{M}$, a WWME $\mathcal{R}$ on $\mathcal{M}$ and DTA $\mathcal{A}$:*

$$Pr(\mathcal{M} \models \mathcal{A}) = Pr(\mathcal{M}/_{\mathcal{R}} \models \mathcal{A})$$

6   Metric Temporal Logic

In this section we show that the quotient MAs obtained under WMEs and WMMEs can be used for verifying Metric Temporal Logic (MTL) formulae. Note that expressive power of MTL is different from that of DTA. We now recall the syntax and semantics of Metric Temporal Logic [9, 28].

---

[5] For any MA $\mathcal{M}$ and DTA $\mathcal{A}$, the set $Paths^{\mathcal{M}}(\mathcal{A})$ is measurable [11, 17, 33].

Definition 25 (Syntax of MTL). *Let AP be a set of atomic propositions, then the formulas of MTL are built from AP using Boolean connectives, and time-constrained versions of the* until *operator U as follows:*

$$\varphi ::= tt \mid a \mid \neg\varphi \mid \varphi \wedge \varphi \mid \varphi\, U^I \varphi$$

where $I \subseteq \mathbb{R}_{\geq 0}$ is a non-empty interval with rational bounds, and $a \in AP$.

Next, we define the semantics of MTL formulas over MA paths.

Definition 26 (Semantics of MTL formulas). *The meaning of MTL formulas is defined by means of a satisfaction relation, denoted by $\models$, between a MA $\mathcal{M}$, one of its paths π, MTL formula φ, and time $t \in \mathbb{R}_{\geq 0}$. Let $\pi = s_0 \xrightarrow{\sigma_0, t_0} s_1 \ldots s_{n-1} \xrightarrow{\sigma_{n-1}, t_{n-1}} s_n \ldots$ be a finite or infinite path of $\mathcal{M}$, then $(\pi, t) \models \varphi$ is defined inductively by:*

$$
\begin{aligned}
&(\pi, t) \models tt \\
&(\pi, t) \models a &&iff\ a \in L(\pi@t) \\
&(\pi, t) \models \neg\varphi &&iff\ not(\pi, t) \models \varphi \\
&(\pi, t) \models \varphi_1 \wedge \varphi_2 &&iff\ (\pi, t) \models \varphi_1\ and\ (\pi, t) \models \varphi_2 \\
&(\pi, t) \models \varphi_1\, U^I \varphi_2 &&iff\ \exists t' \in t+I.\ ((\pi, t') \models \varphi_2 \wedge \forall t \leq t'' < t'.\,(\pi, t'') \models \varphi_1)\,.
\end{aligned}
$$

Let $Paths^{\mathcal{M}}(\varphi) = \{\pi \in Paths^{\mathcal{M}} \mid \pi \models \varphi\}$[6].

Definition 27 (Probability of MTL paths). *For MA $\mathcal{M}$ and MTL formula φ, let $Pr(\mathcal{M} \models \varphi) = Pr(Paths^{\mathcal{M}}(\varphi))$.*

$Pr(\mathcal{M} \models \varphi)$ denote the probability of all paths of $\mathcal{M}$ that satisfy an MTL formula φ.

Theorem 6 (Preservation of MTL under WME) *Let $\mathcal{M}$ be a MA and $\mathcal{R}$ be a WME on $\mathcal{M}$. Then for any MTL formula φ:*

$$Pr(\mathcal{M} \models \varphi) = Pr(\mathcal{M}/_{\mathcal{R}} \models \varphi)$$

Theorem 7 (Preservation of MTL under WWME). *Let $\mathcal{M}$ be a MA and $\mathcal{R}$ be a WWME on $\mathcal{M}$. Then for any MTL formula φ:*

$$Pr(\mathcal{M} \models \varphi) = Pr(\mathcal{M}/_{\mathcal{R}} \models \varphi)$$

7   Conclusions and Future Work

This paper presented two equivalence relations for closed MA models. We defined the quotient system under these relations and investigated their relationship with (weak) bisimulation. Finally, we have proved that smaller models obtained under

---

[6] Note that paths satisfying an MTL formula φ can be written as a set of cylinder sets [33].

these equivalences can be used for verification as they preserve the probability of linear real-time objectives. Our work can be extended in several directions. We plan to investigate the relationship between WWME and late weak bisimulation for MAs [34]. We also plan to investigate the relationship between WME and trace semantics for MAs [32]. It would be interesting to study if our definition of WME can be extended to open MA models with multiple action transitions. Another interesting direction of research is to develop and implement an efficient quotienting algorithm and validate it on some academic case studies.

References

1. Aldini, A., Bernardo, M.: Expected-delay-summing weak bisimilarity for Markov automata. In: QAPL, EPTCS, vol. 194, pp. 1–15 (2015)
2. Alur, R., Dill, D.L.: A theory of timed automata. Theor. Comput. Sci. **126**(2), 183–235 (1994)
3. Bernardo, M.: Non-bisimulation-based Markovian behavioral equivalences. J. Log. Algebr. Program. **72**(1), 3–49 (2007)
4. Bernardo, M.: Towards state space reduction based on t-lumpability-consistent relations. In: Thomas, N., Juiz, C. (eds.) EPEW 2008. LNCS, vol. 5261, pp. 64–78. Springer, Heidelberg (2008). https://doi.org/10.1007/978-3-540-87412-6_6
5. Böde, E., et al.: Compositional dependability evaluation for STATEMATE. IEEE Trans. Softw. Eng. **35**(2), 274–292 (2009)
6. Boudali, H., Crouzen, P., Haverkort, B.R., Kuntz, M., Stoelinga, M.: Architectural dependability evaluation with arcade. In: DSN, pp. 512–521. IEEE Computer Society (2008)
7. Boudali, H., Crouzen, P., Stoelinga, M.: A compositional semantics for dynamic fault trees in terms of interactive Markov chains. In: Namjoshi, K.S., Yoneda, T., Higashino, T., Okamura, Y. (eds.) ATVA 2007. LNCS, vol. 4762, pp. 441–456. Springer, Heidelberg (2007). https://doi.org/10.1007/978-3-540-75596-8_31
8. Boudali, H., Crouzen, P., Stoelinga, M.: Dynamic fault tree analysis using input/output interactive Markov chains. In: DSN, pp. 708–717. IEEE Computer Society (2007)
9. Bouyer, P.: From Qualitative to Quantitative Analysis of Timed Systems. Mémoire d'habilitation, Université Paris 7, Paris, France, January 2009
10. Bozzano, M., Cimatti, A., Katoen, J., Nguyen, V.Y., Noll, T., Roveri, M.: Safety, dependability and performance analysis of extended AADL models. Comput. J. **54**(5), 754–775 (2011)
11. Chen, T., Han, T., Katoen, J.-P., Mereacre, A.: Quantitative model checking of continuous-time Markov chains against timed automata specifications. In: LICS, pp. 309–318 (2009)
12. Coste, N., Hermanns, H., Lantreibecq, E., Serwe, W.: Towards performance prediction of compositional models in industrial GALS designs. In: Bouajjani, A., Maler, O. (eds.) CAV 2009. LNCS, vol. 5643, pp. 204–218. Springer, Heidelberg (2009). https://doi.org/10.1007/978-3-642-02658-4_18
13. Deng, Y., Hennessy, M.: On the semantics of Markov automata. In: Aceto, L., Henzinger, M., Sgall, J. (eds.) ICALP 2011. LNCS, vol. 6756, pp. 307–318. Springer, Heidelberg (2011). https://doi.org/10.1007/978-3-642-22012-8_24
14. Deng, Y., Hennessy, M.: On the semantics of Markov automata. Inf. Comput. **222**, 139–168 (2013)

15. Eisentraut, C., Godskesen, J.C., Hermanns, H., Song, L., Zhang, L.: Probabilistic bisimulation for realistic schedulers. In: Bjørner, N., de Boer, F. (eds.) FM 2015. LNCS, vol. 9109, pp. 248–264. Springer, Cham (2015). https://doi.org/10.1007/978-3-319-19249-9_16

16. Eisentraut, C., Hermanns, H., Zhang, L.: On probabilistic automata in continuous time. In: LICS, pp. 342–351 (2010)

17. Fu, H.: Approximating acceptance probabilities of CTMC-paths on multi-clock deterministic timed automata. In: HSCC, pp. 323–332. ACM (2013)

18. Guck, D., Hatefi, H., Hermanns, H., Katoen, J.-P., Timmer, M.: Modelling, reduction and analysis of Markov automata. In: Joshi, K., Siegle, M., Stoelinga, M., D'Argenio, P.R. (eds.) QEST 2013. LNCS, vol. 8054, pp. 55–71. Springer, Heidelberg (2013). https://doi.org/10.1007/978-3-642-40196-1_5

19. Guck, D., Hatefi, H., Hermanns, H., Katoen, J., Timmer, M.: Analysis of timed and long-run objectives for Markov automata. LMCS **10**(3), 1–29 (2014)

20. Guck, D., Timmer, M., Hatefi, H., Ruijters, E., Stoelinga, M.: Modelling and analysis of Markov reward automata. In: Cassez, F., Raskin, J.-F. (eds.) ATVA 2014. LNCS, vol. 8837, pp. 168–184. Springer, Cham (2014). https://doi.org/10.1007/978-3-319-11936-6_13

21. Hatefi, H., Hermanns, H.: Model checking algorithms for Markov automata. In: ECEASST, vol. 53 (2012)

22. Hermanns, H.: Interactive Markov Chains: And the Quest for Quantified Quality. Springer, Heidelberg (2002). https://doi.org/10.1007/3-540-45804-2

23. Hermanns, H., Katoen, J.-P.: The how and why of interactive Markov chains. In: de Boer, F.S., Bonsangue, M.M., Hallerstede, S., Leuschel, M. (eds.) FMCO 2009. LNCS, vol. 6286, pp. 311–337. Springer, Heidelberg (2010). https://doi.org/10.1007/978-3-642-17071-3_16

24. Hermanns, H., Katoen, J., Neuhäußer, M.R., Zhang, L.: GSPN model checking despite confusion. Technical report, RWTH Aachen University (2010)

25. Mateescu, R., Serwe, W.: A study of shared-memory mutual exclusion protocols using CADP. In: Kowalewski, S., Roveri, M. (eds.) FMICS 2010. LNCS, vol. 6371, pp. 180–197. Springer, Heidelberg (2010). https://doi.org/10.1007/978-3-642-15898-8_12

26. Meyer, J.F., Movaghar, A., Sanders, W.H.: Stochastic activity networks: structure, behavior, and application. In: PNPM, pp. 106–115. IEEE Computer Society (1985)

27. Neuhäußer, M.R.: Model checking non-deterministic and randomly timed systems. Ph.D. dissertation, RWTH Aachen University (2010)

28. Ouaknine, J., Worrell, J.: Some recent results in metric temporal logic. In: Cassez, F., Jard, C. (eds.) FORMATS 2008. LNCS, vol. 5215, pp. 1–13. Springer, Heidelberg (2008). https://doi.org/10.1007/978-3-540-85778-5_1

29. Segala, R.: Modelling and Verification of Randomized Distributed Real Time Systems. Ph.D. thesis, MIT (1995)

30. Sharma, A.: Reduction Techniques for Non-deterministic and Probabilistic Systems. Ph.D. dissertation, RWTH Aachen (2015)

31. Sharma, A.: Interactive Markovian equivalence. In: Reinecke, P., Di Marco, A. (eds.) EPEW 2017. LNCS, vol. 10497, pp. 33–49. Springer, Cham (2017). https://doi.org/10.1007/978-3-319-66583-2_3

32. Sharma, A.: Trace relations and logical preservation for Markov automata. In: Jansen, D.N., Prabhakar, P. (eds.) FORMATS 2018, LNCS 11022, pp. 162–178. Springer, Cham (2018)

33. Sharma, A., Katoen, J.-P.: Weighted lumpability on Markov chains. In: Clarke, E., Virbitskaite, I., Voronkov, A. (eds.) PSI 2011. LNCS, vol. 7162, pp. 322–339. Springer, Heidelberg (2012). https://doi.org/10.1007/978-3-642-29709-0_28
34. Song, L., Zhang, L., Godskesen, J.C.: Late weak bisimulation for Markov automata. CoRR, abs/1202.4116 (2012)
35. Timmer, M., Katoen, J.-P., van de Pol, J., Stoelinga, M.I.A.: Efficient modelling and generation of Markov automata. In: Koutny, M., Ulidowski, I. (eds.) CONCUR 2012. LNCS, vol. 7454, pp. 364–379. Springer, Heidelberg (2012). https://doi.org/10.1007/978-3-642-32940-1_26
36. Wolf, V., Baier, C., Majster-Cederbaum, M.E.: Trace machines for observing continuous-time Markov chains. ENTCS **153**(2), 259–277 (2006)

Timed Words

Distance on Timed Words
and Applications

Eugene Asarin[1], Nicolas Basset[2], and Aldric Degorre[1(✉)]

[1] IRIF, University Paris Diderot and CNRS, Paris, France
aldric.degorre@irif.fr
[2] VERIMAG, University Grenoble Alpes and CNRS, Grenoble, France

Abstract. We introduce and study a new (pseudo) metric on timed words having several advantages:
- it is global: it applies to words having different number of events;
- it is realistic and takes into account imprecise observation of timed events; thus it reflects the fact that the order of events cannot be observed whenever they are very close to each other;
- it is suitable for quantitative verification of timed systems: we formulate and solve quantitative model-checking and quantitative monitoring in terms of the new distance, with reasonable complexity;
- it is suitable for information-theoretical analysis of timed systems: due to its pre-compactness the quantity of information in bits per time unit can be correctly defined and computed.

1 Introduction

Timed words are sequences of events (from a finite alphabet Σ) with their dates (from $\mathbb{R}^+$). Such words, sets thereof (timed languages) and automata working on them (timed automata) constitute a relevant abstraction level for modelling and verification of real-time systems and an attractive research area since the founding work [1].

It is commonly accepted that timed words can be produced or observed with a certain precision, and several works considered approximate verification of timed systems, fixing a distance and a precision on timed words. In most cases the uniform distance on dates (or delays) for words with n events is considered, see e.g. tube languages [11], or robustness [14]. In [4,7] we have studied symbolic dynamics of timed systems w.r.t. a similar distance, and in [3] we have applied it to the following question: "what is the amount of information in timed words of language L, of length n, with precision ε".

However, on the information theory side, all the distances considered up to now are well adapted to analysis of quantity of information for a fixed number of events n, or its asymptotic behaviour w.r.t. n. But those distances are not suitable for the analysis on information for a given time T (or asymptotically w.r.t. $T \to \infty$). To perform such an analysis, we need a unique distance on timed words with different numbers of events. Furthermore, this metric should

© Springer Nature Switzerland AG 2018
D. N. Jansen and P. Prabhakar (Eds.): FORMATS 2018, LNCS 11022, pp. 199–214, 2018.
https://doi.org/10.1007/978-3-030-00151-3_12

be compact (for a given duration T), if we want the amount of information transmitted in T seconds with precision ε to be finite.

On the practical side, if we observed timed words with some finite precision (say $0.01s$), then it would be difficult to distinguish the order of close events, e.g. detect the difference between

$$w_1 = (a, 1), (b, 2), (c, 2.001) \text{ and } w_2 = (a, 1.001), (c, 1.999), (b, 2.001).$$

Moreover, it is even difficult to count the number of events that happen in a short lapse of time, e.g. the words w_1, w_2 look very similar to

$$w_3 = (a, 1), (c, 1.999), (c, 2), (b, 2.001), (c, 2.0002).$$

A slow observer, when receiving timed words w_1, w_2, w_3 will just sense an a at the date ≈ 1 and b and c at the date ≈ 2.

As the main contribution of this paper, we introduce a metric on timed words (with non-fixed number of events) for which w_1, w_2, w_3 are very close to each other. We believe that this metric is natural and sets a ground for approximate model-checking and information theory of timed languages w.r.t. time (and not only number of events).

We present the first technical results concerning this distance:

– its simple geometrical properties;
– techniques of quantitative model-checking and monitoring, and complexity estimates thereof (the complexity of standard problems is quite moderate: PSPACE or sometimes NP);
– proof of compactness of this distance, and analysis of information contents of some important languages.

The paper is structured as follows: after some preliminaries in Sect. 2 we introduce our main new notion of distance between timed words in Sect. 3. We analyse problems of quantitative model-checking (with respect to this distance) in Sect. 4 and those of information content in Sect. 5. We conclude with some perspectives in Sect. 6.

2   Preliminaries

We suppose that the reader is acquainted with timed automata (and region equivalence), [1]. Nonetheless, here we fix notation and provide main definitions. We also provide basic facts and notions on pre-compact spaces and two information measures thereof.

2.1   Timed Words and Timed Languages

A *timed word* of length n over an alphabet Σ is a sequence $w = t_1 a_1 \ldots t_n a_n$, with $a_i \in \Sigma, t_i \in \mathbb{R}$ and $0 \le t_1 \le \ldots \le t_n$. Here t_i represents the dates at which the event a_i occurs (this definition rules out timed words ending by a time delay). We also adopt the convention that $t_0 = 0$. A *timed language* L is a set of timed words.

Timed word projection. The projection $p_\Sigma(u)$ of a timed word u erasing alphabet Σ consists in the word u where the events with labels in Σ are hidden. Recursively:

$$p_\Sigma(\varepsilon) = \varepsilon \; ; \; p_\Sigma(ta) = \begin{cases} ta \text{ if } a \notin \Sigma \\ \varepsilon \text{ if } a \in \Sigma \end{cases} ;$$

$$p_\Sigma(tau) = p_\Sigma(ta)p_\Sigma(u) = \begin{cases} ta \cdot p_\Sigma(u) \text{ if } a \notin \Sigma \\ p_\Sigma(u) \text{ if } a \in \Sigma \end{cases}$$

This definition is lifted to timed languages the natural way: the projection of a language L is the set of the projections of all words $u \in L$.

2.2   Timed Graphs and Timed Automata

A *clock* is a variable ranging over $\mathbb{R}_{\geq 0}$ (non-negative reals). A *clock constraint* $\mathfrak{g} \in G_C$ over a set of clocks C is a conjunction of finitely many inequalities of the form $x \sim c$ or $x \sim y$, where x and y are clocks, $\sim \in \{<, \leq, =, \geq, >\}$ and $c \in \mathbb{Q}_{\geq 0}$. A *clock reset* $\mathfrak{r} \in R_C$ is determined by a subset of clocks $B \subset C$, it resets to 0 all the clocks in B and does not modify the values of the others.

A *timed graph* (TG) is a triple $\Gamma = (V, C, E)$. Its elements are respectively the finite set of locations, the finite set of clocks (let its cardinality be d) and the transition relation (timed edges). A *state* of Γ is a pair $(v, \mathbf{x})$ of a control location $v \in V$ and a vector of clock values $\mathbf{x} \in \mathbb{R}^d$. Elements of $\mathbf{E}$ are *transitions*, i.e. tuples $(v, \mathfrak{g}, \mathfrak{r}, v') \in V \times G_C \times R_C \times V$ denoting the possibility, at location v when the clock vector satisfies the *guard* $\mathfrak{g}$, to apply the clock reset $\mathfrak{r}$ and then go to location v'.

A *timed automaton* (TA) is a tuple $\mathcal{A} = (Q, \Sigma, C, \Delta, q_0, F)$ such that Σ, Q, C are finite sets, $q_0 \in Q$, $F \subset Q \times G_C$ and $\Delta \subset Q \times (\Sigma \cup \{\varepsilon\}) \times G_C \times R_C \times Q$. Hence, if we define $E = \{(q, \mathfrak{g}, \mathfrak{r}, q') | \exists a \in \Sigma \cup \{\varepsilon\} \text{ s.t. } (q, a, \mathfrak{g}, \mathfrak{r}, q') \in \Delta\}$, then (Q, C, E) is a TG called the *underlying timed graph* of $\mathcal{A}$.

Q is the set of locations of the TA, Σ, the alphabet of its symbols, Δ, its transition relation, q_0, its initial location and F, its final condition.

Intuitively, a TA reads a timed word, which will make a pebble move from state to state, starting from $(q_0, \mathbf{0})$, and accepts or rejects the word depending on whether the last visited state satisfies F or not.

More formally, a *run* of $\mathcal{A}$ along a *path* $\pi = \delta_1 \dots \delta_n \in \Delta^n$ has the form

$$(q_{i_0}, \mathbf{x}_0) \xrightarrow{t_1 a_1} (q_{i_1}, \mathbf{x}_1) \xrightarrow{t_2 a_2} \cdots \xrightarrow{t_n a_n} (q_{i_n}, \mathbf{x}_n),$$

where, for all $j \in 1..n$, $\delta_j = (q_{i_{j-1}}, a_j, \mathfrak{g}, \mathfrak{r}, q_{i_j}) \in \Delta$,

- $\mathbf{x}_{j-1} + (t_j - t_{j-1})\mathbb{1} \models \mathfrak{g}$ with $\mathbb{1}$ denoting the vector $(1, \dots, 1)$,
- and $\mathbf{x}_j = \mathfrak{r}(\mathbf{x}_{j-1} + (t_j - t_{j-1})\mathbb{1})$.

When $q_{i_0} = q_0$ is the initial state, $\mathbf{x}_0$ is $\mathbf{0}$ and F contains a couple $(q, \mathfrak{g})$ with $q_{i_n} = q$ and $\mathbf{x}_n$ satisfying $\mathfrak{g}$, then the timed word $p_\varepsilon(t_1 a_1 \dots t_n a_n)$ is said to be *accepted* by $\mathcal{A}$. The set of all such words is the language $L(\mathcal{A})$ accepted by $\mathcal{A}$.

Finally, the *granularity* of a timed graph G is the largest rational number $g(G)$ such that any constant k appearing in the guards of G satisfies $\frac{k}{g(G)} \in \mathbb{N}$.

2.3 Synchronized Product of TA

The *synchronized product* of the TA $\mathcal{A} = (Q_A, \Sigma_A \cup \Sigma_S, C_A, \Delta_A, q_{0A}, F_A)$ and $\mathcal{B} = (Q_B, \Sigma_B \cup \Sigma_S, C_B, \Delta_B, q_{0B}, F_B)$, with Σ_A, Σ_B and Σ_S disjoint alphabets and C_A and C_B disjoint clock sets[1], is the TA

$$\mathcal{A} \otimes_{\Sigma_S} \mathcal{B} = \left(Q_A \times Q_B, \Sigma_A \cup \Sigma_B \cup \Sigma_S, C_A \cup C_B, \dot{\Delta}_A \cup \Delta_S \cup \dot{\Delta}_B, (q_{0A}, q_{0B}), F \right),$$

where $\Delta_S = \{ ((q_A, q_B), s, g_A \wedge g_B, r_A \cup r_B, (q'_A, q'_B))$
$\qquad\qquad | \; \exists s \in \Sigma_S \wedge (q_A, s, g_A, r_A, q'_A) \in \Delta_A \wedge (q_B, s, g_B, r_B, q'_B) \in \Delta_B \};$
$\dot{\Delta}_A = \{ ((q_A, q_B), a, g_A, r_A, (q'_A, q_B))$
$\qquad\qquad | \; a \in \Sigma_A \wedge (q_A, a, g_A, r_A, q'_A) \in \Delta_A \wedge q_B \in Q_B \};$
$\dot{\Delta}_B = \{ ((q_A, q_B), b, g_B, r_B, (q_A, q'_B))$
$\qquad\qquad | \; b \in \Sigma_B \wedge q_A \in Q_B \wedge (q_B, b, g_B, r_B, q'_B) \in \Delta_B \};$
and $F = \{((q_A, q_B), g_A \wedge g_B) \mid (q_A, g_A) \in F_A \wedge (q_B, g_B) \in F_B \}$

We remark that $\mathcal{A}_1 \otimes_\Sigma (\mathcal{A}_2 \otimes_\Sigma \mathcal{A}_3)$ and $(\mathcal{A}_1 \otimes_\Sigma \mathcal{A}_2) \otimes_\Sigma \mathcal{A}_3$ are isomorphic (up to relabelling of the locations), hence, with only a slight abuse of notation, operation $\otimes_\Sigma$ is associative. The same reasoning also holds for commutativity. Thus, for iterating $\otimes_\Sigma$ (with Σ fixed), on $A = \{\mathcal{A}_1, \mathcal{A}_2, \ldots, \mathcal{A}_n\}$, a finite set of TA, we define the notation $\bigotimes_{\mathcal{A} \in A}^{\Sigma} \mathcal{A} = \mathcal{A}_1 \otimes_\Sigma \mathcal{A}_2 \otimes_\Sigma \cdots \otimes_\Sigma \mathcal{A}_n$.

2.4 Pre-compact Spaces, and Their ε-entropy and ε-capacity

We recall some concepts (mostly from [12]). Given a metric space (S, d), i.e. a set S with a distance d, a subset $K \subset S$ is called *ε-net* if for any $x \in S$, there exists some $y \in K$ with $d(x, y) \leq \varepsilon$ (i.e. any point can be ε-approximated by an element of K). The *ε-entropy* of S is defined as the logarithm[2] of the size of the smallest ε-net:

$$\mathcal{H}_\varepsilon(S) = \log \min\{\#K | K \text{ an } \varepsilon\text{-net in } S\}.$$

A subset M of S is called *ε-separated*, if all the distances between points in M are $> \varepsilon$. The *ε-capacity* of S is defined as the logarithm of the size of the largest ε-separated set:

$$\mathcal{C}_\varepsilon(S) = \log \max\{\#M | M \text{ an } \varepsilon\text{-separated set in } S\}.$$

The metric space (S, d) is pre-compact if its ε-entropy (or equivalently its ε-capacity) is finite for any $\varepsilon > 0$.

Both $\mathcal{H}$ and $\mathcal{C}$ characterise the quantity of information needed to describe an arbitrary point in S with precision ε, they give respectively upper and lower bound, as shows the following informal reasoning. Indeed, every point $x \in S$ can

---

[1] Generally, shared clocks could be considered, but they are not needed in this paper.
[2] As usual in information theory, all logarithms are base 2.

be described with precision ε using $\mathcal{H}_\varepsilon$ bits information: it suffices to pick an ε-approximation y in some standard minimal-size ε-net K, and write the number of y in a standard enumeration of K. On the other hand, ε-precise descriptions of points of a (maximal) 2ε-separated set M should be all distinct, which requires at least $\log \#M = \mathcal{C}_{2\varepsilon}(S)$ bits.

The two information characteristics ($\mathcal{H}$ and $\mathcal{C}$) are tightly related [12]:

$$\mathcal{C}_{2\varepsilon} \leq \mathcal{H}_\varepsilon \leq \mathcal{C}_\varepsilon. \tag{1}$$

3   Distance

Given two timed words $u = (a_1, t_1) \ldots (a_n, t_n)$ and $v = (b_1, s_1) \ldots (b_m, s_m)$, we define

$$\overrightarrow{d}(u,v) = \overleftarrow{d}(v,u) = \max_i \min_j \{|t_i - s_j| : b_j = a_i\};$$

$$d(u,v) = \max(\overrightarrow{d}(u,v), \overleftarrow{d}(u,v)).$$

In words, $\overrightarrow{d}(u,v)$ is small whenever for each event in u, there exists the same event in v, happening at a close date.

As explained in the introduction, this distance formalizes the idea of a slow observer who cannot distinguish events which are too close to each other.

Function d is strongly related to the classical Hausdorff distance (between sets in metric spaces). Indeed, in the case of a one-letter alphabet, $d((a, t_1) \ldots (a, t_n), (a, s_1) \ldots (a, s_m))$ coincides with Hausdorff distance between two sets of dates $\{t_1, \ldots, t_n\}$ and $\{s_1, \ldots, s_m\}$.

Let us state basic geometric properties of d, $\overrightarrow{d}$ and $\overleftarrow{d}$. We need a notation: for a timed word v and a date t we denote by $v(t) \subseteq \Sigma$ the set of all letters a such that v contains an event (a, t); also let $\alpha(u) \subseteq \Sigma$ denote the set of all the letters appearing in u.

Proposition 1. – d is symmetrical, $\overrightarrow{d}, \overleftarrow{d}$ are not.
- $d, \overrightarrow{d}, \overleftarrow{d}$ satisfy the triangular inequality.
- $\overrightarrow{d}(u,v) = 0$ whenever for all t it holds that $u(t) \subseteq v(t)$. The criterion for $\overleftarrow{d}$ is symmetrical. Finally, $d(u,v) = 0$ whenever $u(t) = v(t)$ holds for all t.
- $\overrightarrow{d}(u,v) = \infty$ whenever $\alpha(u) \not\subseteq \alpha(v)$. The criterion for $\overleftarrow{d}$ is symmetrical. Finally, $d(u,v) = \infty$ whenever $\alpha(u) \neq \alpha(v)$.

Thus, in fact, d is a pseudo-distance on timed words. Later on, in Sect. 5 we will prove its pre-compactness on timed words of a duration $\leq T$.

We also extend $\overleftarrow{d}$, $\overrightarrow{d}$ and d to distances between an element and a set, and between two sets the usual way. For $\delta \in \{\overleftarrow{d}, \overrightarrow{d}, d\}$, L, L' two timed languages, u a timed word, we define:

- $\delta(u, L) = \min \{\delta(u,v) | v \in L\}$;
- $\delta(L, u) = \min \{\delta(v,u) | v \in L\}$;
- $\delta(L, L') = \min \{\delta(u,v) | u \in L, v \in L'\}$.

4　Quantitative Verification

In this section, we treat the following verification problems:

Quantitative model-checking. Given two timed automata $\mathcal{A}$ and $\mathcal{B}$ we want to compute one of three distances $\overrightarrow{d}(L_{\mathcal{A}}, L_{\mathcal{B}})$; $\overleftarrow{d}(L_{\mathcal{A}}, L_{\mathcal{B}})$; $d(L_{\mathcal{A}}, L_{\mathcal{B}})$. A practical interpretation is as follows: $\mathcal{A}$ represents a timed system; $\mathcal{B}$ recognises the set of bad (erroneous) behaviours. In this case the distances represent the "security margin" between the system and errors. It is similar to robustness from [14] or [10]. The choice of the most appropriate distance for each practical setting is still to be explored.

Quantitative monitoring. Given a timed word w and a timed automaton $\mathcal{B}$ we want to compute one of three distances $\overrightarrow{d}(w, L_{\mathcal{B}})$; $\overleftarrow{d}(w, L_{\mathcal{B}})$; $d(w, L_{\mathcal{B}})$. One practical interpretation is that w is an execution trace (log file, airplane black box record etc.) of a system, (measured with some finite precision $\varkappa$), and $L_{\mathcal{B}}$ is the set of good (admissible) behaviours. Whenever $d(w, L_{\mathcal{B}}) > \varkappa$ we can be sure that the system behaviour was erroneous. Symmetrically, if $L_{\mathcal{B}}$ is the set of bad behaviours, and $d(w, L_{\mathcal{B}}) > \varkappa$ we can be sure that the system behaviour was correct.

4.1　Reachability Problems

In our complexity analysis we will use a couple of results about reachability on timed graphs: one is well-known, the other less so.

We say that $(G, I, F) \in$ TREACH whenever G is a timed graph, I, F are subsets of its vertices (for technical reasons we suppose them disjoint), and there exists a path in G which starts in I (with all clocks equal to 0) and terminates by a transition to F.

Theorem 1 ([1,9]). *The problem* TREACH *is* PSPACE-*complete.*

A variant of TREACH with bounded length of path is easier. We say that $(G, I, F, b) \in$ TREACH$_B$ whenever G is a timed graph, I, F, disjoint subsets of its vertices and b a natural number in unary representation; and there exists a feasible path of length $\leq b$ in G which starts in I (with all clocks equal to 0) and terminates by a transition to F.

Proposition 2. TREACH$_B$ *is in* NP.

Proof. The non-deterministic algorithm will first guess a path (of some length $\ell \leq b$) in the timed graph G from I to F. Feasibility of the path corresponds to existence of a sequence of dates $t_1, \ldots, t_\ell$, satisfying a polynomially sized system of difference constraints, which can be checked polynomially. □

Last, the following result concerns reachability in small time.

Proposition 3. *In a timed graph G, if a state $(q', \mathbf{x}')$ is reachable from a state $(q, \mathbf{x})$, within time $t < g(G)$, by some path π, then it is also reachable within exactly the same time via a path π' of polynomial size. Moreover, such a π' can be chosen such that it contains the same set of transitions as π.*

Proof. Without loss of generality, we assume $g(G) = 1$. Let k be the number of clocks, ℓ the number of locations (vertices) and tr the number of transitions (edges). Consider a path π in G from $(q, \mathbf{x})$ to $(q', \mathbf{x}')$ of duration t. We define the subset of *important* transitions in π which includes, for each clock c (with initial value x)

- the first transition such that $c > x$ (just before taking the transition);
- the same for $c = \lceil x \rceil$ and for $c > \lceil x \rceil$;
- the transition when c is reset for the first or last time.

For each clock there are at most five important transitions (some of them can be absent or coincide), thus altogether there are at most $5k$ of those.

Without changing the important transitions in π, we simplify the periods between those as follows.

During the period between two important transitions the clock vector stays in the same region. Thus if in such a period some location p of G is entered twice, the segment of π of duration τ from p to p can be removed, and replaced by staying in p during the same time τ. After removing all such useless fragments we get a new path π' without repeated locations between two important transitions. Its maximal size is $5k + (5k + 1)\ell$. The duration of π' is t, by construction.

To prove that π' leads again from $(q, \mathbf{x})$ to $(q', \mathbf{x}')$, it suffices to notice that all resets removed from π are not important because they happen between the first and the last reset of the same clock.

If we want π' and π to contain the same set of edges, the simplification should be a bit less aggressive: instead of removing the whole path fragment from p to p we preserve enough loops (at most tr) to visit the same set of transitions. □

4.2 Timed Automata for Neighbourhoods

We present now the key construction for quantitative verification with respect to our distances: for each distance $\delta \in \{\overleftarrow{d}, \overrightarrow{d}, d\}$, for any TA $\mathcal{B}$ and any rational number $\varkappa > 0$, we want to construct an automaton (resp. $\overleftarrow{\mathcal{B}}_\varkappa$, $\overrightarrow{\mathcal{B}}_\varkappa$ and $\mathcal{B}_\varkappa$) that recognizes the $\varkappa$-neighbourhood of $L_\mathcal{B}$, *i.e.* the language

$$\mathcal{N}_\delta(L_\mathcal{B}, \varkappa) = \{w | \exists v \, (v \in L_\mathcal{B} \wedge \delta(w, v) < \varkappa)\}.$$

We build these three automata as products of several components:

- $\mathcal{A}_v$ guesses the word v, check that $v \in L_\mathcal{B}$ and communicates with other components about timed events in v. No wonder, it is very similar to $\mathcal{B}$: it has the same states and clocks. To each transition in $\mathcal{B}$ corresponds a transition in $\mathcal{A}_v$ as presented on Fig. 1.
- For each letter $a \in \Sigma$, automaton $\mathcal{A}_{a\leftarrow}$ checks that every occurrence of a in the guessed v is $\varkappa$-close to its occurrence in the input w, see Fig. 2, left.
- Similarly, for each $a \in \Sigma$, automaton $\mathcal{A}_{a\rightarrow}$ checks that every occurrence of a in the input w is $\varkappa$-close to its occurrence in the guessed v, see Fig. 2, right.

Fig. 1. A transition in $\mathcal{B}$ (left) and its variant in $\mathcal{A}_v$ (right)

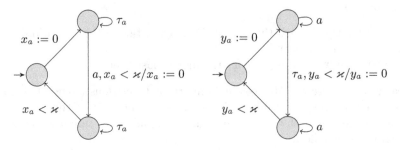

Fig. 2. Timed automata $\mathcal{A}_{a\leftarrow}$ (left) and $\mathcal{A}_{a\rightarrow}$ (right)

Formally, let $\mathcal{A}_{\leftarrow} = \bigotimes^{\emptyset}_{a\in\Sigma} \mathcal{A}_{a\leftarrow}$ and $\mathcal{A}_{\rightarrow} = \bigotimes^{\emptyset}_{a\in\Sigma} \mathcal{A}_{a\rightarrow}$. Then $\mathcal{B}_{\varkappa}$, $\overrightarrow{\mathcal{B}}_{\varkappa}$ and $\overleftarrow{\mathcal{B}}_{\varkappa}$ are defined respectively as the products $\left(\mathcal{A}_{\leftarrow} \otimes_{\{\tau_a|a\in\Sigma\}} \mathcal{A}_v \otimes_{\{\tau_a|a\in\Sigma\}} \mathcal{A}_{\rightarrow}\right)$, $\left(\mathcal{A}_v \otimes_{\{\tau_a|a\in\Sigma\}} \mathcal{A}_{\rightarrow}\right)$ and $\left(\mathcal{A}_{\leftarrow} \otimes_{\{\tau_a|a\in\Sigma\}} \mathcal{A}_v\right)$ where we replace all τ_a by ε.

Proposition 4. *Timed automata* $\overrightarrow{\mathcal{B}}_{\varkappa}$; $\overleftarrow{\mathcal{B}}_{\varkappa}$; $\mathcal{B}_{\varkappa}$ *recognise respectively $\varkappa$-neighbourhoods of $L_{\mathcal{B}}$ with respect to distances* $\overleftarrow{d}$, $\overrightarrow{d}$, d.

4.3   Quantitative Timed Model-Checking

Proposition 5. *Given timed automata $\mathcal{A}$ and $\mathcal{B}$ and a precision $\varkappa > 0$ (represented as ratio of two integers), deciding whether $d(L_A, L_B) < \varkappa$ is* PSPACE-*complete. The same is true for* $\overrightarrow{d}$ *and* $\overleftarrow{d}$.

Proof. **PSPACE-easyness.** Consider first the case of distance d. The inequality $d(L_A, L_B) < \varkappa$ holds iff L_A and $L_{\mathcal{B}_{\varkappa}}$ have a nonempty intersection. We can build a timed automaton C for this intersection using the standard product construction. The size of C is polynomial, it uses ε-transitions and constants proportional to 1 and to $\varkappa$. To get rid of non-integers, we can multiply everything by the denominator of $\varkappa$, and the problem is just reduced to reachability between (initial and final states) in a polynomial-sized timed graph, which is in PSPACE.

The cases of $\overrightarrow{d}$ and $\overleftarrow{d}$ are similar, they just use $\overrightarrow{\mathcal{B}}_{\varkappa}$ and $\overleftarrow{\mathcal{B}}_{\varkappa}$ instead of $\mathcal{B}_{\varkappa}$.

PSPACE-hardness. We reduce the TREACH question for a timed graph G to the question of the form $d(L_A, L_B) < \varkappa$. We choose the trivial event alphabet $\Sigma = \{a\}$, take $\mathcal{A}$ the same as G with all transitions labeled by a; and $\mathcal{B}$ an automaton for the universal timed language over Σ and choose the constant $\varkappa > 0$ arbitrarily. In this case $d(L_A, L_B) = 0 < \varkappa$ whenever the final state is reachable in G, otherwise $d(L_A, L_B) = \infty > \varkappa$. This concludes the reduction and the PSPACE-hardness for d; the cases of $\overrightarrow{d}$ and $\overleftarrow{d}$ are similar.   □

4.4 Quantitative Timed Monitoring

Proposition 6. *Given a timed word w (with timings represented as rationals), a timed automaton $\mathcal{B}$ and a precision $\varkappa > 0$, deciding whether $d(w, L_\mathcal{B}) < \varkappa$ is* PSPACE-*complete. The same is true for $\overrightarrow{d}$ and $\overleftarrow{d}$.*

Proof. **PSPACE-easyness.** Build a timed automaton $\mathcal{A}$ (with rational constants) recognizing only w, thus $d(w, L_\mathcal{B}) < \varkappa$ iff $d(L_\mathcal{A}, L_\mathcal{B}) < \varkappa$, the latter condition is PSPACE-easy as stated in the previous proposition.

PSPACE-hardness. Again we reduce TREACH. We chose the trivial event alphabet $\Sigma = \{a\}$, take $\mathcal{B}$ the same as G with all transitions labeled by a; and $w = (a, 0)$. The constant $\varkappa$ is chosen very large, an upper bound for the diameter of the region graph of $\mathcal{B}$ ($\varkappa$ can still be written in a polynomial number of bits). Whenever the final state is reachable in G, the language $L_\mathcal{B}$ contains some word v (containing only letters a) of duration smaller than $\varkappa$. In this case $d(w, L_\mathcal{B}) \leq d(w, v) < \varkappa$. If the final state is unreachable in G, then $L_\mathcal{B} = \emptyset$ and hence $d(w, L_\mathcal{B}) = \infty > \varkappa$. This concludes the reduction and the PSPACE-hardness for d; the cases of $\overrightarrow{d}$ and $\overleftarrow{d}$ are similar. $\qquad\square$

The case when $\varkappa$ is small is easier. Let us define the granularity $g(w)$ of a timed word $w = (a_1, t_1) \ldots (a_n, t_n)$ as $\min\{t_{s+1} - t_s | t_s < t_{s+1}\}$ (with $t_0 = 0$), i.e. the minimal non-0 interval between events.

Proposition 7. *Given a timed word w (with timings represented as rationals), a timed automaton $\mathcal{B}$ and a positive precision $\varkappa < \min(g(\mathcal{B}), g(w))/2$, deciding whether $d(w, L_\mathcal{B}) < \varkappa$ is* NP-*complete. The same is true for $\overleftarrow{d}$. For $\overrightarrow{d}$, the problem is* PSPACE-*complete even for small $\varkappa$.*

Proof. **NP-easyness for $\overleftarrow{d}$.** We first show (with $\varkappa$ as small as required) that
(*) the inequality $\overleftarrow{d}(w, L_\mathcal{B}) < \varkappa$ is equivalent to existence of some
$v \in L_\mathcal{B}$ of polynomially bounded length, such that $\overleftarrow{d}(w, v) < \varkappa$.
Let $t_1 < \cdots < t_N$ be distinct dates of events in w. We denote $t_i^- = t_i - \varkappa$ and $t_i^+ = t_i + \varkappa$. Due to the bound on $\varkappa$, the intervals (t_i^-, t_i^+) are of length < 1 and disjoint. The inequality $\overleftarrow{d}(w, L_\mathcal{B}) < \varkappa$ is equivalent to existence of $u \in L_\mathcal{B}$ with $\overleftarrow{d}(w, u) < \varkappa$. In other words, u should satisfy three requirements:
- u is accepted by $\mathcal{B}$;
- for each i, within the interval (t_i^-, t_i^+), the word u only contains letters from $w(t_i)$;
- no events happen in u outside of intervals (t_i^-, t_i^+).

The fragment accepting run of $\mathcal{B}$ on u within the interval (t_i^-, t_i^+) can be considered as a path in timed graph consisting of transitions in $\mathcal{B}$ labeled by letters from $w(t_i)$. This path (and the corresponding fragment of u) can thus be simplified (using Proposition 3) to a polynomially bounded length. Proceeding with such a simplification for every i will transform the totality of u to the required polynomially bounded v. The property (*) is proved.
As in previous easiness proofs, we build a timed automaton $\mathcal{A}$ for $\{w\}$, then another one for $L_\mathcal{A} \cap L_{\overline{\mathcal{B}}_\varkappa}$, and check existence of a polynomially bounded accepted word v with complexity NP as stated by Proposition 2.

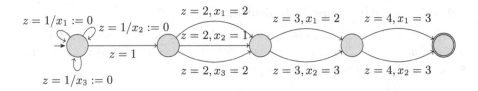

Fig. 3. Timed automaton encoding the 3CNF $(p_1 \vee \bar{p}_2 \vee p_3) \wedge (\bar{p}_1 \vee p_2) \wedge (\bar{p}_1 \vee \bar{p}_3)$

NP-easyness for d is proved similarly, but the variant of Proposition 2 where the simplified path has the same set of transitions should be used.

NP-hardness for d **and** $\overleftarrow{d}$**.** We proceed by reduction of 3SAT. Given a 3CNF $\bigwedge_{i=1}^{k} C_i$ with n boolean variables $p_1, \ldots, p_n$, we take $w = (a, 1)(a, 2) \ldots (a, k+1)$. The timed automaton $\mathcal{B}$ over alphabet $\{a\}$ has clocks $x_1, \ldots, x_n$ (which will encode boolean variables) and a special clock z which is never reset and ensures that all transitions of $\mathcal{B}$ happen every time unit. A gadget works during the first time unit and gives to each clock x_i a value 0 or 1 (this corresponds to possible boolean values of p_i). Afterwards, there are no more resets, hence $x_i = z - 1$ encodes $p_i = 0$ while $x_i = z$ encodes $p_i = 1$. At transition $i + 1$ the clause C_i is checked (one of boolean literals should have a required value), see example on Fig. 3.

Whenever the formula is satisfiable, the language of $\mathcal{B}$ contains w, and $d(w, L_{\mathcal{B}}) = 0 < \varkappa$, otherwise $L_{\mathcal{B}} = \emptyset$ and hence $d(w, L_{\mathcal{B}}) = \infty > \varkappa$. This concludes the reduction. The case of $\overleftarrow{d}$ is similar.

PSPACE-hardness for $\overrightarrow{d}$**.** The hardness argument is quite similar to that of Proposition 6, and also proceeds by reduction of TREACH in a timed graph G to the question of the form $\overrightarrow{d}(w, L_{\mathcal{B}}) < \varkappa$ (for any positive $\varkappa$). We chose the trivial event alphabet $\Sigma = \{a\}$, the word $w = (a, 1)$. The timed automaton $\mathcal{B}$ has its first transition (labeled by a and resetting all clocks) at time 1, afterwards it follows the graph G with all transitions labeled by a. Whenever the final state is reachable in G, the language $L_{\mathcal{B}}$ contains some word v starting with $(a, 1)$. In this case $\overrightarrow{d}(w, L_{\mathcal{B}}) = 0 < \varkappa$. If the final state is unreachable in G, then $L_{\mathcal{B}} = \emptyset$ and hence $\overrightarrow{d}(w, L_{\mathcal{B}}) = \infty > \varkappa$. This concludes the reduction. □

5   Information in Timed Words

In [3–5,7] we have answered the following question:

> Given a timed regular language L, what is the maximal amount of information in $w \in L$, observed with precision ε (as function of ε and **the number of events** n in w)?

We have explored potential applications including information transmission, data compression, and random generation. However, in the timed setting it is more natural and important to consider the quantity of information (or band-width) w.r.t. **time elapsed**, i.e. the duration T of w. Unfortunately, it was not possible in previous settings, because considering together timed words of the same duration but different number of events is tricky. We proposed a first solution in [6] based on formal summation of volumes in various dimensions but this turns out to be a bit artificial.

In this section, we show that our new distances on timed words provide a natural framework for a thorough study of quantity of information in timed words and languages w.r.t. **time elapsed**. This quantity can be characterised as ε-capacity (or ε-entropy), as described in Sect. 2.4, of sets of words in L of duration $\leq T$. Two features of our distances are crucial: (1) they can be applied to words with different numbers of events; (2) the relevant sets endowed with these distances are compact.

We cannot yet compute the ε-capacity (or ε-entropy) of an arbitrary timed regular language. Instead, we address two important examples:

- the most important one is the universal timed language U_T^{Σ} consisting of all timed words on event alphabet Σ (with s elements) of duration $\leq T$. We show that it is indeed compact (and hence all other closed languages of bounded duration are); and compute its ε-entropy. Naturally, since all timed words are considered, the entropy is quite large.
- In many practical situations, the words to consider have some special properties and thus are constrained to belong to some sublanguage, and their bandwidth is lower. The most natural constraint concerns the minimal interval separating the events (or the maximal frequency thereof). For that reason, we consider the timed language F_b^{Σ} of all the words over an alphabet Σ with the minimal interval b between events (in particular, simultaneous events are forbidden). We come up with tight bounds on its ε-entropy, without surprise it grows much more slowly than for the universal language.

Information in the Universal Timed Language. We consider the universal timed language U_T^{Σ} and start with a simple construction of a finite subset $M_{T,N}^{\Sigma} \subset U_T^{\Sigma}$, explore its net/separated properties and deduce tight bounds on ε-capacity and ε-entropy of U_T^{Σ}.

The set of timed words $M_{T,N}^{\Sigma}$ is built as follows. We distribute uniformly N active instants t_k on the interval $[0,T]$, taking $t_k = \frac{(2k-1)T}{2N}$ for $k = 1..N$. Then a timed word w belongs to $M_{T,N}^{\Sigma}$ whenever

- all events in w happen at active instants t_k only;
- within any fixed active instant t_k, the events in Σ happen in alphabetic order, and each letter in Σ happens at most once (in this instant).

It is easy to see that the cardinality of $M_{T,N}^{\Sigma}$ is 2^{sN}, indeed for each of N active instants there are 2^s possible choices (corresponding to subsets of Σ).

Proposition 8. *The set $M_{T,N}^{\Sigma}$ described above is an ε-separated in U_T^{Σ} whenever $\varepsilon < T/N$. It is an ε-net whenever $\varepsilon \geq T/2N$.*

Given T and ε, we can choose $N = \lceil T/2\varepsilon \rceil$, which yields $N - 1 < T/2\varepsilon \leq N$ which implies two bounds:

- $\varepsilon \geq T/2N$, hence $\varepsilon \geq T/2N$ and $M_{T,N}^\Sigma$ is an ε-net, and thus $\mathcal{H}_\varepsilon(U_T^\Sigma) \leq \log \#M_{T,N}^\Sigma = sN$.
- On the other hand, $2\varepsilon < T/(N-1)$, so $M_{T,N-1}^\Sigma$ is 2ε-separated, hence $\mathcal{C}_{2\varepsilon}(U_T^\Sigma) \geq \log \#M_{T,N-1}^\Sigma = s(N-1)$.

Together with (1) this gives $s(N-1) \leq \mathcal{C}_{2\varepsilon}(U_T^\Sigma) \leq \mathcal{H}_\varepsilon(U_T^\Sigma) \leq sN$. This implies the following result

Theorem 2. *ε-capacity and ε-entropy of U_T^Σ satisfy:*

$$s(\lceil T/2\varepsilon \rceil - 1) \leq \mathcal{H}_\varepsilon(U_T^\Sigma) \leq s\lceil T/2\varepsilon \rceil;$$
$$s(\lceil T/\varepsilon \rceil - 1) \leq \mathcal{C}_\varepsilon(U_T^\Sigma) \leq s\lceil T/\varepsilon \rceil.$$

Consequently, for $\varepsilon \to 0$ this gives the asymptotical estimates:

$$\mathcal{H}_\varepsilon(U_T^\Sigma) \approx sT/2\varepsilon; \quad \mathcal{C}_\varepsilon(U_T^\Sigma) \approx sT/\varepsilon.$$

Thus, the maximal bandwidth in timed words on Σ, observed with precision ε, equals $|\Sigma|/\varepsilon$ bits per time unit.

Information in bounded frequency language F_b^Σ. We recall that the timed language F_b^Σ contains all the words over an alphabet Σ with the minimal interval b between events (in particular, simultaneous events are forbidden). To simplify a bit the reasoning, we also suppose that the first event occurs after b seconds. We let $F_{b,T,\varepsilon}^\Sigma$ be the restriction of $F_{b,T}^\Sigma$ to timed words with events happening at dates multiple of ε. This set constitutes both an $\varepsilon/2$-net and an ε'-separated subset of $F_{b,T}^\Sigma$ for every $0 < \varepsilon' < \varepsilon$:

Lemma 1. *For every $0 < \varepsilon' < \varepsilon$, the set $F_{b,T,\varepsilon}^\Sigma$ is an $\varepsilon/2$-net and is ε'-separated.*

Hence, by evaluating the cardinality of $F_{b,T,\varepsilon}^\Sigma$, we will learn about $\varepsilon/2$-entropy and ε-entropy of $F_{b,T}^\Sigma$.

Lemma 2. *For every $\varepsilon > 0$, it holds that $|F_{b,T,\varepsilon}^\Sigma| = \sum_{n=0}^{\lfloor T/b \rfloor} s^n \binom{\lfloor (T-nb)/\varepsilon \rfloor + n}{n}$.*

Proof. We decompose the set $F_{b,T,\varepsilon}^\Sigma$ w.r.t. the number n of events per timed word. This number n goes from 0 to $\lfloor T/b \rfloor$ and for each n, there are s^n choices for the events that should be multiplied by the number of possible choices of a sequence of dates belonging to the set $\{b \leq t_1 \leq \cdots \leq t_n \leq T \mid t_{i+1} - t_i \geq b \wedge t_i \in \varepsilon \mathbb{N} \text{ for } i \leq n\}$. The latter set can be mapped to the set $\{0 < k_1 < \cdots < k_n \leq (T-nb)/\varepsilon + n \mid k_i \in \mathbb{N} \text{ for } i \leq n\}$ by the bijection $(t_1, t_2, \ldots, t_n) \mapsto ((t_1 - b)/\varepsilon + 1, (t_2 - 2b)/\varepsilon + 2, \ldots, (t_n - nb)/\varepsilon + n)$. This set has $\binom{\lfloor (T-nb)/\varepsilon \rfloor + n}{n}$ elements. Summing up over all n from 0 to $\lfloor T/b \rfloor$ we get the desired result.

As a consequence of the two previous lemmas we obtain:

Theorem 3. *For every $0 < \varepsilon' < \varepsilon$, the set $F_{b,T,\varepsilon}^{\Sigma}$ is an $\varepsilon/2$-net and is ε'-separated. The information measurements for $F_{b,T}^{\Sigma}$ are tightly linked as follows: for every $0 < \varepsilon' < \varepsilon$,*

$$\mathcal{C}_{\varepsilon}(F_{b,T}^{\Sigma}) \leq \mathcal{H}_{\varepsilon/2}(F_{b,T}^{\Sigma}) \leq \log|F_{b,T,\varepsilon}^{\Sigma}| \leq \mathcal{C}_{\varepsilon'}(F_{b,T}^{\Sigma}).$$

The following asymptotic equality holds when $\varepsilon \to 0$:

$$\log|F_{b,T,\varepsilon}^{\Sigma}| = \mathfrak{n}\log(1/\varepsilon) + \log\left(\frac{(se\,((T/\mathfrak{n}) - b))^{\mathfrak{n}}}{\sqrt{2\pi\mathfrak{n}}}\right) + o(1) \text{ with } \mathfrak{n} = \lceil T/b \rceil - 1.$$

Proof. The sequence of inequalities is a consequence of Lemma 1, the definitions of entropy and capacity and the classical inequalities (1). To find the asymptotic expansion of $\log|F_{b,T,\varepsilon}^{\Sigma}|$ up to $o(1)$ we start from Lemma 2.

For $n \leq \lceil T/b \rceil - 1 < T/b$ we have

$$\binom{\lfloor (T - nb)/\varepsilon \rfloor + n}{n} \sim (\lfloor (T - nb)/\varepsilon \rfloor + n)^n /n! \sim (T - nb)^n /(n!\varepsilon^n).$$

When $n = T/b$, the term is equal to $s^n = O(1)$ which is negligible compared to the other terms.

Thus

$$|F_{b,T,\varepsilon}^{\Sigma}| \sim \sum_{n=0}^{\lceil T/b \rceil - 1} s^n \left(\frac{T - nb}{\varepsilon}\right)^n /n!,$$

and this polynomial in $1/\varepsilon$ is equivalent to its last term when $\varepsilon \to 0$:

$$|F_{b,T,\varepsilon}^{\Sigma}| \sim s^{\mathfrak{n}} \left(\frac{T - \mathfrak{n}b}{\varepsilon}\right)^{\mathfrak{n}} /\mathfrak{n}! \text{ with } \mathfrak{n} = \lceil T/b \rceil - 1.$$

Using Stirling formula $\mathfrak{n}! \sim (\mathfrak{n}/e)^{\mathfrak{n}}\sqrt{2\pi\mathfrak{n}}$ we obtain:

$$|F_{b,T,\varepsilon}^{\Sigma}| \sim \frac{(se\,((T/\mathfrak{n}) - b))^{\mathfrak{n}}}{\sqrt{2\pi\mathfrak{n}}} \left(\frac{1}{\varepsilon}\right)^{\mathfrak{n}} \text{ with } \mathfrak{n} = \lceil T/b \rceil - 1.$$

Taking logarithms gives the desired asymptotic expansion. $\qquad\square$

Note that the second term of the asymptotic estimate is not bounded when T is allowed to vary and to approach a multiple of b from below. For this reason, below we also provide hard bounds for $\log|F_{b,T,\varepsilon}^{\Sigma}|$ that are not as tight w.r.t. variations of parameter ε but behave better w.r.t. parameter T.

Proposition 9. *For every $\varepsilon < 1/2b$ and[3] $T \geq b$, the following inequalities hold:*

$$\left(\left\lfloor \frac{T}{b} \right\rfloor - 1\right) \log \left\lfloor \frac{1}{\varepsilon} \right\rfloor - \left\lfloor \frac{T}{b} \right\rfloor \log \left\lfloor \frac{T}{b} \right\rfloor \leq \log|F_{b,T,\varepsilon}^{\Sigma}| \leq \left\lfloor \frac{T}{b} \right\rfloor \log \frac{1}{\varepsilon} + \left\lfloor \frac{T}{b} \right\rfloor \log 6bes.$$

---

[3] when $T < b$, the set of interest $F_{b,T}^{\Sigma}$ is empty.

Proof. First, let us state an equality about binomial coefficients: it holds that

$$\sum_{n=0}^{N} \binom{A+n}{n} = \binom{A+N+1}{N}, \tag{2}$$

where A, N and $n < N$ are given natural numbers. The above is true because

$$\sum_{n=0}^{N} \binom{A+n}{n} = \sum_{n=0}^{N} \binom{A+n}{A} = \sum_{n=A}^{A+N} \binom{n}{A} = \binom{A+N+1}{A+1} = \binom{A+N+1}{N},$$

where the third equality is known as the Hockey-Stick identity.

Now we prove the upper-bound using Lemma 2. We first treat the case where $\lfloor T/b \rfloor = 1$, that is $b \le T < 2b$. In this case, Lemma 2 gives

$$|F_{b,T,\varepsilon}^{\Sigma}| = s\binom{\lfloor (T-b)/\varepsilon \rfloor + 1}{1} = s(\lfloor (T-b)/\varepsilon \rfloor + 1) \le s(b/\varepsilon + 1) \le 2sb/\varepsilon.$$

So $\log |F_{b,T,\varepsilon}^{\Sigma}| \le \log(1/\varepsilon) + \log 2sb \le \lfloor T/b \rfloor \log(1/\varepsilon) + \lfloor T/b \rfloor \log 6bes$.

Now we treat the case where $T \ge 2b$ (still proving the upper bound).

$$\sum_{n=0}^{\lfloor T/b \rfloor} s^n \binom{\lfloor (T-nb)/\varepsilon \rfloor + n}{n}$$

$$\le s^{\lfloor T/b \rfloor} \sum_{n=0}^{\lfloor T/b \rfloor} \binom{\lfloor T/\varepsilon \rfloor + n}{n} = s^{\lfloor T/b \rfloor} \binom{\lfloor T/\varepsilon \rfloor + \lfloor T/b \rfloor + 1}{\lfloor T/b \rfloor},$$

where the last equality is given by (2). By using the inequality $\binom{N}{m} \le N^m/m!$, we obtain the following upper bound:

$$\binom{\lfloor T/\varepsilon \rfloor + \lfloor T/b \rfloor + 1}{\lfloor T/b \rfloor} \le (\lfloor T/\varepsilon \rfloor + \lfloor T/b \rfloor + 1)^{\lfloor T/b \rfloor} / \lfloor T/b \rfloor! \le \lfloor 3T/\varepsilon \rfloor^{\lfloor T/b \rfloor} / \lfloor T/b \rfloor!,$$

where the latter inequality holds because by assumption $\varepsilon \le 1/2b \le 1$, and so $\lfloor 3T/\varepsilon \rfloor \ge 1 \ge \lfloor T/b \rfloor$.

We now use a formula due to Robbins [13]: $N! \ge N^N e^{-N} \sqrt{2\pi N} e^{1/(12N+1)}$ for every $N > 0$. We instantiate this formula for $N = \lfloor T/b \rfloor$ and take its log. We obtain the following upper bound: $-\log(\lfloor T/b \rfloor!) \le -\lfloor T/b \rfloor \log \lfloor T/b \rfloor + \lfloor T/b \rfloor \log e$ and deduce $\log |F_{b,T,\varepsilon}^{\Sigma}| \le \lfloor T/b \rfloor \log (\lfloor 3T/\varepsilon \rfloor / \lfloor T/b \rfloor) + \lfloor T/b \rfloor \log e + \lfloor T/b \rfloor \log s$.

Note that $1/\lfloor T/b \rfloor \le 1/(T/b - 1) = (1/T)/(1/b - 1/T) \le (1/T)/(1/b - 1/2b) = (1/T)/(1/2b)$, where the second inequality holds due to the assumption $T \ge 2b$ which is equivalent to $1/b - 1/T \ge 1/2b$. Hence $\log (\lfloor 3T/\varepsilon \rfloor / \lfloor T/b \rfloor) \le \log(1/\varepsilon) + \log 6b$. Summing up we get the desired inequality:

$$\log |F_{b,T,\varepsilon}^{\Sigma}| \le \lfloor T/b \rfloor \log(1/\varepsilon) + \lfloor T/b \rfloor \log 6bes.$$

Now we prove the left-most inequality:

$$|F_{b,T,\varepsilon}^{\Sigma}| = \sum_{n=0}^{\lfloor T/b \rfloor} s^n \binom{\lfloor (T-nb)/\varepsilon \rfloor + n}{n} \ge \sum_{n=0}^{\lfloor T/b \rfloor - 1} \binom{\lfloor 1/\varepsilon \rfloor + n}{n}.$$

We use again (2) and now the fact that $\binom{N}{m} \geq (N-m)^m/m!$

$$|F^\Sigma_{b,T,\varepsilon}| = \sum_{n=0}^{\lfloor T/b \rfloor -1} \binom{\lfloor 1/\varepsilon \rfloor + n}{n} = \binom{\lfloor 1/\varepsilon \rfloor + \lfloor T/b \rfloor}{\lfloor T/b \rfloor - 1} \geq \lfloor 1/\varepsilon \rfloor^{\lfloor T/b \rfloor - 1}/(\lfloor T/b \rfloor - 1)!$$

Taking the log we obtain the sought inequality. □

6   Conclusion and Further Work

The three contributions of this paper constitute only the beginning of exploration of a new kind of distance on timed words. Below we draw some research perspectives.

Distance definition. We believe that depending on practical setting, variants of our distance could be appropriate. First, a sort of cost matrix allowing replacement of an a by a b at some cost can be allowed (to compare with edit distance from [8]). Second, a dependence structure over events can be introduced, so that the observer cannot notice swapping independent a and b (when they are close in time), but does observe a swap of a and c.

This work can be seen as a step towards resolution of Open question 5 in the research program of [2], we refer the reader to that work for a general discussion.

Quantitative verification. To make practical quantitative model-checking and monitoring sketched in Sect. 4, methodology, practical algorithms and tools should be developed.

Information in timed languages. The approach introduced opens the way to a thorough study of quantity of information in timed words and languages w.r.t. time elapsed; extending the analysis of Sect. 5 to all timed regular languages is the first challenge. The practical applications to timed data transmission should also be explored.

Acknowledgements. The authors thank James Worrell and François Laroussinie for their valuable advice on complexity analysis.

References

1. Alur, R., Dill, D.L.: A theory of timed automata. Theor. Comput. Sci. **126**, 183–235 (1994). https://doi.org/10.1016/0304-3975(94)90010-8
2. Asarin, E.: Challenges in timed languages: from applied theory to basic theory (column: concurrency). Bull. EATCS **83**, 106–120 (2004). https://eatcs.org/images/images/bulletin/beatcs83.pdf
3. Asarin, E., Basset, N., Béal, M.P., Degorre, A., Perrin, D.: Toward a timed theory of channel coding. In: Jurdziński, M., Ničković, D. (eds.) FORMATS 2012. LNCS, vol. 7595, pp. 27–42. Springer, Heidelberg (2012). https://doi.org/10.1007/978-3-642-33365-1_4

4. Asarin, E., Basset, N., Degorre, A.: Entropy of regular timed languages. Inf. Comput. **241**, 142–176 (2015). https://doi.org/10.1016/j.ic.2015.03.003
5. Asarin, E., Degorre, A.: Volume and entropy of regular timed languages: discretization approach. In: Bravetti, M., Zavattaro, G. (eds.) CONCUR 2009. LNCS, vol. 5710, pp. 69–83. Springer, Heidelberg (2009). https://doi.org/10.1007/978-3-642-04081-8_6
6. Asarin, E., Degorre, A.: Two size measures for timed languages. In: Lodaya, K., Mahajan, M. (eds.) Proceedings of FSTTCS. LIPIcs, vol. 8, pp. 376–387 (2010). https://doi.org/10.4230/LIPIcs.FSTTCS.2010.376
7. Basset, N.: Timed symbolic dynamics. In: Sankaranarayanan, S., Vicario, E. (eds.) FORMATS 2015. LNCS, vol. 9268, pp. 44–59. Springer, Cham (2015). https://doi.org/10.1007/978-3-319-22975-1_4
8. Chatterjee, K., Ibsen-Jensen, R., Majumdar, R.: Edit distance for timed automata. In: Fränzle, M., Lygeros, J. (eds.) Proceedings of HSCC, pp. 303–312. ACM (2014). https://doi.org/10.1145/2562059.2562141
9. Courcoubetis, C., Yannakakis, M.: Minimum and maximum delay problems in real-time systems. Form. Method. Syst. Des. **1**(4), 385–415 (1992). https://doi.org/10.1007/BF00709157
10. Donzé, A., Maler, O.: Robust satisfaction of temporal logic over real-valued signals. In: Chatterjee, K., Henzinger, T.A. (eds.) FORMATS 2010. LNCS, vol. 6246, pp. 92–106. Springer, Heidelberg (2010). https://doi.org/10.1007/978-3-642-15297-9_9
11. Gupta, V., Henzinger, T.A., Jagadeesan, R.: Robust timed automata. In: Maler, O. (ed.) HART 1997. LNCS, vol. 1201, pp. 331–345. Springer, Heidelberg (1997). https://doi.org/10.1007/BFb0014736
12. Kolmogorov, A., Tikhomirov, V.: ε-entropy and ε-capacity of sets in function spaces. Uspekhi Mat. Nauk **14**(2), 3–86 (1959). Russian, English translation in [15]
13. Robbins, H.: A remark on Stirling's formula. Am. Math. Mon. **62**(1), 26–29 (1955). https://doi.org/10.2307/2308012
14. Sankur, O., Bouyer, P., Markey, N., Reynier, P.-A.: Robust controller synthesis in timed automata. In: D'Argenio, P.R., Melgratti, H. (eds.) CONCUR 2013. LNCS, vol. 8052, pp. 546–560. Springer, Heidelberg (2013). https://doi.org/10.1007/978-3-642-40184-8_38
15. Shiryayev, A. (ed.): Selected works of A.N. Kolmogorov, vol. 3. Springer, Dordrecht (1993). https://doi.org/10.1007/978-94-017-2973-4

Online Timed Pattern Matching
Using Automata

Alexey Bakhirkin[1]([✉]), Thomas Ferrère[2], Dejan Nickovic[3], Oded Maler[1],
and Eugene Asarin[4]

[1] Univ. Grenoble Alpes, CNRS, Grenoble INP, VERIMAG, 38000 Grenoble, France
{alexey.bakhirkin,Oded.Maler}@univ-grenoble-alpes.fr
[2] IST Austria, Klosterneuburg, Austria
thomas.ferrere@ist.ac.at
[3] AIT Austrian Institute of Technology, Vienna, Austria
Dejan.Nickovic@ait.ac.at
[4] IRIF, Université Paris Diderot, Paris, France
asarin@irif.fr

Abstract. We provide a procedure for detecting the sub-segments of
an incrementally observed Boolean signal w that match a given temporal pattern φ. As a pattern specification language, we use timed regular
expressions, a formalism well-suited for expressing properties of concurrent asynchronous behaviors embedded in metric time. We construct a
timed automaton accepting the timed language denoted by φ and modify
it slightly for the purpose of matching. We then apply zone-based reachability computation to this automaton while it reads w, and retrieve all
the matching segments from the results. Since the procedure is automaton based, it can be applied to patterns specified by other formalisms
such as timed temporal logics reducible to timed automata or directly
encoded as timed automata. The procedure has been implemented and
its performance on synthetic examples is demonstrated.

1 Introduction and Motivation

Complex cyber-physical systems and reactive systems in general exhibit temporal behaviors that can be viewed as dense-time signals or discrete-time sequences
and time-series. The correctness and performance of such systems is based on
properties satisfied by these behaviors. In formal verification, a system model
is used to generate *all* possible behaviors and check for their inclusion in the
language defined by the specifications. In runtime verification, interpreted as
lightweight simulation-based verification, property satisfaction by *individual* system behaviors is checked. In many situations, we would like to monitor the ongo-
ing behavior of a real system, already deployed and running, rather than traces of

This research was supported in part by the Austrian Science Fund (FWF) under
grants S11402-N23 (RiSE/SHiNE) and Z211-N23 (Wittgenstein Award), and by
the European Research Council under the European Union's Seventh Framework
Programme (FP/2007-2013)/ERC Grant Agreement nr. 306595 "STATOR".

D. N. Jansen and P. Prabhakar (Eds.): FORMATS 2018, LNCS 11022, pp. 215–232, 2018.
https://doi.org/10.1007/978-3-030-00151-3_13

a simulation model during design time. In this context we want to detect property violation and other patterns of interest such as suspicious activities, degradation of performance and other alarming signs known to precede unpleasant or even catastrophic situations. The detection of such patterns and the reaction to them can be the basis of another level of supervisory control that reacts to situations as they occur without achieving the challenging and often impossible task of verifying offline against all possible scenarios. In fact, in the software engineering literature for safety-critical systems there is an actuator-monitor decomposition (*safety bag*) where one module computes the reaction while the other checks the results. Such an architecture has been proposed recently as a way to handle autonomous systems such as driver-free cars [15].

Properties traditionally used in verification often correspond to complete behaviors or their prefixes that start from time zero. In pattern matching one is interested in segments that may start and end in any time point. To be useful, the detection of patterns should be done *online*, as soon as they occur. In this paper we provide an automaton-based online pattern matching procedure where patterns are specified using timed regular expressions, a formalism suitable for describing patterns in concurrent and asynchronous behaviors. Before moving to our contribution, let us make a brief survey of some well-known classical results on string pattern matching. A regular expression φ defines a regular language $\mathcal{L}(\varphi)$ consisting of sequences that match it. It can be transformed into a non-deterministic automaton $\mathcal{A}_\varphi$ that recognizes $\mathcal{L}(\varphi)$ in the sense that $\mathcal{L}(\varphi)$ is exactly the set of words w that admit a run from an initial to a final state. [19] The existence for such an accepting run in $\mathcal{A}_\varphi$ can be checked by exploring the finitely many such runs associated with w. As a byproduct of classifying w, the automaton can classify any prefix $w[0..j]$ of w for $j < k$, just by observing the states reachable by the runs at time j. It is worth noting that the determinization procedure (subset construction) due to Rabin and Scott [21] corresponds to a breadth-first exploration of these runs for all words, combined with the fact that runs that reach the same state can be merged (see Fig. 3). A simple modification of $\mathcal{A}_\varphi$, to our knowledge first described in [23], allows also to find all sub-segments $w[i..j]$ of w that match φ. First, a counter t' is used which increments each time a symbol is read – such a counter exists anyway in any implementation of a membership tester as a pointer to the current symbol in the sequence. Then a new initial state s is added to $\mathcal{A}_\varphi$, and in this state the automaton can self-loop indefinitely and postpone the selection of the point in time when it starts reading w. When it moves to the original initial state of $\mathcal{A}_\varphi$, it records the start time in an auxiliary variable t (see Figs. 1 and 2 for an example). Then whenever there is a run reaching an accepting state with $t = r$ and $t' = r'$, one can conclude that $w[r..r']$ matches φ. This modification, also pointed to in [1], enabled the later implementation of fast and reliable string matching tools [2,20] which are now standard. The application of regular expressions since extends beyond text processing but also occurs, e.g. in DNA analysis and programming languages.

To reason about the dynamic behaviors of complex systems, cyber-physical or not, one needs a language richer than traditional expressions [26]. To start with,

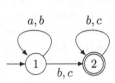

Fig. 1. A non-deterministic automaton for $(a \cup b)^* \cdot (b \cup c)^+$.

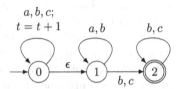

Fig. 2. A non-deterministic matching automaton for $(a \cup b)^* \cdot (b \cup c)^+$. Note the new initial state and the counter t.

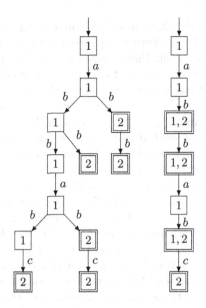

Fig. 3. Runs of the automaton in Fig. 1. *Left* – all runs for the word *abbabc*. *Right* – breadth-first on-the-fly subset construction.

the behaviors of such systems, unlike sequential text, are multi-dimensional by nature, involving several state variables and components working in parallel. In principle, it is possible to express patterns in the behavior of such systems using a global product alphabet, but such a flattening of the structure is impractical for both readability and complexity reasons. Instead we use a more symbolic variant of regular expressions (first used in the timed setting in [27], see also the proposal [13] to add timing to the regular expressions of the industrial specification language PSL which admits variables) where one can refer to state variables and write expressions like $p \cdot q$ rather than $(pq \cup p\bar{q}) \cdot (pq \cup \bar{p}q)$. Needless to say, the whole practice of verification, starting with temporal logic specifications, via compositional system descriptions to their symbolic model-checking [9] is based on such an approach, which seems to be less developed in formal language theory. To reason about what happens in various parts of the system, we also employ intersection in our syntax. In the one-dimensional untimed case it does not increase the expressive power, but affects the complexity of online membership testing since the minimal DFA translating such expressions can be exponentially larger [12]. The second observation is that system components need not be synchronized and they may operate on different time scales. Consequently, reasoning in discrete time with a pre-selected time step is wasteful and we use instead the timed regular expressions of [4,5], a formalism tailored for specifying properties of timed behaviors such as Boolean signals [4] or time-event sequences [5], where value changes and events can occur anywhere along the time axis. Thus the expression $p \cap (\text{true} \cdot q \cdot \text{true})$ is matched by any segment of a Boolean signal where p holds continuously and a burst of q occurs anywhere inside this segment. Using duration constraints we can refine the patterns, for example the expression $p \cap (\text{true} \cdot \langle q \rangle_{[a,\infty]} \cdot \text{true})$ considers only q-bursts that last for at least a time. The problem of timed pattern matching has been introduced and solved in [27]: find all the sub-segments of a multi-dimensional Boolean signal of a bounded variability that match a timed regular expression. This work was automaton-free and worked inductively on the structure of the formula in an offline manner. An online version of that procedure has been developed in [28] based on a novel extension of Brzozowski derivatives [8] to timed regular expressions and dense time signals. Both works, which have been implemented in the tool Montre [25] did not use the full syntax of timed regular expressions and hence did not match the expressive power of timed automata (see [14]). In this paper we explore an alternative automaton-based procedure whose scope of application is wider than the expressions used in [27,28] as it works with any timed language definable by a timed automaton and is agnostic about the upstream pattern specification language. Let us mention another recent automaton-based approach is the one of [29], a real-time extension of the Boyer-Moore pattern matching method. In contrast to our work, the procedure in [29] works on TA defined over time-event sequences and it requires pre-computing the region graph from the TA specification. The same authors improve this result in [30], by using a more efficient variant of the Boyer-Moore algorithm and by replacing the region automaton by the more efficient zone-simulation graph.

The essence of our contribution is the following. Starting with an expression φ, we build a non deterministic timed automaton $\mathcal{A}_\varphi$ which accepts $\mathcal{L}(\varphi)$. Then by a small modification, similar to the discrete case, we convert it to a matching automaton $\mathcal{A}'_\varphi$ with two additional clocks x_0 and x_s that record, respectively the time since the beginning of the signal (absolute time) and the time since we started reading it. Then, given a bounded variability Boolean signal we compute the reachability tree of the automaton whose nodes are pairs of the form (q, Z) where Z is a zone in the extended clock space of $\mathcal{A}'_\varphi$. This tree captures all (possibly uncountably many) runs induced by w. By projecting zones associated with accepting states of the automaton on x_0 and $x_0 - x_s$, we retrieve the matches. We combine this procedure with incremental observation of the input signal to obtain an online matching procedure. We implemented this procedure using the zone library of IF [7].

2   Preliminaries

Signals. Let $\mathbb{B} = \{0, 1\}$ and let $P = \{p_1, \ldots, p_n\}$ be a set of propositions. A state over P is an element of 2^P or equivalently a Boolean vector $u \in \mathbb{B}^n$ assigning the truth value for any $p \in P$. The time domain $\mathbb{T}$ is taken to be the set of non-negative reals. A Boolean signal w of duration $|w| = d$ is a right-continuous function $w : [0, d) \to \mathbb{B}^n$ whose value at time t is denoted by $w[t]$. We use $w[t..t']$ to denote the part of signal w between absolute times t and t'. The concatenation of two signals w and w' of respective durations d and d' is the signal ww' of duration $d + d'$ defined as $ww'[t] = w[t]$ for all $t < d$, $ww'[t] = w'[t - d]$ for all $t \in [d, d + d')$. We consider signals of finite variability, which can be written as a finite concatenation of constant signals. The empty signal of duration zero is denoted ϵ. We use $w\|w'$ to denote the parallel composition of two signals of the same duration defined over disjoint sets of propositions.

Timed Regular Expressions. To specify sets of signals we use the timed regular expressions (TRE) of [4], augmented with the use of a structured alphabet represented by a set P of atomic propositions [27]. The set of state constraints, denoted by $\Sigma(P)$ is simply the set of Boolean formulas over P. The syntax of TRE is given by the grammar

$$\varphi ::= \epsilon \mid \sigma \mid \varphi \cup \varphi \mid \varphi \cap \varphi \mid \varphi \cdot \varphi \mid \varphi^+ \mid \langle \varphi \rangle_I \mid \exists p.\varphi$$

where $\sigma \in \Sigma(P)$ and $I \subseteq \mathbb{T}$ is an integer-bounded interval. As customary, iterations of φ are denoted in exponent with $\varphi^0 \equiv \epsilon$ and $\varphi^k \equiv \varphi^{k-1} \cdot \varphi$ for $k \geq 1$. The Kleene star is defined as $\varphi^* \equiv \epsilon \cup \varphi^+$.

Any TRE φ is associated with a set of signals, the timed language $\mathcal{L}(\varphi)$, via the following inductive definitions:

$\mathcal{L}(\epsilon) = \{\epsilon\}$ $\mathcal{L}(\varphi_1 \cdot \varphi_2) = \{w_1 \cdot w_2 \mid w_i \in \mathcal{L}(\varphi_i), i = 1, 2\}$

$\mathcal{L}(\sigma) = \{w \mid \forall t \in [0, |w|)\ w[t] \models \sigma\}$ $\mathcal{L}(\varphi^+) = \bigcup_{k=1}^{\infty} \mathcal{L}(\varphi^k)$

$\mathcal{L}(\varphi_1 \cup \varphi_2) = \mathcal{L}(\varphi_1) \cup \mathcal{L}(\varphi_2)$ $\mathcal{L}(\langle \varphi \rangle_I) = \{w \mid w \in \mathcal{L}(\varphi) \wedge |w| \in I\}$

$\mathcal{L}(\varphi_1 \cap \varphi_2) = \mathcal{L}(\varphi_1) \cap \mathcal{L}(\varphi_2)$ $\mathcal{L}(\exists p.\varphi) = \{w \mid \exists w' \text{ over } \{p\}, w\|w' \in \mathcal{L}(\varphi)\}$

Note that signals in $\mathcal{L}(\sigma)$ need not be a constant, for example $\mathcal{L}(p_i)$ consists of all signals in which p_i is constantly true but p_j, for $j \neq i$ may go up and down. Note also that the semantics of σ does not specify any duration, and in this sense it resembles σ^* in classical regular expressions. The duration restriction is expressed using the $\langle \varphi \rangle_I$ operation. The $\exists p.\varphi$ operation corresponds to the renaming operation in [4] which has been proven in [14] to be necessary in order to match the expressive power of timed automata.

Timed Automata. We use a variant of timed automata, finite-state automata extended with real-valued clock variables, as acceptors of timed languages over signals. Unlike the automata introduced originally in [3] and used in [5], which are event-based with alphabet symbols associated with transitions, we use a state-based approach [4] where signal values are associated with time passage inside states. Let $X = \{x_1, \ldots, x_m\}$ be a set of clock variables. A *clock constraint* is a Boolean combination of inequalities of the form $x \bowtie c$ where $c \in \mathbb{N}$ is a constant, $x \in X$ is a clock variable, and $\bowtie \in \{<, \leq, =, \geq, >\}$ is a comparison sign. The set of clock constraints over X is written $\Phi(X)$. A *valuation* $v \in \mathbb{T}^m$ associates any $x \in X$ with a delay denoted $v(x) \in \mathbb{T}$.

Definition 1 (Timed Automaton). *A timed automaton over signals is a tuple $\mathcal{A} = (P, X, L, S, i, o, \Delta)$ with locations L, initial locations $S \subseteq L$, input* *labeling* $i : L \rightarrow \Sigma(P)$, *output labeling* $o : L \rightarrow \Phi(X)$, *and set of edges* $\Delta \subseteq L \times \Phi(X) \times 2^X \times L$.

A state (configuration) of the automaton is a pair (ℓ, v) where ℓ is a location and v is a clock valuation. The behavior of the automaton while reading a signal consists of an alternation of two types of steps:

- A time step $(\ell, v) \overset{w}{\rightsquigarrow} (\ell, v + r)$ where the automaton consumes a signal w of duration r while advancing all clocks in the same pace provided that the signal satisfies continuously the state invariant specified by the input label: $\forall t \in [0, r) \; w[t] \models i(\ell)$;
- A discrete step $(\ell, v) \overset{\delta}{\rightarrow} (\ell', v')$ for some transition $\delta = (\ell, \varphi, R, \ell') \in \Delta$ such that $v \models \varphi$ (clocks satisfy transition guard) and $v' = v[R \leftarrow 0]$ (clocks in R are reset while taking the transition).

A *run* of automaton $\mathcal{A}$ over a signal w is a sequence

$$(\ell_0, 0) \overset{w_0}{\rightsquigarrow} (\ell_0, v_0) \overset{\delta_1}{\rightarrow} (\ell_1, v_1') \overset{w_1}{\rightsquigarrow} (\ell_1, v_1) \overset{\delta_2}{\rightarrow} \ldots \overset{\delta_n}{\rightarrow} (\ell_n, v_n') \overset{w_n}{\rightsquigarrow} (\ell_n, v_n)$$

of discrete and time steps such that $w = w_1 w_2 \ldots w_n$, starting with an initial configuration, that is, $\ell_0 \in S$ and $v_0(x) = 0$ for all $x \in X$. A run is accepting if it ends in an accepting configuration: $v_n \models o(\ell_n)$. The language $\mathcal{L}(\mathcal{A})$ is the set of signals admitting an accepting run.

The object that we are going to compute is the *match set* of a signal w with respect to a timed language $\mathcal{L}$ defined either by an automaton $\mathcal{A}$ or a timed regular expression: $\mathcal{M}(w, \mathcal{L}) = \{(t, t') : w[t..t'] \in \mathcal{L}\}$. In [27] it has been proved that for an expression φ, $\mathcal{M}(w, \mathcal{L}(\varphi))$ is a finite union of two-dimensional zones. Our results extend it to languages accepted by timed automata where (t, t') belong to the match set if $w[t..t']$ admits an accepting run in $\mathcal{A}$.

Translating TRE into Automata. We now demonstrate, following [4], how a timed regular expression translates into a timed automaton accepting the same language. The construction is rather straightforward and the reader is referred to [4] for a more lengthy intuitive presentation. The construction of an automaton $\mathcal{A}_\varphi = (P, X_\varphi, L_\varphi, S_\varphi, i_\varphi, o_\varphi, \Delta_\varphi)$ accepting $\mathcal{L}(\varphi)$, is obtained by structural induction. In the description that follows we assume that automata given by induction hypothesis have disjoint sets of locations, but may share the same clocks except for the case of intersection.

- Empty word: $\mathcal{A}_\epsilon$ is defined by letting $X_\epsilon = \{x\}$, $L_\epsilon = S_\epsilon = \{\ell\}$, $i_\epsilon(\ell) \equiv \mathsf{true}$, $o_\epsilon(\ell) \equiv (x = 0)$, and $\Delta_\epsilon = \emptyset$.
- State expressions: $\mathcal{A}_\sigma$ is defined by $X_\sigma = \emptyset$, $L_\sigma = S_\sigma = \{\ell\}$, $i_\sigma(\ell) \equiv \sigma$, $o_\sigma(\ell) \equiv \top$, and $\Delta_\sigma = \emptyset$.
- Union: $\mathcal{A}_{\varphi \cup \psi}$ is defined as the component-wise union of $\mathcal{A}_\varphi$ and $\mathcal{A}_\psi$.
- Intersection: $\mathcal{A}_{\varphi \cap \psi}$ is given by $X_{\varphi \cap \psi} = X_\varphi \uplus X_\psi$, $L_{\varphi \cap \psi} = L_\varphi \times L_\psi$, $S_{\varphi \cap \psi} = S_\varphi \times S_\psi$, with input labels $i_{\varphi \cap \psi}(\ell, m) = i_\varphi(\ell) \wedge i_\psi(m)$ for every $\ell \in L_\varphi, m \in L_\psi$, similarly for output labels. For a pair of edges $(\ell, \beta, Q, \ell') \in \Delta_\varphi, (m, \gamma, R, m') \in \Delta_\psi$, $\mathcal{A}_{\varphi \cap \psi}$ has the edges $((\ell, m), \beta, Q, (\ell', m))$, $((\ell, m), \gamma, R, (\ell, m'))$, and $((\ell, m), \beta \wedge \gamma, Q \cup R, (\ell', m'))$.

- Concatenation: we let $X_{\varphi \cdot \psi} = X_\varphi \cup X_\psi$, $L_{\varphi \cdot \psi} = L_\varphi \cup L_\psi$ and $S_{\varphi \cdot \psi} = S_\varphi$. Labels are given by $i_{\varphi \cdot \psi}(\ell) \equiv i_\varphi(\ell)$ if $\ell \in \mathcal{L}_\varphi$, $i_{\varphi \cdot \psi}(\ell) \equiv i_\psi(\ell)$ otherwise; $o_{\varphi \cdot \psi}(\ell) \equiv \mathsf{false}$ if $\ell \in L_\varphi$, $o_{\varphi \cdot \psi}(\ell) \equiv o_\psi(\ell)$ otherwise. Edges are given by $\Delta_{\varphi \cdot \psi} = \Delta_\varphi \cup \Delta_\psi \cup \{(f, o_\varphi(f), X_\psi, s) \mid f \in L_\varphi, s \in S_\psi\}$.
- Iteration: $\mathcal{A}_{\varphi+}$ is obtained from $\mathcal{A}_\varphi$ by adding edges $(f, o_\varphi(f), X_\varphi, s)$ for every pair $f \in L_\varphi$ and $s \in S_\varphi$.
- Duration constraint: $\mathcal{A}_{\langle \varphi \rangle_I}$ is obtained by using a fresh clock $x \notin X_\varphi$ and replacing output labels ϕ with $\varphi \wedge (x \in I)$ in every location.
- Existential quantification: $\mathcal{A}_{\exists p.\varphi}$ is obtained by replacing input labels σ with $\sigma[p \leftarrow \mathsf{true}] \vee \sigma[p \leftarrow \mathsf{false}]$ in every location.

The above procedure yields the following:

Theorem 1 (TRE $\Rightarrow$ TA). *For any TRE of containing m atomic expressions and n duration constraints, one can construct an equivalent timed automaton with n clocks and 2^m locations.*

The exponential blow-up in the number of locations is solely due to the intersection operator, with repeated application of the product construction, and would otherwise vanish. For a proof of the other direction, TA $\Rightarrow$ TRE, see [4,5].

3   Membership and Matching Using Timed Automata

In this section we present a zone-based algorithm for testing membership of a signal in the language accepted by a timed automaton; then show how it can be extended to find and extract the match set of the signal in that language.

3.1   Checking Acceptance by Non-deterministic Timed Automata

The automata constructed from expressions, as well as other typical timed automata, are non-deterministic. Part of this non-determinism is dense, coming from modeling duration uncertainty using intervals, and also from different factorizations of a signal segment into two concatenated expressions. Unlike classical automata, it can be shown that some timed automata cannot be determinized [3] and even determinizability of a given automaton is an undecidable problem [11]. However, these results are concerned with converting the non-deterministic TA into a deterministic one, equivalent with respect to *all* possible inputs which include signals of arbitrary variability and hence the number of clocks cannot be bounded. In contrast, exploring all the (uncountably many) possible runs of a non-deterministic timed automaton while reading a *given* signal of finite duration and variability is feasible, as has already been demonstrated [16,18,24] in the context of testing, using what has been termed on-the-fly subset construction. The procedure described in the sequel shows how despite their dense non-determinism, timed automata can be effectively used as membership testers for bounded-variability signals and eventually as online pattern matching devices. To this end we use a variant of the standard zone-based reachability algorithm for simulating uncountably many runs in parallel. This algorithm underlies all timed automata verification tools [6,7,10], see [17,31]. The procedure computes the simulation/reachability graph whose nodes are symbolic states of the form (ℓ, Z) where ℓ is a location and Z is a zone in the space of clock valuations.

Definition 2 (Zone). *Let X be a set of clock variables. A* difference constraint *is an inequality of the form $x - y \prec c$ for $x, y \in X$, $c \in \mathbb{T}$, and $\prec \in \{<, \leq\}$. A* zone *is a polytope definable as a conjunction of clock and difference constraints.*

Zones are known to be closed under intersection, projection, resets and forward time projection defined as $Z^{\nearrow} = \{v + t \mid v \in Z \wedge t \geq 0\}$. These operations are implemented as simple operations on the difference bound matrix (DBM) representing the zone.

Let $\mathcal{A} = (P, X, L, S, i, o, \Delta)$ be a timed automaton and let $\mathcal{A}'$ be the automaton obtained from $\mathcal{A}$ by adding an auxiliary clock x_0 which is never reset since the beginning and hence it keeps track of the absolute time. We will consider zones in the extended clock space, and denote extended clock valuations as (v_0, v). It is not hard to see that a configuration $(\ell, (v_0, v))$ is reachable in $\mathcal{A}'$ iff the input prefix $w[0..v_0]$ admits a run to (ℓ, v) in $\mathcal{A}$.

Definition 3 (Discrete Successor). *Let Z be a zone and let $\delta = (\ell, \varphi, R, \ell') \in \Delta$ be a transition. The δ-successor of Z is the zone*

$$Succ^{\delta} Z = \{v' : \exists v \in Z \ v \models \varphi \wedge v' = v[R \leftarrow 0]\}$$

While doing zone-based time passage in a zone, we need to restrict ourselves to segments of the signal that satisfy the input constraints of the location and this is made possible through the use of absolute time.

Definition 4 (Temporal Scope). *The temporal scope of a signal w in location ℓ is the set of time points where w satisfies the input constraint of ℓ:*

$$\mathcal{J}(\ell, w) = \{t : w[t] \models i(\ell)\}.$$

For a bounded variability signal, $\mathcal{J}(\ell, w)$ is a sequence $J_1, \ldots, J_k$ of disjoint intervals of the form $J_i = [\alpha_i, \beta_i)$.

When a symbolic state (ℓ, Z) is reached via a discrete transition, we need to split Z into zones on which time can progress, using the following operation.

$$E(\ell, Z) = \{Z \wedge \alpha \leq x_0 \leq \beta \mid [\alpha, \beta) \in \mathcal{J}(\ell, w)\}.$$

The procedure *Succ* (Algorithm 1) computes the successors of a symbolic state by one discrete transition and one time passage. The whole reachability algorithm (Algorithm 2) applies this procedure successively to all reachable symbolic states. It accepts as arguments the automaton $\mathcal{A}$, the signal w, and the set I of states from which to start the exploration. When calling *Reach* for the first time, we set I to be $\{(\ell, 0) \mid \ell \in S\}$. When *Reach* terminates, it outputs the set Q_{reach}

Algorithm 1. $Succ(\ell, Z)$

Require: A timed automaton $\mathcal{A}$ and symbolic state (ℓ, Z);
Require: An input signal w for which $\mathcal{J}(\ell, w)$ has been computed for every location.
Ensure: The set Q of successors of (ℓ, Z) by one transition and one time step.
  $Q := \emptyset$
  $Q_1 := \{Succ^\delta(\ell, Z) \mid \delta \in \Delta\}$ {Discrete successors}
  for all non-empty $(\ell', Z') \in Q_1$ **do**
    $Q_2 := \{\ell'\} \times E(\ell', Z')$ {Compute the sub-zones of Z' in which time can progress}
    for all non-empty $(\ell'', Z'') \in Q_2$ **do**
      $Q := Q \cup \{(\ell'', Z''^\nearrow \wedge x_0 \leq \beta_i)\}$ {Apply time passage until the corresponding upper bound}
    end for
  end for
  return Q

Algorithm 2. $Reach(\mathcal{A}, w, I)$

Require: A timed automaton $\mathcal{A}$, signal w, set of initial states I;
Ensure: The set Q_{reach} of all symbolic states reachable while reading w
  $Q_{\text{reach}} := P := I$ {Initialization of visited and pending symbolic states}
  while $P \neq \emptyset$ **do**
    pick and **remove** $(\ell, Z) \in P$
    $Q_1 := Succ(\ell, Z)$
    for all $(\ell', Z') \in Q_1$ **do**
      if $(\ell', Z') \notin Q_{\text{reach}}$ **then**
        $Q_{\text{reach}} := Q_{\text{reach}} \cup \{(\ell', Z')\}$ {Add to visited}
        $P := P \cup \{(\ell', Z')\}$ {Add to pending}
      end if
    end for
  end while
  return Q_{reach}

---

of reachable symbolic states. From Q_{reach}, we can extract the set of accepting states by intersecting its elements with the output labels of locations: $Q_{\text{acc}} = \{(\ell, Z_a) \mid Z_a = Z \wedge o(\ell) \wedge Z_a \neq \emptyset \wedge (\ell, Z) \in Q\}$. If a configuration $(\ell, (v, v_0))$ is reachable and accepting (belongs to some element of Q_{acc}), then the prefix $w[0..v(x_0)]$ is accepted by the automaton.

Theorem 2 (Termination). *Given a finite-variability signal, Algorithm 2 terminates.*

Termination follows from the fact that the set of symbolic states is finite in our case. We can scale the signal so that all the switching points come at integer times, then, we can use zones with integer coefficients in Algorithm 2. The largest possible value of a clock and thus the largest constant that can appear in a reachable symbolic state is the duration of the signal, hence the number of possible symbolic states is finite.

Algorithm 3. $ReachOnline(\mathcal{A}, w_i, Q_r^{i-1})$

Require: A timed automaton $\mathcal{A}$, signal segment w_i defined on $[t_i, t_{i+1})$, previous set of reachable states Q_r^{i-1};
Ensure: The set Q_r^i contains the states reachable while reading w_i
$\quad I = \{(\ell, Z') \mid Z' = Z \wedge x_0 = t_i \wedge Z' \neq \emptyset \wedge (\ell, Z) \in Q_r^{i-1}\}$ {States that are reachable when w_i starts}
$\quad$ **return** $Reach(\mathcal{A}, w_i, I)$

Theorem 3 (Completeness). *There exists a run of the automaton $\mathcal{A}$:*

$$(\ell_0, 0) \overset{w_0}{\rightsquigarrow} (\ell_0, v_0) \overset{\delta_1}{\longrightarrow} (\ell_1, v_1') \overset{w_1}{\rightsquigarrow} (\ell_1, v_1) \overset{\delta_2}{\longrightarrow} \ldots \overset{\delta_n}{\longrightarrow} (\ell_n, v_n') \overset{w_n}{\rightsquigarrow} (\ell_n, v_n)$$

if and only if the configuration (ℓ_n, v_n) belongs to Q_{reach}.

By induction on the number of discrete transitions, every reachable configuration is eventually visited by the algorithm as part of some symbolic state.

3.2 Checking Acceptance Online

Algorithm 2 can be used to perform reachability computation in an online way. We can arbitrarily split the input signal w into segments $w_1, w_2, \cdots, w_n$ and present them one by one to the procedure *ReachOnline* (Algorithm 3). After processing segment w_i, the procedure returns the set of states reachable after reading $w_1 \cdots w_i$. From the previous set of reachable states, *ReachOnline* extracts the states which are reachable at the start of the new segment (those where the absolute time clock satisfies $x_0 = |w_1 \cdots w_i|$) and passes them on as initial states for *Reach*. More formally, we build the sequence

$$Q_r^1 = ReachOnline(A, w_1, \{(\ell, 0) \mid \ell \in S\}),$$
$$Q_r^2 = ReachOnline(A, w_2, Q_r^1),$$
$$\cdots$$
$$Q_r^n = ReachOnline(A, w_n, Q_r^{n-1})$$

and take the set of reachable states Q_{reach} to be $\bigcup_{i=1}^n Q_r^i$.

One useful property of *ReachOnline* in terms of memory use is that when processing a segment of the signal, it does not need to store previously processed segments and, after the new initial states are extracted, it does not need to store previously computed reachable states. Another property of *ReachOnline* is that it does not care about how we split w into segments. Segments may have different duration, different number of switching points, etc. The way we split the signal affects the performance though. As the segment size gets smaller, the number of times Algorithm 2 is called increases, but the cost to process a segment decreases. The influence of this parameter on performance is discussed in Sect. 4.

3.3 From Acceptance to Matching

To compute the segments of w which are accepted by an automaton $\mathcal{A}$, we first construct a matching automaton $\mathcal{A}'$ similar to the one used in the discrete case. It can stay indefinitely in an added initial state before it moves to an initial state of $\mathcal{A}$, resets a clock x_s and starts reading the remaining part of w. The automaton also uses the absolute time clock x_0 used for acceptance, see Fig. 4.

Definition 5 (Matching Timed Automaton). *Let* $\mathcal{A} = (P, X, L, S, i, o, \Delta)$ *be a timed automaton. Then the corresponding matching automaton is* $\mathcal{A}' = (P, X', L', S', i', o', \Delta')$, *where* $X' = X \cup \{x_0, x_s\}$; $L' = L \cup \{\ell_s\}$; $S' = \{\ell_s\}$, $i' = i \cup \{\ell_s \mapsto \text{true}\}$, $o' = o \cup \{\ell_s \mapsto \text{false}\}$; $\Delta' = \Delta \cup \{(\ell_s, \text{true}, X' - \{x_0\}, \ell) \mid \ell \in S\}$.

The start time of reading the segment is constantly maintained by the difference $x_0 - x_s$. As a generalization of the case of acceptance, w admits a run that ends in an extended configuration $(\ell, (v, v_0, v_s))$ in $\mathcal{A}'$ iff the signal segment $w[v_0 - v_s..v_0]$ admits a run in $\mathcal{A}$ that leads to (ℓ, v). Thus Algorithms 2 and 3 applied to $\mathcal{A}'$ compute the reachable symbolic states in the extended clock space. Projecting zones associated with accepting locations on x_0 and x_s we can can extract the matches. From Theorems 2 and 3 it follows that the for a given TRE and expression, the match set can be described by a finite set of zones. This extends the result obtained in [27] to arbitrary TA.

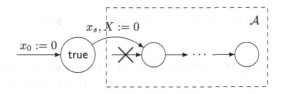

Fig. 4. Matching automaton $\mathcal{A}'$ for a property automaton $\mathcal{A}$.

3.4 Example

Let us illustrate the matching algorithm with a simple example. As the pattern specification, we use the expression $\varphi = p \cdot q$, and we translate it to the automaton shown in Fig. 5. As input, we use the signal w from Fig. 6. The signal is split into two segments: w_1 defined in the interval $[0, 4)$, and w_2 defined in the interval $[4, 8)$. We run the matching algorithm presenting it one segment at a time.

When the segment w_1 arrives, we start the exploration with the symbolic state $(\ell_\top, x_0 = 0)$ and immediately apply the time transition to it. We can stay in the location $\ell_\top$ until the end of the segment, thus we add to the reachability tree the state $s_1 = (\ell_\top, x_0 \in [0, 4])$. Next, from s_1, we execute the discrete transition that leads to ℓ_p. Changing the location, resetting the clock x_s and constraining the zone to the interval where p holds, produces the state $(\ell_p, x_0 \in [1, 3] \wedge x_s = 0 \wedge x_0 - x_s \in [1, 3])$. Then, applying time elapse until the end of p produces the state $s_2 = (\ell_p, x_0 \in [1, 3] \wedge x_s = [0, 2] \wedge x_0 - x_s \in [1, 3])$ that we

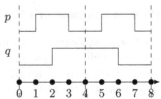

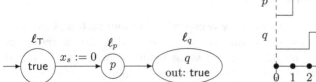

Fig. 5. Matching automaton for the expression $p \cdot q$.

Fig. 6. Example of a signal.

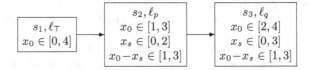

Fig. 7. Reachable symbolic states after reading the first fragment of the signal.

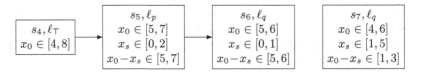

Fig. 8. Reachable symbolic states after reading the second fragment of the signal. States corresponding to the previous fragment were discarded.

add to the reachability tree. Finally, we execute from s_2 the discrete transition to ℓ_q. After changing the location and restricting to the interval where q holds, we get the state $(\ell_q, x_0 \in [2,3] \wedge x_s \in [0,2] \wedge x_0 - x_s \in [1,3])$. After applying time elapse until the end of q (the end of the fragment in this case), we get the state $s_3 = (\ell_q, x_0 \in [2,4] \wedge x_s \in [0,3] \wedge x_0 - x_s \in [1,3])$ that we add to the tree. We would like to point out again that time transitions from different states are not synchronized. When s_2 was created, we allowed x_0 to advance until time 3. When executing the transition to ℓ_q, we discover that it could happen "in the past", between time 2 and 3; but also that after taking the transition, we can stay in ℓ_q until time 4. At this point, there are no more states to explore, and we report the matches in the observed signal prefix. In this example, the matches are described by the state s_3 intersected with its output label true. Possible values of $x_0 - x_s$ in s_3 are the possible start times of the match, and possible values of x_0 are the end times. For us, the match should start between time 1 and 3, while p holds, and end between time 2 and 4, while q holds (Figs. 7 and 8).

We now proceed to read w_2. We extract from the reachability tree all states that correspond to reading the first segment until the end, that is, states with valuations that lie on the hyperplane $x_0 = 4$. From state s_0, we extract $(\ell_T, x_0 = 4)$. Applying time transition to it results in the state $s_4 = (\ell_T, x_0 \in [4,8])$ that we add to the tree. From state s_3, we extract $(\ell_q, x_0 = 4 \wedge x_s \in [1,3] \wedge x_0 - x_s \in [1,3])$. Applying time transition to it results in the state $s_7 = (\ell_q, x_0 \in [4,6] \wedge x_s \in [1,5] \wedge x_0 - x_s \in [1,3])$ that we add to the tree. At this point, we can discard the previous segment of the signal and the reachability tree corresponding to it; they will no longer be used. Then, we restart the exploration from s_4 and s_7, which discovers two more states: s_5 and s_6. Both s_6 and s_7 correspond to ℓ_q and describe newly discovered matches. State s_6 corresponds to the matches that start and end between time 5 and 6, when q still holds and p holds again. State s_7 corresponds to matches that start between time 11 and 3, that is, in the previous segment) and end before time 6 in the current segment.

4   Implementation and Experiments

We implemented a prototype of the algorithm in C++, using the zone library of the tool IF [7]. We evaluate the performance of the prototype using a number of patterns and periodic signals of different length. We summarize the experimental results in Table 1. The columns "Expression" and "Signal" give the expression and the shape of the signal. Different expressions and signal shapes are discussed in more detail below. To present time-related parameters in a uniform way, we measure them in integer time units. The column "Seg" gives the length of the signal segment (in time units) that is presented at once to the reachability algorithm. We run every experiment with 2–3 segment lengths: presenting the whole signal at once ("offline") and presenting a fixed number of time units, based on the period of the signal. The last three columns show the results for different length of the signal: 10K, 100K, and 1 million time units. A cell of the table shows the run time of the matching algorithm in seconds and the number of explored symbolic states. The three parameters: signal length, signal shape, and segment length influence the performance of the algorithm in a connected way. The longer are the stable periods of the signal, the fewer switching points it has within a given length; but at the same time, if the segment length is small, longer stable periods become split into more segments. Time figures were obtained on a PC with a Core i7-3630QM and 8 GB RAM.

Signals. We use three different periodic signal shapes. The signal $wave_2$ has two components, p_0 and p_1, which are square waves with the period of 2 time units, p_1 being the negation of p_0. The signal $wave_{200}$ has four components, p_0 to p_3, which are square waves with the period of 200 time units, shifted in time by different amount. The signal $wave_{30/32}$ has two components, p_0 and p_1. The component p_0 has the period of 30 time units, in every period it has hi value for 5 time units. The component p_1 has the period of 32 time units, in every period it has hi value for 4 time units.

Simple Expressions. Expressions φ_1 to φ_4 are examples of basic regular operators: concatenation, disjunction, and duration constraint.

Intersection Example. Intersection allows to assert that multiple properties should hold during the same interval. To evaluate it, we use the expression

$$\varphi_5 = (\langle p \rangle_{[4,5]} \cdot \neg p) \cap (\neg q \cdot \langle q \rangle_{[4,5]}) \cap (\text{true} \cdot \langle p \wedge q \rangle_{[1,2]} \cdot \text{true})$$

It denotes a pattern where p holds at the beginning and between 4 to 5 time units, q holds at the end between 4 to 5 time units, and in between p and q hold together for at least 1 to 2 time units. This could be an example of one resource (such as power source) replacing another in a redundant architecture. We cannot express this property without intersection; it would require duration constraints with unbalanced parentheses [4].

Quantification Example. Existential quantification allows to express synchronization with a signal which is not part of the input, but is itself described by a regular expression. To evaluate quantification, we use the expression

$$\varphi_6 = \exists r. (((\langle \neg r \rangle_{[98,98]} \cdot \langle r \rangle_{[1,3]})^+$$
$$\cap (\neg p \cdot (\neg p \wedge \neg r) \cdot (p \wedge r) \cdot p \cdot (p \wedge \neg r) \cdot (\neg p \wedge r))^+)$$

It denotes a signal p that changes its value on the rising edge of a virtual clock, denoted by r, that occurs every 100 ± 1 time units (note how we use $(\neg p \wedge \neg r) \cdot (p \wedge r)$ to synchronize the rising edges of p and r). In the experiments, we use this property for prefix matching. We fix the start of the match to the start of the signal and use our algorithm to find matching prefixes.

Discussion. The run time of the matching algorithm is determined by the number of symbolic states that it explores, which depends on the structure of the expression, the input signal, and the way the signal is split into segments when presented to the matching algorithm. In our experiments, we focused on the case when the length of a segment given to the algorithm is greater than or equal to the length of a stable state of the signal. For example, for the signal $wave_{200}$, we normally observe two cases: when the algorithm receives the whole signal immediately, and when the signal is split into segments 100 time units in length, which is the half-period of the signal. In this setup, for a variety of regular expressions we observe two properties of the algorithm: (1) the number of explored configurations (and thus the runtime) is linear in the length of the signal; and (2) going from offline to online matching (with the length of a segment greater or equal to the length of a stable state) increases the number of explored configurations only by a small constant factor. That said, one can always come up with adversarial examples, where the match set (and thus the number of explored configurations) requires at least quadratic number of zones in the length of the signal. One way to construct adversarial examples is to synchronize the start and end of a match with some event, e.g., a raising or a falling edge. In our experiments, this happens in the property φ_6. For the signal $wave_{200}$, every sequence of one or more full signal periods is a match, and the set of all matches

Table 1. Evaluation results.

Expression	Signal	Seg	Signal length		
			10K	100K	1M
$\varphi_1 = p_0 \cdot p_1$	$wave_2$	offline	0.1s, 10K	0.96s, 100K	16s, 1M
		1	0.14s, 30K	1.4s, 300K	21s, 3M
	$wave_{200}$	signal	<0.01s, 100	0.02s, 1K	0.1s, 10K
		100	<0.01s, 350	0.03s, 3.5K	0.18, 35K
		25	0.02s, 2.4K	0.1s, 24K	0.84s, 240K
$\varphi_2 = \langle p_0 \rangle_{[0,20]} \cdot \langle p_1 \rangle_{[0,20]}$ $\cdot \langle p_2 \rangle_{[0,20]}$	$wave_{200}$	offline	<0.01s, 150	0.03s, 1.5K	0.22s, 15K
		100	<0.01s, 450	0.06s, 4.5K	0.4s, 45K
$\varphi_3 = (p_0 \cup p_1) \cdot (p_2 \cup p_3)$	$wave_{200}$	offline	<0.01s, 300	0.03s, 3K	0.24s, 30K
		100	0.01s, 900	0.05s, 9K	0.4s, 90K
$\varphi_4 = \langle p_1 \cdot (p_0 \cdot p_2)^+ \rangle_{[0,1000]}$	$wave_{200}$	offline	<0.01s, 250	0.03s, 2.5K	0.26s, 25K
		100	<0.01s, 500	0.04s, 5K	0.3s, 50K
φ_5 (see text)	$wave_{30/32}$	offline	0.02s, 800	0.1s, 8K	1s, 80K
		30	0.03s, 1.4K	0.14s, 14K	1.4s, 140K
φ_6 (prefix match, see text)	$wave_{200}$	offline	0.01s, 400	0.04, 4K	0.24s, 40K
		100	0.03s, 6.3K	2.7s, 500K	TO

is described by a quadratic number of zones. For this reason, we only do prefix matching in that experiment. Another way to construct adversarial examples is to perform "oversampling" and split every stable state of the input signal into a large number of segments. As a result, every zone in the match set may be split in a quadratic number of smaller zones, since the matches that start and/or end in different segments cannot be part of the same zone in the current algorithm. We can observe this effect for the property φ_1 and the signal $wave_{200}$. Reducing the segment length from 100 to 25 time units causes oversampling and increases the number of explored configurations by a factor of $8 = 4^2/2$. In future work, we wish to address this issue, as it is reminiscent of the issue of interleaving in reachability of timed automata, which was addressed in [22].

Removing Inactive Clocks. The cost of zone operations is in the worst case cubic in the number of clocks (normalization is cubic, but is not required for some operations), thus it is important to remove clocks as soon as they are no longer needed. For automata produced from TREs, this is not difficult to do, since every clock is tied to a duration constraint and thus has a clearly defined set of locations where it is active (x_0 and x_s are always active). When taking a transition, we erase (existentially quantify) clocks that are not active in the target location.

Introducing Clock Invariants. The simple encoding of duration constraints that we describe may lead, during state exploration, to the creation of *doomed* symbolic states that may never lead to an accepting state. When time transition is applied to a state, we may increase a clock past a bound that will be much later checked by a guard of some transition. In the meantime, we may start exploring the successors of the doomed state, which are also doomed, then their successors, etc. To reduce the amount of such redundant work, in our implementation, we let locations have clock invariants. They are produced from the upper bounds of duration constraints and we use them to constrain the result of time transitions.

5   Conclusion

We presented a novel algorithm for timed pattern matching of Boolean signals. We are particularly interested in patterns described by timed regular expressions, but our result applies to arbitrary timed automata. The algorithm can be applied online, without restriction on how the input signal is split into incrementally presented segments. The prototype implementation shows promising results, but also points out some pessimistic scenarios. In future work, we plan to improve the performance of matching with the major goal being to improve the handling of small signal segments by adapting partial order reduction techniques; we also expect that some constant factor can be gained by improving the quality of the code. In another direction, we wish to perform a more in-depth case study to be able to adapt the algorithm to the specifics of real applications.

References

1. Aho, A.V., Hopcroft, J.E.: The Design and Analysis of Computer Algorithms. Pearson Education India, Noida (1974)
2. Aho, A.V., Kernighan, B.W., Weinberger, P.J.: The AWK Programming Language. Addison-Wesley Longman Publishing Co., Inc., Boston (1987)
3. Alur, R., Dill, D.L.: A theory of timed automata. Theor. Comput. Sci. **126**(2), 183–235 (1994)
4. Asarin, E., Caspi, P., Maler, O.: A Kleene theorem for timed automata. In: Logic in Computer Science, pp. 160–171. IEEE (1997)
5. Asarin, E., Caspi, P., Maler, O.: Timed regular expressions. J. ACM **49**(2), 172–206 (2002)
6. Behrmann, G., et al.: Uppaal 4.0. In: Third International Conference on Quantitative Evaluation of Systems, QEST 2006, pp. 125–126. IEEE (2006)
7. Bozga, M., Fernandez, J.-C., Ghirvu, L., Graf, S., Krimm, J.-P., Mounier, L.: If: an intermediate representation and validation environment for timed asynchronous systems. In: Wing, J.M., Woodcock, J., Davies, J. (eds.) FM 1999. LNCS, vol. 1708, pp. 307–327. Springer, Heidelberg (1999). https://doi.org/10.1007/3-540-48119-2_19
8. Brzozowski, J.A.: Derivatives of regular expressions. J. ACM (JACM) **11**(4), 481–494 (1964)
9. Clarke, E.M., Grumberg, O., Peled, D.A.: Model Checking (1999)
10. Daws, C., Olivero, A., Tripakis, S., Yovine, S.: The tool KRONOS. In: Alur, R., Henzinger, T.A., Sontag, E.D. (eds.) HS 1995. LNCS, vol. 1066, pp. 208–219. Springer, Heidelberg (1996). https://doi.org/10.1007/BFb0020947

11. Finkel, O.: Undecidable problems about timed automata. In: Asarin, E., Bouyer, P. (eds.) FORMATS 2006. LNCS, vol. 4202, pp. 187–199. Springer, Heidelberg (2006). https://doi.org/10.1007/11867340_14

12. Gelade, W.: Succinctness of regular expressions with interleaving, intersection and counting. In: Ochmański, E., Tyszkiewicz, J. (eds.) MFCS 2008. LNCS, vol. 5162, pp. 363–374. Springer, Heidelberg (2008). https://doi.org/10.1007/978-3-540-85238-4_29

13. Havlicek, J., Little, S.: Realtime regular expressions for analog and mixed-signal assertions. In: Proceedings of the International Conference on Formal Methods in Computer-Aided Design, pp. 155–162. FMCAD Inc. (2011)

14. Herrmann, P.: Renaming is necessary in timed regular expressions. In: Rangan, C.P., Raman, V., Ramanujam, R. (eds.) FSTTCS 1999. LNCS, vol. 1738, pp. 47–59. Springer, Heidelberg (1999). https://doi.org/10.1007/3-540-46691-6_4

15. Koopman, P., Wagner, M.: Challenges in autonomous vehicle testing and validation. SAE Int. J. Transp. Saf. 4(1), 15–24 (2016)

16. Krichen, M., Tripakis, S.: Conformance testing for real-time systems. Form. Method. Syst. Des. 34(3), 238–304 (2009)

17. Larsen, K.G., Pettersson, P., Yi, W.: Uppaal in a nutshell. Int. J. Softw. Tools Technol. Transf. (STTT) 1(1), 134–152 (1997)

18. Larsen, K.G., Mikucionis, M., Nielsen, B.: Online testing of real-time systems using UPPAAL. In: Grabowski, J., Nielsen, B. (eds.) FATES 2004. LNCS, vol. 3395, pp. 79–94. Springer, Heidelberg (2005). https://doi.org/10.1007/978-3-540-31848-4_6

19. McNaughton, R., Yamada, H.: Regular expressions and state graphs for automata. IRE Trans. Electron. Comput. 1, 39–47 (1960)

20. Pike, R.: The text editor Sam. Softw.: Pract. Exp. 17(11), 813–845 (1987)

21. Rabin, M.O., Scott, D.: Finite automata and their decision problems. IBM J. Res. Dev. 3(2), 114–125 (1959)

22. Ben Salah, R., Bozga, M., Maler, O.: On interleaving in timed automata. In: Baier, C., Hermanns, H. (eds.) CONCUR 2006. LNCS, vol. 4137, pp. 465–476. Springer, Heidelberg (2006). https://doi.org/10.1007/11817949_31

23. Thompson, K.: Programming techniques: regular expression search algorithm. Commun. ACM 11(6), 419–422 (1968)

24. Tripakis, S.: Fault diagnosis for timed automata. In: Damm, W., Olderog, E.-R. (eds.) FTRTFT 2002. LNCS, vol. 2469, pp. 205–221. Springer, Heidelberg (2002). https://doi.org/10.1007/3-540-45739-9_14

25. Ulus, D.: MONTRE: a tool for monitoring timed regular expressions. In: Majumdar, R., Kunčak, V. (eds.) CAV 2017. LNCS, vol. 10426, pp. 329–335. Springer, Cham (2017). https://doi.org/10.1007/978-3-319-63387-9_16

26. Ulus, D.: Pattern Matching with Time: Theory and Applications. Ph.D. thesis, University of Grenobles-Alpes (UGA) (2018)

27. Ulus, D., Ferrère, T., Asarin, E., Maler, O.: Timed pattern matching. In: Legay, A., Bozga, M. (eds.) FORMATS 2014. LNCS, vol. 8711, pp. 222–236. Springer, Cham (2014). https://doi.org/10.1007/978-3-319-10512-3_16

28. Ulus, D., Ferrère, T., Asarin, E., Maler, O.: Online timed pattern matching using derivatives. In: Chechik, M., Raskin, J.-F. (eds.) TACAS 2016. LNCS, vol. 9636, pp. 736–751. Springer, Heidelberg (2016). https://doi.org/10.1007/978-3-662-49674-9_47

29. Waga, M., Akazaki, T., Hasuo, I.: A Boyer-Moore type algorithm for timed pattern matching. In: Fränzle, M., Markey, N. (eds.) FORMATS 2016. LNCS, vol. 9884, pp. 121–139. Springer, Cham (2016). https://doi.org/10.1007/978-3-319-44878-7_8

30. Waga, M., Hasuo, I., Suenaga, K.: Efficient online timed pattern matching by automata-based skipping. In: Abate, A., Geeraerts, G. (eds.) FORMATS 2017. LNCS, vol. 10419, pp. 224–243. Springer, Cham (2017). https://doi.org/10.1007/978-3-319-65765-3_13
31. Yovine, S.: Model checking timed automata. In: Rozenberg, G., Vaandrager, F.W. (eds.) EEF School 1996. LNCS, vol. 1494, pp. 114–152. Springer, Heidelberg (1998). https://doi.org/10.1007/3-540-65193-4_20

Continuous Dynamical Systems

Duality-Based Nested Controller Synthesis from STL Specifications for Stochastic Linear Systems

Susmit Jha[1], Sunny Raj[2(✉)], Sumit Kumar Jha[2], and Natarajan Shankar[1]

[1] Computer Science Laboratory, SRI International, Menlo Park, USA
{susmit.jha,shankar}@sri.com
[2] Computer Science Department, University of Central Florida, Orlando, USA
{sraj,jha}@eecs.ucf.edu

Abstract. We propose an automatic synthesis technique to generate provably correct controllers of stochastic linear dynamical systems for Signal Temporal Logic (STL) specifications. While formal synthesis problems can be directly formulated as exists-forall constraints, the quantifier alternation restricts the scalability of such an approach. We use the duality between a system and its proof of correctness to partially alleviate this challenge. We decompose the controller synthesis into two subproblems, each addressing orthogonal concerns - stabilization with respect to the noise, and meeting the STL specification. The overall controller is a nested controller comprising of the feedback controller for noise cancellation and an open loop controller for STL satisfaction. The correct-by-construction compositional synthesis of this nested controller relies on using the guarantees of the feedback controller instead of the controller itself. We use a linear feedback controller as the stabilizing controller for linear systems with bounded additive noise and over-approximate its ellipsoid stability guarantee with a polytope. We then use this over-approximation to formulate a mixed-integer linear programming (MILP) problem to synthesize an open-loop controller that satisfies STL specifications.

1 Introduction

Cyber-physical systems can be conceptually decomposed into a physical plant and a controller. The complex interaction between the plant and the controller often necessitates an hierarchical control. While high-level decisions are typically made by a supervisory controller, traditional control laws such as PID control are typically used at low levels. These controllers at different levels are often designed in isolation, and then plugged into a hierarchical framework to build an ad hoc implementation that can be evaluated through simulations and in-the-field experiments. For safety-critical systems, design of such hierarchical controller often relies on the worst-case characterization of independently designed controllers in each layer, which leads to overly conservative design with

© Springer Nature Switzerland AG 2018
D. N. Jansen and P. Prabhakar (Eds.): FORMATS 2018, LNCS 11022, pp. 235–251, 2018.
https://doi.org/10.1007/978-3-030-00151-3_14

low performance. This problem is becoming even more acute with the growing complexity of cyber-physical systems. Hence, there is a pressing need for automatic synthesis techniques that can co-design controllers at different layers in a synergistic way for an optimal yet safe hierarchical control of cyber-physical systems.

Safety-critical applications of cyber-physical systems necessitate providing assurance and safety certification of the controllers. Approaches based on barrier certificates [5,33] and Lyapunov functions [15] are applicable to proving stability, asymptotic convergence, and safety of continuous control laws but their extensions to hierarchical controls and stochastic dynamics is difficult. Automatic synthesis of controllers from high-level specifications [10,13,27,30] either in the open-loop setting or model-predictive and reactive setting have also been studied [12,35]. These methods ensure that the synthesized controllers are correct by construction. While these techniques based on mixed integer linear programming (MILP) have been shown to scale well, they are limited to linear deterministic dynamics. More recently, extensions to uncertainty in dynamics and observations have also been proposed [19] using a chance-constraint programming formulation. But these methods are restricted to Gaussian noise and use a less scalable semi-definite programming formulation. Further, these offline synthesis methods try to be robust to worst-case noise which makes them very conservative. Thus, safe controller design for high-level temporal properties in presence of noisy dynamics remains a challenge.

In this paper, we study the problem of synthesizing safe control for linear, discrete-time plant with bounded disturbance against high-level temporal logic specifications expressed in signal temporal logic (STL). A natural paradigm for designing controllers for reach-avoid properties in presence of noise comprises of designing an open-loop controller ignoring noise, followed by a tracking controller to drive the trajectory towards the reference trajectory in presence of noise. We formulate a bottom-up approach to controller synthesis which does not ignore the interdependencies between the two controllers. We first synthesize a stabilizing controller to reject noisy disturbances and then use its stability certificate to formulate a less conservative robust open-loop controller synthesis problem for STL specifications using MILP. The novel contributions in this paper are as follows:

- We extend the MILP based controller synthesis approach for signal temporal logic (STL) specifications to dynamics with bounded noise.
- We present a new approach for nesting controllers that allows composing correctness guarantee of the low-level noise-canceling controller during synthesis, enabling a compositional proof of correctness of the overall nested controller.
- We experimentally validated the effectiveness of the controller synthesis approach on a set of case-studies.

We discuss related work and background in Sects. 2 and 3. We formulate the controller synthesis problem in Sect. 4. We present the proposed synthesis approach in Sect. 5 and experimental evaluation in Sect. 6.

2   Related Work

We briefly discuss related work on formal synthesis of controllers from high-level specifications, and compare and contrast with our proposed approach.

Synthesis of safe control using reachability analysis has been extensively studied in literature where the specification is restricted to reach-avoid properties requiring that a particular target state be reached while avoiding unsafe states [28,29,39]. More recently, safe control optimization techniques have been developed which allow exploration of control parameter space and online learning of optimal controller while remaining safe [2,4]. These techniques rely on learning probabilistic model of uncertainty either offline or online at runtime and computation of reachable sets. Our approach is orthogonal to techniques for estimating or modeling uncertainty, and we focus on the synthesis of safe control for an additive noise model. The control of stochastic systems has also been extensively investigated beginning with the work of Pontryagin [31] and Bellman [3], and extending to more recent literature [8,18,23,33,34]. The goal of these techniques is to determine a control policy that maximizes the probability of remaining within a safe set during a finite time horizon [1]. In contrast, we consider a bounded noise model and require deterministic safety with respect to high-level temporal specifications.

Temporal logic such as linear temporal logic have been used for high-level specification of goals. Controller design with respect to high-level specifications for linear dynamics model has been studied in [12,21,40,41], and extended to polynomial systems [9] and other nonlinear systems using piecewise linear approximation [6,16,42]. The synthesis techniques can be broadly classified into automata theoretic and constraint-based approaches. Automata theoretic techniques for controller synthesis from temporal specifications such as LTL are based on discrete, finite-state and symbolic abstraction of the system. Then, the solution of a two player game on the abstracted game graph is obtained by composing the discrete abstraction with a discrete controller. While these techniques can be used with nonlinear dynamics in principle, the discrete abstraction severely limits their scalability for high dimensional models. Our approach is closer to constraint-solving based methods. While extension of satisfiability solving to deal with continuous dynamics has been studied in literature [11,22], we adopt the use of mixed-integer linear programming for solving the open loop synthesis problem which is sufficient for modeling linear dynamics. We use signal temporal logic (STL) for specifying the requirements of the controller. STL has been proposed as an extension of linear temporal logic for specifying behavior of continuous and hybrid systems [10]. It combines dense time modalities with numerical predicates over continuous state variables. Automatic synthesis of controllers from STL properties using mixed integer linear programming has proved to be an efficient and scalable approach [35], and more recently, it has been recently extended to chance-constraints [17,19,36]. While these previous extensions require computationally expensive second order cone programming, we present an MILP formulation of STL controller synthesis for linear dynamical system with additive but bounded noise. Further, we demonstrate the nested controller synthesis approach that uses an online noise canceling controller in conjunction with an offline open loop controller. This nested approach leads to less conservative formulation than a direct offline robust formulation that considers worst-case noise.

Invariant based methods that rely on generating barrier certificates or Lyapunov invariants [5,15] have been also well-studied in literature. Invariant based control can be combined with other high-performance controllers to provide guarantees in a Simplex architecture [38]. More recently, it has been extended to synthesize switching control [24,32] for a family of dynamical systems by formulating a finite game graph that consists of the switching surfaces as the existential nodes and the choices of the dynamics as the universal nodes. Instead of switching between different modes or two different controllers, we use the invariant guarantee provided by the noise-canceling lower-level controller to formulate a nested safe but less conservative open-loop synthesis problem. Our work is closest to nested controller synthesis methods [14,37]. Our approach considers general STL properties and is not limited to reach avoid properties. Further, we use the guarantee provided by the low-level controller as a dual to synthesize the nested open loop STL controller without explicitly composing the two controllers.

3 Preliminarie

We consider a discrete-time linear system Σ of the form

$$\mathbf{x}_{t+1} = A\mathbf{x}_t + B\mathbf{u}_t + \omega_t \tag{1}$$

where $A \in \mathbb{R}^{n \times n}$ is the dynamics matrix, $\mathbf{x}_t \in X \subseteq \mathbb{R}^n$ is the system state, $B \in \mathbb{R}^{n \times m}$ is the control input matrix, $\mathbf{u}_t \in U \subseteq \mathbb{R}^m$ is the controller input, and $\omega_t \in D \subseteq \mathbb{R}^n$ is the bounded additive noise disturbance. $\mathbb{R}$ denotes the set of reals, X, U are closed polytopes that represents the set of all possible states and feasible control inputs. D represents bounded noise, that is,

$$\forall \omega \in D \quad \omega^T M^T M \omega \leq \Omega^2 \tag{2}$$

If M is identity, the above is the familiar 2-norm bound. We choose a generic M-norm since noise in different dimensions may have asymmetric significance. The set of initial states of the system is denoted by $\mathbf{X}_0$. We denote a sequence of control inputs $\mathbf{u}_0, \mathbf{u}_1, \ldots, \mathbf{u}_{N-1}$ of length N by $\overline{\mathbf{u}}_N$, and a sequence of noise disturbances $\omega_0, \omega_1, \ldots, \omega_{N-1}$ of length N by $\overline{\omega}_N$. We say $\overline{\omega}_N \in D^N$ if $\omega_i \in D$ for $i \in [0, N-1]$, and $\overline{\mathbf{u}}_N \in U^N$ if $\mathbf{u}_i \in U$ for $i \in [0, N-1]$. Starting from an initial state $\mathbf{x}_0 \in \mathbf{X}_0$ and applying the control inputs $\overline{\mathbf{u}}_N$ and noise disturbances $\overline{\omega}_N$, the horizon-N trajectory of the system $\mathbf{x}_0\mathbf{u}_0, \mathbf{x}_1\mathbf{u}_1, \ldots, \mathbf{x}_N\mathbf{u}_N$ is denoted by $\tau(\mathbf{x}_0, \overline{\mathbf{u}}_N, \overline{\omega}_N)$.

For specifying the requirements on the controlled dynamical system, we use signal temporal logic (STL). Let $\mathbb{B}$ denotes the set of Boolean values $\top, \bot$ denoting true and false respectively. An STL formula can be constructed recursively using the following grammar:

$$\phi := \pi^\mu \mid \neg\phi \mid \phi_1 \wedge \phi_2 \mid G_{[a,b]}\phi \mid F_{[a,b]}\phi \mid \phi_1 U_{[a,b]}\phi_2$$

where π^{μ} is an atomic predicate $X \times U \rightarrow \mathbb{B}$ whose truth value is determined by the sign of a signal $\mu : X \times U \rightarrow \mathbb{R}$. $\tau(\mathbf{x}_0, \overline{\mathbf{u}}_N, \overline{\omega}_N) \models \phi$ denotes that the trajectory $\tau(\mathbf{x}_0, \overline{\mathbf{u}}_N, \overline{\omega}_N)$ satisfies an STL formula ϕ. When the arguments are obvious from context, we also denote it by $\tau \models \phi$ and $\tau[i]$ denotes the i-th element $\mathbf{x}_i \; \mathbf{u}_i$ in the sequence. Informally, $\tau \models G_{[a,b]}\phi$ if ϕ holds at every time step between a and b. $\tau \models F_{[a,b]}\phi$ if ϕ holds at some time step between a and b. $\tau \models \phi_1 U_{[a,b]}\phi_2$ holds if ϕ_1 holds at every time step before ϕ_2 holds and ϕ_2 holds at some time step between a and b. Formally, the validity of a formula ϕ with respect to the run τ is defined inductively as follows:

$$
\begin{aligned}
\tau \models \phi &\iff & \tau[0] \models \phi \\
\tau[t_k] \models \pi^{\mu} &\iff & \mu(\mathbf{x}_k, \mathbf{u}_k) > 0 \\
\tau[t_k] \models \neg\phi &\iff & \tau[t_k] \not\models \phi \\
\tau[t_k] \models \phi_1 \wedge \phi_2 &\iff & \tau[t_k] \models \phi_1 \wedge \tau[t_k] \models \phi_2 \\
\tau[t_k] \models G_{[a,b]}\phi &\iff & \forall t \in [t_k + a, t_k + b] \; \tau[t] \models \phi \\
\tau[t_k] \models F_{[a,b]}\phi &\iff & \exists t \in [t_k + a, t_k + b] \; \tau[t] \models \phi \\
\tau[t_k] \models \phi_1 U_{[a,b]}\phi_2 &\iff & \exists t_1 \in [t_k + a, t_k + b] \; (\tau[t_1] \models \phi_2 \\
& & \wedge \forall t_2 \in [t_k + a, t_1]\tau[t_2] \models \phi_1)
\end{aligned}
$$

Bounded-time STL contains no unbounded temporal operators and the bound of ϕ is the maximum over the sum of all nested upper bounds on the trajectory operators. The bound of ϕ is a conservative bound on the trajectory length required to decide its satisfiability.

Typical properties such as reach-avoid can be easily encoded as an STL formula. For example, if we require a vehicle to reach a particular destination region while avoiding obstacles. The STL specification for a vehicle starting in state $\mathbf{x}_0$ and reaching $\mathcal{R}^{dest}$ within T time-steps while avoiding obstacles $\mathcal{R}^{obs_1}, \ldots, \mathcal{R}^{obs_k}$ is $F_{[0,T]}\mathcal{R}^{dest}(\mathbf{x}) \wedge G_{[0,T]}(\neg\mathcal{R}^{obs_1}(\mathbf{x}) \wedge \ldots \neg \wedge \mathcal{R}^{obs_k}(\mathbf{x}))$. Any region of interest $\mathcal{R}$ (destination or an obstacle) can be approximated using a union of polytopes, represented by a disjunction of conjunction of linear constraints. For soundness, the choice of under or over approximation depends on the region being approximated. For example, one would under-approximate the destination region while over-approximating the obstacles to ensure that a feasible trajectory with respect to this approximation can safely reach within the destination region while avoiding the obstacles. So, we restrict the atomic predicates in the signal temporal logic formulas to be linear inequalities, that is, the signals μ are restricted to be linear combinations of state variables and control inputs.

We use mixed integer linear programming (MILP) encoding of an STL formula [35]. A variable z_t^{ϕ} is introduced for an STL formula ϕ with horizon N, and MILP constraints are formulated on this variable such that $z_t^{\phi} = 1$ if and only if ϕ holds at time t. Let M be sufficiently large and ϵ be sufficiently small, the MILP constraints corresponding to z_t^{ϕ} can be generated as follows:

$$not(z, z') \qquad \equiv z = 1 - z'$$

$$and(z, [z_1, \ldots, z_n]) \qquad \equiv \bigwedge_{i=1}^{n}(z \le z_i) \wedge z \ge \sum_{i=1}^{n} z_i - n + 1$$

$$or(z, [z_1, \ldots, z_n]) \qquad \equiv \bigwedge_{i=1}^{n}(z \ge z_i) \wedge z \le \sum_{i=1}^{n} z_i$$

$$\mathbf{encode}(\mu(\mathbf{x}, \mathbf{u}) > 0, t) \quad \equiv \mu(\mathbf{x}_t, \mathbf{u}_t) \le M z_t^{\mu} - \epsilon \wedge -\mu(\mathbf{x}_t, \mathbf{u}_t) \le M(1 - z_t^{\mu}) - \epsilon$$

$$\mathbf{encode}(\neg\phi, t) \qquad \equiv not(z_t^{\neg\phi}, z_t^{\phi}) \wedge \mathbf{encode}(\phi, t)$$

$$\mathbf{encode}(\phi_1 \wedge \phi_2, t) \qquad \equiv and(z_t^{\phi_1 \wedge \phi_2}, [z_t^{\phi_1}, z_t^{\phi_2}]) \wedge \mathbf{encode}(\phi_1, t) \wedge \mathbf{encode}(\phi_2, t)$$

$$\mathbf{encode}(\phi_1 \vee \phi_2, t) \qquad \equiv or(z_t^{\phi_1 \vee \phi_2}, [z_t^{\phi_1}, z_t^{\phi_2}]) \wedge \mathbf{encode}(\phi_1, t) \wedge \mathbf{encode}(\phi_2, t)$$

$$\mathbf{encode}(G_{[a,b]}\phi, t) \qquad \equiv and(z_t^{G_{[a,b]}\phi}, [z_{t+a}^{\phi} \cdots z_{t+b}^{\phi}]) \wedge \bigwedge_{t'=a}^{b} \mathbf{encode}(\phi, t + t')$$

$$\mathbf{encode}(F_{[a,b]}\phi, t) \qquad \equiv or(z_t^{F_{[a,b]}\phi}, [z_{t+a}^{\phi} \cdots z_{t+b}^{\phi}]) \wedge \bigwedge_{t'=a}^{b} \mathbf{encode}(\phi, t + t')$$

$$\mathbf{encode}(\phi_1 U_{[a,b]}\phi_2, t) \quad \equiv \mathbf{encode}(\; G_{[0,a]}\phi_1 \wedge F_{[a,b]}\phi_2 \wedge F_{[a,a]}(\phi_1 U \phi_2), t \;)$$

$$\mathbf{encode}(\phi_1 U \phi_2, t) \qquad \equiv or(z_t^{\phi_2}, and(z_t^{\phi_1}, z_{t+1}^{\phi_1 U \phi_2})) \wedge \mathbf{encode}(\phi_1, t) \wedge \mathbf{encode}(\phi_2, t)$$
$$\wedge \; if(t < N) \; then \; \mathbf{encode}(\phi_1 U \phi_2, t + 1) \; else \; z_N^{\phi_1 U \phi_2} = z_N^{\phi_2}$$

We also briefly review the linear state feedback control used for stabilizing a system. Given a system $\mathbf{x}_{t+1} = A\mathbf{x}_t + B\mathbf{u}_t$, let the feedback controller be given by $\mathbf{u}_t = -K\mathbf{x}_t$. The dynamics of the controlled system is given by

$$\mathbf{x}_{t+1} = (A - BK)\mathbf{x}_t$$

This system is stable if and only if the spectral radius of $(A - BK)$ is less than 1, that is, $(A - BK)$ is contracting. The linear stabilizing feedback controller synthesis problem is to solve the following problem:

$$\exists K \; \exists P \succeq 0 \; (A - BK)^T P(A - BK) \prec P$$

Unfortunately, this is not a semi-definite program (SDP) since the matrix inequality is not linear in the decision variables P and K.

4   Problem Definition

In this section, we formulate the problem of synthesizing safe control for a stochastic linear dynamical system so that the system satisfies the given STL specification.

Controller Synthesis Problem: Given a system Σ of the form: $\mathbf{x}_{t+1} = A\mathbf{x}_t + B\mathbf{u}_t + \omega_t$ with initial state $\mathbf{x}_0$, a high-level signal temporal logic (STL) specification ϕ with horizon N, the controller synthesis problem is as follows:

$$\exists \mathbf{u}_0 \forall \omega_0 \forall \mathbf{x}_1 \exists \mathbf{u}_1 \forall \omega_1 \forall \mathbf{x}_2 \ldots \exists \mathbf{u}_{N-1} \forall \omega_{N-1} \forall \mathbf{x}_N \quad \tau(\mathbf{x}_0, \overline{\mathbf{u}}_N, \overline{\omega}_N) \models \phi$$

where $\mathbf{x}_t \in X, \mathbf{u}_t \in U, \omega_t \in D = \{\omega \mid \omega^T M^T M \omega \leq \Omega^2\}$. The control inputs are generated by a controller $\mathtt{cntlr}(\mathbf{x}_0, \phi, \mathbf{x}_t, X, U, D)$ which maps the initial state, STL specification, and current state to the control input assuming that the disturbance $\omega_t \in D$ and ensuring that the states $x_t \in X$ and control inputs $u_t \in U$. We use this controller function for Skolemization and elimination of the existential quantifiers on the control inputs. The controller synthesis problem can then be written as an exists-forall problem:

$$\exists \mathtt{cntlr} \; \forall \omega_0 \forall \mathbf{x}_1 \forall \omega_1 \forall \mathbf{x}_2 \ldots \forall \omega_{N-1} \forall \mathbf{x}_N \;\; \tau(x_0, \overline{\mathbf{u}}_N, \overline{\omega}_N) \models \phi \text{ where } \mathbf{x}_t \in X, \mathbf{u}_t \in U,$$

$$\mathbf{u}_t = \mathtt{cntlr}(\mathbf{x}_0, \phi, \mathbf{x}_t, X, U, D), \; \mathbf{x}_{t+1} = A\mathbf{x}_t + B\mathbf{u}_t + \omega_t, \; \omega_t^T M^T M \omega_t \leq \Omega^2 \quad (3)$$

Instead of requiring the controller to have to store the entire history of states and the noise, we have restricted the controller $\mathtt{cntlr}$ to generate a control input using only the current state, the initial state and the STL specification, in addition to the sets X, U and D. The goal is to synthesize such a controller which can satisfy the STL specification even in presence of noise (Fig. 1).

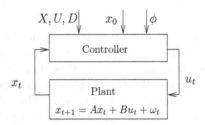

Fig. 1. Controller has access to the STL specification ϕ to be satisfied, an initial state $\mathbf{x}_0$ of the system, the bounding sets X, U and D. It continuously receives the current state $\mathbf{x}_t$ of the system. It produces control inputs $\mathbf{u}_t$ which can be computed offline (for example, in open-loop control), online (for example, in feedback control) or a combination of offline and online (for example, in nested control presented in Sect. 5). The presence of noise ω_t makes completely offline safe control synthesis very conservative as the synthesis algorithm has to consider worst-case accumulative effect of noise.

5   Controller Synthesis

We first describe over-approximation of elliptical bounds on the noise that will be used in controller synthesis. Given $\mathcal{D}_M^\Omega = \omega^T M^T M \omega \leq \Omega^2$ which restricts the noise in an ellipse, we can over approximate this ellipse using hyperboxes that are axis-parallel or parallel to orthogonal[1] eigenvectors (sketched for two dimensions in Fig. 2). We construct an over-approximation of possible disturbances $\mathcal{OA}(M, \Omega) \supseteq \mathcal{D}_M^\Omega$ by taking the intersection of the two over-approximations.

Before presenting the nested controller synthesis approach, we discuss two straightforward solutions to the synthesis problem by direct application of standard control theoretic techniques.

---

[1] Eigenvectors are orthogonal since $M^T M$ is symmetric.

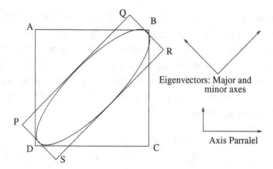

Fig. 2. Given an elliptical $\mathcal{D}_M^\Omega$ in two dimensions defined by $\omega^T M^T M \omega \leq \Omega^2$, $ABCD$ is the axis parallel hyperbox $\mathcal{P}_M^\Omega$ over-approximating the ellipse. The eigenvectors of the ellipse correspond to the major and minor axes of the ellipse. $PQRS$ is the hyperbox $\mathcal{E}_M^\Omega$ over-approximating the ellipse by bounding the eigenvectors. $\mathcal{OA}(M, \Omega) = \mathcal{P}_M^\Omega \cap \mathcal{E}_M^\Omega$ is the polytope corresponding to the intersection of these two hyperboxes represented by the conjunction of linear constraints of both hyberboxes.

Open Loop Robust Controller. The synthesis problem can be solved using a robust controller that considers the worst-case noise and synthesizes control with respect to it for the given horizon N. This method aims at jointly addressing the satisfiability of the mission specification in STL and robustness with respect to bounded noise without decomposing the problem. The following mixed-integer linear constraints formulate the finite horizon open loop robust controller synthesis problem:

$$\forall t \in [0, N] \; \mathbf{x}_{t+1} = A\mathbf{x}_t + B\mathbf{u}_t + \omega_t$$
$$\texttt{encode}(\phi, 0), \omega \in \mathcal{OA}(M, \Omega), \mathbf{x} \in X, \mathbf{u} \in U$$

where $\texttt{encode}$ is MILP encoding of the specification ϕ, $\mathcal{OA}(M, \Omega)$ is the polytope overapproximation of the disturbance set D, and X, U are conjunction of linear constraints restricting the states and control inputs to allowed polytopes. Consequently, the state at time t in the above formulation is given by $\mathbf{x}_t = A^t \mathbf{x}_0 + (A^{t-1} B \mathbf{u}_0 + A^{t-2} B \mathbf{u}_1 + \ldots + B \mathbf{u}_t) + (A^{t-1} \omega_0 + A^{t-2} \omega_1 + \ldots + \omega_t)$. This considers the worst-case noise irrespective of the actual noise experienced at runtime and consequently leads to very conservative controller design.

Tracking Controller. The second alternative is to decompose the synthesis problem by first ignoring the noise and synthesizing an open-loop controller to satisfy the STL specification. At runtime, a tracking controller can be used to ensure that the system tracks the noise-free state trajectory corresponding to the open-loop controller synthesis problem. The open loop controller is synthesized by solving the following mixed integer linear program:

$$\forall t \in [0, N] \; \mathbf{x}_{t+1} = A\mathbf{x}_t + B\mathbf{u}_t$$
$$\texttt{encode}(\phi, 0), \mathbf{x} \in X, \mathbf{u} \in U$$

The satisfiable solution to these linear constraints yield $\mathbf{x}_t$ and $\mathbf{u}_t$ for $t \in [0, N]$. Once we have these reference signals, we use the standard pole placement method to design a feedback controller that tracks this reference. In practice, solving the feasibility problem corresponding to the linear program yields *borderline* solutions which just barely satisfy the constraints. This is the consequence of search methods used to solve these problems. This makes it even more difficult to design tracking controller which prevents the trajectory from failing the STL specification in presence of noise.

Nested Controller. While a closed loop solution is needed to be not overly conservative, we also require it to have correctness guarantees similar to the open loop robust controller. We accomplish this by first designing a noise stabilizing controller and then using its robustness guarantees to synthesize the open loop control inputs that robustly satisfies the STL. In rest of this section, we describe this two step design of nested controller in detail:

Feedback Controller: Given the linear dynamical system $\mathbf{x}_{t+1} = A\mathbf{x}_t + B\mathbf{u}_t^{fb} + \omega_t$ and a linear feedback stabilization controller $\mathbf{u}_t^{fb} = -K\mathbf{x}_t$, the deviation from the reference trajectory is given by

$$\mathbf{x}_{t+1} - \mathbf{x}_{t+1}^{ref} = (A - BK)(\mathbf{x}_t - \mathbf{x}_t^{ref}) + \omega_t$$

We need to find K such that $A - BK$ is stable. While this problem of stabilizing linear systems can be solved using a variety of control theoretic methods, this choice is orthogonal to the nested control approach proposed in this paper. We use pole placement approach [20] similar to the tracking controller and ensure that the poles lie in the left half plane. This guarantees that $A - BK$ is stable and the spectral radius $\rho(A - BK) < 1$.

Lemma 1. *Given a feedback control matrix K that stabilizes $A - BK$, the transform $A - BK$ is a contracting transform and $\forall \mathbf{d} \; \mathbf{d}^T (A - BK)^T M^T M (A - BK)\mathbf{d} \leq \mathbf{d}^T M^T M \mathbf{d}$.*

While this contraction could be provided as a stability guarantee to be used by the open loop controller synthesis in the second step, we can further refine this guarantee by considering a new shape of the ellipsoid invariant that ensures maximum contraction due to the feedback controller K. This refinement of guarantee is important for obtaining less conservative yet correct open loop controller. The following semidefinite programming problem yields the optimal shape M' and the corresponding contraction rate κ.

$$\min_{M', \kappa} \kappa \quad \text{subject to } (A - BK)^T M'^T M'(A - BK) \preceq \kappa^2 \, M'^T M'$$

Lemma 2. *Given a feedback control matrix K that stabilizes $A - BK$ and the solution of the above optimization problem M', κ, $\forall \mathbf{d} \; \mathbf{d}^T (A - BK)^T M'^T M'(A - BK)\mathbf{d} \leq \kappa^2 \, \mathbf{d}^T M'^T M'\mathbf{d}$.*

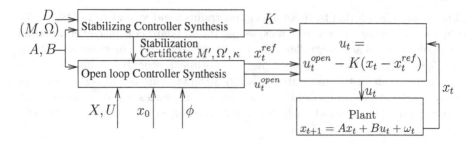

Fig. 3. Nested Controller for STL satisfaction in presence of noise. The stabilizing controller uses the noise bound D to find the required feedback controller K and obtain corresponding stability guarantee. The open loop controller synthesis only relies on the stability guarantee provided by the stabilizing feedback controller.

Noise Reshaping: We solve the following optimization problem to reshape the bounds on the noise to conform to optimum shape discovered above.

$$\min_{\Omega'} \Omega' \quad \text{subject to } \forall \mathbf{d} \ \mathbf{d}^T M^T M \mathbf{d} \leq \Omega^2 \Rightarrow \mathbf{d}^T M'^T M' \mathbf{d} \leq \Omega'^2$$

The implication between quadratic constraints allow the use of S-lemma [7] to formulate a semidefinite programming formulation. After we have obtained the bound Ω'^2, we can extend the guarantee provided by the feedback controller for t timesteps as given in Theorem 1. The proof of theorem follows from Lemma 2 and the repeated use of triangular inequality.

Theorem 1. *Given a feedback control matrix K that stabilizes $A - BK$, the optimal shape and bound of stabilization guarantee M', κ and corresponding noise bound Ω', the state $\mathbf{x}_t$ at time step t satisfies $(\mathbf{x}_t - \mathbf{x}_t^{ref})^T M'^T M' (\mathbf{x}_t - \mathbf{x}_t^{ref}) \leq S(\kappa, t)\Omega'$ where $\kappa < 1$ since K stabilizes $A - BK$ and $S(\kappa, t) = (1 + \kappa^2 + \ldots + \kappa^t)$.*

In solving for the feedback controller K, we did not have to fix the reference trajectory and as long as we use this feedback controller at runtime with $\mathbf{u}^{fb} = -K(\mathbf{x}_t - \mathbf{x}_t^{ref})$, Theorem 1 guarantees the upper bound on possible deviation from any chosen reference trajectory $\mathbf{x}^{ref}$. We will use this guarantee in synthesizing the open loop STL controller $\mathbf{u}^{open}$ and selecting the corresponding $\mathbf{x}^{ref}$. The stabilization certificate provided by the feedback control synthesis step to the open loop control synthesis step is a triplet (M', Ω', κ).

STL Controller: Figure 3 summarizes the overall synthesis approach and illustrates how the runtime control $\mathbf{u}_t$ is obtained by adding the open loop control input and the feedback control input. We recall the Eq. 3 that summarizes the exists-forall formulation of the controller synthesis problem, and decompose the controller into two controllers. The first controller is an open loop controller that lays a reference trajectory while the second controller is the feedback controller described earlier to stabilize against noise.

$$\exists \mathtt{cntlr}^{fb} \, \exists \mathtt{cntlr}^{open} \, \forall \omega_0 \forall \mathbf{x}_1 \forall \omega_1 \forall \mathbf{x}_2 \dots \forall \omega_{N-1} \forall \mathbf{x}_N \, \tau(x_0, \overline{\mathbf{u}}_N, \overline{\omega}_N) \models \phi$$

$$\mathbf{u}_t^{fb} = \mathtt{cntlr}^{fb}(\mathbf{x}_t, \mathbf{x}_t^{ref}, D), \mathbf{u}_t^{ref} = \mathtt{cntlr}^{open}(\mathbf{x}_0, \phi, X, U, \mathtt{cntlr}^{fb})$$

$$\text{where } \mathbf{x}_t \in X, \mathbf{u}_t = \mathbf{u}_t^{ref} + \mathbf{u}_t^{fb} \in U, \omega_t \in \mathcal{D}_M^\Omega, \mathbf{x}_{t+1} = A\mathbf{x}_t + B\mathbf{u}_t + \omega_t$$

Instead of generating the open loop controller taking into account the feedback controller, we use duality to only require the stabilization guarantee (M', Ω', κ) to be available to the feedback controller. This guarantee can be used to eliminate the forall quantification over noise in the above formulation, and using Theorem 1, we obtain the following:

$$\exists \mathtt{cntlr}^{open} \, \forall \mathbf{x}_1 \forall \mathbf{x}_2 \dots \forall \mathbf{x}_N \, \tau(x_0, \overline{\mathbf{u}}_N, \overline{\omega}_N) \models \phi$$

$$\mathbf{u}_t^{ref} = \mathtt{cntlr}^{open}(\mathbf{x}_0, \phi, X, U, M', \Omega', \kappa), (\mathbf{x}_t - \mathbf{x}_t^{ref}) \in \mathcal{D}_M'^{S(\kappa,t)\Omega'}$$

$$\text{where } \mathbf{x}_t \in X, \mathbf{u}_t = \mathbf{u}_t^{ref} + \mathbf{u}_t^{fb} \in U, \mathbf{x}_{t+1} = A\mathbf{x}_t + B\mathbf{u}_t + \omega_t$$

Finally, we use the polytope approximation $\mathcal{OA}(M', S(\kappa, t)\Omega')$ of the elliptical constraint $\mathcal{D}_M'^{S(\kappa,t)\Omega'}$ as described earlier to obtain the following MILP program that solves the open loop controller synthesis problem using the stability guarantee of the feedback controller:

$$\forall t \in [0, N] \, \mathbf{x}_{t+1}^{ref} = A\mathbf{x}_t + B\mathbf{u}_t^{ref}, (\mathbf{x}_t - \mathbf{x}_t^{ref}) \in \mathcal{OA}(M', S(\kappa, t)\Omega')$$

$$\mathtt{encode}(\phi, 0), \mathbf{x}_t \in X, \mathbf{u}_t = \mathbf{u}_t^{ref} - K(\mathbf{x}_t - \mathbf{x}_t^{ref}) \in U$$

The following theorem summarizes the soundness of the proposed approach to synthesize nested controller.

Theorem 2. *Given a dynamical system* $\mathbf{x}_{t+1} = A\mathbf{x}_t + B\mathbf{u}_t + \omega_t$ *with bounds on state, control and noise* (X, U, D), *if the MILP formulation of the synthesis problem is feasible and finds a controller* $\mathbf{u}_t = \mathbf{u}_t^{ref} + \mathbf{u}_t^{fb}$, *then the system starting at* $\mathbf{x}_0$ *satisfies the STL specification* ϕ *even in the presence of bounded noise.*

6 Case Studies

In this section, we present three case-studies to demonstrate the effectiveness and efficiency of the proposed approach to synthesize nested controller. All experiments were conducted on 8-core 2.8 GHz Intel® Xeon® CPU with 16 GB RAM using Matlab®. The first case-study involves controlling a vehicle moving in a map with obstacles. The second case-study is on smart grid control adapted from [26], and the third is indoor climate control case-study [25, 35].

6.1 Case Study 1: Simple Vehicle Model

In this case study, we consider a robot that is expected to navigate in a 2-dimensional grid. The dynamics in each dimension, x and y, is given by a simple double integrator model. It starts at the bottom left corner and is required to

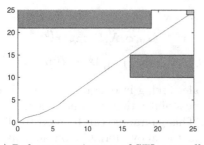
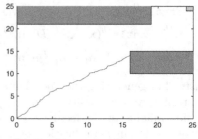

(a) Reference trajectory of STL controller   (b) Tracking controller is not safe

Fig. 4. The open loop STL controller synthesis results into barely satisfying trajectory and the tracking controller is unable to prevent the vehicle from colliding with the obstacles. The obstacles are shown in red and the final destination region in green. (Color figure online)

reach the top right corner within 10 time units. The robot must avoid the two obstacles shown as red rectangles in Fig. 4. This requirement can be captured by the corresponding signal temporal logic property $F_{[0,10]}(24 \leq x_t \leq 25 \land 24 \leq y_t \leq 25) \land G_{[0,10]}(\neg(0 \leq x_t \leq 19 \land 21 \leq y_t \leq 25) \land \neg(16 \leq x_t \leq 25 \land 10 \leq y_t \leq 15))$. The control input to the model is the acceleration. The bounded noise w is given by an uniform distribution between 0.2 and -0.2 added to the x and y dimensions of the position.

Figure 4(a) shows the trajectory of the robot obtained by an open loop STL controller in a noise-free environment. The resulting trajectory of the robot correctly satisfies the specification; however, there is little tolerance for error in the trajectory as it almost grazes past one of the obstacles. This is a consequence of how constraint solvers work in general. MILP solvers are good at finding a satisfying instance for given set of constraints but they are likely to find barely satisfying instances than robustly satisfying trajectories. In fact, the introduction of noise w into the robot dynamics causes the robot to crash into one of the obstacles, as shown in Fig. 4(b). A traditional tracking controller fails to safely follow the reference trajectory in presence of noise.

The offline robust controller synthesis does not find a feasible safe controller. So, we relax the specification to $F_{[0,5]}(13 \leq x_t \leq 15 \land 13 \leq y_t \leq 15) \land G_{[0,5]}(\neg(0 \leq x_t \leq 19 \land 21 \leq y_t \leq 25) \land \neg(16 \leq x_t \leq 25 \land 10 \leq y_t \leq 15))$ requiring the vehicle to reach the unit square region around $15, 15$ instead of $25, 25$. We also reduced the noise to 0.1. We plot the resultant trajectory and the bounds on the uncertainty region around the trajectory in Fig. 5. This illustrates how the robust controller conservatively models noise during offline synthesis and fails to find a safe controller for the original specification. The proposed nested controller synthesis approach can find a safe controller in 8 min 39 s for the original specification and the noise model, and a significant fraction of this runtime (3 min 46 s) is spent in formulating the MILP problem.

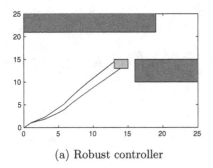
(a) Robust controller

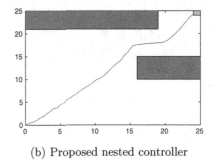
(b) Proposed nested controller

Fig. 5. Robust controller with reduced noise is able to synthesize a safe controller for relaxed specification – the uncertainty region illustrates the conservativeness of the robust controller synthesis method. It fails to solve the original problem. The nested controller is able to generate a safe controller even in the presence of noise.

6.2   Case Study 2: Smart Grid Control

Our second case study is the smart grid model described in [26]. Each grid area contains a turbine, a generator and a governor. An automatic generation control (AGC) regulates the grid frequency using a proportional integral control. The AGC also ensures that the net interchange power between neighboring areas is maintained at predefined values. The Area Control Error (ACE) measures the difference between the predefined and actual electrical generation within an area while compensating for frequency differences. The system is described using a 13×13 dimensional A matrix and a 12×4 dimensional B matrix with two sources of noise and two control inputs. Our controller synthesizes both the control inputs while responding to changes in both sources of noise. Our model also requires that the magnitude of the control input to the system stay bounded by 0.6 and should evolve slowly with no more than a difference of 0.2 between two control inputs. A specification of interest is to ensure that the absolute value of the ACE falls below 0.1 within 60 time units. A tracking controller is unable to satisfy the specification, as shown in Fig. 6(a). We synthesize a nested STL-feedback controller for holding the absolute value of ACE below 0.1 against perturbations in the area-wise power demand. The synthesis of nested controller took 11 min 28 s. Figure 6(b) shows that the nested controller satisfies the specification despite the noise.

6.3   Case Study 3: Indoor Climate Control

Indoor climate control is a well-studied benchmark [25,35] against which controllers have been designed using STL specifications. In this benchmark, a building with 4 rooms is modeled using a resistor-capacitor network. The rate of change of temperature of the ith room depends on the difference between the temperature of this room and its neighboring rooms, the air flow into the room,

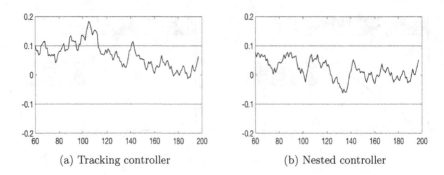

(a) Tracking controller   (b) Nested controller

Fig. 6. Tracking controller is unable to maintain safety while the proposed nested controller keeps the system safe even in the presence of noise.

the heat dissipation from windows, and the heat noise within the room from biological and electro-mechanical entities. While the original system is nonlinear, Euler's discretization method can be used to obtain a linear discrete-time system. We use such a linearization presented in [25] and also use their additive uncertainty model. The specification for controller synthesis is to "maintain a comfortable room temperature whenever the room is occupied". Formally, the specification can be written as a persistence STL property $F_{[0,T_{settle}]}G_{[0,T_{max}]}(T_t > 72+\delta \wedge T_t < 72-\delta)$ where $T_{settle} = 250, T_{max} = 500, \delta = 0.1$ in our experiments. Figure 7 shows the results obtained using the tracking controller synthesis and the nested controller synthesis method proposed in the paper. The synthesis of nested controller took 14 min 24 s. While the tracking controller is unable to satisfy the specification, the synthesized nested controller performs well in presence of runtime noise. Figure 7(b) shows a sample run of the system with the synthesized nested controller.

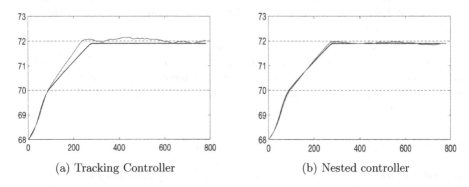

(a) Tracking Controller   (b) Nested controller

Fig. 7. Indoor Climate Controller with the persistence specification to reach a target temperature zone and stay within it. Nested controller is able to satisfy the specification while tracking controller cannot do so. The robust control synthesis could not generate a controller to keep the temperature within the tight bounds in the specification.

7 Conclusion

We proposed a novel approach to generate provably correct controllers of stochastic linear dynamical systems for STL specifications. Our approach decomposes the synthesis problem into orthogonal subproblems of meeting the STL specification, and noise-cancellation. It uses the duality between a system and its proof of correctness to compose their solutions and construct a safe nested controller. We first synthesize a stabilizing controller to reject noise at runtime, and then use its stability guarantee to formulate a less conservative robust open-loop controller synthesis problem for STL specifications using mixed integer linear programming. We experimentally validated the effectiveness of the proposed controller synthesis approach on a set of case-studies, and compared it with robust and tracking control methods. The proposed nested controller is less conservative than robust controllers, and is guaranteed to maintain safety in contrast to tracking controllers. In future work, we are investigating extensions to parametric systems where the guarantee from identical individual controllers for sub-systems can be used to synthesize a higher-level supervisory safe controller.

Acknowledgements. The authors acknowledge support from the National Science Foundation (NSF) Cyber-Physical Systems #1740079 project, NSF Software & Hardware Foundation #1750009 and #1438989 projects, US ARL Cooperative Agreement W911NF-17-2-0196, and DARPA under contract FA8750-16-C-0043.

References

1. Abate, A., Prandini, M., Lygeros, J., Sastry, S.: Probabilistic reachability and safety for controlled discrete time stochastic hybrid systems. Automatica **44**(11), 2724–2734 (2008)
2. Akametalu, A.K., Fisac, J.F., Gillula, J.H., Kaynama, S., Zeilinger, M.N., Tomlin, C.J.: Reachability-based safe learning with Gaussian processes. In: 53rd IEEE Conference on Decision and Control, pp. 1424–1431. IEEE (2014)
3. Bellman, R., Bellman, R.E., Bellman, R.E.: Introduction to the Mathematical Theory of Control Processes, vol. 2. IMA (1971)
4. Berkenkamp, F., Schoellig, A.P.: Safe and robust learning control with Gaussian processes. In: 2015 European Control Conference (ECC), pp. 2496–2501. IEEE (2015)
5. Blanchini, F.: Set invariance in control. Automatica **35**(11), 1747–1767 (1999)
6. Bogomolov, S., Schilling, C., Bartocci, E., Batt, G., Kong, H., Grosu, R.: Abstraction-based parameter synthesis for multiaffine systems. In: Piterman, N. (ed.) HVC 2015. LNCS, vol. 9434, pp. 19–35. Springer, Cham (2015). https://doi.org/10.1007/978-3-319-26287-1_2
7. Boyd, S., El Ghaoui, L., Feron, E., Balakrishnan, V.: Linear Matrix Inequalities in System and Control Theory, vol. 15. SIAM, Philadelphia (1994)
8. Cassandras, C.G., Lygeros, J.: Stochastic Hybrid Systems, vol. 24. CRC Press, Boca Raton (2006)
9. Dang, T., Dreossi, T., Piazza, C.: Parameter synthesis through temporal logic specifications. In: Bjørner, N., de Boer, F. (eds.) FM 2015. LNCS, vol. 9109, pp. 213–230. Springer, Cham (2015). https://doi.org/10.1007/978-3-319-19249-9_14

10. Donzé, A., Maler, O.: Robust satisfaction of temporal logic over real-valued signals. In: Chatterjee, K., Henzinger, T.A. (eds.) FORMATS 2010. LNCS, vol. 6246, pp. 92–106. Springer, Heidelberg (2010). https://doi.org/10.1007/978-3-642-15297-9_9
11. Eggers, A., Fränzle, M., Herde, C.: SAT modulo ODE: a direct SAT approach to hybrid systems. In: Cha, S.S., Choi, J.-Y., Kim, M., Lee, I., Viswanathan, M. (eds.) ATVA 2008. LNCS, vol. 5311, pp. 171–185. Springer, Heidelberg (2008). https://doi.org/10.1007/978-3-540-88387-6_14
12. Fainekos, G.E., Girard, A., Kress-Gazit, H., Pappas, G.J.: Temporal logic motion planning for dynamic robots. Automatica 45(2), 343–352 (2009). https://doi.org/10.1016/j.automatica.2008.08.008
13. Fainekos, G.E., Pappas, G.J.: Robustness of temporal logic specifications for continuous-time signals. Theor. Comput. Sci. 410(42), 4262–4291 (2009)
14. Fan, C., Mathur, U., Mitra, S., Viswanathan, M.: Controller synthesis made real: reach-avoid specifications and linear dynamics. In: Chockler, H., Weissenbacher, G. (eds.) CAV 2018. LNCS, vol. 10981. Springer, Cham (2018). https://doi.org/10.1007/978-3-319-96145-3_19
15. Haddad, W.M., Chellaboina, V.: Nonlinear Dynamical Systems and Control: A Lyapunov-Based Approach. Princeton University Press, Princeton (2011)
16. Huang, Z., Wang, Y., Mitra, S., Dullerud, G.E., Chaudhuri, S.: Controller synthesis with inductive proofs for piecewise linear systems: an SMT-based algorithm. In: 2015 54th IEEE Conference on Decision and Control (CDC), pp. 7434–7439, December 2015
17. Jha, S., Raman, V.: Automated synthesis of safe autonomous vehicle control under perception uncertainty. In: Rayadurgam, S., Tkachuk, O. (eds.) NFM 2016. LNCS, vol. 9690, pp. 117–132. Springer, Cham (2016). https://doi.org/10.1007/978-3-319-40648-0_10
18. Jha, S., Raman, V.: On optimal control of stochastic linear hybrid systems. In: Fränzle, M., Markey, N. (eds.) FORMATS 2016. LNCS, vol. 9884, pp. 69–84. Springer, Cham (2016). https://doi.org/10.1007/978-3-319-44878-7_5
19. Jha, S., Raman, V., Sadigh, D., Seshia, S.A.: Safe autonomy under perception uncertainty using chance-constrained temporal logic. J. Autom. Reason. 60(1), 43–62 (2018). https://doi.org/10.1007/s10817-017-9413-9
20. Kautsky, J., Nichols, N.K., Van Dooren, P.: Robust pole assignment in linear state feedback. Int. J. Control 41(5), 1129–1155 (1985)
21. Kloetzer, M., Belta, C.: A fully automated framework for control of linear systems from temporal logic specifications. IEEE Trans. Autom. Control 53(1), 287–297 (2008). https://doi.org/10.1109/TAC.2007.914952
22. Kong, S., Gao, S., Chen, W., Clarke, E.: dReach: δ-reachability analysis for hybrid systems. In: Baier, C., Tinelli, C. (eds.) TACAS 2015. LNCS, vol. 9035, pp. 200–205. Springer, Heidelberg (2015). https://doi.org/10.1007/978-3-662-46681-0_15
23. Koutsoukos, X., Riley, D.: Computational methods for reachability analysis of stochastic hybrid systems. In: Hespanha, J.P., Tiwari, A. (eds.) HSCC 2006. LNCS, vol. 3927, pp. 377–391. Springer, Heidelberg (2006). https://doi.org/10.1007/11730637_29
24. Liu, J., Prabhakar, P.: Switching control of dynamical systems from metric temporal logic specifications. In: IEEE International Conference on Robotics and Automation (2014)
25. Maasoumy, M., Razmara, M., Shahbakhti, M., Vincentelli, A.S.: Handling model uncertainty in model predictive control for energy efficient buildings. Energy Build. 77, 377–392 (2014). https://doi.org/10.1016/j.enbuild.2014.03.057. http://www.sciencedirect.com/science/article/pii/S0378778814002771

26. Maasoumy, M., Sanandaji, B.M., Sangiovanni-Vincentelli, A., Poolla, K.: Model predictive control of regulation services from commercial buildings to the smart grid. In: 2014 American Control Conference (ACC), pp. 2226–2233. IEEE (2014)

27. Maler, O., Nickovic, D., Pnueli, A.: Real time temporal logic: past, present, future. In: Pettersson, P., Yi, W. (eds.) FORMATS 2005. LNCS, vol. 3829, pp. 2–16. Springer, Heidelberg (2005). https://doi.org/10.1007/11603009_2

28. Mitchell, I., Tomlin, C.J.: Level set methods for computation in hybrid systems. In: Lynch, N., Krogh, B.H. (eds.) HSCC 2000. LNCS, vol. 1790, pp. 310–323. Springer, Heidelberg (2000). https://doi.org/10.1007/3-540-46430-1_27

29. Mitchell, I.M., Bayen, A.M., Tomlin, C.J.: A time-dependent hamilton-jacobi formulation of reachable sets for continuous dynamic games. IEEE Trans. Autom. Control 50(7), 947–957 (2005)

30. Ouaknine, J., Worrell, J.: Some recent results in metric temporal logic. In: Cassez, F., Jard, C. (eds.) FORMATS 2008. LNCS, vol. 5215, pp. 1–13. Springer, Heidelberg (2008). https://doi.org/10.1007/978-3-540-85778-5_1

31. Pontryagin, L.: Optimal control processes. Usp. Mat. Nauk 14(3), 3–20 (1959)

32. Prabhakar, P., García Soto, M.: Formal synthesis of stabilizing controllers for switched systems. In: Proceedings of the 20th International Conference on Hybrid Systems: Computation and Control, HSCC 2017, pp. 111–120. ACM, New York (2017). http://doi.acm.org/10.1145/3049797.3049822

33. Prajna, S., Jadbabaie, A., Pappas, G.J.: A framework for worst-case and stochastic safety verification using barrier certificates. IEEE Trans. Autom. Control 52(8), 1415–1428 (2007)

34. Prandini, M., Hu, J.: Stochastic reachability: theory and numerical approximation. Stochast. Hybrid Syst. Autom. Control Eng. Ser. 24, 107–138 (2006)

35. Raman, V., Donz, A., Maasoumy, M., Murray, R.M., Sangiovanni-Vincentelli, A., Seshia, S.A.: Model predictive control with signal temporal logic specifications. In: 53rd IEEE Conference on Decision and Control, pp. 81–87, December 2014. https://doi.org/10.1109/CDC.2014.7039363

36. Sadigh, D., Kapoor, A.: Safe control under uncertainty with probabilistic signal temporal logic. In: Robotics: Science and Systems XII (2016). http://www.roboticsproceedings.org/rss12/p17.html

37. Schrmann, B., Althoff, M.: Optimal control of sets of solutions to formally guarantee constraints of disturbed linear systems. In: 2017 American Control Conference (ACC), pp. 2522–2529, May 2017

38. Seto, D., Krogh, B.H., Sha, L., Chutinan, A.: Dynamic control system upgrade using the simplex architecture. IEEE Control Syst. 18(4), 72–80 (1998)

39. Summers, S., Kamgarpour, M., Lygeros, J., Tomlin, C.: A stochastic reach-avoid problem with random obstacles. In: Proceedings of the 14th International Conference on Hybrid Systems: Computation and Control, pp. 251–260. ACM (2011)

40. Tabuada, P., Pappas, G.J.: Linear time logic control of discrete-time linear systems. IEEE Trans. Autom. Control 51(12), 1862–1877 (2006)

41. Wongpiromsarn, T., Topcu, U., Murray, R.M.: Receding horizon temporal logic planning. IEEE Trans. Autom. Control 57(11), 2817–2830 (2012). https://doi.org/10.1109/TAC.2012.2195811

42. Yordanov, B., Tumova, J., Cerna, I., Barnat, J., Belta, C.: Temporal logic control of discrete-time piecewise affine systems. IEEE Trans. Autom. Control 57(6), 1491–1504 (2012)

Safe Over- and Under-Approximation of Reachable Sets for Autonomous Dynamical Systems

Meilun Li[1], Peter N. Mosaad[2], Martin Fränzle[2], Zhikun She[1(✉)], and Bai Xue[3]

[1] School of Mathematics and Systems Science, Beihang University, Beijing, China
{meilun.li,zhikun.she}@buaa.edu.cn
[2] Department of Computing Science, Carl von Ossietzky Universität Oldenburg,
Oldenburg, Germany
{peter.nazier.mosaad,fraenzle}@informatik.uni-oldenburg.de
[3] State Key Laboratory of Computer Science, Institute of Software, CAS,
Beijing, China
xuebai@ios.ac.cn

Abstract. We present a method based on the Hamilton-Jacobi framework that is able to compute over- and under-approximations of reachable sets for autonomous dynamical systems beyond polynomial dynamics. The method does not resort to user-supplied candidate polynomials, but rather relies on an expansion of the evolution function whose convergence in compact state space is guaranteed. Over- and under-approximations of the reachable state space up to any designated precision can consequently be obtained based on truncations of that expansion. As the truncations used in computing over- and under-approximations as well as their associated error bounds agree, double-sided enclosures of the true reach-set can be computed in a single sweep. We demonstrate the precision of the enclosures thus obtained by comparison of benchmark results to related simulations.

1 Introduction

Reachable set computation for dynamical systems is a fundamental task within methods for the automatic discharge of various proof obligations such as safety verification or rigorous system falsification [29]. Such methods can in turn be applied to a wide range of system design problems, for example, aircraft collision avoidance [11] and robot control [27].

For cases involving simple dynamics, the reachable sets at any time point can be computed explicitly [3,28]. In most real cases, however, exact reachable sets are not straightforward to obtain either due to the computational complexity

This work was partially supported by the National Natural Science Foundation of China under Grants 11371047, 11422111.

M. Li—The author was supported by the China Scholarship Council for 1 year study at Carl von Ossietzky University of Oldenburg.

D. N. Jansen and P. Prabhakar (Eds.): FORMATS 2018, LNCS 11022, pp. 252–270, 2018.
https://doi.org/10.1007/978-3-030-00151-3_15

of exact computation or due to inherent lack of closed-form computational representations. Consequently, many researchers are interested in computational approximation of reachable sets, with an obvious trade-off between tightness of the approximation and computational effort. A further consideration is that such approximations ought to support reliable logical verdicts concerning safety of the system under consideration, which leads to the notion of (guaranteed) over- or under-approximation. Over-approximation of the reachable set can reliably be employed in the verification of safety, as empty intersection of an over-approximate reach-set with the set of unsafe states implies unreachability of the unsafe states under exact dynamics. Various methods for computing such guaranteed over-approximation are discussed in the literature such as abstraction methods [2,6,30,32–34], simulation-based methods adding appropriate bloating to simulations [7,9,14,18,28], methods based on support-functions [10,12,16,31], and methods based on Taylor expansions [1,4]. Under-approximation computation is usually applied to rigorously falsify a safety property by validating reachability of some undesirable (i.e., unsafe) target state. A number of results are about linear systems [13,17,22,23,25], and methods for nonlinear systems have only emerged in recent years [5,15,21,24,37].

In this paper we present a novel methodology to compute over- and under-approximations of reachable sets for autonomous dynamical systems (ADS). We first introduce the concept of an evolution function for describing the time-evolution of the reach set corresponding to the dynamics of the ADS and show that its sub-level sets can be used to describe reachable sets. Then we employ the Hamilton-Jacobi formulation of the evolution function and we prove that the evolution function of analytic ADS has a special form of expansion permitting truncation. We prove convergence of these truncations over compact state-space, and are consequently able to provide over- and under-approximations of arbitrary desired precision by manipulating truncations of certain degree of t, which we name a t-expansion. Based on this convergence result, we design a computational framework for guaranteed over- and under-approximations of reachable sets, whose correctness is also proved in this paper. For a given system and desired precision, the framework utilizes a global optimization method seeking an extremum to check whether the reach sets derived from the truncated evolution function satisfy the precision limit.

Ample prior research about reachable-set approximation is related to the Hamilton-Jacobi framework. [19] directly describes reachable sets as the zero sub-level sets of the viscosity solutions of time-dependent Hamilton-Jacobi-Isaacs partial differential equations and then uses methods from the level-set literature [26] to numerically approximate these. [35] uses the *advection operator* A_t to describe reachable sets and then converts it to a semi-definite program encoding the first-order Taylor approximation B_t of A_t. [36] uses a semi-definite programming method to compute solutions of relaxed Hamilton-Jacobi inequalities to obtain over- and under-approximations of reachable sets. Our work is different from the above in the following ways. First, the expansion of the evolution function exhibits the very same form introduced in this paper for all analytic

ADS, not only for polynomial ADS. Consequently, our framework facilitates the analysis of a wider class of systems than just polynomial ADS. Second, different from the optimization based methods in [36] which use a candidate polynomial, we directly build our approximations from the expansion of a general evolution function whose convergence in compact state space is guaranteed. This implies that theoretically we can directly, without manual intervention and guess-work, compute an approximation with any designated precision bound. In particular we overcome the shortcoming induced by candidate polynomials that the performance of such template-based methods heavily depends on appropriate choice of the candidate polynomial. Third, as illustrated later in the paper, we can create both over- and under-approximations within a single computation because they satisfy the same criterion and share the same precision bound.

2   Preliminaries

The class of systems we consider in this paper is the set of *autonomous dynamical systems*.

Definition 1. *An* autonomous dynamical system (ADS) *is of the form*

$$\dot{\mathbf{x}} = \mathbf{f}(\mathbf{x}), \tag{1}$$

where $\mathbf{x} \in \mathbb{R}^n$ *is an n-dimensional vector and* $\mathbf{f}(\mathbf{x}) : \mathbb{R}^n \to \mathbb{R}^n$ *is a function. A solution of system (1) starting from* $\mathbf{x}_0 \in \mathbb{R}^n$ *is defined as* $\phi(\mathbf{x}_0, t)$ *satisfying*

$$\begin{cases} \phi(\mathbf{x}_0, 0) = \mathbf{x}_0 \\ \dfrac{\partial \phi(\mathbf{x}_0, t)}{\partial t} = \mathbf{f}(\phi(\mathbf{x}_0, t)) \end{cases}.$$

In this paper we assume that $\mathbf{f}(\mathbf{x})$ in Eq. (1) satisfies a local Lipschitz condition such that the existence and uniqueness of $\phi(\mathbf{x}_0, t)$ is guaranteed. We use $(T_{\mathbf{x}_0}^-, T_{\mathbf{x}_0}^+)$ to denote the maximal well-defined time interval of $\phi(\mathbf{x}_0, t)$. Notice that $T_{\mathbf{x}_0}^-$ and $T_{\mathbf{x}_0}^+$ can be $-\infty$ and $+\infty$ respectively. To simplify discussion, we define

$$\mathcal{R}^+ \equiv \{(\mathbf{x}, t) | \mathbf{x} \in \mathbb{R}^n \wedge t \in (T_{\mathbf{x}}^-, T_{\mathbf{x}}^+)\},$$
$$\mathcal{R}^- \equiv \{(\mathbf{x}, t) | \mathbf{x} \in \mathbb{R}^n \wedge t \in (-T_{\mathbf{x}}^+, -T_{\mathbf{x}}^-)\}$$

as the maximal definable set of $\phi(\mathbf{x}_0, t)$ and $\phi(\mathbf{x}_0, -t)$ respectively. The next proposition holds for local Lipschitz ADS, and is crucial in our later discussion.

Proposition 1. *If an ADS is local Lipschitz, then* $\phi(\phi(\mathbf{x}_0, t), -t) = \mathbf{x}_0, \forall (\mathbf{x}_0, t) \in \mathcal{R}^+$ *and* $\phi(\phi(\mathbf{x}_0, -t), t) = \mathbf{x}_0, \forall (\mathbf{x}_0, t) \in \mathcal{R}^-$.

Now we define the *evolution function*, similar to the concept of *advection operator* in [35] and *reachable set* in [5], as follows.

Definition 2. *Given a function* $g(\mathbf{x}) : \mathbb{R}^n \to \mathbb{R}$, *the evolution function of the ADS (1) with* $g(\mathbf{x})$ *is defined as*

$$Evo_{\mathbf{f},g}(\mathbf{x}, t) = g(\phi(\mathbf{x}, -t)), \forall (\mathbf{x}, t) \in \mathcal{R}^-.$$

Remark 1. The evolution function $Evo_{\mathbf{f},g}(\mathbf{x}, t)$ satisfies the following property:

$$Evo_{\mathbf{f},g}(\phi(\mathbf{x_0}, t), t) \equiv g(\phi(\phi(\mathbf{x_0}, t), -t)) = g(\mathbf{x_0}), \forall \mathbf{x_0} \in \mathcal{R}^+. \tag{2}$$

A widely used method for set representation is *zero-sublevel set* method. It maps a function over $\mathbb{R}^n$ to a set of states in $\mathbb{R}^n$.

Definition 3. *The* zero-sublevel set $\mu(v(\cdot))$ *of* $v(\mathbf{x}) : \mathbb{R}^n \to \mathbb{R}$, *briefly* $\mu(v)$, *is*

$$\mu(v(\cdot)) = \{\mathbf{x} \in \mathbb{R}^n \mid v(\mathbf{x}) \le 0\}$$

3   Equivalent Definition of the Evolution Function

In this section we show that we can define evolution function with Hamilton-Jacobi framework. The next theorem shows the equivalence of the two ways.

Theorem 1. *Given a function* $g(\mathbf{x}) : \mathbb{R}^n \to \mathbb{R}$ *and an ADS (1), the following two expressions are equivalent:*

1. $U(\mathbf{x}, t)$ *is the evolution function of ADS (1).*
2. $U(\mathbf{x}, t)$ *satisfies*

$$\begin{cases} U(\mathbf{x}, 0) = g(\mathbf{x}), \forall \mathbf{x} \in \mathbb{R}^n, \\ \dfrac{\partial U(\mathbf{x}, t)}{\partial \mathbf{x}} \cdot \mathbf{f}(\mathbf{x}) + \dfrac{\partial U(\mathbf{x}, t)}{\partial t} = 0, \forall (\mathbf{x}, t) \in \mathcal{R}^-, \end{cases} \tag{3}$$

where $\cdot$ *is the inner product operator of two vectors with the same dimension.*

Proof. $1 \to 2$. From (2), $U(\phi(\mathbf{x_0}, t), t) \equiv g(\mathbf{x_0}), \forall (\mathbf{x_0}, t) \in \mathcal{R}^+$. Since $\mathbf{x_0}$ and t are independent, for any given $\mathbf{x_0} \in \mathbb{R}$, the value of $U(\phi(\mathbf{x_0}, t), t)$ doesn't change with t. Therefore,

$$0 \equiv \frac{dU(\phi(\mathbf{x_0}, t), t)}{dt} = \frac{\partial U(\mathbf{x}, t)}{\partial \mathbf{x}}|_{\phi(\mathbf{x_0}, t)} \cdot \mathbf{f}(\phi(\mathbf{x_0}, t)) + \frac{\partial U(\phi(\mathbf{x_0}, t), t)}{\partial t}.$$

Because the range of $\phi(\mathbf{x_0}, t)$ is $\mathbb{R}^n$, for each $(\mathbf{x}, t) \in \mathcal{R}^-$, we have

$$\frac{\partial U(\mathbf{x}, t)}{\partial \mathbf{x}} \cdot \mathbf{f}(\mathbf{x}) + \frac{\partial U(\mathbf{x}, t)}{\partial t} \equiv 0,$$

which is the second equation in (3).

Besides, from definition of evolution function, we have $U(\mathbf{x}, 0) \equiv g(\phi(\mathbf{x}, 0)) \equiv g(\mathbf{x}), \forall \mathbf{x} \in \mathbb{R}^n$, which is the first equation in (3). Thus we complete the proof of $1 \to 2$.

$2 \rightarrow 1$. For any given $\mathbf{x}_0 \in \mathbb{R}^n$, consider the derivative of $U(\phi(\mathbf{x}_0,t),t), t \in (T_{\mathbf{x}_0}^-, T_{\mathbf{x}_0}^+)$. By Eq. (3) we have

$$\frac{dU(\phi(\mathbf{x}_0,t),t)}{dt} = \frac{\partial U(\mathbf{x},t)}{\partial \mathbf{x}}|_{\phi(\mathbf{x}_0,t)} \cdot \mathbf{f}(\phi(\mathbf{x}_0,t)) + \frac{\partial U(\phi(\mathbf{x}_0,t),t)}{\partial t} = 0, \quad (4)$$

which means the value of $U(\phi(\mathbf{x}_0,t),t)$ doesn't change with t. Thus

$$U(\phi(\mathbf{x}_0,t),t) = U(\phi(\mathbf{x}_0,0),0) = U(\mathbf{x}_0,0) = g(\mathbf{x}_0), \forall (\mathbf{x}_0,t) \in \mathcal{R}^+.$$

For arbitrary $(\mathbf{x},t) \in \mathcal{R}^-$, since ADS (1) is Lipschitz, we can find a unique $\mathbf{y} = \phi(\mathbf{x},-t)$, and $\mathbf{x} = \phi(\mathbf{y},t) \in \mathcal{R}^+$. Then $U(\mathbf{x},t) = U(\phi(\mathbf{y},t),t) = g(\mathbf{y}) = g(\phi(\mathbf{x},-t))$, which means that $U(\mathbf{x},t)$ is the evolution function of ADS (1) with $g(\mathbf{x})$. □

4 t-expansion of Evolution Function

In this section, we develop the relationship between reachability of ADS and evolution function, and show that the evolution function has a special form, named t-expansion, which is the basis of our approximation framework.

Definition 4. *For given initial state set $\mathbf{X}_0$ and time t such that $(\mathbf{x},t) \in \mathcal{R}^+, \forall \mathbf{x} \in \mathbf{X}_0$, the reachable set of ADS (1) from $\mathbf{X}_0$ for t, denoted as $Reach_{\mathbf{f},\mathbf{X}_0}^t$, is defined as*

$$Reach_{\mathbf{f},\mathbf{X}_0}^t = \{\phi(\mathbf{x}_0,t) \in \mathbb{R}^n | \mathbf{x}_0 \in \mathbf{X}_0\}.$$

$Reach_{\mathbf{f},\mathbf{X}_0}^t$ *is a forward reachable set if $t \geq 0$, and $Reach_{\mathbf{f},\mathbf{X}_0}^t$ is a backward reachable set if $t \leq 0$.*

Remark 2. If $\mathbf{X}_0$ is the zero-sublevel set of a function $g(\mathbf{x})$, we use $Reach_{\mathbf{f},g}^t$ as the abbreviation of $Reach_{\mathbf{f},\mu(g)}^t$.

From the definition of $Reach_{\mathbf{f},g}^t$ and evolution function, the following proposition is easy to obtain.

Proposition 2. *For ADS (1) and $g(\mathbf{x}) : \mathbb{R}^n \rightarrow \mathbb{R}$, $Reach_{\mathbf{f},g}^t = \mu(Evo_{\mathbf{f},g}(\cdot,t))$.*

Proposition 2 shows that computation of reachable set of ADS can be converted to computation of evolution function. However the analytic solution to (1) or (3) are hard to get. In the following theorem, we show that if $\mathbf{f}$ and g are analytic, the evolution function $Evo_{\mathbf{f},g}(\mathbf{x},t)$ has a special form, i.e. t-expansion as we named.

Theorem 2. *For ADS (1) and $g(\mathbf{x}) : \mathbb{R}^n \rightarrow \mathbb{R}$, if both $\mathbf{f}(\mathbf{x})$ and $g(\mathbf{x})$ are analytic, the evolution function $Evo_{\mathbf{f},g}(\mathbf{x},t)$ is of the form*

$$Evo_{\mathbf{f},g}(\mathbf{x},t) = \sum_{i=0}^{+\infty} \frac{\mathcal{M}_i^{\mathbf{f},g}(\mathbf{x})}{i!}(-t)^i, \quad (5)$$

where $\mathcal{M}_n^{f,g}(\mathbf{x})$ is defined inductively as

$$
\begin{cases}
\mathcal{M}_0^{f,g}(\mathbf{x}) = g(\mathbf{x}), \forall \mathbf{x} \in \mathbb{R}^n, \\
\mathcal{M}_{i+1}^{f,g}(\mathbf{x}) = \dfrac{\partial \mathcal{M}_i^{f,g}(\mathbf{x})}{\partial \mathbf{x}} \cdot f(\mathbf{x}), \forall \mathbf{x} \in \mathbb{R}^n.
\end{cases}
\tag{6}
$$

Proof. Denote $U(\mathbf{x},t) \equiv \sum_{i=0}^{+\infty} \frac{\mathcal{M}_i^{f,g}(\mathbf{x})}{i!}(-t)^i$. According to Theorem 1, we only need to prove that $U(\mathbf{x},t)$ satisfies condition (3).

First, since $U(\mathbf{x},t) = g(\mathbf{x}) + \sum_{i=1}^{+\infty} \frac{\mathcal{M}_i^{f,g}(\mathbf{x})}{i!}(-t)^i$, we immediately have that $U(\mathbf{x},0) = g(\mathbf{x}), \forall \mathbf{x} \in \mathbb{R}^n$, which is the first equation in condition (3).

Second, from definition of $U(\mathbf{x},t)$, for arbitrary $(\mathbf{x},t) \in \mathcal{R}^-$ we have

$$
\frac{\partial U(\mathbf{x},t)}{\partial \mathbf{x}} \cdot f(\mathbf{x}) = [\frac{\partial}{\partial \mathbf{x}} \sum_{i=0}^{+\infty} \frac{\mathcal{M}_i^{f,g}(\mathbf{x})}{i!}(-t)^i] \cdot f(\mathbf{x}) = \sum_{i=0}^{+\infty} \frac{(-t)^i}{i!} \frac{\partial \mathcal{M}_i^{f,g}(\mathbf{x})}{\partial \mathbf{x}} \cdot f(\mathbf{x})
$$

$$
= \sum_{i=0}^{+\infty} \frac{(-t)^i}{i!} \mathcal{M}_{i+1}^{f,g}(\mathbf{x})
$$

and

$$
\frac{\partial U(\mathbf{x},t)}{\partial t} = \frac{\partial}{\partial t} \sum_{j=0}^{+\infty} \frac{\mathcal{M}_j^{f,g}(\mathbf{x})}{j!}(-t)^j = \frac{\partial g(\mathbf{x})}{\partial t} + \frac{\partial}{\partial t} \sum_{j=1}^{+\infty} \frac{\mathcal{M}_j^{f,g}(\mathbf{x})}{j!}(-t)^j
$$

$$
= 0 + \sum_{j=1}^{+\infty} \mathcal{M}_j^{f,g}(\mathbf{x}) \frac{d}{dt} \frac{(-t)^j}{j!}
$$

$$
= -\sum_{j=1}^{+\infty} \mathcal{M}_j^{f,g}(\mathbf{x}) \frac{(-t)^{j-1}}{(j-1)!}.
$$

Letting $i = j - 1$ in $\frac{\partial U(\mathbf{x},t)}{\partial t}$, we have

$$
\frac{\partial U(\mathbf{x},t)}{\partial t} = -\sum_{i=0}^{+\infty} \mathcal{M}_{i+1}^{f,g}(\mathbf{x}) \frac{(-t)^i}{i!} = -\frac{\partial U(\mathbf{x},t)}{\partial \mathbf{x}} \cdot f(\mathbf{x}).
$$

Therefore $\frac{\partial U(\mathbf{x},t)}{\partial \mathbf{x}} \cdot f(\mathbf{x}) + \frac{\partial U(\mathbf{x},t)}{\partial t} = 0, \forall (\mathbf{x},t) \in \mathcal{R}^-$, which is the second equation in condition (3). □

We denote $Evo_{f,g}^N(\mathbf{x},t)$ as finite truncation of $Evo_{f,g}(\mathbf{x},t)$ till degree N, i.e. $Evo_{f,g}^N(\mathbf{x},t) \equiv \sum_{i=0}^{N} \frac{(-1)^i \mathcal{M}_i^{f,g}(\mathbf{x})}{i!} t^i$, and define $Evo_{f,g}^{+\infty}(\mathbf{x},t) \equiv \sum_{i=0}^{+\infty} \frac{(-1)^i \mathcal{M}_i^{f,g}(\mathbf{x})}{i!} t^i$.

Since we assume ADS (1) is local Lipschitz, the uniqueness of evolution function is guaranteed, which also ensures the uniqueness of solution to (3) via Theorem 1. Thus $Evo_{f,g}^{+\infty}(\mathbf{x},t)$ is the unique solution to (3).

For fixed $\mathbf{x} \in \mathbb{R}^n$, $Evo_{\mathbf{f},g}^{+\infty}(\mathbf{x}, t)$ is the Taylor expansion of $Evo_{\mathbf{f},g}(\mathbf{x}, t)$ over t, and $(-1)^i \mathcal{M}_i^{\mathbf{f},g}(\mathbf{x})$'s are the Taylor coefficients. Notice that Taylor expansion of a function may not globally convergent to the function. Defining

$$\mathcal{C}^- = \{(\mathbf{x}, t) | \mathbf{x} \in \mathbb{R}^n \wedge Evo_{\mathbf{f},g}^{+\infty}(\mathbf{x}, t) = Evo_{\mathbf{f},g}(\mathbf{x}, t)\},$$
$$\mathcal{C}^+ = \{(\mathbf{x}, t) | (\mathbf{x}, -t) \in \mathcal{C}^-\}.$$

we have the following proposition.

Proposition 3. *Given ADS (1), for any $(\mathbf{x}, t) \in \mathcal{C}^-$, we have*

$$\lim_{N \to +\infty} Evo_{\mathbf{f},g}^N(\mathbf{x}, t) = Evo_{\mathbf{f},g}(\mathbf{x}, t).$$

5   Over- and Under-Approximations of Reachable Sets

From Propositions 2 and 3, we can see that $Evo_{\mathbf{f},g}^N(\mathbf{x}, t)$ can be used to simulate $Reach_{\mathbf{f},g}^t$ in 2-dimensional analytic ADS (1) with analytic solution. In this section, we employ $Evo_{\mathbf{f},g}^N(\mathbf{x}, t)$ to obtain over- and under-approximations of $Reach_{\mathbf{f},g}^t$.

5.1   EFOU Framework

We define over- and under-approximation of set and function.

Definition 5. *For two sets S_1 and S_2, we say S_1 is an over- (under-, resp.) approximation of S_2 iff $S_1 \supseteq (\subseteq)S_2$. For two n-dimensional functions $f_1(\mathbf{x})$ and $f_2(\mathbf{x})$, we say $f_1(\mathbf{x})$ is an over- (under-, resp.) approximation of $f_2(\mathbf{x})$ if $\mu(f_1) \supseteq (\subseteq)\mu(f_2)$.*

Consider a compact set $S \subseteq \mathcal{C}^-$, From Proposition 3, given an arbitrary $\epsilon > 0$, for each $(\mathbf{x}, t) \in S$ there exists $0 \le M_{(\mathbf{x},t)} \in \mathbb{N}$ such that for all $N_{(\mathbf{x},t)} \ge M_{(\mathbf{x},t)}$ we have $| Evo_{\mathbf{f},g}^{N_{(\mathbf{x},t)}}(\mathbf{x}, t) - Evo_{\mathbf{f},g}(\mathbf{x}, t) | \le \epsilon$. Since S is compact, we can then find $M = \sup_{(\mathbf{x},t) \in S} M_{(\mathbf{x},t)}$ such that $| Evo_{\mathbf{f},g}^N(\mathbf{x}, t) - Evo_{\mathbf{f},g}(\mathbf{x}, t) | \le \epsilon, \forall N \ge M$. Therefore the inequalities

$$Evo_{\mathbf{f},g}^N(\mathbf{x}, t) - \epsilon \le Evo_{\mathbf{f},g}(\mathbf{x}, t) \le Evo_{\mathbf{f},g}^N(\mathbf{x}, t) + \epsilon \tag{7}$$

hold over S, yielding the existence of over- and under-approximations of the evolution function bounded by arbitrary precision. But we still need a constructive criterion to decide on the expansion degree N necessary to reach the precision ϵ.

Theorem 3. *For ADS (1) and $g(\mathbf{x}) : \mathbb{R}^n \to \mathbb{R}$, if both $\mathbf{f}(\mathbf{x})$ and $g(\mathbf{x})$ are analytic, for any $(\mathbf{x}, t) \in \mathcal{C}^-$ and $N \in \mathbb{N}$, we have*

$$Evo_{\mathbf{f},g}(\mathbf{x}, t) = Evo_{\mathbf{f},g}^N(\mathbf{x}, t) - \int_0^t \frac{(r - t)^N}{N!} \mathcal{M}_{N+1}^{\mathbf{f},g}(\phi(\mathbf{x}, -r)) dr. \tag{8}$$

Proof. Similar to Theorem 2, for any $N \geq 1$, we have

$$\frac{\partial Evo_{\mathbf{f},g}^N(\mathbf{x},t)}{\partial \mathbf{x}} \cdot \mathbf{f}(\mathbf{x}) = \sum_{i=0}^{N} \frac{(-t)^i}{i!} \mathcal{M}_{i+1}^{\mathbf{f},g}(\mathbf{x})$$

and

$$\frac{\partial Evo_{\mathbf{f},g}^N(\mathbf{x},t)}{\partial t} = -\sum_{i=0}^{N-1} \mathcal{M}_{i+1}^{\mathbf{f},g}(\mathbf{x}) \frac{(-t)^i}{i!}.$$

Therefore

$$\frac{\partial Evo_{\mathbf{f},g}^N(\mathbf{x},t)}{\partial \mathbf{x}} \cdot \mathbf{f}(\mathbf{x}) + \frac{\partial Evo_{\mathbf{f},g}^N(\mathbf{x},t)}{\partial t} = \frac{(-t)^N}{N!} \mathcal{M}_{N+1}^{\mathbf{f},g}(\mathbf{x}), N \geq 1. \qquad (9)$$

And it is easy to check that Eq. (9) also holds when $N = 0$.

Now, for arbitrary $N \in \mathbb{N}$ and any given $\mathbf{x}_0 \in \mathbb{R}^n$, consider the derivative of $Evo_{\mathbf{f},g}^N(\phi(\mathbf{x}_0,t),t)$, we have

$$\frac{dEvo_{\mathbf{f},g}^N(\phi(\mathbf{x}_0,t),t)}{dt} = \frac{\partial Evo_{\mathbf{f},g}^N(\mathbf{y},t)}{\partial \mathbf{y}} \Big|_{\phi(\mathbf{x}_0,t)} \cdot \mathbf{f}(\phi(\mathbf{x}_0,t)) + \frac{\partial Evo_{\mathbf{f},g}^N(\phi(\mathbf{x}_0,t),t)}{\partial t}$$

$$= \frac{(-t)^N}{N!} \mathcal{M}_{N+1}^{\mathbf{f},g}(\phi(\mathbf{x}_0,t)).$$

Thus for any $(\mathbf{x}_0,t) \in \mathcal{C}^+$,

$$Evo_{\mathbf{f},g}^N(\phi(\mathbf{x}_0,t),t) = Evo_{\mathbf{f},g}^N(\phi(\mathbf{x}_0,0),0) + \int_0^t \frac{(-s)^N}{N!} \mathcal{M}_{N+1}^{\mathbf{f},g}(\phi(\mathbf{x}_0,s))ds$$

$$= Evo_{\mathbf{f},g}^N(\mathbf{x}_0,0) + \int_0^t \frac{(r-t)^N}{N!} \mathcal{M}_{N+1}^{\mathbf{f},g}(\phi(\mathbf{x}_0,t-r))dr$$

$$= g(\mathbf{x}_0) + \int_0^t \frac{(r-t)^N}{N!} \mathcal{M}_{N+1}^{\mathbf{f},g}(\phi(\phi(\mathbf{x}_0,t),-r))dr$$

$$= Evo_{\mathbf{f},g}(\phi(\mathbf{x}_0,t),t) + \int_0^t \frac{(r-t)^N}{N!} \mathcal{M}_{N+1}^{\mathbf{f},g}(\phi(\phi(\mathbf{x}_0,t),-r))dr.$$

Therefore we can immediately have that

$$Evo_{\mathbf{f},g}(\mathbf{x},t) = Evo_{\mathbf{f},g}^N(\mathbf{x},t) - \int_0^t \frac{(r-t)^N}{N!} \mathcal{M}_{N+1}^{\mathbf{f},g}(\phi(\mathbf{x},-r))dr, \forall (\mathbf{x},t) \in \mathcal{C}^-.$$

$\square$

We can estimate the value of $\int_0^t \frac{(r-t)^N}{N!} \mathcal{M}_{N+1}^{\mathbf{f},g}(\phi(\mathbf{x},-r))dr$ in different ways. The idea is that if we can determine the range of $\mathcal{M}_{N+1}^{\mathbf{f},g}(\phi(\mathbf{x},-r))$ then we can estimate the integration, as shown in Propositions 4 and 5.

Proposition 4. *Given ADS (1), $g(\mathbf{x}) : \mathbb{R}^n \to \mathbb{R}$, degree N and time bound T, if for a set of states $S \supseteq \bigcup_{t \in [0,T]} Reach_{\mathbf{f},g}^t$ and for some $M \geq 0$ we have $\mid \mathcal{M}_{N+1}^{\mathbf{f},g}(\mathbf{x}) \mid \leq \frac{N!}{T^{N+1}} \frac{M}{2}, \forall \mathbf{x} \in S$, then $Evo_{\mathbf{f},g}^N(\mathbf{x},t) - \frac{Mt}{2T} (Evo_{\mathbf{f},g}^N(\mathbf{x},t) + \frac{Mt}{2T})$ is an over- (under-, resp.) approximation of $Evo_{\mathbf{f},g}(\mathbf{x},t)$, and the precisions for both approximations are bounded by $\frac{Mt}{T}$.*

Proof. From Proposition 2, for all $\mathbf{x} \in \mu(Evo_{\mathbf{f},g}(\cdot,t))$, an $\mathbf{x}_0$ exists such that $\mathbf{x} = \phi(\mathbf{x}_0, t)$. Thus for all $r \in [0,t]$, $\phi(\mathbf{x}, -r) = \phi(\mathbf{x}_0, t - r) \in Reach_{\mathbf{f},g}^{t-r} \subseteq \bigcup_{t \in [0,T]} Reach_{\mathbf{f},g}^t \subseteq S$. Therefore $\mid \mathcal{M}_{N+1}^{\mathbf{f},g}(\phi(\mathbf{x}, -r)) \mid \leq \frac{M \cdot N!}{2 \cdot T^{N+1}}$.

Then from Eq. 8,

$$\mid Evo_{\mathbf{f},g}(\mathbf{x},t) - Evo_{\mathbf{f},g}^N(\mathbf{x},t) \mid = \mid \int_0^t \frac{(r-t)^N}{N!} \mathcal{M}_{N+1}^{\mathbf{f},g}(\phi(\mathbf{x}, -r)) dr \mid$$

$$\leq \int_0^t \mid \frac{(r-t)^N}{N!} \mathcal{M}_{N+1}^{\mathbf{f},g}(\phi(\mathbf{x}, -r)) \mid dr \leq \int_0^t \frac{T^N}{N!} \frac{N!}{T^{N+1}} \frac{M}{2} dr = \frac{Mt}{2T}.$$

From the above inequality we can immediately have that $Evo_{\mathbf{f},g}^N(\mathbf{x},t) - \frac{Mt}{2T}$ $(Evo_{\mathbf{f},g}^N(\mathbf{x},t) + \frac{Mt}{2T})$ is an over- (under-, resp.) approximation of $Evo_{\mathbf{f},g}(\mathbf{x},t)$, and

$$\begin{cases} Evo_{\mathbf{f},g}(\mathbf{x},t) - \dfrac{Mt}{T} \leq Evo_{\mathbf{f},g}^N(\mathbf{x},t) - \dfrac{Mt}{2T} \leq Evo_{\mathbf{f},g}(\mathbf{x},t) \\[2ex] Evo_{\mathbf{f},g}(\mathbf{x},t) \leq Evo_{\mathbf{f},g}^N(\mathbf{x},t) + \dfrac{Mt}{2T} \leq Evo_{\mathbf{f},g}(\mathbf{x},t) + \dfrac{Mt}{T} \end{cases}$$

for all $\mathbf{x} \in \mu(Evo_{\mathbf{f},g}(\cdot,t))$, which means the precisions of both over and under approximations are bounded by $\frac{Mt}{T}$. □

Proposition 5. *Given ADS (1), $g(\mathbf{x}) : \mathbb{R}^n \to \mathbb{R}$, degree N and time bound T, if for a set of states $S \supseteq \bigcup_{t \in [0,T]} Reach_{\mathbf{f},g}^t$ we have $A \leq \mathcal{M}_{N+1}^{\mathbf{f},g}(\mathbf{x}) \leq B, \forall \mathbf{x} \in S$, then for all $t \in [0,T]$,*

1. *if N is even, $Evo_{\mathbf{f},g}^N(\mathbf{x},t) + A\frac{t^{N+1}}{(N+1)!}$ is an over-approximation of $Evo_{\mathbf{f},g}(\mathbf{x},t)$, and $Evo_{\mathbf{f},g}^N(\mathbf{x},t) + B\frac{t^{N+1}}{(N+1)!}$ is an under-approximation of $Evo_{\mathbf{f},g}(\mathbf{x},t)$;*

2. *if N is odd, $Evo_{\mathbf{f},g}^N(\mathbf{x},t) - B\frac{t^{N+1}}{(N+1)!}$ is an over-approximation of $Evo_{\mathbf{f},g}(\mathbf{x},t)$, and $Evo_{\mathbf{f},g}^N(\mathbf{x},t) - A\frac{t^{N+1}}{(N+1)!}$ is an under-approximation of $Evo_{\mathbf{f},g}(\mathbf{x},t)$;*

3. *the precisions for both over- and under-approximations in 1 and 2 are bounded by $(B - A)\frac{t^{N+1}}{(N+1)!}$.*

Proof. First we prove 1 and $1 \to 3$.

For any fixed t, following a similar manner in proof of Proposition 4, we have that for all $r \in [0,t]$ and all $\mathbf{x} \in \mu(Evo_{\mathbf{f},g}(\cdot,t))$, $A \leq \mathcal{M}_{N+1}^{\mathbf{f},g}(\phi(\mathbf{x}, -r)) \leq B$.

Now, if N is even, $(r - t)^N \leq 0$. Thus for all $\mathbf{x} \in \mu(Evo_{\mathbf{f},g}(\cdot,t))$

$$B\frac{(r-t)^N}{N!} \leq \frac{(r-t)^N}{N!} \mathcal{M}_{N+1}^{\mathbf{f},g}(\phi(\mathbf{x}, -r)) \leq A\frac{(r-t)^N}{N!},$$

which implies that

$$-B\frac{t^{N+1}}{N+1} \leq \int_0^t \frac{(r-t)^N}{N!} \mathcal{M}_{N+1}^{\mathbf{f},g}(\phi(\mathbf{x}, -r)) dr \leq -A\frac{t^{N+1}}{N+1}.$$

Together with Eq. 8, we have

$$Evo_{\mathbf{f},g}^N(\mathbf{x},t) + A\frac{t^{N+1}}{(N+1)!} \le Evo_{\mathbf{f},g}(\mathbf{x},t) \le Evo_{\mathbf{f},g}^N(\mathbf{x},t) + B\frac{t^{N+1}}{(N+1)!} \quad (10)$$

for all $\mathbf{x} \in \mu(Evo_{\mathbf{f},g}(\cdot,t))$, which is the result of *1*.

Further, from Eq. 10, we can immediately have

$$\begin{cases} Evo_{\mathbf{f},g}(\mathbf{x},t) - (B - A)\dfrac{t^{N+1}}{(N+1)!} \le Evo_{\mathbf{f},g}^N(\mathbf{x},t) + A\dfrac{t^{N+1}}{(N+1)!} \le Evo_{\mathbf{f},g}(\mathbf{x},t) \\[3mm] Evo_{\mathbf{f},g}(\mathbf{x},t) \le Evo_{\mathbf{f},g}^N(\mathbf{x},t) + B\dfrac{t^{N+1}}{(N+1)!} \le Evo_{\mathbf{f},g}(\mathbf{x},t) + (B - A)\dfrac{t^{N+1}}{(N+1)!} \end{cases}$$

for all $\mathbf{x} \in \mu(Evo_{\mathbf{f},g}(\cdot,t))$, which means that *1 → 3*.

In a similar way we can prove *2* and *2 → 3*. □

Propositions 4 and 5 can both be used to generate over- (under-, resp.) approximations of evolution functions, and consequently also under- (over-, resp.) approximations of reachable sets. The difference is that Proposition 4 builds first-order approximations over t, while Proposition 5 generates $(N+1)$'st-order ones. In fact, if we can estimate the lower and upper bounds of $\mathcal{M}_N^{\mathbf{f},g}(\mathbf{x})$, we can build over- and under-approximations with any order over t between 1 and N.

Algorithm 1 provides a framework to simultaneously compute over- and under-approximations of evolution functions via their t-expansions for given precision ϵ. It calls **EFOUCore** to process the main computation steps. **SFinder** is an algorithm to find S in both Propositions 4 and 5. **BoundFinder** calculates the minimum(L) and supremum(U) of $\mathcal{M}_N^{\mathbf{f},g}(\mathbf{x})$ in S. Details of implementation are given in Sect. 6.

The implementation differences induced by Propositions 4 and 5 can be found in **TermCri** and **OUBuilder**. **OUBuilder** is to build the term representing over- and under-approximations except for $Evo_{\mathbf{f},g}^N(\mathbf{x},t)$. Outputs of **OUBuilder** are the terms in over- and under-approximations except the truncation part, and are generated according to the results of Propositions 4 and 5. For example, $T_o(t)$ and $T_u(t)$ are of the form $-\frac{Mt}{2T}$ and $\frac{Mt}{2T}$ via Proposition 4. For Proposition 5 the construction of $T_o(t)$ and $T_u(t)$ are similar but more complex since the results rely on N.

TermCri is to decide whether the current $Evo_{\mathbf{f},g}^N(\mathbf{x},t)$ can be modified to approximations satisfying the required precision. For Proposition 4, **TermCri** returns *True* when $\max(|L|,|U|) \le \frac{\epsilon \cdot N!}{2 \cdot T^{N+1}}$ and *False* otherwise. For Proposition 5, **TermCri** returns *True* when $(U - L) \le \frac{\epsilon \cdot (N+1)!}{T^{N+1}}$ and *False* otherwise. Since $(U - L) \le 2 \cdot \max(|L|,|U|)$, we can infer that **TermCri** instantiated with Proposition 5 employs a more relaxed criterion than the one with Proposition 4. Therefore it may generate $Evo_{\mathbf{f},g}^N(\mathbf{x},t)$ with smaller N and find approximations of required precision faster.

5.2   Improvements of EFOU Framework

EFOU framework can be improved in different ways to increase its efficiency. The improved framework **EFOU$^+$** is shown in Algorithm 3, and its improvements are explained in detail as follows.

First, in **EFOU$^+$**, the termination of the algorithm is guaranteed. **EFOU** faces the problem that if T is too large to maintain $Evo_{\mathbf{f},g}^N(\mathbf{x},t)$ converge. In a single iteration, since we limit the maximal expansion time N_{max} and the threshold of time interval T_{min}, the expansion will terminate if the degree of t is greater than N_{max}. If expansion of degree N_{max} is not enough, **EFOU$^+$** uses heuristic strategy to shrink ΔT and try to find solution within corresponding new time interval. Thus all computation is guaranteed to be limited in $\mathcal{C}^-$.

Different from **EFOU**, **EFOU$^+$** divides the time interval $[0,T]$ into K segments and computes piecewise over- and under-approximations of the evolution function. Such division empirically helps **EFOU$^+$** to find approximations of the desired approximation accuracy upon relatively smaller expansion degrees. The outputs of **EFOU$^+$** are built according to the results of all time intervals, i.e. for $t \leq T'$ and $0 \leq i \leq K$, $P_o(\mathbf{x},t) = P_o^i(\mathbf{x},t - T^-(i))$, and $P_u(\mathbf{x},t) = P_o^i(\mathbf{x},t - T^-(i))$, for $t \in [T^-(i), T^+(i)]$, where $T^-(i)$ and $T^+(i)$ are the bound of time interval in the i-th iteration of expansion.

Furthermore, the function **Simp** is called to reduce the scale of expansions. The idea is to separate the command of precision into two parts. One part of precision is designated to limit the error of $Evo_{\mathbf{f},Init}^N(\mathbf{x},t)$, and the remaining should be satisfied when reducing the size of $Evo_{\mathbf{f},Init}^N(\mathbf{x},t)$. The parameter $r \in (0,1]$ is used to control the bound of precision pertaining to the first part.

Another property of the piecewise truncation is used in Algorithm 3, that is, since $Tail_o + Tail_o'(t)$ and $Tail_u + Tail_u'(t)$ are independent on $\mathbf{x}$, only the terms in $Tr(\mathbf{x},t)$ $(= Evo_{\mathbf{f},Init}^N(\mathbf{x},t)$ in each iteration $i)$ affect the performance of **TermCri** in the next iteration. Therefore the over- and under-approximations can be generated in a single sweep. For the same reason, **Simp** for both over- and under-approximations actually returns the same result and can be called only once for simplification for both $P_o^i(\mathbf{x},t)$ and $P_u^i(\mathbf{x},t)$. Besides, since **EFOU$^+$** separates the time interval, **Simp** can reduce a moderate amount of terms in $Evo_{\mathbf{f},Init}^i(\mathbf{x},t)$ to simplify the computation if K is large.

6   Examples and Discussions

6.1   Examples

In the sequel we present selected examples of polynomial systems to demonstrate the performance of **EFOU$^+$**. Please note that the **EFOU$^+$** framework solves not only polynomial systems, but actually any ADS with analytic $\mathbf{f}(\mathbf{x})$ and $g(\mathbf{x})$.

In the examples we show the **Simp** method we use, however, it is tailored towards polynomial systems only. For each term in $Func(\mathbf{x},t)$, i.e., the first input of **Simp**, we rank the monomials with degrees in descending order, find an enclosure for each monomial with an interval in S with interval algorithm,

---

Algorithm 1. EFOU Framework

Input: $\mathbf{f}(\mathbf{x}), g(\mathbf{x}), T, \epsilon, K, r$;
Output: $P_o(\mathbf{x}, t), P_u(\mathbf{x}, t)$.

1: $S := \mathbf{SFinder}(\mathbf{f}, g, T)$;
2: $[Trunc(\mathbf{x}, t), Tail_o(t), Tail_u(t)] := \mathbf{EFOUCore}(\mathbf{f}(\mathbf{x}), g(\mathbf{x}), S, T, \epsilon)$;
3: **return** $Trunc(\mathbf{x}, t) + Tail_o(t), Trunc(\mathbf{x}, t) + Tail_u(t)$.

Algorithm 2. EFOUCore

Input: $\mathbf{f}(\mathbf{x}), g(\mathbf{x}), S, T, \epsilon$;
Output: $Evo_{\mathbf{f}, g}^N(\mathbf{x}, t), Tail_o(t), Tail_u(t)$.

1: $APPR(\mathbf{x}, t) := g(\mathbf{x})$;
2: $N := 0$;
3: $M(\mathbf{x}) := \frac{\partial g(\mathbf{x})}{\partial \mathbf{x}} \cdot \mathbf{f}(\mathbf{x})$;
4: $[L, U] := \mathbf{BoundFinder}(M(\mathbf{x}), S)$;
5: **while not** $\mathbf{TermCri}(L, U, T, N, \epsilon)$ **do**
6:     $APPR(\mathbf{x}, t) := APPR(\mathbf{x}, t) + \frac{(-t)^{N+1}}{(N+1)!} M(\mathbf{x})$;
7:     $N := N + 1$;
8:     $M(\mathbf{x}) := \frac{\partial M(\mathbf{x})}{\partial \mathbf{x}} \cdot \mathbf{f}(\mathbf{x})$;
9:     $[L, U] := \mathbf{BoundFinder}(M(\mathbf{x}), R)$;
10: $[T_o(t), T_u(t)] := \mathbf{OUBuilder}(L, U, N)$;
11: **return** $APPR(\mathbf{x}, t), T_o(t), T_u(t)$.

Algorithm 3. EFOU$^+$ Framework

Input: $\mathbf{f}(\mathbf{x}), g(\mathbf{x}), T, T_{min}, N_{max}, \epsilon, K, r$;
Output: $P_o(\mathbf{x}, t), P_u(\mathbf{x}, t), T'$.

1: Initialize $\Delta T := T/K$, $\Delta \epsilon := \epsilon/K$, $Init(\mathbf{x}) := g(\mathbf{x})$, $Tail_o := 0$, $Tail_u := 0$;
2: $i := 1$;
3: **while** $i \leq K$ **do**
4:     $S := \mathbf{SFinder}(\mathbf{f}(\mathbf{x}), Init(\mathbf{x}), \Delta T)$;
5:     $[Tr(\mathbf{x}, t), Tail_o'(t), Tail_u'(t)] := \mathbf{EFOUCore}^+(\mathbf{f}(\mathbf{x}), Init(\mathbf{x}), S, \Delta T, N_{max}, r\Delta\epsilon)$;
6:     **while** $Tr(\mathbf{x}, t) = 0$ **and** $\frac{\Delta T}{2} \geq T_{min}$ **do**
7:       Set $\Delta T := \frac{\Delta T}{2}$, compute corresponding K and $\Delta \epsilon$;
8:       $[Tr(\mathbf{x}, t), Tail_o'(t), Tail_u'(t)] := \mathbf{EFOUCore}^+(\mathbf{f}(\mathbf{x}), Init(\mathbf{x}), S, \Delta T, N_{max}, r\Delta\epsilon)$;
9:     **if** $Tr(\mathbf{x}, t) = 0$ **and** $\frac{\Delta T}{2} \leq T_{min}$ **then**
10:       Construct $P_o(\mathbf{x}, t)$ and $P_u(\mathbf{x}, t)$ from all $P_o^j(\mathbf{x}, t)$ and $P_u^j(\mathbf{x}, t), 1 \leq j \leq i$;
11:       Compute the corresponding time T';
12:       **return** $P_o(\mathbf{x}, t), P_u(\mathbf{x}, t), T'$.
13:     $Tr(\mathbf{x}, t) := \mathbf{Simp}(Tr(\mathbf{x}, t), S, \Delta T, \frac{(1-r)\Delta\epsilon}{2})$;
14:     $P_o^i(\mathbf{x}, t) := Tr(\mathbf{x}, t) + Tail_o - \frac{(1-r)\Delta\epsilon}{2} + Tail_o'(t)$;
15:     $P_u^i(\mathbf{x}, t) := Tr(\mathbf{x}, t) + Tail_u + \frac{(1-r)\Delta\epsilon}{2} + Tail_u'(t)$;
16:     $Tail_o := Tail_o + Tail_o'(\Delta T)$;
17:     $Tail_u := Tail_u + Tail_u'(\Delta T)$;
18:     $Init(\mathbf{x}) := Tr(\mathbf{x}, \Delta T)$ and $i := i + 1$;
19: Construct $P_o(\mathbf{x}, t)$ and $P_u(\mathbf{x}, t)$ from all $P_o^i(\mathbf{x}, t)$ and $P_u^i(\mathbf{x}, t)$;
20: **return** $P_o(\mathbf{x}, t), P_u(\mathbf{x}, t), T$.

Algorithm 4. Simp

Input: $Func(\mathbf{x}, t), S, T, \epsilon$;
Output: $SimpFunc(\mathbf{x}, t)$.

1: Gather some monomials in $Func(\mathbf{x}, t)$ whose sum will not exceed ϵ over $S \times [0, T]$ and restore the sum in $R(\mathbf{x}, t)$;
2: $SimpFunc(\mathbf{x}, t) := Func(\mathbf{x}, t) - R(\mathbf{x}, t)$;
3: **return** $SimpFunc(\mathbf{x}, t)$.

Algorithm 5. EFOUCore$^+$

Input: $\mathbf{f}(\mathbf{x}), g(\mathbf{x}), S, T, N_{max}, \epsilon$;
Output: $Evo_{f,g}^{N}(\mathbf{x}, t), Tail_o(t), Tail_u(t)$.

1: Initialize $APPR(\mathbf{x}, t) := g(\mathbf{x})$, $N := 0$ and $M(\mathbf{x}) := \frac{\partial g(\mathbf{x})}{\partial \mathbf{x}} \cdot \mathbf{f}(\mathbf{x})$;
2: $[L, U] :=$ **BoundFinder**$(M(\mathbf{x}), S)$;
3: **while not TermCri**(L, U, T, N, ϵ) **and** $N \leq N_{max}$ **do**
4:     $APPR(\mathbf{x}, t) := APPR(\mathbf{x}, t) + \frac{(-t)^{N+1}}{(N+1)!} M(\mathbf{x})$;
5:     $N := N + 1$;
6:     $M(\mathbf{x}) := \frac{\partial M(\mathbf{x})}{\partial \mathbf{x}} \cdot \mathbf{f}(\mathbf{x})$;
7:     $[L, U] :=$ **BoundFinder**$(M(\mathbf{x}), S)$;
8: $[T_o(t), T_u(t)] :=$ **OUBuilder**(L, U, N);
9: **if not TermCri**$(L, U, T, N - 1, \epsilon)$ **then**
10:     **return** $0, T_o(t), T_u(t)$;
11: **return** $APPR(\mathbf{x}, t), T_o(t), T_u(t)$.

---

and compute the length for each interval. Then, with the same order, we gather the terms until the sum of lengths of the collected terms exceeds the bound.

In **SFinder**, we here use the same strategy as VNODE-LP [8] to compute S. In **TermCri**, we use a **Matlab** tool *DIRECT* [20] to compute L and U. *DIRECT* is a global extremum optimizer developed by Donald R. Jones. It can be utilized to solve optimization problem with constraints and rectangular bounds on variables for systems with Lipschitz constraints. Here we use its function to compute global minima and maxima of functions within rectangular bounds, and output the results as L and U respectively.

Example 1. Consider the Van der Pol system

$$\mathbf{f}(x, y) = \begin{cases} \dot{x} = y \\ \dot{y} = \frac{1}{2}(1 - x^2)y - x \end{cases}$$

and initial states $\mu(g(x, y))$ where $g(x, y) = (x+1)^2 + (y-3)^2 - 0.1^2$. We compute an over- and an under-approximation of reachable sets $Reach_{f,g}^{t}$ with $t \in [0, 1]$. The initial length of the time interval is 0.05 and the initial precision for each computation is 5×10^{-4}. We use $N_{max} = 10$ and $T_{min} = 0.01$. The results are shown in Fig. 1. The blue/red/black lines represent over-/under-/simulated approximations, resp., and the simulation results are generated by *RK4*. The

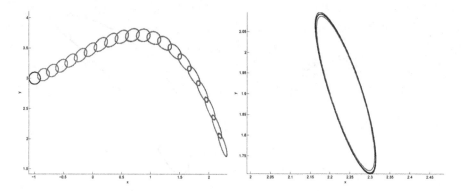

Fig. 1. Results for Example 1. (Color figure online)

left sub-figure in Fig. 1 shows the results for $t = 0.1k, k = 1, ..., 10$, and the right one shows a zoom-in view for $t = 1$.

Example 2. We consider the ADS

$$\mathbf{f}(x, y) = \begin{cases} \dot{x} = \frac{1}{2}xy - 3y \\ \dot{y} = -\frac{2}{5}x^2 + 2y \end{cases}$$

and initial states $\mu(g(x, y))$ where $g(x, y) = (x-1)^2 + (y-1)^2 - 0.2^2$. We compute an over- and an under-approximation of reachable sets $Reach_{\mathbf{f},g}^t$ with $t \in [0, 0.9]$. The initial length of the time interval is 5×10^{-4} and the initial precision for each computation is 2×10^{-5}. We use $N_{max} = 10$ and $T_{min} = 10^{-4}$. The results are shown in Fig. 2. The blue/red/black lines represent over-/under-/simulated approximations, resp., and the simulation results are generated by $RK4$. The left sub-figure in Fig. 2 shows the results for $t = 0.1k, k = 1, ..., 9$, and the right one shows a zoom-in view for $t = 0.9$.

Example 3. We consider the ADS in [36]

$$\mathbf{f}(x, y) = \begin{cases} \dot{x} = y \\ \dot{y} = \frac{x}{5} + y - \frac{x^2 y}{5} \end{cases}$$

and initial states $\mu(g(x, y))$ where $g(x, y) = x^2 + y^2 - 0.2^2$. We compute an over- and an under-approximation of reachable sets $Reach_{\mathbf{f},g}^t$ with $t \in [0, 2]$. The Initial length of the time interval is 5×10^{-3} and the initial precision for each computation is 5×10^{-3}. We use $N_{max} = 10$ and $T_{min} = 10^{-3}$. The results are shown in Fig. 3. The blue/red/black lines represent over-/under-/simulated approximations, resp., and the simulation results are generated by $RK4$. The left sub-figure in Fig. 3 shows the results for $t = 1$ and $t = 2$, and the right one shows a zoom-in view of top-right part of the left sub-figure for $t = 2$.

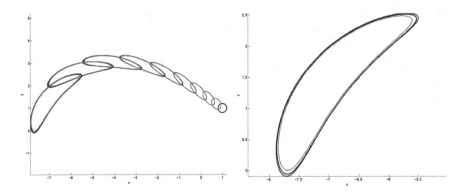

Fig. 2. Results for Example 2. (Color figure online)

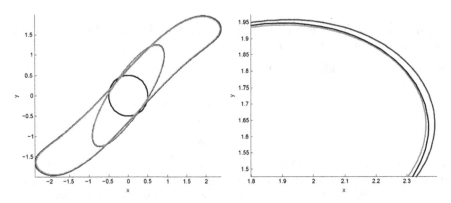

Fig. 3. Results for Example 3. (Color figure online)

6.2   Discussions

In the examples, we can see that the final results are close to the real reachable sets indicated by simulation sample. In all examples we have set the precisions rather strict, nevertheless **EFOU**$^+$ automatically computed matching results.

However, **EFOU**$^+$ does not scale well for nonlinear polynomial systems featuring high polynomial degrees. When the t-expansion continues, the number of terms in $\mathcal{M}_i^{f,g}(\mathbf{x})$ increases accordingly. *DIRECT* therefore needs correspondingly more time and computational resource to find solutions of the desired accuracy.

7   Conclusion

In this paper, we have exposed a novel method based on the well-known Hamilton-Jacobi framework. Our method is to compute over- and under-approximations of reachable sets for autonomous dynamical systems. By not relying on any manually chosen templates and instead fitting a generally convergent scheme, the method constitutes considerable progress with regard to automatic construction of over- and under-approximations of the reachable statespace up to any designated precision. Such general convergence is obtained based on adequate truncations of the expansion of the evolution function. We have confirmed the efficacy of our method as well as the precision of the enclosures obtained by comparing our benchmark results to simulations.

For future work, we will extend our current implementation of the **EFOU$^+$** framework by generalizing it to non-polynomial ADS and integrating other efficient global extremum optimizers. Also, we will explore other applications of t-expansions of the evolution function in the fields of system falsification, control synthesis, and oscillation exclusion of ADS.

References

1. Althoff, M.: Reachability analysis of nonlinear systems using conservative polynomialization and non-convex sets. In: Belta, C., Ivancic, F. (eds.) Proceedings of the 16th International Conference on Hybrid Systems: Computation and Control, HSCC 2013, Philadelphia, PA, USA, 8–11 April 2013, pp. 173–182. ACM (2013)
2. Althoff, M., Stursberg, O., Buss, M.: Reachability analysis of nonlinear systems with uncertain parameters using conservative linearization. In: Proceedings of the 47th IEEE Conference on Decision and Control, CDC 2008, Cancún, México, 9–11 December 2008, pp. 4042–4048. IEEE (2008)
3. Anai, H., Weispfenning, V.: Reach set computations using real quantifier elimination. In: Di Benedetto, M.D., Sangiovanni-Vincentelli, A. (eds.) HSCC 2001. LNCS, vol. 2034, pp. 63–76. Springer, Heidelberg (2001). https://doi.org/10.1007/3-540-45351-2_9
4. Chen, X., Ábrahám, E., Sankaranarayanan, S.: Taylor model flowpipe construction for non-linear hybrid systems. In: Proceedings of the 33rd IEEE Real-Time Systems Symposium, RTSS 2012, San Juan, PR, USA, 4–7 December 2012, pp. 183–192. IEEE Computer Society (2012)
5. Chen, X., Sankaranarayanan, S., Ábrahám, E.: Under-approximate flowpipes for non-linear continuous systems. In: Formal Methods in Computer-Aided Design, FMCAD 2014, Lausanne, Switzerland, 21–24 October 2014, pp. 59–66. IEEE (2014)
6. Dreossi, T., Dang, T., Piazza, C.: Parallelotope bundles for polynomial reachability. In: Abate, A., Fainekos, G.E. (eds.) Proceedings of the 19th International Conference on Hybrid Systems: Computation and Control, HSCC 2016, Vienna, Austria, 12–14 April 2016, pp. 297–306. ACM (2016)
7. Duggirala, P.S., Mitra, S., Viswanathan, M.: Verification of annotated models from executions. In: Proceedings of the International Conference on Embedded Software, EMSOFT 2013, Montreal, QC, Canada, 29 September–4 October 2013, pp. 26:1–26:10. IEEE (2013)
8. Eggers, A., Ramdani, N., Nedialkov, N., Fränzle, M.: Improving SAT modulo ODE for hybrid systems analysis by combining different enclosure methods. In: Barthe, G., Pardo, A., Schneider, G. (eds.) SEFM 2011. LNCS, vol. 7041, pp. 172–187. Springer, Heidelberg (2011). https://doi.org/10.1007/978-3-642-24690-6_13

9. Fan, C., Qi, B., Mitra, S., Viswanathan, M., Duggirala, P.S.: Automatic reachability analysis for nonlinear hybrid models with C2E2. In: Chaudhuri, S., Farzan, A. (eds.) CAV 2016. LNCS, vol. 9779, pp. 531–538. Springer, Cham (2016). https://doi.org/10.1007/978-3-319-41528-4_29

10. Frehse, G., Bogomolov, S., Greitschus, M., Strump, T., Podelski, A.: Eliminating spurious transitions in reachability with support functions. In: Girard, A., Sankaranarayanan, S. (eds.) Proceedings of the 18th International Conference on Hybrid Systems: Computation and Control, HSCC 2015, Seattle, WA, USA, 14–16 April 2015, pp. 149–158. ACM (2015)

11. Frehse, G., et al.: SpaceEx: scalable verification of hybrid systems. In: Gopalakrishnan, G., Qadeer, S. (eds.) CAV 2011. LNCS, vol. 6806, pp. 379–395. Springer, Heidelberg (2011). https://doi.org/10.1007/978-3-642-22110-1_30

12. Frehse, G., Kateja, R., Le Guernic, C.: Flowpipe approximation and clustering in space-time. In: Proceedings of the 16th International Conference on Hybrid Systems: Computation and Control, HSCC 2013, pp. 203–212. ACM, New York (2013)

13. Girard, A., Le Guernic, C., Maler, O.: Efficient computation of reachable sets of linear time-invariant systems with inputs. In: Hespanha, J.P., Tiwari, A. (eds.) HSCC 2006. LNCS, vol. 3927, pp. 257–271. Springer, Heidelberg (2006). https://doi.org/10.1007/11730637_21

14. Girard, A., Pappas, G.J.: Verification using simulation. In: Hespanha, J.P., Tiwari, A. (eds.) HSCC 2006. LNCS, vol. 3927, pp. 272–286. Springer, Heidelberg (2006). https://doi.org/10.1007/11730637_22

15. Goubault, E., Mullier, O., Putot, S., Kieffer, M.: Inner approximated reachability analysis. In: Fränzle, M., Lygeros, J. (eds.) 17th International Conference on Hybrid Systems: Computation and Control (part of CPS Week), HSCC 2014, Berlin, Germany, 15–17 April 2014, pp. 163–172. ACM (2014)

16. Le Guernic, C., Girard, A.: Reachability analysis of hybrid systems using support functions. In: Bouajjani, A., Maler, O. (eds.) CAV 2009. LNCS, vol. 5643, pp. 540–554. Springer, Heidelberg (2009). https://doi.org/10.1007/978-3-642-02658-4_40

17. Hamadeh, A.O., Goncalves, J.M.: Reachability analysis of continuous-time piecewise affine systems. Automatica 44(12), 3189–3194 (2008)

18. Huang, Z., Mitra, S.: Computing bounded reach sets from sampled simulation traces. In: Dang, T., Mitchell, I.M. (eds.) Hybrid Systems: Computation and Control (part of CPS Week 2012), HSCC 2012, Beijing, China, 17–19 April 2012, pp. 291–294. ACM (2012)

19. Isidori, A., Byrnes, C.I.: Output regulation of nonlinear systems. IEEE Trans. Autom. Control 35(2), 131–140 (1990)

20. Jones, D.R.: Direct global optimization algorithm. In: Floudas, C.A., Pardalos, P.M. (eds.) Encyclopedia of Optimization, 2nd edn, pp. 725–735. Springer, Boston (2009). https://doi.org/10.1007/978-0-387-74759-0

21. Korda, M., Henrion, D., Jones, C.N.: Inner approximations of the region of attraction for polynomial dynamical systems. In: Tarbouriech, S., Krstic, M. (eds.) 9th IFAC Symposium on Nonlinear Control Systems, NOLCOS 2013, Toulouse, France, 4–6 September 2013, pp. 534–539. International Federation of Automatic Control (2013)

22. Kurzhanski, A.B., Varaiya, P.: On ellipsoidal techniques for reachability analysis. Part II: internal approximations box-valued constraints. Optim. Methods Softw. 17(2), 207–237 (2002)

23. Lal, R., Prabhakar, P.: Bounded error flowpipe computation of parameterized linear systems. In: Girault, A., Guan, N. (eds.) 2015 International Conference on Embedded Software, EMSOFT 2015, Amsterdam, Netherlands, 4–9 October 2015, pp. 237–246. IEEE (2015)

24. Lhommeau, M., Jaulin, L., Hardouin, L.: Inner and outer approximation of capture basin using interval analysis. In: Zaytoon, J., Ferrier, J., Andrade-Cetto, J., Filipe, J. (eds.) Proceedings of the Fourth International Conference on Informatics in Control, Automation and Robotics, Signal Processing, Systems Modeling and Control, ICINCO 2007, Angers, France, 9–12 May 2007, pp. 5–9. INSTICC Press (2007)

25. Maidens, J.N., Kaynama, S., Mitchell, I.M., Oishi, M.M.K., Dumont, G.A.: Lagrangian methods for approximating the viability kernel in high-dimensional systems. Automatica 49(7), 2017–2029 (2013)

26. Mitchell, I.M.: The flexible, extensible and efficient toolbox of level set methods. J. Sci. Comput. 35(2), 300–329 (2008)

27. Mitsch, S., Ghorbal, K., Vogelbacher, D., Platzer, A.: Formal verification of obstacle avoidance and navigation of ground robots. CoRR, abs/1605.00604 (2016)

28. Nghiem, T., Sankaranarayanan, S., Fainekos, G.E., Ivancic, F., Gupta, A., Pappas, G.J.: Monte-carlo techniques for falsification of temporal properties of non-linear hybrid systems. In: Johansson, K.H., Yi, W. (eds.) Proceedings of the 13th ACM International Conference on Hybrid Systems: Computation and Control, HSCC 2010, Stockholm, Sweden, 12–15 April 2010, pp. 211–220. ACM (2010)

29. Plaku, E., Kavraki, L.E., Vardi, M.Y.: Hybrid systems: from verification to falsification. In: Damm, W., Hermanns, H. (eds.) CAV 2007. LNCS, vol. 4590, pp. 463–476. Springer, Heidelberg (2007). https://doi.org/10.1007/978-3-540-73368-3_48

30. Prabhakar, P., Duggirala, P.S., Mitra, S., Viswanathan, M.: Hybrid automata-based CEGAR for rectangular hybrid systems. Formal Methods Syst. Des. 46(2), 105–134 (2015)

31. Prajna, S., Jadbabaie, A.: Safety verification of hybrid systems using barrier certificates. In: Alur, R., Pappas, G.J. (eds.) HSCC 2004. LNCS, vol. 2993, pp. 477–492. Springer, Heidelberg (2004). https://doi.org/10.1007/978-3-540-24743-2_32

32. Ratschan, S., She, Z.: Safety verification of hybrid systems by constraint propagation-based abstraction refinement. ACM Trans. Embedded Comput. Syst. 6(1), 1–23 (2007). Article No. 8

33. Sankaranarayanan, S.: Automatic abstraction of non-linear systems using change of bases transformations. In: Caccamo, M., Frazzoli, E., Grosu, R. (eds.) Proceedings of the 14th ACM International Conference on Hybrid Systems: Computation and Control, HSCC 2011, Chicago, IL, USA, 12–14 April 2011, pp. 143–152. ACM (2011)

34. Tiwari, A., Khanna, G.: Nonlinear systems: approximating reach sets. In: Alur, R., Pappas, G.J. (eds.) HSCC 2004. LNCS, vol. 2993, pp. 600–614. Springer, Heidelberg (2004). https://doi.org/10.1007/978-3-540-24743-2_40

35. Wang, T.C., Lall, S., West, M.: Polynomial level-set method for polynomial system reachable set estimation. IEEE Trans. Autom. Control 58(10), 2508–2521 (2013)

36. Xue, B., Fränzle, M., Zhan, N.: Under-approximating reach sets for polynomial continuous systems. In: Proceedings of the 21st International Conference on Hybrid Systems: Computation and Control (Part of CPS Week), HSCC 2018, pp. 51–60. ACM, New York (2018)
37. Xue, B., She, Z., Easwaran, A.: Under-approximating backward reachable sets by polytopes. In: Chaudhuri, S., Farzan, A. (eds.) CAV 2016. LNCS, vol. 9779, pp. 457–476. Springer, Cham (2016). https://doi.org/10.1007/978-3-319-41528-4_25

Tropical Abstractions of Max-Plus Linear Systems

Muhammad Syifa'ul Mufid[1]([✉]), Dieky Adzkiya[2], and Alessandro Abate[1]

[1] Department of Computer Science, University of Oxford, Oxford, UK
{muhammad.syifaul.mufid,alessandro.abate}@cs.ox.ac.uk
[2] Department of Mathematics, Institut Teknologi Sepuluh Nopember,
Surabaya, Indonesia
dieky@matematika.its.ac.id

Abstract. This paper describes the development of finite abstractions of Max-Plus-Linear (MPL) systems using tropical operations. The idea of tropical abstraction is inspired by the fact that an MPL system is a discrete-event model updating its state with operations in the tropical algebra. The abstract model is a finite-state transition system: we show that the abstract states can be generated by operations on the tropical algebra, and that the generation of transitions can be established by tropical multiplications of matrices. The complexity of the algorithms based on tropical algebra is discussed and their performance is tested on a numerical benchmark against an existing alternative abstraction approach.

Keywords: MPL system · Tropical algebra · Definite form
Difference-bound matrix · Abstraction · Reachability

1 Introduction

Tropical mathematics has been a rapidly growing subject since it was firstly introduced [15]. It has branches in mathematical fields such as tropical geometry [11] and tropical algebra [15]. The latter denotes an algebraic structure that uses max or min for addition and + for multiplication, respectively - hence, it is well known as max-plus or min-plus algebra. In this paper, we use the former operation to define the tropical algebra.

A class of discrete-event system (DES) based on tropical algebra is the Max-Plus-Linear (MPL) one [5]. Models of MPL systems involve tropical operations, namely max and +. The state space of these models represents the timing of events that are synchronised over the max-plus algebra. This means that the next event will occur right after the last of the previous events has finished.

The connections between max-plus algebra and timed systems have been explored in the recent past. First, the dynamics of timed event graphs (a special case of timed Petri nets where all places have exactly one upstream and one

© Springer Nature Switzerland AG 2018
D. N. Jansen and P. Prabhakar (Eds.): FORMATS 2018, LNCS 11022, pp. 271–287, 2018.
https://doi.org/10.1007/978-3-030-00151-3_16

downstream transition) can be expressed via MPL systems [5,10]. Second, max-plus polyhedra can be used as data structures in reachability analysis of timed automata [12]: such data structures display a similarity with Difference-Bound Matrices (DBMs) [7].

Finite abstractions of MPL system have been firstly introduced in [3]. These abstraction procedures start by transforming a given MPL system into a Piece-Wise Affine (PWA) model [9]. The PWA model is characterised by several domains (PWA regions) and the corresponding affine dynamics. The resulting abstract states are the partitions corresponding to the PWA regions. Finally, the transition relation between pairs of abstract states depends on the trajectory of the original MPL system. This abstraction technique enables one to perform model checking over an MPL system; one of the applications is safety analysis [3]. Interested readers are referred to [1,3,4] and the VeriSiMPL toolbox [2].

This paper introduces the idea of Tropical Abstractions of MPL systems. The approach is inspired by the fact that an MPL system is a DES that is natively updated via tropical operations. We will show that the abstraction of MPL systems can be established by tropical operations and with algorithms exclusively based on tropical algebra. We argue by experiments that this has clear computational benefits on existing abstraction techniques.

The paper is outlined as follows. Section 2 is divided into three parts. The first part explains the basic of MPL systems including the properties of its state matrix. We introduce the notion of region matrix and of its conjugate, which play a significant role in the abstraction procedures. The notion of definite form and its generalisation are explained in the second part. Finally, we introduce a new definition of DBM as a tropical matrix.

Equipped with these notions, all algorithms of the tropical abstraction procedure are explained in Sect. 3, which contains the novel contributions of this paper. The comparison of the algorithms performance against the state of the art is presented in Sect. 4. The paper is concluded with Sect. 5. The proofs of the propositions are contained in an extended version of this paper [13].

2   Models and Preliminaries

2.1   Max-Plus-Linear Systems

In tropical algebra, $\mathbb{R}_{\max}$ is defined as $\mathbb{R} \cup \{-\infty\}$. This set is equipped with two binary operations, $\oplus$ and $\otimes$, where

$$a \oplus b := \max\{a, b\} \quad \text{and} \quad a \otimes b := a + b,$$

for all $a, b \in \mathbb{R}_{\max}$. The algebraic structure $(\mathbb{R}_{\max}, \oplus, \otimes)$ is a semiring with $\varepsilon := -\infty$ and $e := 0$ as the null and unit element, respectively [5].

The notation $\mathbb{R}_{\max}^{m \times n}$ represents the set of $m \times n$ tropical matrices whose elements are in $\mathbb{R}_{\max}$. Tropical operations can be extended to matrices as follows. If $A, B \in \mathbb{R}_{\max}^{m \times n}, C \in \mathbb{R}_{\max}^{n \times p}$ then

$$[A \oplus B](i,j) = A(i,j) \oplus B(i,j) \text{ and } [A \otimes C](i,j) = \bigoplus_{k=1}^{n} A(i,k) \otimes C(k,j)$$

for all i, j in the corresponding dimension.

Given a natural number m, the tropical power of $A \in \mathbb{R}_{\max}^{n \times n}$ is denoted by $A^{\otimes m}$ and corresponds to $A \otimes \ldots \otimes A$ (m times). As we find in standard algebra, the zero power $A^{\otimes 0}$ is an $n \times n$ identity matrix I_n, where all diagonals and non-diagonals are e and ε, respectively.

An (autonomous) MPL system is defined as

$$x(k + 1) = A \otimes x(k), \tag{1}$$

where $A \in \mathbb{R}_{\max}^{n \times n}$ is the matrix system and $x(k) = [x_1(k) \ldots x_n(k)]^\top$ is the state variables [5]. Traditionally, x represents the time stamps of the discrete-events, while k corresponds to an event counter.

Definition 1 (Precedence Graph [5]). *The precedence graph of A, denoted by $\mathcal{G}(A)$, is a weighted directed graph with nodes $1, \ldots, n$ and an edge from j to i with weight $A(i, j)$ if $A(i, j) \neq \varepsilon$.*

Definition 2 (Regular (Row-Finite) Matrix [10]). *A matrix $A \in \mathbb{R}_{\max}^{n \times n}$ is called regular (or row-finite) if there is at least one finite element in each row.*

The following notations deal with a row-finite matrix $A \in \mathbb{R}_{\max}^{n \times n}$. The coefficient $g = (g_1, \ldots, g_n) \in \{1, \ldots, n\}^n$ is called *finite coefficient* iff $A(i, g_i) \neq \varepsilon$ for all $1 \leq i \leq n$. We define the *region matrix* of A w.r.t. the finite coefficient g as

$$A_g(i, j) = \begin{cases} A(i, j), & \text{if } g_i = j \\ \varepsilon, & \text{otherwise.} \end{cases} \tag{2}$$

One can say that A_g is a matrix that keeps the finite elements of A indexed by g. The *conjugate* of A is A^c, where

$$A^c(i, j) = \begin{cases} -A(j, i), & \text{if } A(j, i) \neq \varepsilon \\ \varepsilon, & \text{otherwise.} \end{cases} \tag{3}$$

2.2 Definite Forms of Tropical Matrices

The concept of *definite form* over a tropical matrix was firstly introduced in [17]. Consider a given $A \in \mathbb{R}_{\max}^{n \times n}$ and let α be one of the maximal permutations[1] of A. The definite form of A w.r.t. α is $\overline{A}_\alpha$, where

$$\overline{A}_\alpha(i, j) = A(i, \alpha(j)) \otimes A(j, \alpha(j))^{\otimes -1} = A(i, \alpha(j)) - A(j, \alpha(j)). \tag{4}$$

In this paper, we allow for a generalisation of the notion of definite form. We generate the definite form from the finite coefficients introduced above. Notice that the maximal permutation is a special case of finite coefficient $g = (g_1, \ldots, g_n)$ when all g_i are different. Intuitively, the definite form over a finite coefficient g is established by; (1) column arrangement of A using g i.e.

---

[1] A permutation α is called maximal if $\bigotimes_{i=1}^n A(i, \alpha(i)) = \text{per}(A)$, where $\text{per}(A)$ is the permanent of A [6, 17].

$B(\cdot, j) = A(\cdot, g_j)$ and then (2) subtracting each column by the corresponding diagonal element i.e. $\overline{A}_g(\cdot, j) = B(\cdot, j) - B(j, j)$ for all $j \in \{1, \ldots, n\}$.

Furthermore, we define two types of definite forms. We call the definite form introduced in [17] to be a *column-definite* form. We define as an additional form the *row-definite* form $_g\overline{A}$. The latter form is similar to the former, except that now the row arrangement is used, namely $B(g_i, \cdot) = A(i, \cdot)$ for all $i \in \{1, \ldots, n\}$. Notice that, in a row arrangement, one could find two or more different rows of A are moved into the same row at B. As a consequence, some rows of B remain empty. In these cases, ε is used to fill the empty rows. For rows with multiple entries, we take the maximum point-wise after subtracting by the corresponding diagonal element.

Example 1. Consider a tropical matrix

$$A = \begin{bmatrix} \varepsilon & 1 & 3 \\ 5 & \varepsilon & 4 \\ 7 & 8 & \varepsilon \end{bmatrix}.$$

and a finite coefficient $g = (2, 1, 1)$. The row-definite form for g is

$$A = \begin{bmatrix} \varepsilon & ① & 3 \\ ⑤ & \varepsilon & 4 \\ ⑦ & 8 & \varepsilon \end{bmatrix} \dashrightarrow \begin{bmatrix} 5 & \varepsilon & 4 \\ 7 & 8 & \varepsilon \\ \varepsilon & 1 & 3 \\ \varepsilon & \varepsilon & \varepsilon \end{bmatrix} \dashrightarrow \begin{bmatrix} 0 & \varepsilon & -1 \\ 0 & 1 & \varepsilon \\ \varepsilon & 0 & 2 \\ \varepsilon & \varepsilon & \varepsilon \end{bmatrix} \dashrightarrow {}_g\overline{A} = \begin{bmatrix} 0 & 1 & -1 \\ \varepsilon & 0 & 2 \\ \varepsilon & \varepsilon & \varepsilon \end{bmatrix}.$$

On the other hand, the column-definite form w.r.t. g is

$$A = \begin{bmatrix} \varepsilon & ① & 3 \\ ⑤ & \varepsilon & 4 \\ ⑦ & 8 & \varepsilon \end{bmatrix} \dashrightarrow \begin{bmatrix} 1 & \varepsilon & \varepsilon \\ \varepsilon & 5 & 5 \\ 8 & 7 & 7 \end{bmatrix} \dashrightarrow \overline{A}_g = \begin{bmatrix} 0 & \varepsilon & \varepsilon \\ \varepsilon & 0 & -2 \\ 7 & 2 & 0 \end{bmatrix}.$$

Notice that, the elements at the 3rd row of $_g\overline{A}$ are all ε. □

The generation of definite forms is formulated as tropical operations as follows:

Proposition 1. *The column-definite and row-definite form of $A \in \mathbb{R}_{\max}^{n \times n}$ w.r.t. a finite coefficient g are $\overline{A}_g = A \otimes A_g^c$ and $_g\overline{A} = A_g^c \otimes A$, respectively.* □

2.3 Difference Bound Matrices as Tropical Matrices

Definition 3 (Difference Bound Matrices). *A DBM in $\mathbb{R}^n$ is the intersection of sets defined by $x_i - x_j \sim_{i,j} d_{i,j}$, where $\sim_{i,j} \in \{>, \geq\}$ and $d_{i,j} \in \mathbb{R} \cup \{-\infty\}$ for $0 \leq i, j \leq n$. The variable x_0 is set to be equal to 0.* □

The dummy variable x_0 is used to allow for the single-variable relation $x_i \sim c$, which can be written as $x_i - x_0 \sim c$. Definition 3 slightly differs from [7] as we use operators $\{>, \geq\}$ instead of $\{<, \leq\}$. The reason for this alteration is to transfer DBMs into the tropical domain.

A DBM in $\mathbb{R}^n$ can be expressed as a pair of matrices (D, S). The element $D(i, j)$ stores the bound variable $d_{i,j}$, while S represents the *sign matrix* of the operator i.e. $S(i, j) = 1$ if $\sim_{i,j}\ =\ \geq$ and 0 otherwise. In case of $i = j$, it is more convenient to put $D(i, i) = 0$ and $S(i, i) = 1$, as it corresponds to $x_i - x_i \geq 0$.

Under Definition 3, each DBM D in $\mathbb{R}^n$ is an $(n + 1)$-dimensional tropical matrix. Throughout this paper, we may not include the sign matrix whenever recalling a DBM. Operations and properties in tropical algebra can be used for DBM operations such as intersection, computation of the canonical-form, and emptiness checking. Such DBM operations are key for developing abstraction procedures.

Proposition 2. *The intersection of DBM D_1 and D_2 is equal to $D_1 \oplus D_2$.* $\square$

The sign matrix for $D_1 \oplus D_2$ is determined separately as it depends on the operator of the tighter bound. More precisely, suppose that S_1, S_2 and S are the sign matrices of D_1, D_2 and of $D_1 \oplus D_2$ respectively, then

$$S(i, j) = \begin{cases} S_1(i, j), & \text{if } D_1(i, j) > D_2(i, j) \\ S_2(i, j), & \text{if } D_1(i, j) < D_2(i, j) \\ \min\{S_1(i, j), S_2(i, j)\}, & \text{if } D_1(i, j) = D_2(i, j). \end{cases}$$

Any DBM admits a graphical representation, the potential graph, by interpreting the DBM as a weighted directed graph [14]. Because each DBM is also a tropical matrix, the potential graph of D can be viewed as $\mathcal{G}(D)$.

The canonical-form of a DBM D, denoted as $\mathsf{cf}(D)$, is a DBM with the tightest possible bounds [7]. The advantage of the canonical-form representation is that emptiness checking can be evaluated very efficiently. Indeed, for a canonical DBM (D, S), if there exist $0 \leq i \leq n$ such that $D(i, i) > 0$ or $S(i, i) = 0$ then the DBM corresponds to an empty set. Computing $\mathsf{cf}(D)$ is done by the all-pairs shortest path (APSP) problem over the corresponding potential graph [7,14]. (As we alter the definition of the DBM, it is now equal to all-pairs longest path (APLP) problem). One of the prominent algorithms is Floyd-Warshall [8] which has a cubic complexity w.r.t. its dimension.

On the other hand, in tropical algebra sense, $[D^{\otimes m}](i, j)$ corresponds to the maximal total weights of a path with length m from j to i in $\mathcal{G}(D)$. Furthermore, $[\bigoplus_{m=0}^{n+1} D^{\otimes m}](i, j)$ is equal to the maximal total weights of a path from j to i. Thus, $\bigoplus_{m=0}^{n+1} D^{\otimes m}$ is indeed the solution of APLP problem. Proposition 3 provides an alternative computation of the canonical form of a DBM D based on tropical algebra. Proposition 4 relates non-empty canonical DBMs with the notion of definite matrix. A tropical matrix A is called definite if $\mathrm{per}(A) = 0$ and all diagonal elements of A are zero [6].

Proposition 3. *Given a DBM D, the canonical form of D is $\mathsf{cf}(D) = \bigoplus_{m=0}^{n+1} D^{\otimes m}$, where n is the number of variables excluding x_0.* $\square$

Proposition 4. *Suppose D is a canonical DBM. If D is not empty then it is definite.* $\square$

3 MPL Abstractions Using Tropical Operations

3.1 Related Work

The notion of abstraction of an MPL system has been first discussed in [3]. The procedure starts by transforming the MPL system characterised by $A \in \mathbb{R}_{\max}^{n \times n}$ into a PWA system [3, Algorithm 2], and then considering the partitions associated to the obtained PWA system [3, Algorithm 6]. The abstract states associated to the partitions are represented by DBMs. The transitions are then generated using one-step forward-reachability analysis [3]: first, the image of each abstract state w.r.t. the MPL system is computed; then, each image is intersected with partitions associated to other abstract states; finally, transition relations are defined for each non-empty intersection. This procedure is summarised in [3, Algorithm 7].

The computation of image and of inverse image of a DBM is described in [1]. These computations are used to perform forward and backward reachability analysis, respectively. The worst-case complexity of both procedures is $O(n^3)$, where n is the number of variables in D excluding x_0. A more detailed explanation about image and inverse image computation of a DBM is in Sect. 3.3.

3.2 Generation of the Abstract States

We begin by recalling the PWA representation of an MPL system characterised by a row-finite matrix $A \in \mathbb{R}_{\max}^{n \times n}$. It is shown in [9] that each MPL system can be expressed as a PWA system. The PWA system comprises of convex domains (or PWA regions) and has correspondingly affine dynamics. The PWA regions are generated from the coefficient $g = (g_1, \ldots, g_n) \in \{1, \ldots, n\}^n$. As shown in [3], the PWA region corresponding to coefficient g is

$$R_g = \bigcap_{i=1}^{n} \bigcap_{j=1}^{n} \{\mathbf{x} \in \mathbb{R}^n | x_{g_i} - x_j \geq A(i,j) - A(i,g_i)\}. \tag{5}$$

Notice that, if g is not a finite coefficient, then R_g is empty. However, a finite coefficient might lead to an empty set. Recall that the DBM R_g in (5) is not always in canonical form.

Definition 4 (Adjacent Regions [3, Definition 3.10]**).** *Two non-empty regions generated by* (5) *R_g and $R_{g'}$ are called adjacent, denoted by $R_g > R_{g'}$, if there exists a single $i \in \{1, \ldots, n\}$ such that $g_i > g_i'$ and $g_j = g_j'$ for each $j \neq i$.* □

The affine dynamic of a non-empty R_g is

$$x_i(k+1) = x_{g_i}(k) + A(i,g_i), \quad i = 1, \ldots, n. \tag{6}$$

Notice that Eq. (6) can be expressed as $x(k+1) = A_g \otimes x(k)$, where A_g is a region matrix that corresponds to a finite coefficient g. As mentioned before, a

PWA region R_g is also a DBM. The DBM R_g has no dummy variable x_0. For simplicity, we are allowed to consider R_g as a matrix, that is $R_g \in \mathbb{R}_{\max}^{n \times n}$. We show that R_g is related to the row-definite form w.r.t. g.

Proposition 5. *For each finite coefficient g, $R_g = {}_g\overline{A} \oplus I_n$.*   □

Algorithm 1 provides a procedure to generate the PWA system from a row-finite $A \in \mathbb{R}_{\max}^{n \times n}$. It consists of: (1) generating region matrices (line 3) and their conjugates (line 4), (2) computing the row-definite form (line 5), and (3) emptiness checking of DBM R_g (lines 6–7). The first two steps are based on tropical operations while the last one is using the Floyd-Warshall algorithm.

Algorithm 1. Generation of the PWA system using tropical operations

---

    Input : $A \in \mathbb{R}_{\max}^{n \times n}$, a row-finite tropical matrix
    Output: R,A, a PWA system over $\mathbb{R}^n$
               where **R** is a set of regions and **A** represent a set of affine
    dynamics

1 **for** $g \in \{1, \dots, n\}^n$ **do**
2   **if** g is a finite coefficient **then**
3   generate A_g according to (2)
4   generate A_g^c from A_g according to (3)
5         $R_g := (A_g^c \otimes A) \oplus I_n$
6         $R_g := \mathsf{cf}(R_g)$
7   **if** R_g is not empty **then**
8 | $\mathbf{R} := \mathbf{R} \cup \{R_g\}, \mathbf{A} := \mathbf{A} \cup \{A_g\}$
9   **end**
10   **end**
11 **end**

The complexity of Algorithm 1 depends on line 6; that is $O(n^3)$. The worst-case complexity of Algorithm 1 is $O(n^{n+3})$ because there are n^n possibilities at line 1. However, we do not expect to incur this worst-case complexity, especially when a row-finite A has several ε elements in each row.

In [3], the abstract states are generated via refinement of PWA regions. Notice that, for each pair of adjacent regions R_g and $R_{g'}$, $R_g \cap R_{g'} \neq \emptyset$. The intersection of adjacent regions is removed from the region with the lower index. Mathematically, if $R_g > R_{g'}$ then $R_{g'} := R_{g'} \setminus R_g$.

Instead of removing the intersection of adjacent regions, the partition of PWA regions can be established by choosing the sign matrix for R_g i.e. S_g. As we can see in (5), all operators are $\geq$. Thus, by (5), $S_g(i,j) = 1$ for all $i, j \in \{1, \dots, n\}$. In this paper, we use a rule to decide the sign matrix of R_g as follows

$$
S_g(i,j) = \begin{cases} 1, & \text{if } R_g(i,j) > 0 \text{ or} \\ & \quad R_g(i,j) = 0 \text{ and } i \leq j, \\ 0, & \text{if } R_g(i,j) < 0 \text{ or} \\ & \quad R_g(i,j) = 0 \text{ and } i > j. \end{cases} \tag{7}
$$

This rule guarantees empty intersection for each pair of region.

Algorithm 2 is a modification of Algorithm 1 by applying rule in (7) before checking the emptiness of R_g. Notation $R_g := (R_g, S_g)$ in line 7 is to emphasise that DBM R_g is now associated with S_g. It generates the partitions of PWA regions which represent the abstract states of an MPL system characterised by $A \in \mathbb{R}_{\max}^{n \times n}$. The worst-case complexity of Algorithm 2 is similar to that of Algorithm 1.

Algorithm 2. Generation of partition from region of PWA system by tropical operations

---

Input : $A \in \mathbb{R}_{\max}^{n \times n}$, a row-finite tropical matrix
Output: $\mathbf{R}, \mathbf{A}$, a PWA system over $\mathbb{R}^n$
        where $\mathbf{R}$ is a set of regions and $\mathbf{A}$ represent a set of affine
dynamics

1 **for** $g \in \{1, \ldots, n\}^n$ **do**
2   **if** g is a finite coefficient **then**
3   generate A_g according to (2)
4   generate A_g^c from A_g according to (3)
5        $R_g := A_g^c \otimes A$
6   generate sign matrix S_g from R_g according to (7)
7        $R_g := (R_g, S_g)$
8        $R_g := \mathsf{cf}(R_g)$
9   **if** R_g is not empty **then**
10           $\mathbf{R} := \mathbf{R} \cup \{R_g\}, \mathbf{A} := \mathbf{A} \cup \{A_g\}$
11   **end**
12   **end**
13 **end**

Remark 1. The resulting R_g in Algorithms 1 and 2 is an n-dimensional matrix which represents a DBM without dummy variable x_0. This condition violates Definition 3. To resolve this, the system matrix $A \in \mathbb{R}_{\max}^{n \times n}$ is extended into $(n + 1)$-dimensional matrix by adding the 0th row and column

$$A(0, \cdot) = [0 \quad \varepsilon \quad \ldots \quad \varepsilon], \quad A(\cdot, 0) = A(0, \cdot)^\top.$$

As a consequence, the finite coefficient g is now an $(n + 1)$-row vector $g = (g_0, g_1, \ldots, g_n)$ where g_0 is always equal to 0. For the rest of this paper, all matrices are indexed starting from zero.   □

As explained in [3], each partition of PWA regions is treated as an abstract state. Therefore, the number of abstract states is equivalent to the cardinality of partitions. Suppose $\hat{R}$ is the set of abstract states, then $\hat{R}$ is a collection of all non-empty R_g generated by Algorithm 2.

3.3   Computation of Image and Inverse Image of DBMs

This section describes a procedure to compute the image of DBMs w.r.t. affine dynamics. First, we recall the procedures from [1]. Then, we develop new procedures based on tropical operations.

The image of a DBM D is computed by constructing a DBM $\mathbf{D}$ consisting of D and its corresponding affine dynamics. The DBM $\mathbf{D}$ corresponds to variables $x_1, x_2, \ldots,$ and their primed version $x_1', x_2', \ldots,$. Then, the canonical-form DBM $cf(\mathbf{D})$ is computed. The image of D is established by removing all inequalities with non-primed variables in $cf(\mathbf{D})$. This procedure has complexity $O(n^3)$ [1].

Example 2. Let us compute the image of $D = \{\mathbf{x} \in \mathbb{R}^3 | x_1 - x_2 \geq 6, x_1 - x_3 > -1, x_2 - x_3 \geq 2\}$ w.r.t. its affine dynamics $x_1' = x_2 + 1, x_2' = x_1 + 5, x_3' = x_1 + 2$. The DBM generated from D and the affine dynamics is $\mathbf{D} = \{[\mathbf{x}^\top \ (\mathbf{x}')^\top]^\top \in \mathbb{R}^6 | x_1 - x_2 \geq 6, x_1 - x_3 > -1, x_2 - x_3 \geq 2, x_1' - x_2 = 1, x_2' - x_1 = 5, x_3' - x_1 = 2\}$. The canonical-form representation of $\mathbf{D}$ is $cf(\mathbf{D}) = \{[\mathbf{x}^\top \ (\mathbf{x}')^\top]^\top \in \mathbb{R}^6 | x_1 - x_2 \geq 6, x_1 - x_3 \geq 8, x_2 - x_3 \geq 2, x_1' - x_1 \leq -5, x_1' - x_2 = 1, x_1' - x_3 \geq 3, x_2' - x_1 = 5, x_2' - x_2 \geq 11, x_2' - x_3 \geq 13, x_3' - x_1 = 2, x_1' - x_2' \leq -10, x_1' - x_3' \leq -7, x_2' - x_3' = 3\}$. The image of D over the given affine dynamics is generated by removing all inequalities containing x_1, x_2 or x_3, i.e. $\{\mathbf{x}' \in \mathbb{R}^3 | x_1' - x_2' \leq -10, x_1' - x_3' \leq -7, x_2' - x_3' = 3\}$. □

The above procedure can be improved by manipulating DBM D directly from the affine dynamics. By (6), one could write $x_i' = x_{g_i} + A_g(i, g_i)$ where x_i and x_i' represent the current and next variables, respectively. For each pair (i, j), we have $x_i' - x_j' = x_{g_i} - x_{g_j} + A_g(i, g_i) - A_g(j, g_j)$. This relation ensures that the bound of $x_i' - x_j'$ can be determined uniquely from $x_{g_i} - x_{g_j}$ and $A_g(i, g_i) - A_g(j, g_j)$.

Proposition 6. *The image of a DBM D w.r.t. affine dynamics $x_i' = x_{g_i} + A_g(i, g_i)$ for $1 \leq i \leq n$ is a set $D' = \bigcap_{i=1}^n \bigcap_{j=1}^n \{\boldsymbol{x}' \in \mathbb{R}^n | x_i' - x_j' = x_{g_i} - x_{g_j} + A_g(i, g_i) - A_g(j, g_j)\}$, where the bound of $x_{g_i} - x_{g_j}$ is taken from D.* □

Example 3. We compute the image of $D = \{\mathbf{x} \in \mathbb{R}^3 | x_1 - x_2 \geq 6, x_1 - x_3 > -1, x_2 - x_3 \geq 2\}$ with the same affine dynamics $x_1' = x_2 + 1, x_2' = x_1 + 5, x_3' = x_1 + 2$. From the affine dynamics and D, we have $x_1' - x_2' = x_2 - x_1 - 4 \leq -10$, $x_1' - x_3' = x_2 - x_1 - 1 \leq -7$, and $x_2' - x_3' = 3$ which yields a set $\{\mathbf{x}' \in \mathbb{R}^3 | x_1' - x_2' \leq -10, x_1' - x_3' \leq -7, x_2' - x_3' = 3\}$. □

Algorithm 3 shows a procedure to generate the image of (D, S) w.r.t. the affine dynamics represented by $\mathbf{x}' = A_g \otimes \mathbf{x}$. It requires DBM (D, S) located in a PWA region R_g. This means that there is exactly one finite coefficient g such that $(D, S) \subseteq R_g$. The complexity of Algorithm 3 is in $O(n^2)$ as the addition step at 4 line has complexity of $O(1)$.

Algorithm 3. Computation of the image of DBM D w.r.t. $\mathbf{x}' = A_g \otimes \mathbf{x}$

Input : (D, S), a DBM in $\mathbb{R}^n$

          g, the corresponding finite coefficient such that $(D, S) \subseteq R_g$

          A_g, a region matrix which represents the affine dynamics

Output: (D', S'), image of D w.r.t. $\mathbf{x}' = A_g \otimes \mathbf{x}$

1 **Initialize** (D', S') with $\mathbb{R}^n$

2 **for** $i \in \{0, \ldots, n\}$ **do**

3   **for** $j \in \{0, \ldots, n\}$ **do**

4         $D'(i, j) := D(g_i, g_j) + A_g(i, g_i) - A_g(j, g_j)$

5         $S'(i, j) := S(g_i, g_j)$

6   **end**

7 **end**

As an alternative, we also show that the image of a DBM can be computed by tropical matrix multiplications with the corresponding region matrix A_g.

Proposition 7. *The image of DBM D in $\mathbb{R}^n$ w.r.t. the affine dynamics $\boldsymbol{x}' = A_g \otimes \boldsymbol{x}$ is $D' = A_g \otimes D \otimes A_g^c$.* $\qquad\square$

The procedure to compute the image of DBM D w.r.t. MPL system can be viewed as the extension of Algorithm 3. First, the DBM D is intersected with each region of the PWA system. Then, for each nonempty intersection we apply Algorithm 3. The worst-case complexity is $O(|\hat{R}|n^2)$.

In [1], the procedure to compute the inverse image of D' w.r.t. affine dynamics involves: (1) constructing DBM $\mathbf{D}$ that consists of D' and its corresponding affine dynamics, (2) generating the canonical form of $\mathbf{D}$ and (3) removing all inequalities with primed variables. The complexity of computing the inverse image using this procedure is $O(n^3)$ as it involves the emptiness checking of a DBM [1].

Example 4. Let us compute the inverse image of $D' = \{\mathbf{x}' \in \mathbb{R}^3 | x_1' - x_2' \leq -10, x_1' - x_3' \leq -7, x_2' - x_3' = 3\}$ w.r.t. affine dynamics $x_1' = x_2 + 1, x_2' = x_1 + 5, x_3' = x_1 + 2$. The DBM generated from D' and the affine dynamic is $\mathbf{D}' = \{[\mathbf{x}^\top \ (\mathbf{x}')^\top]^\top \in \mathbb{R}^6 | x_1' - x_2' \leq -10, x_1' - x_3' \leq -7, x_2' - x_3' = 3, x_1' - x_2 = 1, x_2' - x_1 = 5, x_3' - x_1 = 2\}$. The canonical-form of $\mathbf{D}$ is cf$(\mathbf{D}) = \{[\mathbf{x}^\top \ (\mathbf{x}')^\top]^\top \in \mathbb{R}^6 | x_1 - x_2 \geq 6, x_1' - x_1 \leq -5, x_1' - x_2 = 1, x_1' - x_3 \geq 3, x_2' - x_1 = 5, x_2' - x_2 \geq 11, x_3' - x_1 = 2, x_3' - x_2 \geq 8, x_1' - x_2' \leq -10, x_1' - x_3' \leq -7, x_2' - x_3' = 3\}$. The inverse image of D' over the given affine dynamic is computed by removing all inequalities containing x_1', x_2' or x_3', i.e. $\{\mathbf{x} \in \mathbb{R}^3 | x_1 - x_2 \geq 6\}$. $\qquad\square$

The inverse image of D' can be established by manipulating D' from the affine dynamics. Notice that, from (6), we have $x_{g_i} - x_{g_j} = x_i' - x_j' + A_g(j, g_j) - A_g(i, g_i)$. Unlike the previous case, it is possible that $x_{g_i} - x_{g_j}$ has multiple bounds. This happens because there is a case $g_{i_1} = g_{i_2}$ but $i_1 \neq i_2$. In this case, the bound of $x_{g_i} - x_{g_j}$ is taken from the tightest bound among all possibilities.

Proposition 8. *The inverse image of DBM D' w.r.t. affine dynamics $x_i' = x_{g_i} + A_g(i, g_i)$ for $i \in \{1, \ldots, n\}$ is a set $D = \bigcap_{i=1}^n \bigcap_{j=1}^n \{\boldsymbol{x} \in \mathbb{R}^n | x_{g_i} - x_{g_j} = x_i' - x_j' + A_g(j, g_j) - A_g(i, g_i)\}$ where the bound of $x_i' - x_j'$ is taken from D'.* $\qquad\square$

Algorithm 4 shows the steps to compute the inverse image of DBM D' over the affine dynamics $\mathbf{x}' = A_g \otimes \mathbf{x}$. It has similarity with Algorithm 3 except it updates the value of $D(g_i, g_j)$ and $S(g_i, g_j)$ for all $i, j \in \{0, \ldots, n\}$. The variables b and s in lines 4–5 represent the new bound of $x_{g_i} - x_{g_j}$; that is, $x_{g_i} - x_{g_j} \geq b$ if $s = 1$ and $x_{g_i} - x_{g_j} > b$ if $s = 0$. If the new bound is larger then it replaces the old one. In case of they are equal, we only need to update the operator.

Algorithm 4. Computation of the inverse image of DBM D' w.r.t. $\mathbf{x}' = A_g \otimes \mathbf{x}$

    Input   : (D', S'), a DBM in $\mathbb{R}^n$
               g, the corresponding finite coefficient such that $(D, S) \subseteq R_g$
               A_g, a region matrix which represents the affine dynamics
    Output: (D, S), inverse image of D w.r.t. $\mathbf{x}' = A_g \otimes \mathbf{x}$
1 **Initialize** (D, S) with $\mathbb{R}^n$
2 **for** $i \in \{0, \ldots, n\}$ **do**
3   **for** $j \in \{0, \ldots, n\}$ **do**
4         $b := D'(i, j) + A_g(j, g_j) - A_g(i, g_i)$
5         $s := S'(i, j)$
6   **if** $b > D(g_i, g_j)$ **then**
7             $D(g_i, g_j) := b$
8             $S(g_i, g_j) := s$
9   **else if** $b = D(g_i, g_j)$ **then**
10            $S(g_i, g_j) := \min\{s, S(g_i, g_j)\}$
11   **end**
12   **end**
13 **end**

Similar to Algorithms 3, Algorithm 4 has complexity in $O(n^2)$. In tropical algebra, the procedure of Algorithm 4 can be expressed as tropical matrix multiplications using a region matrix and its conjugate.

Proposition 9. *The inverse image of DBM D' in $\mathbb{R}^n$ w.r.t. affine dynamic $\mathbf{x}' = A_g \otimes \mathbf{x}$ is $D = (A_g^c \otimes D' \otimes A_g) \oplus I_{n+1}$.* $\square$

The procedure to compute the inverse image of DBM D' w.r.t. MPL system can be viewed as the extension of Algorithm 4. First, we compute the inverse image of DBM D' w.r.t. all affine dynamics. Then each inverse image is intersected with the corresponding PWA region. The worst-case complexity is $O(|\hat{R}|n^2)$.

3.4 Generation of the Abstract Transitions

As we mentioned before, the transition relations are generated by one-step forward-reachability analysis, and involve the image computation of each abstract state. Suppose $\hat{R} = \{\hat{r}_1, \ldots, \hat{r}_{|\hat{R}|}\}^2$ is the set of abstract states generated

---

^{2} $\hat{R}$ is the collection of non-empty R_g. We use small letter $\hat{r}_i$ for sake of simplicity.

by Algorithm 2. There is a transition from $\hat{r}_i$ to $\hat{r}_j$ if $\mathsf{Im}(\hat{r}_i) \cap \hat{r}_j \neq \emptyset$, where $\mathsf{Im}(\hat{r}_i) = \{A \otimes \mathbf{x} | \mathbf{x} \in \hat{r}_i\}$ which can be computed by Algorithm 3. Notice that, each abstract state corresponds to an unique affine dynamics.

The procedure to generate the transitions is summarized in Algorithm 5. It spends most time for emptiness checking at line 5. Therefore, the worst-case complexity is in $O(n^3 |\hat{R}|^2)$, where n is the dimension of A in Algorithm 2.

Algorithm 5. Generation of the transitions via one-step forward reachability.

Input : $\hat{R} = \{\hat{r}_1, \ldots, \hat{r}_{|\hat{R}|}\}$, the set of abstract states generated by Algorithm 2

Output: $T \subseteq \hat{R} \times \hat{R}$, a transition relation

1 **Initialize** T with an empty set
2 **for** $i \in \{1, \ldots, |\hat{R}|\}$ **do**
3   **for** $j \in \{1, \ldots, |\hat{R}|\}$ **do**
4   compute $\mathsf{Im}(\hat{r}_i)$ by Algorithm 3
5   **if** $\mathsf{Im}(\hat{r}_i) \cap \hat{r}_j \neq \emptyset$ **then**
6              $T := T \cup \{(\hat{r}_i, \hat{r}_j)\}$
7   **end**
8   **end**
9 **end**

Example 5. Matrix A in Example 1 has 8 finite coefficients. The abstract states generated by Algorithm 2 are $\hat{r}_1 = \{\mathbf{x} \in \mathbb{R}^3 | x_1 - x_2 \geq 1, x_1 - x_3 \geq 3, x_2 - x_3 \geq 2\}$, $\hat{r}_2 = \{\mathbf{x} \in \mathbb{R}^3 | x_1 - x_2 < 1, x_1 - x_3 > -1, x_2 - x_3 \geq 2\}$, $\hat{r}_3 = \{\mathbf{x} \in \mathbb{R}^3 | x_1 - x_2 \leq -3, x_1 - x_3 \leq -1, x_2 - x_3 \geq 2\}$, $\hat{r}_4 = \{\mathbf{x} \in \mathbb{R}^3 | x_1 - x_2 \geq 1, x_1 - x_3 > -1, x_2 - x_3 < 2\}$, $\hat{r}_5 = \{\mathbf{x} \in \mathbb{R}^3 | -3 < x_1 - x_2 < 1, -1 < x_1 - x_3 < 3, -2 < x_2 - x_3 < 2\}$, $\hat{r}_6 = \{\mathbf{x} \in \mathbb{R}^3 | x_1 - x_2 \geq 1, x_1 - x_3 \leq -1, x_2 - x_3 \leq -2\}$, and $\hat{r}_7 = \{\mathbf{x} \in \mathbb{R}^3 | x_1 - x_2 < 1, x_1 - x_3 \leq -1, x_2 - x_3 < 2\}$, which correspond to finite coefficients $(2,1,1), (2,1,2), (2,3,2), (3,1,1), (3,1,2), (3,3,1)$, and $(3,3,2)$, respectively. The only finite coefficient that leads to an empty set is $(2,3,1)$. Figure 1 shows the illustrations of abstract states and transition relations. $\square$

4   Computational Benchmarks

We compare the run-time of abstraction algorithms in this paper with the procedures in VeriSiMPL 1.4 [2]. For increasing n, we generate matrices $A \in \mathbb{R}_{\max}^{n \times n}$ with two finite elements in each row, with value ranging between 1 and 100. The location and value of the finite elements are chosen randomly. The computational benchmark has been implemented on the Oxford University ARC server [16].

We run the experiments for both procedures (VeriSiMPL 1.4 and Tropical) using MATLAB R2017a with parallel computing. Over 10 different MPL systems

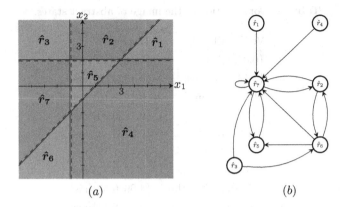

Fig. 1. (*a*) Plot of partitions (and corresponding abstract states), projected on the plane $x_3 = 0$. The solid and dashed lines represent $\geq$ and $>$, respectively. (*b*) Transition relations among abstract states.

Table 1. Generation of abstract states and transitions.

n	VeriSiMPL 1.4.		Tropical	
	Time for generating abstract states	Time for generating transitions	Time for generating abstract states	Time for generating transitions
3	$\{7.51, 9.82\}$[ms]	$\{0.13, 0.21\}$[sec]	$\{4.04, 8.39\}$[ms]	$\{0.12, 0.17\}$[sec]
4	$\{11.29, 15.58\}$[ms]	$\{0.20, 0.29\}$[sec]	$\{5.23, 16.10\}$[ms]	$\{0.17, 0.22\}$[sec]
5	$\{18.51, 28.19\}$[ms]	$\{0.20, 0.21\}$[sec]	$\{5.16, 6.89\}$[ms]	$\{0.19, 0.20\}$[sec]
6	$\{49.22, 55.10\}$[ms]	$\{0.21, 0.22\}$[sec]	$\{9.99, 11.44\}$[ms]	$\{0.20, 0.21\}$[sec]
7	$\{90.88, 118.94\}$[ms]	$\{0.24, 0.26\}$[sec]	$\{15.88, 20.67\}$[ms]	$\{0.22, 0.24\}$[sec]
8	$\{0.21, 0.28\}$[sec]	$\{0.32, 0.44\}$[sec]	$\{0.04, 0.04\}$[sec]	$\{0.27, 0.38\}$[sec]
9	$\{0.52, 0.69\}$[sec]	$\{0.72, 1.07\}$[sec]	$\{0.07, 0.10\}$[sec]	$\{0.60, 0.91\}$[sec]
10	$\{1.25, 1.88\}$[sec]	$\{2.62, 4.48\}$[sec]	$\{0.14, 0.17\}$[sec]	$\{2.38, 4.22\}$[sec]
11	$\{3.87, 5.14\}$[sec]	$\{17.62, 29.44\}$[sec]	$\{0.35, 0.39\}$[sec]	$\{17.17, 28.88\}$[sec]
12	$\{8.34, 14.22\}$[sec]	$\{1.20, 2.24\}$[min]	$\{0.61, 0.71\}$[sec]	$\{1.10, 2.19\}$[min]
13	$\{26.17, 45.17\}$[sec]	$\{5.05, 10.45\}$[min]	$\{1.21, 1.37\}$[sec]	$\{4.98, 10.40\}$[min]
14	$\{1.81, 4.24\}$[min]	$\{41.14, 112.09\}$[min]	$\{0.06, 0.07\}$[min]	$\{40.61, 110.06\}$[min]
15	$\{10.29, 23.18\}$[min]	$\{2.63, 7.57\}$[hr]	$\{0.11, 0.17\}$[min]	$\{2.57, 7.65\}$[hr]

for each dimension, Table 1 shows the running time to generate the abstract states and transitions. Each entry represents the average and maximal values.

With regards to the generation of abstract states, the tropical algebra based algorithm is much faster than VeriSiMPL 1.4. As the dimension increases, we see an increasing gap of the running time. For a 12-dimensional MPL system over 10 independent experiments, the time needed to compute abstract states using tropical based algorithm is less than 1 s. In comparison, average running time using VeriSiMPL 1.4 for the same dimension is 8.34 s.

Table 2. Computation of the image of abstract states.

n	VeriSiMPL 1.4.	Tropical
3	$\{0.84, 1.13\}$[ms]	$\{0.16, 0.23\}$[ms]
4	$\{1.13, 1.76\}$[ms]	$\{0.13, 0.20\}$[ms]
5	$\{1.53, 2.40\}$[ms]	$\{0.14, 0.16\}$[ms]
6	$\{5.32, 6.68\}$[ms]	$\{0.18, 0.20\}$[ms]
7	$\{11.22, 15.19\}$[ms]	$\{0.31, 0.44\}$[ms]
8	$\{26.05, 46.94\}$[ms]	$\{0.71, 1.19\}$[ms]
9	$\{70.31, 92.87\}$[ms]	$\{2.37, 3.37\}$[ms]
10	$\{153.07, 183.08\}$[ms]	$\{4.06, 6.57\}$[ms]
11	$\{380.01, 477.94\}$[ms]	$\{5.58, 8.19\}$[ms]
12	$\{0.79, 1.13\}$[sec]	$\{0.02, 0.03\}$[sec]
13	$\{1.96, 3.13\}$[sec]	$\{0.03, 0.04\}$[sec]
14	$\{5.51, 9.60\}$[sec]	$\{0.06, 0.16\}$[sec]
15	$\{14.33, 23.82\}$[sec]	$\{0.49, 0.87\}$[sec]

For the generation of transitions, the running time of tropical algebra-based algorithm is slightly faster than that of VeriSiMPL 1.4. We remind that the procedure to generate transitions involves the image computation of each abstract state. In comparison to the 2nd and 4th columns of Tables 1 and 2 shows the running time to compute the image of abstract states. Each entry represents the average and maximum of running time. It shows that our proposed algorithm for computing the image of abstract states is faster than VeriSiMPL 1.4.

We also compare the running time algorithms when applying forward- and backward-reachability analysis. We generate the forward reach set [3, Definition 4.1] and backward reach set [3, Definition 4.3] from an initial and a final set, respectively. In more detail, suppose $\mathcal{X}_0$ is the set of initial conditions; the forward reach set $\mathcal{X}_k$ is defined recursively as the image of $\mathcal{X}_{k-1}$, namely $\mathcal{X}_k = \{A \otimes \mathbf{x} \mid \mathbf{x} \in \mathcal{X}_{k-1}\}$. On the other hand, suppose $\mathcal{Y}_0$ is a set of final conditions. The backward reach set $\mathcal{Y}_{-k}$ is defined via the inverse image of $\mathcal{Y}_{-k+1}$, $\mathcal{Y}_{-k} = \{\mathbf{y} \in \mathbb{R}^n \mid A \otimes \mathbf{y} \in \mathcal{Y}_{-k+1}\}$, where n is the dimension of A.

We select $\mathcal{X}_0 = \{\mathbf{x} \in \mathbb{R}^n \mid 0 \leq x_1, \ldots, x_n \leq 1\}$ and $\mathcal{Y}_0 = \{\mathbf{y} \in \mathbb{R}^n \mid 90 \leq y_1, \ldots, y_n \leq 100\}$ as the sets of initial and final conditions, respectively. The experiments have been implemented to compute $\mathcal{X}_1, \ldots, \mathcal{X}_N$ and $\mathcal{Y}_{-1}, \ldots, \mathcal{Y}_{-N}$ for $N = 10$. Notice that it is possible that the inverse image of $\mathcal{Y}_{-k+1}$ results in an empty set: in this case, the computation of backward reach sets is terminated, since $\mathcal{Y}_{-k} = \ldots = \mathcal{Y}_{-N} = \emptyset$. (If this termination happens, it applies for both VeriSiMPL 1.4 and the algorithms based on tropical algebra.)

Table 3 reports the average computation of PWA system and reach sets over 10 independent experiments for each dimension. In general, algorithms based on tropical algebra outperform those of VeriSiMPL 1.4. For a 15-dimensional MPL

Table 3. Reachability analysis.

n	VeriSiMPL 1.4.			Tropical		
	Time for generating PWA system	Time for generating forward reach sets	Time for generating backward reach sets	Time for generating PWA system	Time for generating forward reach sets	Time for generating backward sets
3	2.55[ms]	11.37[ms]	5.73[ms]	1.70[ms]	8.33[ms]	5.63[ms]
4	4.31[ms]	9.87[ms]	27.00[ms]	1.37[ms]	7.72[ms]	28.48[ms]
5	9.23[ms]	11.77[ms]	3.62[ms]	1.88[ms]	9.25[ms]	2.89[ms]
6	23.44[ms]	18.49[ms]	9.76[ms]	3.80[ms]	13.81[ms]	7.35[ms]
7	49.59[ms]	35.68[ms]	21.53[ms]	7.84[ms]	32.02[ms]	17.92[ms]
8	108.75[ms]	85.27[ms]	34.05[ms]	16.84[ms]	73.63[ms]	28.62[ms]
9	0.25[sec]	0.18[sec]	0.09[sec]	0.03[sec]	0.17[sec]	0.07[sec]
10	0.48[sec]	0.28[sec]	0.17[sec]	0.08[sec]	0.25[sec]	0.14[sec]
11	1.19[sec]	0.77[sec]	1.35[sec]	0.18[sec]	0.76[sec]	1.13[sec]
12	2.52[sec]	1.14[sec]	0.88[sec]	0.38[sec]	1.01[sec]	0.70[sec]
13	7.02[sec]	3.96[sec]	2.78[sec]	1.09[sec]	3.56[sec]	1.95[sec]
14	8.15[sec]	5.54[sec]	4.61[sec]	1.54[sec]	5.24[sec]	2.98[sec]
15	20.60[sec]	19.23[sec]	12.39[sec]	4.21[sec]	18.37[sec]	7.16[sec]
16	46.92[sec]	60.19[sec]	36.00[sec]	9.62[sec]	58.70[sec]	20.41[sec]
18	2.98[min]	3.91[min]	2.61[min]	0.83[min]	3.83[min]	1.35[min]
20	15.74[min]	21.03[min]	15.21[min]	4.84[min]	20.86[min]	7.51[min]

system, the average time to generate PWA system using VeriSiMPL 1.4 is just over 20 s. In comparison, the computation time for tropical algorithm is under 5 s.

Tropical algorithms also show advantages to compute reach sets. As shown in Table 3, the average computation time for forward and backward-reachability analysis is slightly faster when using tropical procedures. There is evidence that the average time to compute the backward reach sets decreases as the dimension increases. This happens because the computation is terminated earlier once there is a $k \leq N$ such that $\mathcal{Y}_{-k} = \emptyset$. Notice that, this condition occurs for both VeriSiMPL 1.4 and the new algorithms based on tropical algebra.

We summarise the worst-complexity of abstraction procedures via VeriSiMPL 1.4 and our proposed algorithms in Table 4 – recall that in VeriSiMPL 1.4 the generation of abstract states involves two procedures: the generation of PWA systems and the refinement of PWA regions.

Table 4. The worst-case complexity of abstraction procedures.

Procedures	VeriSiMPL 1.4	Tropical
Generating the PWA systems	$O(n^{n+3})$	$O(n^{n+3})$
Generating the abstract states	$O(n^{n+3})$ and $O(n^{2n+1})$	$O(n^{n+3})$
Computing the image of DBMs	$O(n^3)$	$O(n^2)$
Computing the inverse image of DBMs	$O(n^3)$	$O(n^2)$
Generating the abstract transitions	$O(n^3|\hat{R}|^2)$	$O(n^3|\hat{R}|^2)$

5   Conclusions

This paper has introduced the concept of MPL abstractions using tropical operations. We have shown that the generation of abstract states is related to the row-definite form of the given matrix. The computation of image and inverse image of DBMs over the affine dynamics has also been improved based on tropical algebra operations.

The procedure has been implemented on a numerical benchmark and compared with VeriSiMPL 1.4. Algorithm 2 has shown a strong advantage to generate the abstract states especially for high-dimensional MPL systems. Algorithms (Algorithms 3, 4, and 5) for the generation of transitions and for reachability analysis also display an improvement.

For future research, the authors are interested to extend the tropical abstractions for non-autonomous MPL systems [5], with dynamics that are characterised by non-square tropical matrices.

Acknowledgements. The first author is supported by Indonesia Endowment Fund for Education (LPDP), while the third acknowledges the support of the Alan Turing Institute, London, UK.

References

1. Adzkiya, D.: Finite abstractions of max-plus-linear systems: theory and algorithms. Ph.D. thesis, Delft University of Technology (2014)
2. Adzkiya, D., Abate, A.: VeriSiMPL: verification via biSimulations of MPL models. In: Joshi, K., Siegle, M., Stoelinga, M., D'Argenio, P.R. (eds.) QEST 2013. LNCS, vol. 8054, pp. 274–277. Springer, Heidelberg (2013). https://doi.org/10.1007/978-3-642-40196-1_22
3. Adzkiya, D., De Schutter, B., Abate, A.: Finite abstractions of max-plus-linear systems. IEEE Trans. Autom. Control **58**(12), 3039–3053 (2013)
4. Adzkiya, D., De Schutter, B., Abate, A.: Computational techniques for reachability analysis of max-plus-linear systems. Automatica **53**, 293–302 (2015)
5. Baccelli, F., Cohen, G., Olsder, G.J., Quadrat, J.-P.: Synchronization and Linearity: An Algebra for Discrete Event Systems. Wiley, Hoboken (1992)
6. Butkovič, P.: Max-algebra: the linear algebra of combinatorics? Linear Algebra Appl. **367**, 313–335 (2003)

7. Dill, D.L.: Timing assumptions and verification of finite-state concurrent systems. In: Sifakis, J. (ed.) CAV 1989. LNCS, vol. 407, pp. 197–212. Springer, Heidelberg (1990). https://doi.org/10.1007/3-540-52148-8_17

8. Floyd, R.W.: Algorithm 97: shortest path. Commun. ACM **5**(6), 345 (1962)

9. Heemels, W., De Schutter, B., Bemporad, A.: Equivalence of hybrid dynamical models. Automatica **37**(7), 1085–1091 (2001)

10. Heidergott, B., Olsder, G.J., Van der Woude, J.: Max Plus at Work: Modeling and Analysis of Synchronized Systems: A Course on Max-Plus Algebra and Its Applications. Princeton University Press, Princeton (2014)

11. Itenberg, I., Mikhalkin, G., Shustin, E.I.: Tropical Algebraic Geometry, vol. 35. Springer, Basel (2009). https://doi.org/10.1007/978-3-0346-0048-4

12. Lu, Q., Madsen, M., Milata, M., Ravn, S., Fahrenberg, U., Larsen, K.G.: Reachability analysis for timed automata using max-plus algebra. J. Logic Algebraic Program. **81**(3), 298–313 (2012)

13. Mufid, M.S., Adzkiya, D., Abate, A.: Tropical abstractions of max-plus-linear systems (2018). arXiv:1806.04604

14. Péron, M., Halbwachs, N.: An abstract domain extending difference-bound matrices with disequality constraints. In: Cook, B., Podelski, A. (eds.) VMCAI 2007. LNCS, vol. 4349, pp. 268–282. Springer, Heidelberg (2007). https://doi.org/10.1007/978-3-540-69738-1_20

15. Pin, J.-E.: Tropical semirings. Idempotency, pp. 50–69 (1998)

16. Richards, A.: University of Oxford Advanced Research Computing (2015). Zenodo. https://doi.org/10.5281/zenodo.22558

17. Sergeev, S.: Max-plus definite matrix closures and their eigenspaces. Linear Algebra Appl. **421**(2–3), 182–201 (2007)

Author Index

Printed in the United States
By Bookmasters